STOCK TRADER'S ALMANAC 2015

Jeffrey A. Hirsch & Yale Hirsch

WILEY

www.stocktradersalmanac.com

Editor in Chief	Jeffrey A. Hirsch
Editor at Large	Yale Hirsch
Director of Research	Christopher Mistal
Production Editor	Steven Kyritz

For general information about our other products and services, please contact our Customer Care Department within the United States at 800-762-2974, outside the United States at 317-572-3993, or fax 317-572-4002.

Wiley also publishes its books in a variety of electronic formats. Some content that appears in print may not be available in electronic books. For more information about Wiley products, visit our website at www.wiley.com.

ISBN: 978-1-118-91760-2 (paper)
ISBN: 978-1-118-98831-2 (ebk)
ISBN: 978-1-118-98832-9 (ebk)
10 9 8 7 6 5 4 3 2 1

Printed in the U.S.A.

This Forty-Eighth Edition is respectfully dedicated to:

Larry Williams

Larry is a veteran trader and a bit of a Renaissance man. He has been trading stocks and futures for over 50 years. Larry has been a dear friend and trusted colleague since the *Almanac* began 48 years ago. He began following the markets in 1962 and by 1965 was trading actively and writing a newsletter. Since he started in the market, Larry has been on the cutting edge of seasonal and historical market analysis and produced groundbreaking work. This year, the Market Technicians Association presented him with their highest honor, the 2014 Annual Award, citing his "outstanding accomplishments in the field of technical analysis" and for being "a pioneer in technical analysis indicator development."

He developed his Williams %R timing tool in 1966, which is still published in major financial papers and used as a standard indicator on trading websites from MSN's Money Central to Yahoo! Finance. He has created a host of other indicators and techniques that we are all familiar with. He has written many books, including 1973's, *Sure Thing Commodity Trading: How Seasonal Factors Influence Commodity Prices*, the first book ever on the seasonality of commodity prices, and of course his most recent opuses: *Long Term Secrets to Short Term Trading*, *Trade Stocks & Commodities with the Insiders*, and *The Right Stock at the Right Time* (our Best Investment Book of the year in 2004!).

He also wrote a book, *The Mountain of Moses: The Discovery of Mount Sinai*, that suggests Mount Sinai is on the Arabian Peninsula, not the Sinai Peninsula in Egypt. In addition, he ran for Senate twice in his home state of Montana, as well as 76 marathons, and is quite the philanthropist.

One of Jeff's fondest childhood memories is learning how to catch big rainbow trout in Montana from Larry. It's been a pleasure seeing him in recent years at several events.

Find out more at www.ireallytrade.com.

INTRODUCTION TO THE FORTY-EIGHTH EDITION

We are pleased and proud to introduce the Forty-Eighth Edition of the *Stock Trader's Almanac*. The *Almanac* provides you with the necessary tools to invest successfully in the twenty-first century.

J. P. Morgan's classic retort, "Stocks will fluctuate," is often quoted with a wink-of-the-eye implication that the only prediction one can make about the stock market is that it will go up, down, or sideways. Many investors agree that no one ever really knows which way the market will move. Nothing could be further from the truth.

We discovered that while stocks do indeed fluctuate, they do so in well-defined, often predictable patterns. These patterns recur too frequently to be the result of chance or coincidence. How else do we explain that since 1950 all the gains in the market were made during November through April, compared to a loss May through October? (See page 52.)

The *Almanac* is a practical investment tool. It alerts you to those little-known market patterns and tendencies on which shrewd professionals enhance profit potential. You will be able to forecast market trends with accuracy and confidence when you use the *Almanac* to help you understand:

- How our presidential elections affect the economy and the stock market—just as the moon affects the tides. Many investors have made fortunes following the political cycle. You can be sure that money managers who control billions of dollars are also political cycle watchers. Astute people do not ignore a pattern that has been working effectively throughout most of our economic history.

- How the passage of the Twentieth Amendment to the Constitution fathered the January Barometer. This barometer has an outstanding record for predicting the general course of the stock market each year, with only seven major errors since 1950, for an 89.1% accuracy ratio. (See page 16.)

- Why there is a significant market bias at certain times of the day, week, month, and year.

Even if you are an investor who pays scant attention to cycles, indicators, and patterns, your investment survival could hinge on your interpretation of one of the recurring patterns found within these pages. One of the most intriguing and important patterns is the symbiotic relationship between Washington and Wall Street. Aside from the potential profitability in seasonal patterns, there's the pure joy of seeing the market very often do just what you expected.

The *Stock Trader's Almanac* is also an organizer. Its wealth of information is presented on a calendar basis. The *Almanac* puts investing in a business framework and makes investing easier because it:

- Updates investment knowledge and informs you of new techniques and tools.
- Is a monthly reminder and refresher course.
- Alerts you to both seasonal opportunities and dangers.
- Furnishes a historical viewpoint by providing pertinent statistics on past market performance.
- Supplies forms necessary for portfolio planning, record keeping, and tax preparation.

 The WITCH icon signifies THIRD FRIDAY OF THE MONTH on calendar pages and alerts you to extraordinary volatility due to the expiration of equity and index options and index futures contracts. Triple-witching days appear during March, June, September, and December.

 The BULL icon on calendar pages signifies favorable trading days based on the S&P 500 rising 60% or more of the time on a particular trading day during the 21-year period January 1993 to December 2013.

 A BEAR icon on calendar pages signifies unfavorable trading days based on the S&P falling 60% or more of the time for the same 21-year period.

Also, to give you even greater perspective, we have listed next to the date of every day that the market is open the Market Probability numbers for the same 21-year period for the Dow (D), S&P 500 (S), and NASDAQ (N). You will see a "D," "S," and "N" followed by a number signifying the actual Market Probability number for that trading day, based on the recent 21-year period. On pages 121–128 you will find complete Market Probability Calendars, both long-term and 21-year for the Dow, S&P, and NASDAQ, as well as for the Russell 1000 and Russell 2000 indices.

Other seasonalities near the ends, beginnings, and middles of months—options expirations, around holidays, and other significant times—as well as all FOMC Meeting dates are noted for *Almanac* investors' convenience on the weekly planner pages. All other important economic releases are provided in the Strategy Calendar every month in our e-newsletter, *Almanac Investor*, available at our website, *www.stocktradersalmanac.com*.

Last edition, we introduced one-year seasonal pattern charts for Dow, S&P 500, NASDAQ, Russell 1000, and Russell 2000 on pages 171 to 173. There are three charts each for Dow and S&P 500 spanning our entire database starting in 1901 and one each for the younger indices. As 2015 is a pre-presidential election year, each chart contains typical pre-election year performance compared to all years.

For this edition, we reached out to some of our favorite minds on Wall Street to share a brief outlook for 2015. Eighteen brave souls took the plunge and their concise and salient remarks cover three pages on 24, 26, and 28. It is quite a cross section of different disciplines and opinions. We think you'll find them enlightening.

The Notable Events on page 6 provides a handy list of major events of the past year that can be helpful when evaluating things that may have moved the market. Over the past few years, our research had been restructured to flow better with the rhythm of the year. This has also allowed us more room for added data. Again, we have included historical data on the Russell 1000 and Russell 2000 indices. The Russell 2K is an excellent proxy for small and mid-caps, which we have used over the years, and the Russell 1K provides a broader view of large caps. Annual highs and lows for all five indices covered in the *Almanac* appear on pages 149–151 and we've tweaked the Best & Worst section.

In order to cram in all this material, some of our Record Keeping section was cut. We have converted many of these paper forms into computer spreadsheets for our own internal use. As a service to our faithful readers, we are making these forms available at our website, *www.stocktradersalmanac.com*.

Pre-election years are notoriously the best year of the four-year cycle and fifth years of decades are the strongest, so 2015 has some solid history behind it. The Dow has not had a loss in a pre-election year since 1939 (page 20). You can find all the market charts of pre-elections since the Depression on page 32. The last nine fifth years of decades appear on page 34. Learn why a 50% move in the Dow is possible from the 2014 low to the 2015 high on page 36 and never-before-shown Seventh Year of Presidential Terms on page 40. On page 76 is our Best Investment Book of the Year, *Profitable Day and Swing Trading* (Wiley, 2014), which should help increase your trading returns dramatically. Other top books are listed on page 116.

Sector seasonalities include several consistent shorting opportunities and appear on pages 94–98. In response to many reader inquiries about how and what to trade when implementing the Best Months Switching Strategies, we detail some simple techniques, including a sampling of tradable mutual funds and ETFs on page 42.

We are constantly searching for new insights and nuances about the stock market and welcome any suggestions from our readers.

Have a healthy and prosperous 2015.

NOTABLE EVENTS

2013

June 6	Snowden leaks U.S. classified info
July 1	Croatia becomes 28th member of European Union
July 3	Egyptian President Morsi deposed in military coup, protests, and violence
Sep 21	4-day gun battle at Nairobi mall
Oct 1	Affordable Care Act launches
Oct 1	16-day federal gov't shutdown begins
Nov 4	SAC Capital pleads guilty to insider trading
Nov 7	Twitter IPO
Nov 8	Typhoon Haiyan deadliest storm in modern Philippine history
Nov 19	J.P. Morgan Chase pays record $13 billion penalty to settle MBS lawsuits
Nov 21	Ukraine demonstrations after President Yanukovych rejects EU deal in favor of closer ties to Russia
Nov 21	Dow closes above 16,000 for the first time
Nov 24	Historic nuclear accord with Iran
Nov 27	American Airlines merges with U.S. Airways becoming largest U.S. carrier
Dec 18	Fed announces QE taper begins Jan 2014

2014

Jan 1	Latvia adopts Euro and becomes 18th member of Eurozone
Feb 1	Janet Yellen is new Fed Chair
Feb 7	All Bitcoin withdrawals halted by Mt. Gox
Feb 7-23	XXII Olympic Winter Games, Sochi, Russia
Feb 19	Facebook announces acquisition of WhatsApp for $19 billion
Feb 22	Ukrainian parliament removes President Yanukovych
Feb 26	Russian forces move into Crimea
Mar 9	Malaysia Air Flight 370 is lost en route to Beijing
Mar 9	Biggest Bitcoin exchange Mt. Gox files for bankruptcy protection
Mar 21	Russia formally annexes Crimea
Mar 24	Russia temporarily suspended from G8
Apr 27	U.S. President Obama imposes economic sanctions on Russia
May 20	Terrorists in Nigeria detonate bombs at Jos, killing 118
May 28	Apple announces acquisition of Beats Music for $3 billion

2015 OUTLOOK

Historical cycles suggest good things for the stock market in 2015. It's a pre-presidential election year, which is by far and away the best year of the 4-year cycle (pages 20, 32, 130). Since the Dow's last loss in 1939, the third year of the cycle is up 16.0% on average for the Dow and 16.3% for the S&P 500. Since 1971, NASDAQ averages a whopping 30.9% in the third year of the 4-year cycle. The fifth year of the decade is also the best year of the decennial pattern by a long shot with only one loss in the past 13 decades (pages 34 & 129). Years ending in 5 average 28.3% for the Dow and its predecessors since 1885, with S&P 500 averaging 25.3% since 1935 and NASDAQ averaging 25.6% since 1975.

At this writing, we are entering the middle of the worst two quarters of the 4-year cycle, Q2–3 of the midterm year. So far, the three major U.S. equity indices are up about 1–3% for the first two months of Q2, better than average. This is a testament to the strength of the sixth year of the 4-year cycle, a president's second midterm year, as compared to the first midterm year. Since 1901 there have been six previous presidents that have served a sixth and seventh year. Except for 1919 during the post–WWI-armistice rally, seventh years have been a little weaker than other pre-election years, likely due to lower excitement with a president the country has become apathetic toward (page 40).

With the worst two quarters of 4-year cycle solid so far, we expect mild further gains through June and into early July. Even though we issued our Dow and S&P Best Six Months Seasonal MACD Sell Signal (page 54) on April 7, at this writing we are still long many positions in addition to some bond positions and a little downside protection. After a 3–5% rally into July that takes the market up to about Dow 17,500, S&P 2,025, and NASDAQ 4,500, look for major averages to fall 10–15% with a low in the August–October period to the vicinity of Dow 15,000, S&P 1,750, and NASDAQ 3,800.

Then the rally in the best three quarters of the 4-year cycle (midterm Q4 and pre-election Q1–2, page 102) should ensue. But we expect the usual 50% move from the midterm low to the pre-election-year high (page 36) to be below average in the 20–30% range as quantitative easing (QE) tapering winds down, Fed rates hikes loom large, and the economy stalls while Republicans and Democrats begin the next battle for the White House, to a high most likely in the first half of 2015 around Dow 19,000, S&P 2,250, and NASDAQ 5,000, slightly higher or lower than NASDAQ's all-time high.

Then look for a move sideways to slightly higher throughout 2015, with an ultimate high near year-end 2015. Then, the next bear market is likely to begin in earnest, taking the market 30–40% lower into 2017–2018 into the range of Dow 11,500–13,500, S&P 1,350–1,575, and NASDAQ 3,000–3,500. For now, the Fed is still easy and the tape still moving higher, so don't fight either. But chinks are beginning to appear in the armor. Economic numbers have softened and been inconsistent. Market internals are weakening. Sentiment is quite high and the dysfunctional federal government is no help. The next election process promises to be nasty. As the U.S. situation sours, money will move into overseas markets. Our Next Super Boom forecast is still entirely in play. Though we have raised the floor on our initial forecast, the 500+% move to Dow 38,820 by 2025 is still on target. We have elevated the low-end of the range to account for this new easy-money world. We still expect some tough sledding over the next few years in the market.

— *Jeffrey A. Hirsch, June 4, 2014*

THE 2015 STOCK TRADER'S ALMANAC

CONTENTS

10 2015 Strategy Calendar

12 **January Almanac**

14 January's First Five Days: An Early Warning System

16 The Incredible January Barometer (Devised 1972):
Only Seven Significant Errors in 64 Years

18 January Barometer in Graphic Form Since 1950

20 Pre-Presidential Election Years: No Losers in 76 Years

22 **February Almanac**

24 2015 Outlooks from Some of the Best Minds on Wall Street

30 **March Almanac**

32 Market Charts of Pre-Presidential Election Years

34 The Fifth Year of Decades

36 Why a 50% Gain in the Dow Is Possible
from Its 2014 Low to Its 2015 High

38 **April Almanac**

40 Seventh Year of Presidential Terms

42 How to Trade Best Months Switching Strategies

44 The December Low Indicator: A Useful Prognosticating Tool

46 **May Almanac**

48 Down Januarys: A Remarkable Record

50 Top Performing Months Past 64⅓ Years:
Standard & Poor's 500 and Dow Jones Industrials

52 "Best Six Months": Still an Eye-Popping Strategy

54 MACD-Timing Triples "Best Six Months" Results

56 **June Almanac**

58 Top Performing NASDAQ Months Past 43⅓ Years

60 Get More out of NASDAQ's "Best Eight Months" with MACD Timing

62 Triple Returns, Less Trades: Best 6 + 4-Year Cycle

64 **July Almanac**

66 First Month of Quarters Is the Most Bullish

68 2013 Daily Dow Point Changes

70 Don't Sell Stocks on Monday or Friday

72 A Rally for All Seasons

74 **August Almanac**

76 Best Investment Book of the Year: *Profitable Day and Swing Trading*

78 Aura of the Triple Witch—4th Quarter Most Bullish:
Down Weeks Trigger More Weakness Week After

80   Take Advantage of Down Friday/Down Monday Warning
82   **September Almanac**
84   A Correction for All Seasons
86   First-Trading-Day-of-the-Month Phenomenon:
      Dow Gains More One Day than All Other Days
88   Market Behavior Three Days before and Three Days after Holidays
90   **October Almanac**
92   Market Gains More on Super-8 Days Each Month
      than on All 13 Remaining Days Combined
94   Sector Seasonality: Selected Percentage Plays
96   Sector Index Seasonality Strategy Calendar
100   **November Almanac**
102   Fourth Quarter Market Magic
104   Trading the Thanksgiving Market
106   Most of the So-Called "January Effect" Takes Place in Last Half of
      December
108   **December Almanac**
110   January Effect Now Starts in Mid-December
112   Wall Street's Only "Free Lunch" Served before Christmas
114   If Santa Claus Should Fail to Call, Bears May Come to Broad and Wall
116   Year's Top Investment Books
118   2016 Strategy Calendar

DIRECTORY OF TRADING PATTERNS AND DATABANK

121   Dow Jones Industrials Market Probability Calendar 2015
122   <u>Recent</u> Dow Jones Industrials Market Probability Calendar 2015
123   S&P 500 Market Probability Calendar 2015
124   <u>Recent</u> S&P 500 Market Probability Calendar 2015
125   NASDAQ Composite Market Probability Calendar 2015
126   <u>Recent</u> NASDAQ Composite Market Probability Calendar 2015
127   Russell 1000 Index Market Probability Calendar 2015
128   Russell 2000 Index Market Probability Calendar 2015
129   Decennial Cycle: A Market Phenomenon
130   Presidential Election/Stock Market Cycle: The 181-Year Saga Continues
131   Dow Jones Industrials Bull and Bear Markets Since 1900
132   Standard & Poor's 500 Bull and Bear Markets Since 1929/NASDAQ Composite
      Since 1971
133   Dow Jones Industrials 10-Year Daily Point Changes: January and February
134   Dow Jones Industrials 10-Year Daily Point Changes: March and April
135   Dow Jones Industrials 10-Year Daily Point Changes: May and June
136   Dow Jones Industrials 10-Year Daily Point Changes: July and August
137   Dow Jones Industrials 10-Year Daily Point Changes: September and October
138   Dow Jones Industrials 10-Year Daily Point Changes: November and December
139   A Typical Day in the Market
140   Through the Week on a Half-Hourly Basis
141   Tuesday Most Profitable Day of Week
142   NASDAQ Strongest Last 3 Days of Week
143   S&P Daily Performance Each Year Since 1952

144   NASDAQ Daily Performance Each Year Since 1971
145   Monthly Cash Inflows into S&P Stocks
146   Monthly Cash Inflows into NASDAQ Stocks
147   November, December, and January: Year's Best Three-Month Span
148   November Through June: NASDAQ's Eight-Month Run
149   Dow Jones Industrials Annual Highs, Lows, and Closes Since 1901
150   S&P 500 Annual Highs, Lows, and Closes Since 1930
151   NASDAQ, Russell 1000 and 2000 Annual Highs, Lows, and Closes Since 1971
152   Dow Jones Industrials Monthly Percent Changes Since 1950
153   Dow Jones Industrials Monthly Point Changes Since 1950
154   Dow Jones Industrials Monthly Closing Prices Since 1950
155   Standard & Poor's 500 Monthly Percent Changes Since 1950
156   Standard & Poor's 500 Monthly Closing Prices Since 1950
157   NASDAQ Composite Monthly Percent Changes Since 1971
158   NASDAQ Composite Monthly Closing Prices Since 1971
159   Russell 1000 Monthly Percent Changes and Closing Prices Since 1979
160   Russell 2000 Monthly Percent Changes and Closing Prices Since 1979
161   10 Best Days by Percent and Point
162   10 Worst Days by Percent and Point
163   10 Best Weeks by Percent and Point
164   10 Worst Weeks by Percent and Point
165   10 Best Months by Percent and Point
166   10 Worst Months by Percent and Point
167   10 Best Quarters by Percent and Point
168   10 Worst Quarters by Percent and Point
169   10 Best Years by Percent and Point
170   10 Worst Years by Percent and Point
171   Dow Jones Industrials One-Year Seasonal Pattern Charts Since 1901
172   S&P 500 One-Year Seasonal Pattern Charts Since 1930
173   NASDAQ, Russell 1000 & 2000 One-Year Seasonal Pattern Charts Since 1971

STRATEGY PLANNING AND RECORD SECTION

175   Portfolio at Start of 2015
176   Additional Purchases
178   Short-Term Transactions
180   Long-Term Transactions
182   Interest/Dividends Received during 2015/Brokerage Account Data 2015
183   Weekly Portfolio Price Record 2015
185   Weekly Indicator Data 2015
187   Monthly Indicator Data 2015
188   Portfolio at End of 2015
189   If You Don't Profit from Your Investment Mistakes, Someone Else Will;
       Performance Record of Recommendations
190   Individual Retirement Account (IRA):
       Most Awesome Mass Investment Incentive Ever Devised
191   G.M. Loeb's "Battle Plan" for Investment Survival
192   G.M. Loeb's Investment Survival Checklist

2015 STRATEGY CALENDAR

(Option expiration dates circled)

	MONDAY	TUESDAY	WEDNESDAY	THURSDAY	FRIDAY	SATURDAY	SUNDAY
JANUARY	29	30	31	1 JANUARY New Year's Day	2	3	4
	5	6	7	8	9	10	11
	12	13	14	15	(16)	17	18
	19 Martin Luther King Day	20	21	22	23	24	25
	26	27	28	29	30	31	1 FEBRUARY
FEBRUARY	2	3	4	5	6	7	8
	9	10	11	12	13	14 ♥	15
	16 Presidents' Day	17	18 Ash Wednesday	19	(20)	21	22
	23	24	25	26	27	28	1 MARCH
MARCH	2	3	4	5	6	7	8 Daylight Saving Time Begins
	9	10	11	12	13	14	15
	16	17 ♣ St. Patrick's Day	18	19	(20)	21	22
	23	24	25	26	27	28	29
	30	31	1 APRIL	2	3 Good Friday	4 Passover	5 Easter
APRIL	6	7	8	9	10	11	12
	13	14	15 Tax Deadline	16	(17)	18	19
	20	21	22	23	24	25	26
	27	28	29	30	1 MAY	2	3
MAY	4	5	6	7	8	9	10 Mother's Day
	11	12	13	14	(15)	16	17
	18	19	20	21	22	23	24
	25 Memorial Day	26	27	28	29	30	31
JUNE	1 JUNE	2	3	4	5	6	7
	8	9	10	11	12	13	14
	15	16	17	18	(19)	20	21 Father's Day
	22	23	24	25	26	27	28

Market closed on shaded weekdays; closes early when half-shaded.

2015 STRATEGY CALENDAR

(Option expiration dates circled)

MONDAY	TUESDAY	WEDNESDAY	THURSDAY	FRIDAY	SATURDAY	SUNDAY	
29	30	1 JULY	2	3	4 Independence Day	5	
6	7	8	9	10	11	12	JULY
13	14	15	16	(17)	18	19	
20	21	22	23	24	25	26	
27	28	29	30	31	1 AUGUST	2	
3	4	5	6	7	8	9	
10	11	12	13	14	15	16	AUGUST
17	18	19	20	(21)	22	23	
24	25	26	27	28	29	30	
31	1 SEPTEMBER	2	3	4	5	6	
7 Labor Day	8	9	10	11	12	13	SEPTEMBER
14 Rosh Hashanah	15	16	17	(18)	19	20	
21	22	23 Yom Kippur	24	25	26	27	
28	29	30	1 OCTOBER	2	3	4	
5	6	7	8	9	10	11	OCTOBER
12 Columbus Day	13	14	15	(16)	17	18	
19	20	21	22	23	24	25	
26	27	28	29	30	31	1 NOVEMBER Daylight Saving Time Ends	
2	3 Election Day	4	5	6	7	8	NOVEMBER
9	10	11 Veterans' Day	12	13	14	15	
16	17	18	19	(20)	21	22	
23	24	25	26 Thanksgiving	27	28	29	
30	1 DECEMBER	2	3	4	5	6	DECEMBER
7 Chanukah	8	9	10	11	12	13	
14	15	16	17	(18)	19	20	
21	22	23	24	25 Christmas	26	27	
28	29	30	31	1 JANUARY New Year's Day	2	3	

JANUARY ALMANAC

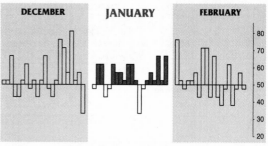

FEBRUARY

S	M	T	W	T	F	S
1	2	3	4	5	6	7
8	9	10	11	12	13	14
15	16	17	18	19	20	21
22	23	24	25	26	27	28

Market Probability Chart above is a graphic representation of the S&P 500 Recent Market Probability Calendar on page 124.

◆ January Barometer predicts year's course with .766 batting average (page 16) ◆ 14 of last 16 pre-presidential election years followed January's direction ◆ Every down January on the S&P since 1950, *without exception*, preceded a new or extended bear market, a flat market, or a 10% correction (page 48) ◆ S&P gains January's first five days preceded full-year gains 85.4% of the time, 12 of last 16 pre-presidential election years followed first five days' direction (page 14) ◆ November, December, and January constitute the year's best three-month span, a 4.3% S&P gain (pages 50 & 147) ◆ January NASDAQ powerful 2.9% since 1971 (pages 58 & 148) ◆ "January Effect" now starts in mid-December and favors small-cap stocks (pages 106 & 110) ◆ 2009 has the dubious honor of the worst S&P 500 January on record.

January Vital Statistics

	DJIA	S&P 500	NASDAQ	Russell 1K	Russell 2K
Rank	6	5	1	5	2
Up	42	40	29	23	20
Down	23	25	15	13	16
Average % Change	1.0%	1.1%	2.9%	1.1%	1.8%
Pre-Election Year	4.2%	4.3%	7.3%	3.6%	3.9%
Best & Worst January					
	% Change	% Change	% Change	% Change	% Change
Best	1976 14.4	1987 13.2	1975 16.6	1987 12.7	1985 13.1
Worst	2009 −8.8	2009 −8.6	2008 −9.9	2009 −8.3	2009 −11.2
Best & Worst January Weeks					
Best	1/9/76 6.1	1/2/09 6.8	1/12/01 9.1	1/2/09 6.8	1/9/87 7.0
Worst	1/24/03 −5.3	1/28/00 −5.6	1/28/00 −8.2	1/28/00 −5.5	1/4/08 −6.5
Best & Worst January Days					
Best	1/17/91 4.6	1/3/01 5.0	1/3/01 14.2	1/3/01 5.3	1/21/09 5.3
Worst	1/8/88 −6.9	1/8/88 −6.8	1/2/01 −7.2	1/8/88 −6.1	1/20/09 −7.0
First Trading Day of Expiration Week: 1980–2014					
Record (#Up–#Down)	24–11	21–14	20–15	20–15	20–15
Current streak	D1	D2	D2	D2	D2
Avg % Change	0.12	0.10	0.13	0.08	0.14
Options Expiration Day: 1980–2014					
Record (#Up–#Down)	18–17	18–17	18–17	18–17	19–16
Current streak	U4	D1	D5	D1	D1
Avg % Change	−0.09	−0.10	−0.16	−0.12	−0.12
Options Expiration Week: 1980–2014					
Record (#Up–#Down)	19–16	15–20	20–15	15–20	19–16
Current streak	U4	D1	U3	D1	U3
Avg % Change	−0.15	−0.07	0.26	−0.08	0.25
Week After Options Expiration: 1980–2014					
Record (#Up–#Down)	18–17	21–14	19–16	21–14	23–12
Current streak	D1	D1	D1	D1	D1
Avg % Change	−0.06	0.14	0.05	0.11	0.15
First Trading Day Performance					
% of Time Up	58.2	49.2	56.8	44.4	47.2
Avg % Change	0.27	0.17	0.23	0.18	0.10
Last Trading Day Performance					
% of Time Up	56.9	61.5	63.6	58.3	75.0
Avg % Change	0.21	0.25	0.28	0.32	0.26

Dow & S&P 1950–April 2014, NASDAQ 1971–April 2014, Russell 1K & 2K 1979–April 2014.

20th Amendment made "lame ducks" disappear.
Now, "As January goes, so goes the year."

MONDAY

D 52.4
S 52.4
N 47.6

29

So much hangs on the decisions of a small number of poorly educated people. That's Democracy. A terrible way to run a country, but every other system is worse.
— Kenneth Martin Follett (Welsh author, *Fall of Giants*, b. 1949)

TUESDAY

D 42.9
S 57.1
N 47.6

30

The death of contrarians has been greatly exaggerated. The reason is that the crowd is the market for most of any cycle. You cannot be contrarian all the time, otherwise you end up simply fighting the tape the whole way up (or down), therefore being wildly wrong.
— Barry L. Ritholtz (Founder/CIO Ritholtz Wealth Management, *Bailout Nation*, *The Big Picture* blog, Bloomberg View 12/20/2013, b. 1961)

Last Trading Day of the Year, NASDAQ Down 11 of last 14
NASDAQ Was Up 29 Years in a Row 1971–1999

WEDNESDAY

D 42.9
S 33.3
N 47.6

31

If the market prefers a system that looks inefficient, that's a good sign that it's more efficient than it looks.
— Matt Levine (Bloomberg View columnist, former investment banker, lawyer, & high school Latin teacher)

New Years Day (*Market Closed*)

THURSDAY

1

At the end of the day, the most important thing is how good are you at risk control. Ninety-percent of any great trader is going to be the risk control.
— Paul Tudor Jones II (Founder Tudor Investment Corporation, b. 1954)

Small Caps Punished First Trading Day of Year
Russell 2000 Down 15 of Last 25, But Up 5 of Last 6

FRIDAY

D 71.4
S 47.6
N 66.7

2

Successful investing is anticipating the anticipations of others.
— John Maynard Keynes (British economist, 1883–1946)

SATURDAY

3

January Almanac Investor Seasonalities: See Pages 94, 96 and 98

SUNDAY

4

JANUARY'S FIRST FIVE DAYS: AN EARLY WARNING SYSTEM

The last 41 up First Five Days were followed by full-year gains 35 times for an 85.4% accuracy ratio and a 14.0% average gain in all 41 years. The five exceptions include flat 1994 and four related to war. Vietnam military spending delayed start of 1966 bear market. Ceasefire imminence early in 1973 raised stocks temporarily. Saddam Hussein turned 1990 into a bear. The war on terrorism, instability in the Mideast, and corporate malfeasance shaped 2002 into one of the worst years on record. The 23 down First Five Days were followed by 12 up years and 11 down (47.8% accurate) and an average gain of 0.2%.

In pre-presidential election years this indicator has a solid record. In the last 16 pre-presidential election years 12 full years followed the direction of the First Five Days; however, 2007 and 2011 did not. The full-month January Barometer (page 16) has an even better record as 14 of the last 16 full years have followed January's direction.

THE FIRST-FIVE-DAYS-IN-JANUARY INDICATOR

Chronological Data / Ranked by Performance

Year	Previous Year's Close	January 5th Day	5-Day Change	Year Change	Rank	Year	5-Day Change	Year Change
1950	16.76	17.09	2.0%	21.8%	1	1987	6.2%	2.0%
1951	20.41	20.88	2.3	16.5	2	1976	4.9	19.1
1952	23.77	23.91	0.6	11.8	3	1999	3.7	19.5
1953	26.57	26.33	-0.9	-6.6	4	2003	3.4	26.4
1954	24.81	24.93	0.5	45.0	5	2006	3.4	13.6
1955	35.98	35.33	-1.8	26.4	6	1983	3.3	17.3
1956	45.48	44.51	-2.1	2.6	7	1967	3.1	20.1
1957	46.67	46.25	-0.9	-14.3	8	1979	2.8	12.3
1958	39.99	40.99	2.5	38.1	9	2010	2.7	12.8
1959	55.21	55.40	0.3	8.5	10	1963	2.6	18.9
1960	59.89	59.50	-0.7	-3.0	11	1958	2.5	38.1
1961	58.11	58.81	1.2	23.1	12	1984	2.4	1.4
1962	71.55	69.12	-3.4	-11.8	13	1951	2.3	16.5
1963	63.10	64.74	2.6	18.9	14	2013	2.2	29.6
1964	75.02	76.00	1.3	13.0	15	1975	2.2	31.5
1965	84.75	85.37	0.7	9.1	16	1950	2.0	21.8
1966	92.43	93.14	0.8	-13.1	17	2004	1.8	9.0
1967	80.33	82.81	3.1	20.1	18	2012	1.8	13.4
1968	96.47	96.62	0.2	7.7	19	1973	1.5	-17.4
1969	103.86	100.80	-2.9	-11.4	20	1972	1.4	15.6
1970	92.06	92.68	0.7	0.1	21	1964	1.3	13.0
1971	92.15	92.19	0.04	10.8	22	1961	1.2	23.1
1972	102.09	103.47	1.4	15.6	23	1989	1.2	27.3
1973	118.05	119.85	1.5	-17.4	24	2011	1.1	-0.003
1974	97.55	96.12	-1.5	-29.7	25	2002	1.1	-23.4
1975	68.56	70.04	2.2	31.5	26	1997	1.0	31.0
1976	90.19	94.58	4.9	19.1	27	1980	0.9	25.8
1977	107.46	105.01	-2.3	-11.5	28	1966	0.8	-13.1
1978	95.10	90.64	-4.7	1.1	29	1994	0.7	-1.5
1979	96.11	98.80	2.8	12.3	30	1965	0.7	9.1
1980	107.94	108.95	0.9	25.8	31	2009	0.7	23.5
1981	135.76	133.06	-2.0	-9.7	32	1970	0.7	0.1
1982	122.55	119.55	-2.4	14.8	33	1952	0.6	11.8
1983	140.64	145.23	3.3	17.3	34	1954	0.5	45.0
1984	164.93	168.90	2.4	1.4	35	1996	0.4	20.3
1985	167.24	163.99	-1.9	26.3	36	1959	0.3	8.5
1986	211.28	207.97	-1.6	14.6	37	1995	0.3	34.1
1987	242.17	257.28	6.2	2.0	38	1992	0.2	4.5
1988	247.08	243.40	-1.5	12.4	39	1968	0.2	7.7
1989	277.72	280.98	1.2	27.3	40	1990	0.1	-6.6
1990	353.40	353.79	0.1	-6.6	41	1971	0.04	10.8
1991	330.22	314.90	-4.6	26.3	42	2007	-0.4	3.5
1992	417.09	418.10	0.2	4.5	43	2014	-0.6	??
1993	435.71	429.05	-1.5	7.1	44	1960	-0.7	-3.0
1994	466.45	469.90	0.7	-1.5	45	1957	-0.9	-14.3
1995	459.27	460.83	0.3	34.1	46	1953	-0.9	-6.6
1996	615.93	618.46	0.4	20.3	47	1974	-1.5	-29.7
1997	740.74	748.41	1.0	31.0	48	1998	-1.5	26.7
1998	970.43	956.04	-1.5	26.7	49	1988	-1.5	12.4
1999	1229.23	1275.09	3.7	19.5	50	1993	-1.5	7.1
2000	1469.25	1441.46	-1.9	-10.1	51	1986	-1.6	14.6
2001	1320.28	1295.86	-1.8	-13.0	52	2001	-1.8	-13.0
2002	1148.08	1160.71	1.1	-23.4	53	1955	-1.8	26.4
2003	879.82	909.93	3.4	26.4	54	2000	-1.9	-10.1
2004	1111.92	1131.91	1.8	9.0	55	1985	-1.9	26.3
2005	1211.92	1186.19	-2.1	3.0	56	1981	-2.0	-9.7
2006	1248.29	1290.15	3.4	13.6	57	1956	-2.1	2.6
2007	1418.30	1412.11	-0.4	3.5	58	2005	-2.1	3.0
2008	1468.36	1390.19	-5.3	-38.5	59	1977	-2.3	-11.5
2009	903.25	909.73	0.7	23.5	60	1982	-2.4	14.8
2010	1115.10	1144.98	2.7	12.8	61	1969	-2.9	-11.4
2011	1257.64	1271.50	1.1	-0.003	62	1962	-3.4	-11.8
2012	1257.60	1280.70	1.8	13.4	63	1991	-4.6	26.3
2013	1426.19	1457.15	2.2	29.6	64	1978	-4.7	1.1
2014	1848.36	1837.49	-0.6	??	65	2008	-5.3	-38.5

Based on S&P 500

JANUARY

Second Trading Day of the Year, Dow Up 14 of Last 21
Santa Claus Rally Ends (Page 114)

MONDAY
D 66.7
S 61.9
N 61.9
5

Between two evils, I always pick the one I never tried before.
— Mae West (American actress and playwright, 1893–1980)

January Ends "Best Three-Month Span" (Pages 50, 56, 147 and 148)

TUESDAY
D 52.4
S 61.9
N 57.1
6

The Stone Age didn't end for lack of stone, and the oil age will end long before the world runs out of oil.
— Sheikh Ahmed Zaki Yamani (Saudi oil minister 1962–1986, b. 1930)

WEDNESDAY
D 47.6
S 42.9
N 52.4
7

The symbol of all relationships among such men, the moral symbol of respect for human beings, is the trader.
— Ayn Rand (Russian-born American novelist and philosopher, from Galt's Speech, *Atlas Shrugged*, 1957, 1905–1982)

January's First Five Days Act as an "Early Warning" (Page 14)

THURSDAY
D 38.1
S 47.6
N 52.4
8

One machine can do the work of fifty ordinary men. No machine can do the work of one extraordinary man.
— Elbert Hubbard (American author, *A Message to Garcia*, 1856–1915)

FRIDAY
D 57.1
S 61.9
N 71.4
9

Things may come to those who wait, but only the things left by those who hustle.
— Abraham Lincoln (16th U.S. President, 1809–1865)

SATURDAY
10

SUNDAY
11

THE INCREDIBLE JANUARY BAROMETER (DEVISED 1972): ONLY SEVEN SIGNIFICANT ERRORS IN 64 YEARS

Devised by Yale Hirsch in 1972, our January Barometer states that as the S&P 500 goes in January, so goes the year. The indicator has registered **only seven major errors since 1950 for an 89.1% accuracy ratio**. Vietnam affected 1966 and 1968; 1982 saw the start of a major bull market in August; two January rate cuts and 9/11 affected 2001; the anticipation of military action in Iraq held down the market in January 2003; 2009 was the beginning of a new bull market following the second worst bear market on record; and the Fed saved 2010 with QE2. (*Almanac Investor* newsletter subscribers receive full analysis of each reading as well as its potential implications for the full year.)

Including the eight flat-year errors (less than +/– 5%) yields a 76.6% accuracy ratio. A full comparison of all monthly barometers for the Dow, S&P, and NASDAQ in our January 18, 2013, blog post at *blog.stocktradersalmanac.com* details January's market forecasting prowess. Bear markets began or continued when Januarys suffered a loss (see page 48). Full years followed January's direction in 14 of the last 16 pre-presidential election years. See page 18 for more.

AS JANUARY GOES, SO GOES THE YEAR

Market Performance in January

	Previous Year's Close	January Close	January Change	Year Change	
1950	16.76	17.05	1.7%	21.8%	
1951	20.41	21.66	6.1	16.5	
1952	23.77	24.14	1.6	11.8	
1953	26.57	26.38	−0.7	−6.6	
1954	24.81	26.08	5.1	45.0	
1955	35.98	36.63	1.8	26.4	
1956	45.48	43.82	−3.6	2.6	flat
1957	46.67	44.72	−4.2	−14.3	
1958	39.99	41.70	4.3	38.1	
1959	55.21	55.42	0.4	8.5	
1960	59.89	55.61	−7.1	−3.0	flat
1961	58.11	61.78	6.3	23.1	
1962	71.55	68.84	−3.8	−11.8	
1963	63.10	66.20	4.9	18.9	
1964	75.02	77.04	2.7	13.0	
1965	84.75	87.56	3.3	9.1	
1966	92.43	92.88	0.5	−13.1	X
1967	80.33	86.61	7.8	20.1	
1968	96.47	92.24	−4.4	7.7	X
1969	103.86	103.01	−0.8	−11.4	
1970	92.06	85.02	−7.6	0.1	flat
1971	92.15	95.88	4.0	10.8	
1972	102.09	103.94	1.8	15.6	
1973	118.05	116.03	−1.7	−17.4	
1974	97.55	96.57	−1.0	−29.7	
1975	68.56	76.98	12.3	31.5	
1976	90.19	100.86	11.8	19.1	
1977	107.46	102.03	−5.1	−11.5	
1978	95.10	89.25	−6.2	1.1	flat
1979	96.11	99.93	4.0	12.3	
1980	107.94	114.16	5.8	25.8	
1981	135.76	129.55	−4.6	−9.7	
1982	122.55	120.40	−1.8	14.8	X
1983	140.64	145.30	3.3	17.3	
1984	164.93	163.41	−0.9	1.4	flat
1985	167.24	179.63	7.4	26.3	
1986	211.28	211.78	0.2	14.6	
1987	242.17	274.08	13.2	2.0	flat
1988	247.08	257.07	4.0	12.4	
1989	277.72	297.47	7.1	27.3	
1990	353.40	329.08	−6.9	−6.6	
1991	330.22	343.93	4.2	26.3	
1992	417.09	408.79	−2.0	4.5	flat
1993	435.71	438.78	0.7	7.1	
1994	466.45	481.61	3.3	−1.5	flat
1995	459.27	470.42	2.4	34.1	
1996	615.93	636.02	3.3	20.3	
1997	740.74	786.16	6.1	31.0	
1998	970.43	980.28	1.0	26.7	
1999	1229.23	1279.64	4.1	19.5	
2000	1469.25	1394.46	−5.1	−10.1	
2001	1320.28	1366.01	3.5	−13.0	X
2002	1148.08	1130.20	−1.6	−23.4	X
2003	879.82	855.70	−2.7	26.4	X
2004	1111.92	1131.13	1.7	9.0	
2005	1211.92	1181.27	−2.5	3.0	flat
2006	1248.29	1280.08	2.5	13.6	
2007	1418.30	1438.24	1.4	3.5	flat
2008	1468.36	1378.55	−6.1	−38.5	
2009	903.25	825.88	−8.6	23.5	X
2010	1115.10	1073.87	−3.7	12.8	X
2011	1257.64	1286.12	2.3	−0.003	flat
2012	1257.60	1312.41	4.4	13.4	
2013	1426.19	1498.11	5.0	29.6	
2014	1848.36	1782.59	−3.6	??	

January Performance by Rank

Rank		January Change	Year's Change	
1	1987	13.2%	2.0%	flat
2	1975	12.3	31.5	
3	1976	11.8	19.1	
4	1967	7.8	20.1	
5	1985	7.4	26.3	
6	1989	7.1	27.3	
7	1961	6.3	23.1	
8	1997	6.1	31.0	
9	1951	6.1	16.5	
10	1980	5.8	25.8	
11	1954	5.1	45.0	
12	2013	5.0	29.6	
13	1963	4.9	18.9	
14	2012	4.4	13.4	
15	1958	4.3	38.1	
16	1991	4.2	26.3	
17	1999	4.1	19.5	
18	1971	4.0	10.8	
19	1988	4.0	12.4	
20	1979	4.0	12.3	
21	2001	3.5	−13.0	X
22	1965	3.3	9.1	
23	1983	3.3	17.3	
24	1996	3.3	20.3	
25	1994	3.3	−1.5	flat
26	1964	2.7	13.0	
27	2006	2.5	13.6	
28	1995	2.4	34.1	
29	2011	2.3	−0.003	flat
30	1972	1.8	15.6	
31	1955	1.8	26.4	
32	1950	1.7	21.8	
33	2004	1.7	9.0	
34	1952	1.6	11.8	
35	2007	1.4	3.5	flat
36	1998	1.0	26.7	
37	1993	0.7	7.1	
38	1966	0.5	−13.1	X
39	1959	0.4	8.5	
40	1986	0.2	14.6	
41	1953	−0.7	−6.6	
42	1969	−0.8	−11.4	
43	1984	−0.9	1.4	flat
44	1974	−1.0	−29.7	
45	2002	−1.6	−23.4	X
46	1973	−1.7	−17.4	
47	1982	−1.8	14.8	X
48	1992	−2.0	4.5	flat
49	2005	−2.5	3.0	flat
50	2003	−2.7	26.4	X
51	2014	−3.6	??	
52	1956	−3.6	2.6	flat
53	2010	−3.7	12.8	X
54	1962	−3.8	−11.8	
55	1957	−4.2	−14.3	
56	1968	−4.4	7.7	X
57	1981	−4.6	−9.7	
58	1977	−5.1	−11.5	
59	2000	−5.1	−10.1	
60	2008	−6.1	−38.5	
61	1978	−6.2	1.1	flat
62	1990	−6.9	−6.6	
63	1960	−7.1	−3.0	flat
64	1970	−7.6	0.1	flat
65	2009	−8.6	23.5	X

X = major error Based on S&P 500

JANUARY

First Trading Day of January Expiration Week, Dow Up 16 of Last 22

MONDAY

D 52.4
S 57.1
N 57.1

12

While markets often make double bottoms, three pushes to a high is the most common topping pattern.
— John Bollinger (Bollinger Capital Management, *Capital Growth Letter, Bollinger on Bollinger Bands*)

TUESDAY

D 57.1
S 57.1
N 61.9

13

The man who can master his time can master nearly anything.
— Winston Churchill (British statesman, 1874–1965)

**January Expiration Week Horrible Since 1999, Dow Down 9 of Last 16
Average Dow loss: –1.3%**

WEDNESDAY

D 52.4
S 52.4
N 52.4

14

The difference between life and the movies is that a script has to make sense, and life doesn't.
— Joseph L. Mankiewicz (Film director, writer, producer, 1909–1993)

THURSDAY

D 61.9
S 61.9
N 47.6

15

The secret to business is to know something that nobody else knows.
— Aristotle Onassis (Greek shipping billionaire, 1906–1975)

**January Expiration Day, Dow Down 10 of Last 16 with Big Losses
Off 2.1% in 2010, Off 2.0% in 2006 and 1.3% in 2003**

FRIDAY

D 57.1
S 61.9
N 71.4

16

A good new chairman of the Federal Reserve Bank is worth a $10 billion tax cut.
— Paul H. Douglas (U.S. Senator Illinois 1949–1967, 1892–1976)

SATURDAY

17

SUNDAY

18

JANUARY BAROMETER IN GRAPHIC FORM SINCE 1950

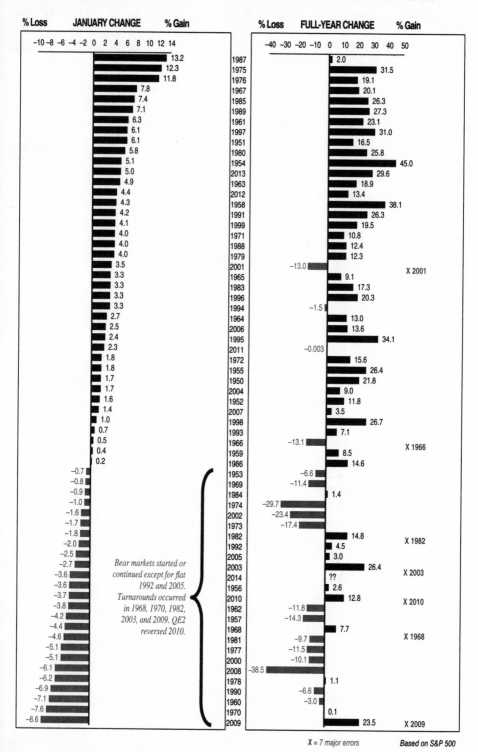

% Loss	JANUARY CHANGE	% Gain	Year	% Loss	FULL-YEAR CHANGE	% Gain	
		13.2	1987		2.0		
		12.3	1975			31.5	
		11.8	1976		19.1		
		7.8	1967		20.1		
		7.4	1985		26.3		
		7.1	1989		27.3		
		6.3	1961		23.1		
		6.1	1997		31.0		
		6.1	1951		16.5		
		5.8	1980		25.8		
		5.1	1954			45.0	
		5.0	2013		29.6		
		4.9	1963		18.9		
		4.4	2012		13.4		
		4.3	1958			38.1	
		4.2	1991		26.3		
		4.1	1999		19.5		
		4.0	1971		10.8		
		4.0	1988		12.4		
		4.0	1979		12.3		
		3.5	2001	−13.0			X 2001
		3.3	1965		9.1		
		3.3	1983		17.3		
		3.3	1996		20.3		
		3.3	1994	−1.5			
		2.7	1964		13.0		
		2.5	2006		13.6		
		2.4	1995			34.1	
		2.3	2011	−0.003			
		1.8	1972		15.6		
		1.8	1955		26.4		
		1.7	1950		21.8		
		1.7	2004		9.0		
		1.6	1952		11.8		
		1.4	2007		3.5		
		1.0	1998		26.7		
		0.7	1993		7.1		
		0.5	1966	−13.1			X 1966
		0.4	1959		8.5		
		0.2	1986		14.6		
−0.7			1953		−6.6		
−0.8			1969		−11.4		
−0.9			1984		1.4		
−1.0			1974	−29.7			
−1.6			2002	−23.4			
−1.7			1973	−17.4			
−1.8			1982		14.8		X 1982
−2.0			1992		4.5		
−2.5			2005		3.0		
−2.7			2003		26.4		X 2003
−3.6			2014		??		
−3.6			1956		2.6		
−3.7			2010		12.8		X 2010
−3.8			1962	−11.8			
−4.2			1957	−14.3			
−4.4			1968		7.7		X 1968
−4.6			1981	−9.7			
−5.1			1977	−11.5			
−5.1			2000	−10.1			
−6.1			2008	−38.5			
−6.2			1978		1.1		
−6.9			1990		−6.6		
−7.1			1960		−3.0		
−7.6			1970		0.1		
−8.6			2009			23.5	X 2009

Bear markets started or continued except for flat 1992 and 2005. Turnarounds occurred in 1968, 1970, 1982, 2003, and 2009. QE2 reversed 2010.

X = 7 major errors   Based on S&P 500

18

JANUARY

Martin Luther King Jr. Day (*Market Closed*)

MONDAY

19

If banking institutions are protected by the taxpayer and they are given free reign to speculate, I may not live long enough to see the crisis, but my soul is going to come back and haunt you.
— Paul A. Volcker (Fed Chairman 1979–1987, Chair Economic Recovery Advisory Board, 2/2/2010, b. 1927)

TUESDAY

D 33.3
S 52.4
N 66.7

20

Banking establishments are more dangerous than standing armies; and that the principle of spending money to be paid by posterity, under the name of funding, is but swindling futurity on a large scale.
— Thomas Jefferson (3rd U.S. President, 1743–7/4/1826, 1816 letter to John Taylor of Caroline)

WEDNESDAY

D 33.3
S 33.3
N 28.6

21

We are like tenant farmers chopping down the fence around our house for fuel when we should be using Nature's inexhaustible sources of energy—sun, wind and tide. I'd put my money on the sun and solar energy. What a source of power! I hope we don't have to wait until oil and coal run out before we tackle that.
— Thomas Alva Edison (American inventor, 1093 patents, 1847–1931)

THURSDAY

D 38.1
S 47.6
N 38.1

22

If you are ready to give up everything else to study the whole history of the market as carefully as a medical student studies anatomy and you have the cool nerves of a great gambler, the sixth sense of a clairvoyant, and the courage of a lion, you have a ghost of a chance.
— Bernard Baruch (Financier, speculator, statesman, presidential adviser, 1870–1965)

FRIDAY

D 38.1
S 52.4
N 57.1

23

The future now belongs to societies that organize themselves for learning. What we know and can do holds the key to economic progress.
— Ray Marshall (b. 1928) and Marc Tucker (b. 1939) (*Thinking for a Living: Education and the Wealth of Nations*, 1992)

SATURDAY

24

SUNDAY

25

PRE-PRESIDENTIAL ELECTION YEARS NO LOSERS IN 76 YEARS

Investors should feel somewhat more secure going into 2015. There hasn't been a down year in the third year of a presidential term since war-torn 1939, Dow off 2.9%. The only severe loss in a pre-presidential election year going back 100 years occurred in 1931 during the Depression.

Electing a president every four years has set in motion a 4-year political stock market cycle. Most bear markets take place in the first or second years after elections (see pages 130–131). Then, the market improves. Typically each administration usually does everything in its power to juice up the economy so that voters are in a positive mood at election time.

Quite an impressive record. Chances are the winning streak will continue and that the market, in pre-presidential election year 2015, will gain ground. Prospects improve considerably if the market takes a breather in 2014 following the robust bull run of 2013.

THE RECORD SINCE 1915

Year	President	
1915	Wilson (D)	World War I in Europe, but Dow up 81.7%.
1919	Wilson (D)	Post-Armistice 45.5% gain through Nov 3 top. Dow +30.5%
1923	Harding/Coolidge (R)	Teapot Dome scandal a depressant. Dow loses 3.3%.
1927	Coolidge (R)	Bull market rolls on, up 28.8%.
1931	Hoover (R)	Depression, stocks slashed in half. Dow −52.7%, S&P −47.1%
1935	Roosevelt (D)	Almost a straight up year, S&P 500 up 41.2%, Dow 38.5%.
1939	Roosevelt (D)	War clouds, Dow −2.9% but 23.7% Apr-Dec gain. S&P −5.5%
1943	Roosevelt (D)	U.S. at war, prospects brighter, S&P +19.4%, Dow +13.8%.
1947	Truman (D)	S&P unchanged, Dow up 2.2%.
1951	Truman (D)	Dow +14.4%, S&P +16.5%.
1955	Eisenhower (R)	Dow +20.8%, S&P +26.4%.
1959	Eisenhower (R)	Dow +16.4%, S&P +8.5%.
1963	Kennedy/Johnson (D)	Dow +17.0%, S&P +18.9%.
1967	Johnson (D)	Dow +15.2%, S&P +20.1%.
1971	Nixon (R)	Dow +6.1%, S&P +10.8%, NASDAQ +27.4%.
1975	Ford (R)	Dow +38.3%, S&P +31.5%, NASDAQ +29.8%.
1979	Carter (D)	Dow +4.2%, S&P +12.3%, NASDAQ +28.1%.
1983	Reagan (R)	Dow +20.3%, S&P +17.3%, NASDAQ +19.9%.
1987	Reagan (R)	Dow +2.3%, S&P +2.0% despite Oct meltdown. NAS −5.4%.
1991	G.H.W. Bush (R)	Dow +20.3%, S&P +26.3%, NASDAQ +56.8%.
1995	Clinton (D)	Dow +33.5%, S&P +34.1%, NASDAQ +39.9%.
1999	Clinton (D)	Millennial fever crescendo: Dow +25.2%, S&P +19.5%, NASDAQ +85.6%.
2003	G.W. Bush (R)	Straight up after fall of Saddam: Dow +25.3% S&P +26.4%, NASDAQ +50.0%
2007	G.W. Bush (R)	Credit bubble fuels all-time market highs before bear starts & Great Recession: Dow: +6.4% S&P: +3.5% NASDAQ: 9.8%
2011	Obama (D)	Debt Ceiling Debacle and U.S. credit rating downgrade: Dow +5.5% S&P −0.003% NASDAQ: −1.8%

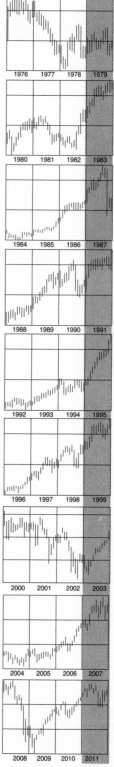

Graph shows Pre-Presidential Election years screened
Based on Dow Jones Industial Average monthly ranges

JANUARY/FEBRUARY

MONDAY

D 61.9
S 57.1
N 47.6

26

The only function of economic forecasting is to make astrology look respectable.
— John Kenneth Galbraith (Canadian/American economist and diplomat, 1908–2006)

FOMC Meeting (2 Days)

TUESDAY

D 61.9
S 52.4
N 76.2

27

We can guarantee cash benefits as far out and at whatever size you like, but we cannot guarantee their purchasing power.
— Alan Greenspan (Fed Chairman 1987–2006, on funding Social Security to Senate Banking Committee 2/15/05)

WEDNESDAY

D 61.9
S 66.7
N 71.4

28

The years teach much which the days never know.
— Ralph Waldo Emerson (American author, poet, and philosopher, *Self-Reliance*, 1803–1882)

THURSDAY

D 47.6
S 52.4
N 42.9

29

We like what's familiar, and we dislike change. So, we push the familiar until it starts working against us big-time—a crisis. Then, MAYBE we can accept change.
— Kevin Cameron (Journalist, *Cycle World*, April 2013)

"January Barometer" 89.1% Accurate (Page 16)
Almanac Investor Subscribers Emailed Official Results (See Insert)

FRIDAY

D 61.9
S 66.7
N 61.9

30

It is totally unproductive to think the world has been unfair to you. Every tough stretch is an opportunity.
— Charlie Munger (Vice-Chairman Berkshire Hathaway, 2007 Wesco Annual Meeting, b. 1924)

SATURDAY

31

February Almanac Investor Seasonalities: See Pages 94, 96 and 98

SUNDAY

1

FEBRUARY ALMANAC

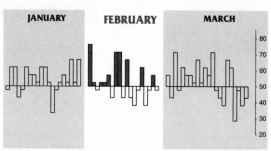

FEBRUARY						
S	M	T	W	T	F	S
1	2	3	4	5	6	7
8	9	10	11	12	13	14
15	16	17	18	19	20	21
22	23	24	25	26	27	28

MARCH						
S	M	T	W	T	F	S
1	2	3	4	5	6	7
8	9	10	11	12	13	14
15	16	17	18	19	20	21
22	23	24	25	26	27	28
29	30	31				

Market Probability Chart above is a graphic representation of the S&P 500 Recent Market Probability Calendar on page 124.

♦ February is the weak link in "Best Six Months" (pages 50, 52, & 147)
♦ RECENT RECORD: S&P up 8, down 7, average change –0.9% last 15 years ♦ Fifth best NASDAQ month in pre-presidential election years average gain 2.4%, up 8, down 3 (page 157), #7 Dow, up 10, down 6, and #7 S&P, up 10, down 6 (pages 153 & 155) ♦ Day before Presidents' Day weekend S&P down 17 of 23, 11 straight 1992–2002, day after down 8 of last 14 (see pages 88 & 133) ♦ Many technicians modify market predictions based on January's market.

February Vital Statistics

	DJIA	S&P 500	NASDAQ	Russell 1K	Russell 2K
Rank	8	9	8	10	7
Up	38	36	24	22	21
Down	27	29	20	14	15
Average % Change	0.1%	–0.03%	0.6%	0.2%	1.1%
Pre-Election Year	1.0%	0.8%	2.4%	1.1%	2.1%
Best & Worst February					
	% Change	% Change	% Change	% Change	% Change
Best	1986 8.8	1986 7.1	2000 19.2	1986 7.2	2000 16.4
Worst	2009 –11.7	2009 –11.0	2001 –22.4	2009 –10.7	2009 –12.3
Best & Worst February Weeks					
Best	2/1/08 4.4	2/6/09 5.2	2/4/00 9.2	2/6/09 5.3	2/1/91 6.6
Worst	2/20/09 –6.2	2/20/09 –6.9	2/9/01 –7.1	2/20/09 –6.9	2/20/09 –8.3
Best & Worst February Days					
Best	2/24/09 3.3	2/24/09 4.0	2/11/99 4.2	2/24/09 4.1	2/24/09 4.5
Worst	2/10/09 –4.6	2/10/09 –4.9	2/16/01 –5.0	2/10/09 –4.8	2/10/09 –4.7
First Trading Day of Expiration Week: 1980–2014					
Record (#Up–#Down)	20–15	24–11	19–16	24–11	20–15
Current streak	D2	U1	U1	U1	U1
Avg % Change	0.27	0.23	0.03	0.20	0.07
Options Expiration Day: 1980–2014					
Record (#Up–#Down)	17–18	14–21	13–22	15–20	15–20
Current streak	D1	D2	D3	D2	U1
Avg % Change	–0.07	–0.15	–0.29	–0.15	–0.10
Options Expiration Week: 1980–2014					
Record (#Up–#Down)	20–15	18–17	18–17	18–17	22–13
Current streak	D2	D1	U1	U5	U5
Avg % Change	0.32	0.11	–0.03	0.11	0.19
Week After Options Expiration: 1980–2014					
Record (#Up–#Down)	16–19	16–19	19–16	16–19	18–17
Current streak	U3	U1	U1	U1	U1
Avg % Change	–0.32	–0.23	–0.22	–0.19	–0.12
First Trading Day Performance					
% of Time Up	61.5	61.5	70.5	66.7	66.7
Avg % Change	0.13	0.14	0.32	0.17	0.33
Last Trading Day Performance					
% of Time Up	50.8	56.9	52.3	58.3	58.3
Avg % Change	0.01	–0.01	–0.05	–0.04	0.10

Dow & S&P 1950–April 2014, NASDAQ 1971–April 2014, Russell 1K & 2K 1979–April 2014.

Either go short, or stay away the day before Presidents' Day.

FEBRUARY

MONDAY

D 76.2
S 76.2
N 81.0

2

When investment decisions need to consider the speed of light, something is seriously wrong.
— Frank M. Bifulco (Senior Portfolio Manager Alcott Capital Management, *Barron's Letters to the Editor*, 5/24/2010)

TUESDAY

D 42.9
S 52.4
N 57.1

3

Every man who knows how to read has it in his power to magnify himself, to multiply the ways in which he exists, to make his life full, significant and interesting.
— Aldous Huxley (English author, *Brave New World*, 1894–1963)

WEDNESDAY

D 47.6
S 47.6
N 47.6

4

Today's Ponzi-style acute fragility and speculative dynamics dictate that he who panics first panics best.
— Doug Noland (Prudent Bear Funds, *Credit Bubble Bulletin*, 10/26/07)

THURSDAY

D 52.4
S 52.4
N 52.4

5

The worst crime against working people is a company that fails to make a profit.
— Samuel Gompers (American labor leader, 1850–1924)

FRIDAY

D 57.1
S 52.4
N 57.1

6

Foolish consistency is the hobgoblin of little minds.
— Ralph Waldo Emerson (American author, poet, and philosopher, *Self-Reliance*, 1803–1882)

SATURDAY

7

SUNDAY

8

2015 OUTLOOKS FROM SOME OF THE BEST MINDS ON WALL STREET

As we do every edition, we've provided our outlook for the coming year on page 6. This year we have invited some of our favorite minds on Wall Street to share their early outlooks with us and our readers. We reached out to all whose opinions and analysis we respect and read on a regular basis and asked if they would share a brief outlook for 2015. The response was overwhelming—and humbling. We want to express our deepest gratitude to all those who were able and willing to stick their necks out and make a call for 2015. In order of receipt:

There are a variety of historical anecdotes that suggest 2015 will be a good year for stocks. But what if history doesn't repeat itself and actually "forgets the words," like singers of the national anthem? Remember that it's usually better to buy than it is to bail. Since WWII, nearly 90% of all declines in excess of 5% got back to breakeven in an average of only four months after hitting bottom. So be less concerned about getting out at the top, and focus more on buying close to the bottom.

–Sam Stovall, Managing Director–U.S. Equities, S&P Capital IQ

I believe 2015 equity results will be determined by the winner of a tug-of-war between liquidity and growth. There's no doubt that liquidity righted the ship back in 2009 and helped propel asset values, but 2015 investors will require tangible, organic growth in revenues and profits fueled by economic activity, to remain invested in domestic equities. The best returns could be harnessed abroad, as central bank stimulus will remain firmly in place in Europe and Japan. Emerging Asia could surprise investors to the upside as well, as several economies have embarked on infrastructure building. We will continue to watch for any diminishment in liquidity by monitoring credit spreads. Like 2014, we're looking for modest, single-digit equity returns in the year ahead.

–Jack Ablin, Chief Investment Officer, BMO Private Bank

Bull markets do not last forever. Noting margin debt is at all-time highs and sentiment and valuation measures are at huge extremes, it makes sense to expect a bear market to begin soon. Given the average 14–15 month duration of the last eight bear markets, if a bear market begins today, the pain will likely not end until the latter part of 2015. Using the average of the last eight bears, we might expect the Dow to eventually trade down as much as 35%–40%. Our official target remains 12471, down roughly 25%.

–Alan M. Newman, Editor, Crosscurrents

Long-term bond yields remain ultra-low, which essentially means that companies can continue to borrow at ultra-low interest rates and aggressively buy back their existing stock. At the current stock buyback pace, the S&P 500 might go "poof" and literally disappear in approximately 18 years. Due to these stock buybacks, the foundation under the stock market remains very strong and the fact that S&P 500's dividend yield is higher than the bank is essentially the icing on the cake. So overall, I remain very bullish, due to the fact that the stock market buybacks and dividend yields prevent any serious correction, so every dip should be viewed as a buying opportunity. I am also especially bullish due to the fact that 2015 should be characterized by steadily improving earnings growth due to improving GDP growth, a continued gridlocked federal government, and the excitement that a new presidential campaign will be unfolding in 2015.

–Louis Navellier, Navellier & Associates

"It" rarely is different, but this time it is. The market is being manipulated by the strongest economic power in the world, the central bank of United States, the only bank with the ability to print money and get away with it (temporarily and not forever, IMHO). If, how, and when that manipulation ends will determine the direction of the stock market. In the absence of that manipulation, the market would crash, but while the manipulation continues, the "tiger by a tail" market can easily continue its stage-managed life in the stratosphere.

–Daniel Turov, Turov Investment Group

(continued on page 26)

MONDAY

D 42.9
S 57.1
N 61.9

9

Even being right 3 or 4 times out of 10 should yield a person a fortune, if he has the sense to cut his losses quickly on the ventures where he has been wrong.
— Bernard Baruch (Financier, speculator, statesman, presidential adviser, 1870–1965)

TUESDAY

D 52.4
S 42.9
N 42.9

10

There are many people who think they want to be matadors [or money managers or traders] only to find themselves in the ring with two thousand pounds of bull bearing down on them, and then discover that what they really wanted was to wear tight pants and hear the crowd roar.
— Terry Pearce (Founder and President of Leadership Communication, b. 1941)

Week Before February Expiration Week, NASDAQ Down 9 of Last 14, 2010 Up 2.0%, 2011 Up 1.5%, 2014 Up 2.9%

WEDNESDAY

D 57.1
S 71.4
N 52.4

11

Any fool can buy. It is the wise man who knows how to sell.
— Albert W. Thomas (Trader, investor, mutualfundmagic.com, *If It Doesn't Go Up, Don't Buy It!*, b. 1927)

THURSDAY

D 61.9
S 71.4
N 61.9

12

There is no one who can replace America. Without American leadership, there is no leadership. That puts a tremendous burden on the American people to do something positive. You can't be tempted by the usual nationalism.
— Lee Hong-koo (South Korean prime minister 1994–1995 and ambassador to U.S. 1998–2000, *NY Times* 2/25/2009)

Day Before Presidents' Day Weekend, S&P Down 17 of Last 23

FRIDAY

D 42.9
S 42.9
N 61.9

13

The principles of successful stock speculation are based on the supposition that people will continue in the future to make the mistakes that they have made in the past.
— Thomas F. Woodlock (*Wall Street Journal* editor, quoted in *Reminiscences of a Stock Operator*, 1866–1945)

Valentine's Day ♥

SATURDAY

14

SUNDAY

15

(continued from page 24)

In the Chinese zodiac, 2015 will be the Year of the Sheep, and we should accordingly expect a sheepish, unconvincing economic recovery. Since the American consumer is running low on real disposable personal income—the fuel for future expenditures—and the middle class (the ultimate driver of the U.S. economy) has eroded to the lower-income spectra, investors shouldn't anticipate a solid state of economic affairs. While employment has been increasing, the majority of the gains remain in low-income positions, of which many members require two or three simply to keep pace with their pre-recession employment situations.

–Richard Yamarone, Bloomberg Senior Economist

Years ending in 5 and years that are the third year of the Presidential Cycle have been overwhelmingly bullish. The last few times those two coincided were 1995, 1975, and 1955. All were sharply higher years, almost without interruption (except for the last few months of 1975, which were modestly lower). So were 1935 and 1915, for that matter. I'm not smart enough to go against that sort of evidence, so I'm predicting a strong market for 2015. Could the Fed's constant interference be a problem someday? Certainly, but I'm betting that it won't be a problem in 2015.

–Lawrence G. McMillan, President, McMillan Analysis

From a low early in the fourth quarter of 2014 (near November 1), expect markets to experience the normal end-of-year rally into 2015 before the next 12-year interval (counted from 2/19/04) begins to exert a downward pull again. The rally from Q4 2014 should continue until June–July 2015, when it will turn down again into a final cyclical bear market low during the summer of 2016.

–Ed Carlson, Seattle Technical Advisors

In 2015, I believe we see a rise in real rates with major downside exposure in the 30-year bond prices. As interest rates increase, this could be the year the U.S. dollar gains value. Watch for a change in legislation that would ease home lending requirements. If this occurs, then 2015 could see a surprise in most homebuilder stocks. Look for emerging foreign markets to improve in 2015. In general, expect market sectors to adhere to historical seasonal supply-and-demand trends. One of the most notable will be to look for a buying opportunity in early February in the energy complex, more specifically the XLE, and refiners. Finally, if the U.S. equity markets have not endured a correction of at least 10% by July 2015, I would be very concerned for an eventual correction as we head into October. This could bring the S&P 500 stock index to test the 1425 level.

–John Person, CTA, President National Futures

Looking toward next year, I will be watching the presidential election cycle. 2015 is a pre-presidential year and according to history, is the year showing the most strength in the market. This pattern has been typically consistent in that a four-year term sees weakness in the first half and strength in the second half—year three, the pre-presidential year, is the strongest on average. Rising global GDP is another indicator that global growth is improving, so this is something I will also be watching, right along with accelerating industrial production (IP), which signals that momentum in the global economy is changing for the better. People in every country want upward mobility and a thriving economy, benefiting demand numbers for cyclicals, commodities, etc.

–Frank Holmes, CEO and Chief Investment Officer, U.S. Global Investors

International markets have been considerably cheaper than the U.S. market for several years. Value opportunities are concentrated in European and emerging markets, and we expect the valuation differences between the United States and these regions to narrow into 2015. This means that U.S. investors should diversify away from the United States and purchase some international equities.

–Jim O'Shaughnessy, Chairman, CEO, and CIO, O'Shaughnessy Asset Management

Stocks will struggle in 2015 with the end of QE and expected rate hikes in 2015. The turning point will be Q1. Long-only stock funds have gotten a free ride. Once Fed liquidity dries up funds will start selling, taking profits and moving into bonds, overseas stocks, and

(continued on page 28)

Presidents' Day (*Market Closed*)

We are all born originals; why is it so many die copies?
— Edward Young (English poet, 1683–1765)

Day After Presidents Day, NASDAQ Down 14 of Last 20
First Trading Day of February Expiration Week Dow Down 7 of Last 10

TUESDAY
D 66.7
S 66.7
N 52.4
17

Nothing is more uncertain than the favor of the crowd.
— Marcus Tullius Cicero (Great Roman Orator, Politician, 106-43 B.C.)

Ash Wednesday

WEDNESDAY
D 52.4
S 42.9
N 42.9
18

When new money is created on a grand scale, it must go somewhere and have some major consequences. One of these will be greatly increased volatility and instability in the economy and financial system.
— J. Anthony Boeckh, Ph.D (Chairman Bank Credit Analyst 1968–2002, *The Great Reflation, Boeckh Investment Letter*)

THURSDAY
D 33.3
S 38.1
N 42.9
19

I'm very big on having clarified principles. I don't believe in being reactive. You can't do that in the markets effectively. I can't. I need perspective. I need a game plan.
— Ray Dalio (Money manager, founder Bridgewater Associates, *Fortune* 3/16/2009, b. 1949)

February Expiration Day, NASDAQ Down 12 of Last 15

FRIDAY
D 52.4
S 47.6
N 38.1
20

You know a country is falling apart when even the government will not accept its own currency.
— Jim Rogers (Financier, *Adventure Capitalist*, b. 1942)

SATURDAY
21

SUNDAY
22

(continued from page 26)

other vehicles. The cumulative effect will be a series of selloffs whose momentum is enhanced by program and algorithmic trading. We expect a 15% to 20% correction, but do not think a crash is in the cards because the Fed remains prepared to step in with new stimulus or a delay in rate hikes. Once the trillions of dollars in stimulus are pulled, the stock market will find itself in extreme overbought conditions just as interest rates start to move higher. This will be the exact opposite of the risk on trade we have seen from 2009 into the beginning of 2014.

–Danny Riley, President and owner, MrTopStep.com

Some classic early-warning signs of a major top have begun to appear in this 62-month-old bull market. For example, the percentage of stocks making new 52-week highs has been diminishing, from 28% in mid-May 2013 to just 8% as of May 27, 2014. A more critical warning sign will occur when the all-issues Advance–Decline Line begins to repeatedly diverge from the major big-cap price indexes—a condition that typically persists for four to six months before the final high in bull market. Thus, caution is warranted for 2015.

–Paul Desmond, Lowry Research

I'm fully invested in dividend-paying stocks and intend to continue doing so, but given that it's 5–6 years of a bull market, who's to say what will happen next year? I'm still thinking a 20% correction is inevitable at some point. But as long as interest rates stay low, CPI stays low, the Fed is accommodating, and the economy seems sluggish, the bull market should continue.

– Mark Skousen, Ph.D., editor, *Forecasts & Strategies*

If you ignore the indicators behind the rise in the S&P and simply look at the chart, there is a measured target on the S&P of 2150–2200. If the market manages to have a correction of some magnitude (at least 10%) in the second half of 2014, it ought to set up a decent push higher in 2015 with the measured target in this area. A correction would help the market hit the refresh button by cleaning out weak holders and placing stock into the hands of strength. Chart patterns rarely repeat exactly, but if we look at a chart of the S&P from the 1970s into the early 1980s, we see a very similar pattern of sideways for a number of years, followed by a breakout and a retest of the breakout (in 1982) and a renewed rise. Therefore a correction in the second half of 2014 provides a similar setup.

– Helene Meisler, Financial Markets Analyst & Columnist, TheStreet.com &
RealMoney.com

By all technical expectations, 2015 should be an up year. With the best record for any yearly performance since 1900, years ending in 5 for the DJIA have been up, *with the exception of a near miss in 2005; the S&P 500, however, was* up *in 2005. So with or without a 4-year cycle decline in 2014, 2015 carries a bright outlook.*

– Louise Yamada, Managing Director, Louise Yamada Technical Research Advisors

In 2015, central banks will be forced to start pulling back. Whether they do so gradually or abruptly, it's bound to lead to a rude awakening for investors who were lulled into an easy-money-fueled stupor. In bond markets of all stripes and colors, expect the beginning of a major, long-term decline in prices and rise in yields. In most major stock market averages, a correction of 10% or more will be very difficult to avoid. But some key sectors—such as domestic energy, aerospace, health care, and food and beverages—will hold up better, while others, especially financial stocks, could take bigger hits. Overall, no matter how you invest or what you invest in, go for quality *and* safety—*the strongest balance sheets, the most consistent track records of historic performance and the highest ratings by independent analysts who are never paid, directly or indirectly, by the companies they cover.*

–Mike Larson, Editor, *Safe Money Report* & Martin D. Weiss, Founder and
Chairman, Weiss Research

Overall, all 2015 will be a bull market. I expect the best buy points for 2015 will be late in 2014, as well as mid-April 2015 and the first few days of October. Times for caution will be the end of February and the Middle of July.

–Larry Williams, Veteran Trader

FEBRUARY/MARCH

MONDAY
D 57.1
S 61.9
N 61.9
23

If you want to raise a crop for one year, plant corn. If you want to raise a crop for decades, plant trees. If you want to raise a crop for centuries, raise men. If you want to plant a crop for eternities, raise democracies.
— Carl A. Schenck (German forester, 1868–1955)

Week After February Expiration Week, Dow Down 10 of Last 16

TUESDAY
D 33.3
S 38.1
N 52.4
24

Pretend that every single person you meet has a sign around his or her neck that says, "Make me feel important." Not only will you succeed in sales, you will succeed in life.
— Mary Kay Ash (Mary Kay Cosmetics)

WEDNESDAY
D 42.9
S 47.6
N 52.4
25

The only title in our democracy superior to that of president is the title of citizen.
— Louis D. Brandeis (U.S. Supreme Court Justice 1916–1939, 1856–1941)

End of February Miserable in Recent Years (Page 22 and 133)

THURSDAY
D 47.6
S 57.1
N 52.4
26

Let me tell you the secret that has led me to my goal. My strength lies solely in my tenacity.
— Louis Pasteur (French chemist, founder of microbiology, 1822–1895)

FRIDAY
D 42.9
S 47.6
N 38.1
27

Another factor contributing to productivity is technology, particularly the rapid introduction of new microcomputers based on single-chip circuits.... The results over the next decade will be a second industrial revolution.
— Yale Hirsch (Creator of *Stock Trader's Almanac*, Smart Money Newsletter 9/22/1976, b. 1923)

SATURDAY
28

March Almanac Investor Seasonalities: See Pages 94, 96 and 98

SUNDAY
1

MARCH ALMANAC

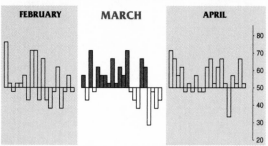

MARCH								APRIL						
S	M	T	W	T	F	S		S	M	T	W	T	F	S
						1					1	2	3	4
2	3	4	5	6	7	8		5	6	7	8	9	10	11
9	10	11	12	13	14	15		12	13	14	15	16	17	18
16	17	18	19	20	21	22		19	20	21	22	23	24	25
23	24	25	26	27	28	29		26	27	28	29	30		
30	31													

Market Probability Chart above is a graphic representation of the S&P 500 Recent Market Probability Calendar on page 124.

♦ Mid-month strength and late-month weakness are most evident above ♦ RECENT RECORD: S&P 14 up, 7 down, average gain 1.5%, third best ♦ Rather turbulent in recent years with wild fluctuations and large gains and losses ♦ March has been taking some mean end-of-quarter hits (page 134), down 1469 Dow points March 9–22, 2001 ♦ Last three or four days Dow a net loser 17 out of last 25 years ♦ NASDAQ hard hit in 2001, down 14.5% after 22.4% drop in February ♦ Fourth best NASDAQ month during pre-presidential election years average gain 3.5%, up 10, down 1.

March Vital Statistics

	DJIA		S&P 500		NASDAQ		Russell 1K		Russell 2K	
Rank	5		4		5		4		6	
Up	43		43		28		25		26	
Down	22		22		16		11		10	
Average % Change	1.1%		1.2%		0.8%		1.1%		1.3%	
Pre-Election Year	2.2%		2.1%		3.5%		2.4%		3.2%	
	Best & Worst March									
	% Change		% Change		% Change		% Change		% Change	
Best	2000	7.8	2000	9.7	2009	10.9	2000	8.9	1979	9.7
Worst	1980	–9.0	1980	–10.2	1980	–17.1	1980	–11.5	1980	–18.5
	Best & Worst March Weeks									
Best	3/13/09	9.0	3/13/09	10.7	3/13/09	10.6	3/13/09	10.7	3/13/09	12.0
Worst	3/16/01	–7.7	3/6/09	–7.0	3/16/01	–7.9	3/6/09	–7.1	3/6/09	–9.8
	Best & Worst March Days									
Best	3/23/09	6.8	3/23/09	7.1	3/10/09	7.1	3/23/09	7.0	3/23/09	8.4
Worst	3/2/09	–4.2	3/2/09	–4.7	3/12/01	–6.3	3/2/09	–4.8	3/27/80	–6.0
	First Trading Day of Expiration Week: 1980–2014									
Record (#Up–#Down)	23–12		23–12		16–19		21–14		18–17	
Current streak	U3		U3		U2		U2		U2	
Avg % Change	0.17		0.04		–0.31		–0.02		–0.35	
	Options Expiration Day: 1980–2014									
Record (#Up–#Down)	18–17		20–15		16–19		18–17		15–19	
Current streak	D3		D2		D3		D2		D3	
Avg % Change	0.05		–0.001		–0.06		–0.001		–0.07	
	Options Expiration Week: 1980–2014									
Record (#Up–#Down)	24–10		23–12		21–14		22–13		19–16	
Current streak	U3		U3		U3		U3		U3	
Avg % Change	0.88		0.72		–0.02		0.65		0.15	
	Week After Options Expiration: 1980–2014									
Record (#Up–#Down)	16–19		12–23		18–17		12–23		17–18	
Current streak	U1		D3		D2		D3		D3	
Avg % Change	–0.19		–0.10		0.08		–0.10		0.02	
	First Trading Day Performance									
% of Time Up	66.2		63.1		61.4		58.3		63.9	
Avg % Change	0.13		0.14		0.20		0.09		0.16	
	Last Trading Day Performance									
% of Time Up	43.1		41.5		65.9		50.0		83.3	
Avg % Change	–0.09		0.01		0.20		0.12		0.41	

Dow & S&P 1950–April 2014, NASDAQ 1971–April 2014, Russell 1K & 2K 1979–April 2014.

March has Ides and St. Patrick's Day;
Begins bullishly, then fades away.

First Trading Day in March, Dow Down 5 of Last 8, –4.2% in 2009,
1996–2006 Up 9 of 11

MONDAY

D 57.1
S 57.1
N 52.4

2

Don't be overly concerned about your heirs. Usually, unearned funds do them more harm than good.
— Gerald M. Loeb (E.F. Hutton, *The Battle for Investment Survival*, predicted 1929 Crash, 1900–1974)

TUESDAY

D 47.6
S 42.9
N 38.1

3

To an imagination of any scope the most far-reaching form of power is not money, it is the command of ideas.
— Oliver Wendell Holmes Jr. (U.S. Supreme Court Justice 1902–1932, *The Mind and Faith of Justice Holmes*, edited by Max Lerner, 1841–1935)

March Historically Strong Early in the Month (Pages 30 and 134)

WEDNESDAY

D 61.9
S 71.4
N 71.4

4

Some men see things as they are and say "why?" I dream things that never were and say "why not?"
— George Bernard Shaw (Irish dramatist, 1856–1950)

THURSDAY

D 42.9
S 47.6
N 38.1

5

Always grab the reader by the throat in the first paragraph, sink your thumbs into his windpipe in the second, and hold him against the wall until the tagline.
— Paul O'Neill (Marketer)

FRIDAY

D 66.7
S 61.9
N 52.4

6

The market is a voting machine, whereon countless individuals register choices which are the product partly of reason and partly of emotion.
— Graham & Dodd

SATURDAY

7

Daylight Saving Time Begins

SUNDAY

8

MARKET CHARTS OF PRE-PRESIDENTIAL ELECTION YEARS

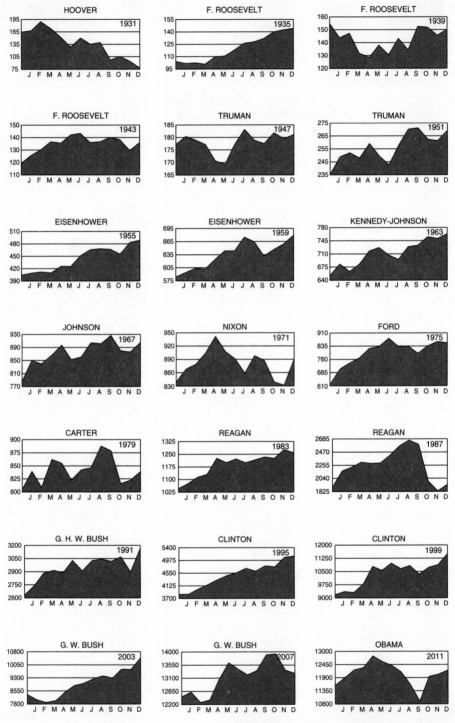

Based on Dow Jones Industrial Average monthly closing prices

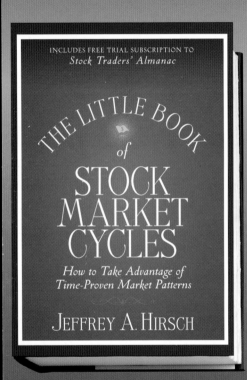

MARCH

MONDAY
D 52.4
S 57.1
N 52.4
9

The facts are unimportant! It's what they are perceived to be that determines the course of events.
— R. Earl Hadady (*Bullish Consensus, Contrary Opinion*)

TUESDAY
D 66.7
S 57.1
N 52.4
10

The words "I am..." are potent words; be careful what you hitch them to. The thing you're claiming has a way of reaching back and claiming you.
— A. L. Kitselman (Author, math teacher)

Dow Down 1469 Points March 9–22 in 2001

WEDNESDAY
D 66.7
S 52.4
N 47.6
11

Don't delay! A good plan, violently executed now, is better than a perfect plan next week. War is a very simple thing, [like stock trading] and the determining characteristics are self-confidence, speed, and audacity.
— General George S. Patton, Jr. (U.S. Army field commander WWII, 1885–1945)

THURSDAY
D 52.4
S 66.7
N 71.4
12

Ideas are easy; it's execution that's hard.
— Jeff Bezos (Amazon.com)

FRIDAY
D 66.7
S 52.4
N 52.4
13

If we did all the things we are capable of doing, we would literally astound ourselves.
— Thomas Alva Edison (American inventor, 1093 patents, 1847–1931)

SATURDAY
14

SUNDAY
15

THE FIFTH YEAR OF DECADES

Fifth years have by far and away the best record, averaging 28.3% for the Dow and its predecessors in the past 130 years (see page 129). There has only been one losing "5" year in 13 decades. 2005 was a post-election year, the weakest of that more influential 4-year cycle, and the Dow was off a mere 0.6%, S&P 500 was up 3.0%. 2015 is a pre-election year, the strongest of the 4-year cycle (page 130), but it is also the seventh year of the president's term, which has not been as strong (page 40).

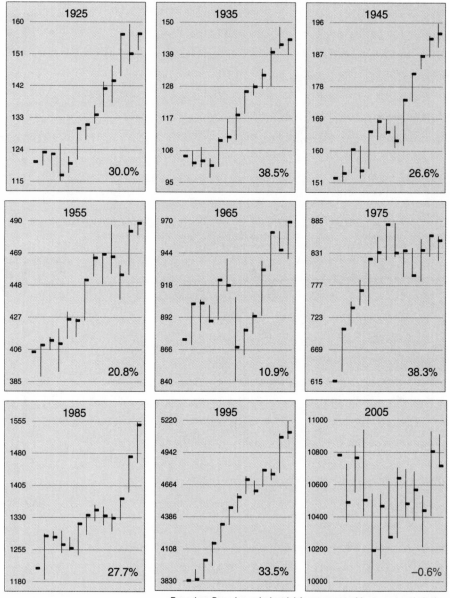

Based on Dow Jones Industrial Average monthly ranges and closing

MARCH

Monday Before March Triple Witching, Dow Up 20 of Last 27

MONDAY

D 61.9
S 61.9
N 47.6

16

It doesn't pay to anticipate the correction; there are already plenty who have been carried out on their shields trying to do that. Rather, we will wait for some confirmed sell signals before altering our still-bullish view.
— Lawrence G. McMillan (Professional trader, author, RIA, OptionStrategist.com, b. 1946)

St. Patrick's Day

Bullish Cluster Highlights March's "Sweet Spot"

TUESDAY

D 52.4
S 57.1
N 57.1

17

I have a simple philosophy. Fill what's empty. Empty what's full. And scratch where it itches.
— Alice Roosevelt Longworth (Writer, daughter of President T. Roosevelt, 1884–1980)

WEDNESDAY

D 66.7
S 71.4
N 61.9

18

What's money? A man is a success if he gets up in the morning and goes to bed at night and in between does what he wants to do.
— Bob Dylan (American singer-songwriter, musician, and artist, b. 1941)

THURSDAY

D 61.9
S 47.6
N 61.9

19

Individualism, private property, the law of accumulation of wealth and the law of competition… are the highest result of human experience, the soil in which, so far, has produced the best fruit.
— Andrew Carnegie (Scottish-born U.S. industrialist, philanthropist, The Gospel of Wealth, 1835–1919)

March Triple Witching Day Mixed Last 28 Years
But, Dow Down 5 of Last 6

FRIDAY

D 38.1
S 42.9
N 33.3

20

The four horsemen of the Investment Apocalypse are fear, greed, hope, and ignorance. And notice, only one of the four is not an emotion—ignorance. These four things have accounted for more losses in the market than any recession or depression, and they will never change. Even if you correct ignorance, the other three will get you every time.
— James P. O'Shaughnessy (Chairman & CEO at O'Shaughnessy Asset Management, b. 1960)

SATURDAY

21

SUNDAY

22

WHY A 50% GAIN IN THE DOW IS POSSIBLE FROM ITS 2014 LOW TO ITS 2015 HIGH

Normally, major corrections occur sometime in the first or second years following presidential elections. In the last 13 midterm election years, bear markets began or were in progress nine times—we experienced bull years in 1986, 2006, and 2010, while 1994 was flat.

The puniest midterm advance, 14.5% from the 1946 low, was during the industrial contraction after World War II. The next four smallest advances were: 1978 (OPEC–Iran) 21.0%, 1930 (economic collapse) 23.4%, 1966 (Vietnam) 26.7%, and 2010 (European debt) 32.3%.

Since 1914, the Dow has gained 48.6% on average from its midterm election year low to its subsequent high in the following pre-election year. A swing of such magnitude is equivalent to a move from 12000 to 18000 or from 15000 to 22500.

POST-ELECTION HIGH TO MIDTERM LOW: –20.9%

Conversely, since 1913, the Dow has dropped –20.9% on average from its post-election-year high to its subsequent low in the following midterm year. The Dow's 2013 post-election-year high is 16576.66. A 20.9% decline would put the Dow back at 13112.14 at the 2014 midterm bottom. Whatever the level, the rally off the 2014 midterm low could be another great buying opportunity.

Pretty impressive seasonality! There is no reason to think the quadrennial Presidential Election/Stock Market Cycle will not continue. Page 130 shows how effectively most presidents "managed" to have much stronger economies in the third and fourth years of their terms than in their first two.

% CHANGE IN DOW JONES INDUSTRIALS BETWEEN THE MIDTERM YEAR LOW AND THE HIGH IN THE FOLLOWING YEAR

	Midterm Year Low			Pre-Election Year High			
	Date of Low		Dow	Date of High		Dow	% Gain
1	Jul 30	1914*	52.32	Dec 27	1915	99.21	89.6%
2	Jan 15	1918**	73.38	Nov 3	1919	119.62	63.0
3	Jan 10	1922**	78.59	Mar 20	1923	105.38	34.1
4	Mar 30	1926*	135.20	Dec 31	1927	202.40	49.7
5	Dec 16	1930*	157.51	Feb 24	1931	194.36	23.4
6	Jul 26	1934*	85.51	Nov 19	1935	148.44	73.6
7	Mar 31	1938*	98.95	Sep 12	1939	155.92	57.6
8	Apr 28	1942*	92.92	Jul 14	1943	145.82	56.9
9	Oct 9	1946	163.12	Jul 24	1947	186.85	14.5
10	Jan 13	1950**	196.81	Sep 13	1951	276.37	40.4
11	Jan 11	1954**	279.87	Dec 30	1955	488.40	74.5
12	Feb 25	1958**	436.89	Dec 31	1959	679.36	55.5
13	Jun 26	1962*	535.74	Dec 18	1963	767.21	43.2
14	Oct 7	1966*	744.32	Sep 25	1967	943.08	26.7
15	May 26	1970*	631.16	Apr 28	1971	950.82	50.6
16	Dec 6	1974*	577.60	Jul 16	1975	881.81	52.7
17	Feb 28	1978*	742.12	Oct 5	1979	897.61	21.0
18	Aug 12	1982*	776.92	Nov 29	1983	1287.20	65.7
19	Jan 22	1986	1502.29	Aug 25	1987	2722.42	81.2
20	Oct 11	1990*	2365.10	Dec 31	1991	3168.84	34.0
21	Apr 4	1994	3593.35	Dec 13	1995	5216.47	45.2
22	Aug 31	1998*	7539.07	Dec 31	1999	11497.12	52.5
23	Oct 9	2002*	7286.27	Dec 31	2003	10453.92	43.5
24	Jan 20	2006	10667.39	Oct 9	2007	14164.53	32.8
25	Jul 2	2010**	9686.48	Apr 29	2011	12810.54	32.3

*Bear Market ended **Bear previous year*   **Average**   **48.6%**

MARCH

Week After Triple Witching, Dow Down 17 of Last 27, 2000 Up 4.9%, 2007 Up 3.1%, 2009 Up 6.8%, 2011 Up 3.1%, Up 7 of Last 11

MONDAY
D 47.6
S 38.1
N 57.1
23

Cannot people realize how large an income is thrift?
— Marcus Tullius Cicero (Great Roman Orator, Politician, 106-43 B.C.)

TUESDAY
D 42.9
S 66.7
N 61.9
24

All free governments are managed by the combined wisdom and folly of the people.
— James A. Garfield (20th U.S. President, 1831–1881)

March Historically Weak Later in the Month (Pages 30 and 134)

WEDNESDAY
D 61.9
S 61.9
N 66.7
25

A cynic is a man who knows the price of everything and the value of nothing.
— Oscar Wilde (Irish-born writer and wit, 1845–1900)

THURSDAY
D 23.8
S 28.6
N 38.1
26

It is the growth of total government spending as a percentage of gross national product—not the way it is financed—that crowds out the private sector.
— Paul Craig Roberts (*Business Week*, 1984, b. 1939)

FRIDAY
D 52.4
S 47.6
N 42.9
27

It is a funny thing about life; if you refuse to accept anything but the best, you very often get it.
— W. Somerset Maugham (English dramatist, novelist, 1874–1965)

SATURDAY
28

April Almanac Investor Seasonalities: See Pages 94, 96 and 98

SUNDAY
29

APRIL ALMANAC

APRIL						
S	M	T	W	T	F	S
		1	2	3	4
5	6	7	8	9	10	11
12	13	14	15	16	17	18
19	20	21	22	23	24	25
26	27	28	29	30		

MAY						
S	M	T	W	T	F	S
					1	2
3	4	5	6	7	8	9
10	11	12	13	14	15	16
17	18	19	20	21	22	23
24	25	26	27	28	29	30
31						

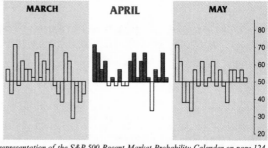

Market Probability Chart above is a graphic representation of the S&P 500 Recent Market Probability Calendar on page 124.

◆ April is still the best Dow month (average 1.9%) since 1950 (page 50) ◆ April 1999, first month ever to gain 1000 Dow points, 856 in 2001, knocked off its high horse in 2002, down 458, 2003 up 488 ◆ Up nine straight, average gain 3.1% ◆ Prone to weakness after mid-month tax deadline ◆ Stocks anticipate great first-quarter earnings by rising sharply before earnings are reported, rather than after ◆ Rarely a dangerous month, recent exceptions are 2002, 2004, and 2005 ◆ "Best Six Months" of the year end with April (page 52) ◆ Pre-presidential election year Aprils even stronger since 1950 (Dow 4.2%, S&P 3.6%, NASDAQ 3.7%) ◆ End of April NASDAQ strength (pages 125 & 126).

April Vital Statistics

	DJIA		S&P 500		NASDAQ		Russell 1K		Russell 2K	
Rank	1		2		4		3		4	
Up	43		45		28		24		22	
Down	22		20		16		12		14	
Average % Change	1.9%		1.5%		1.4%		1.6%		1.6%	
Pre-Election Year	4.2%		3.6%		3.7%		3.0%		3.4%	
Best & Worst April										
		% Change		% Change		% Change		% Change		% Change
Best	1978	10.6	2009	9.4	2001	15.0	2009	10.0	2009	15.3
Worst	1970	−6.3	1970	−9.0	2000	−15.6	2002	−5.8	2000	−6.1
Best & Worst April Weeks										
Best	4/11/75	5.7	4/20/00	5.8	4/12/01	14.0	4/20/00	5.9	4/3/09	6.3
Worst	4/14/00	−7.3	4/14/00	−10.5	4/14/00	−25.3	4/14/00	−11.2	4/14/00	−16.4
Best & Worst April Days										
Best	4/5/01	4.2	4/5/01	4.4	4/5/01	8.9	4/5/01	4.6	4/9/09	5.9
Worst	4/14/00	−5.7	4/14/00	−5.8	4/14/00	−9.7	4/14/00	−6.0	4/14/00	−7.3
First Trading Day of Expiration Week: 1980–2014										
Record (#Up–#Down)	22–13		20–15		19–16		19–16		15–20	
Current streak	U1		U1		U1		U1		U1	
Avg % Change	0.21		0.13		0.11		0.11		−0.03	
Options Expiration Day: 1980–2014										
Record (#Up–#Down)	24–11		24–11		21–14		24–11		23–12	
Current streak	D1		U4		U2		U4		U4	
Avg % Change	0.23		0.21		0.01		0.20		0.25	
Options Expiration Week: 1980–2014										
Record (#Up–#Down)	28–7		25–10		23–12		23–12		26–9	
Current streak	U1		U1		U1		U1		U1	
Avg % Change	1.12		0.90		0.94		0.88		0.78	
Week After Options Expiration: 1980–2014										
Record (#Up–#Down)	23–12		23–12		25–10		23–12		23–12	
Current streak	D1		D1		D1		D1		D1	
Avg % Change	0.41		0.39		0.65		0.40		0.83	
First Trading Day Performance										
% of Time Up	60.0		63.1		47.7		61.1		50.0	
Avg % Change	0.18		0.15		−0.10		0.18		−0.05	
Last Trading Day Performance										
% of Time Up	52.3		56.9		68.2		58.3		69.4	
Avg % Change	0.10		0.09		0.19		0.09		0.15	

Dow & S&P 1950–April 2014, NASDAQ 1971–April 2014, Russell 1K & 2K 1979–April 2014.

April "Best Month" for Dow since 1950;
Day-before-Good Friday gains are nifty.

MARCH/APRIL

Start Looking for the Dow and S&P MACD SELL Signal (Pages 50 and 52)
Almanac Investor Subscribers Emailed When It Triggers (See Insert)

MONDAY
D 52.4
S 38.1
N 47.6

30

With respect to trading Sugar futures, if they give it away for free at restaurants, you probably don't want to be trading it.
— John L. Person (CTA, professional trader, author, speaker, nationalfutures.com, 2/22/2011 TradersExpo, b. 1961)

Last Trading Day of March, Dow Down 15 of Last 26
Russell 2000 Up 15 of Last 20

TUESDAY
D 38.1
S 42.9
N 57.1

31

English stocks... are springing up like mushrooms this year... forced up to a quite unreasonable level and then, for most part, collapse. In this way, I have made over 400 pounds... [Speculating] makes small demands on one's time, and it's worth while running some risk in order to relieve the enemy of his money.
— Karl Marx (German social philosopher and revolutionary, in an 1864 letter to his uncle, 1818–1883)

First Trading Day in April, Dow Up 16 of Last 20

WEDNESDAY
D 76.2
S 71.4
N 61.9

1

Life is like riding a bicycle. You don't fall off unless you stop peddling.
— Claude D. Pepper (U.S. Senator Florida 1936–1951, 1900–1989)

NASDAQ Up 14 Straight Days Before Good Friday

THURSDAY
D 66.7
S 66.7
N 57.1

2

The higher a people's intelligence and moral strength, the lower will be the prevailing rate of interest.
— Eugen von Bohm-Bawerk (Austrian economist, *Capital and Interest*, 1851–1914)

Good Friday (*Market Closed*)

FRIDAY

3

There have been three great inventions since the beginning of time: Fire, the wheel, and central banking.
— Will Rogers (American humorist and showman, 1879–1935)

Passover

SATURDAY

4

Easter

SUNDAY

5

SEVENTH YEAR OF PRESIDENTIAL TERMS

Prior to President Obama, there have been six previous presidents that served a seventh year in office since 1901; Presidents Wilson (1919), Roosevelt (1939), Eisenhower (1959), Reagan (1987), Clinton (1999), and G.W. Bush (2007). President McKinley was elected to a second term, but was assassinated in his fifth year in office. Seventh years are also pre-presidential election years. In the following two charts the one-year seasonal pattern for seventh years is compared to all pre-presidential election years.

DJIA and S&P 500 averaged 13.0% and 5.6% respectively in seventh years, and 1939 was the only negative seventh year for either. DJIA's 30.5% gain in 1919 (on the heels of the big 45.5% post-WWI-armistice rally) lifts its average performance in seventh years when compared to S&P 500. Seventh years follow the typical pre-presidential election year pattern quite closely leading to similar above-average full-year gains. The market crash of October 1987 is clearly visible. It is also interesting to note how the S&P was weaker in all six seventh years of presidential terms. See pages 171 to 173 for additional one-year seasonal pattern charts.

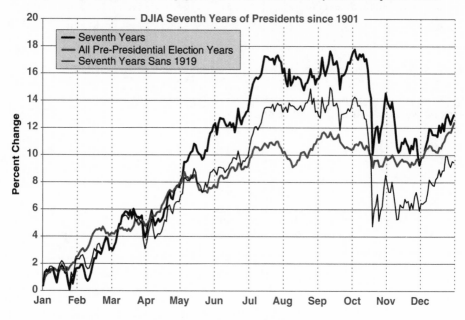

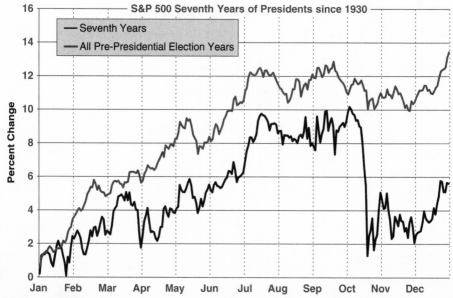

APRIL

Day After Easter, Second Worst Post-Holiday (Page 88)

MONDAY

D 47.6
S 57.1
N 71.4

6

Age is a question of mind over matter. If you don't mind, it doesn't matter.
— Leroy Robert "Satchel" Paige (Negro League and Hall of Fame Pitcher, 1906–1982)

April Is the Best Month for the Dow, Average 1.9% Gain Since 1950

TUESDAY

D 66.7
S 61.9
N 57.1

7

Whatever method you use to pick stocks…, your ultimate success or failure will depend on your ability to ignore the worries of the world long enough to allow your investments to succeed. It isn't the head but the stomach that determines the fate of the stockpicker.
— Peter Lynch (Fidelity Investments, *Beating the Street*, 1994, b. 1944)

WEDNESDAY

D 42.9
S 47.6
N 38.1

8

In the history of the financial markets, arrogance has destroyed far more capital than stupidity.
— Jason Trennert (Managing Partner, Strategas Research Partners, March 27, 2006)

April Is 2nd Best Month for S&P, 4th Best for NASDAQ (Since 1971)

THURSDAY

D 47.6
S 52.4
N 57.1

9

The most important lesson in investing is humility.
— Sir John Templeton (Founder Templeton Funds, philanthropist, 1912–2008)

FRIDAY

D 52.4
S 47.6
N 47.6

10

Some people say we can't compete with Intel. I say, like hell you can't… Dominant companies usually don't change unless they're forced to do so.
— David Patterson (Chip designing force behind R.I.S.C. and R.A.I.D., *WSJ* 8/28/98, b. 1947)

SATURDAY

11

SUNDAY

12

HOW TO TRADE BEST MONTHS SWITCHING STRATEGIES

Our Best Months Switching Strategies found on pages 52, 54, 60, and 62 are simple and reliable with a proven 64-year track record. Thus far we have failed to find a similar trading strategy that even comes close over the past six decades. And to top it off, the strategy has only been improving since we first discovered it in 1986.

Exogenous factors and cultural shifts must be considered. "Backward" tests that go back to 1925 or even 1896 and conclude that the pattern does not work are best ignored. They do not take into account these factors. Farming made August the best month from 1900–1951. Since 1987 it is the worst month of the year for Dow and S&P. Panic caused by financial crisis in 2007–08 caused every asset class aside from U.S. Treasuries to decline substantially. But the bulk of the major decline in equities in the worst months of 2008 was sidestepped using these strategies.

Our Best Months Switching Strategy will not make you an instant millionaire as other strategies claim they can do. What it will do is steadily build wealth over time with half the risk (or less) of a "buy-and-hold" approach.

A sampling of tradable funds for the Best and Worst Months appears in the table below. These are just a starting point and only skim the surface of possible trading vehicles currently available to take advantage of these strategies. Your specific situation and risk tolerance will dictate a suitable choice. If you are trading in a tax-advantaged account such as a company-sponsored 401(k) or Individual Retirement Account (IRA), your investment options may be limited to what has been selected by your employer or IRA administrator. But if you are a self-directed trader with a brokerage account, then you likely have unlimited choices (perhaps too many).

TRADABLE BEST AND WORST MONTHS SWITCHING STRATEGY FUNDS

Best Months		Worst Months	
Exchange Traded Funds (ETF)		**Exchange Traded Funds (ETF)**	
Symbol	Name	Symbol	Name
DIA	SPDR Dow Jones Industrial Average	SHY	iShares Barclays 1–3 Year Treasury Bond
SPY	SPDR S&P 500	IEI	iShares Barclays 3–7 Year Treasury Bond
QQQ	PowerShares QQQ	IEF	iShares Barclays 7–10 Year Treasury Bond
IWM	iShares Russell 2000	TLT	iShares Barclays 20+ Year Treasury Bond
Mutual Funds		**Mutual Funds**	
Symbol	Name	Symbol	Name
VWNDX	Vanguard Windsor Fund	VFSTX	Vanguard Short-Term Investment-Grade Bond Fund
FMAGX	Fidelity Magellan Fund	FBNDX	Fidelity Investment Grade Bond Fund
AMCPX	American Funds AMCAP Fund	ABNDX	American Funds Bond Fund of America
FKCGX	Franklin Flex Cap Growth Fund	FKUSX	Franklin U.S. Government Securities Fund
SECEX	Guggenheim Large Cap Core Fund	SIUSX	Guggenheim U.S. Intermediate Bond Fund

Generally speaking, during the Best Months you want to be invested in equities that offer similar exposure to the companies that constitute Dow, S&P 500, and NASDAQ indices. These would typically be large-cap growth and value stocks as well as technology concerns. Reviewing the holdings of a particular ETF or mutual fund and comparing them to the index members is an excellent way to correlate.

During the Worst Months switch into Treasury bonds, money market funds, or a bear/short fund. **Grizzly Short** (GRZZX) and **AdvisorShares Ranger Equity Bear** (HDGE) are two possible choices. Money market funds will be the safest, but are likely to offer the smallest return, while bear/short funds offer potentially greater returns, but more risk. If the market moves sideways or higher during the Worst Months, a bear/short fund is likely to lose money. Treasuries can offer a combination of decent returns with limited risk.

Additional Worst Month possibilities include precious metals and the companies that mine them. **SPDR Gold Shares** (GLD), **Market Vectors Gold Miners** (GDX), and **ETF Securities Physical Swiss Gold** (SGOL) are a few well recognized names available from the ETF universe.

Become an *Almanac Investor*

Almanac Investor subscribers receive specific buy and sell alerts based upon the Best Months Switching Strategies online and via e-mail. Sector Index Seasonalities, found on page 92, are also put into action throughout the year with corresponding ETF trades. Buy limits, stop losses, and auto-sell price points for the majority of seasonal trades are delivered directly to your inbox. Visit www.stocktradersalmanac.com or see the insert for details and a special offer for new subscribers.

Monday Before Expiration, Dow Up 18 of Last 26, Though Mixed Last 10 Years

MONDAY

D 66.7
S 57.1
N 66.7

13

War is God's way of teaching Americans geography.
— Ambrose Bierce (Writer, satirist, Civil War hero, *The Devil's Dictionary*, 1842–1914?)

TUESDAY

D 57.1
S 47.6
N 47.6

14

There are ways for the individual investor to make money in the securities markets. Buying value and holding long term while collecting dividends has been proven over and over again.
— Robert M. Sharp (Author, *The Lore and Legends of Wall Street*)

Income Tax Deadline, *Generally Bullish, Dow Down Only Six Times Since 1981*

WEDNESDAY

D 66.7
S 47.6
N 47.6

15

All great truths begin as blasphemies.
— George Bernard Shaw (Irish dramatist, 1856–1950)

April Prone to Weakness After Tax Deadline (Pages 38 and 134)

THURSDAY

D 66.7
S 61.9
N 42.9

16

There are two kinds of people who lose money: those who know nothing and those who know everything.
— Henry Kaufman (German-American economist, b. 1927, to Robert Lenzner in *Forbes* 10/19/98, who added, "With two Nobel Prize winners in the house, Long-Term Capital clearly fits the second case.")

April Expiration Day Dow Up 14 of Last 18

FRIDAY

D 57.1
S 66.7
N 52.4

17

In nature there are no rewards or punishments; there are consequences.
— Horace Annesley Vachell (English writer, *The Face of Clay*, 1861–1955)

SATURDAY

18

SUNDAY

19

THE DECEMBER LOW INDICATOR: A USEFUL PROGNOSTICATING TOOL

When the Dow closes below its December closing low in the first quarter, it is frequently an excellent warning sign. Jeffrey Saut, managing director of investment strategy at Raymond James, brought this to our attention a few years ago. The December Low Indicator was originated by Lucien Hooper, a *Forbes* columnist and Wall Street analyst back in the 1970s. Hooper dismissed the importance of January and January's first week as reliable indicators. He noted that the trend could be random or even manipulated during a holiday-shortened week. Instead, said Hooper, "Pay much more attention to the December low. If that low is violated during the first quarter of the New Year, watch out!"

Eighteen of the 32 occurrences were followed by gains for the rest of the year—and 16 full-year gains—after the low for the year was reached. For perspective we've included the January Barometer readings for the selected years. Hooper's "Watch Out" warning was absolutely correct, though. All but two of the instances since 1952 experienced further declines, as the Dow fell an additional 10.9% on average when December's low was breached in Q1. As was the case in 2014, when the December Low was breached and the January Barometer was down 21 previous times the Dow fell 14%.

Only three significant drops occurred (not shown) when December's low was not breached in Q1 (1974, 1981, and 1987). Both indicators were wrong only five times, and nine years ended flat. If the December low is not crossed, turn to our January Barometer for guidance. It has been virtually perfect, right nearly 100% of these times (view the complete results at *www.stocktradersalmanac.com*).

YEARS DOW FELL BELOW DECEMBER LOW IN FIRST QUARTER

Year	Previous Dec Low	Date Crossed	Crossing Price	Subseq. Low	% Change Cross-Low	Rest of Year % Change	Full Year % Change	Jan Bar
1952	262.29	2/19/52	261.37	256.35	−1.9%	11.7%	8.4%	1.6%[2]
1953	281.63	2/11/53	281.57	255.49	−9.3	−0.2	−3.8	−0.7[3]
1956	480.72	1/9/56	479.74	462.35	−3.6	4.1	2.3	−3.6[1, 2, 3]
1957	480.61	1/18/57	477.46	419.79	−12.1	−8.7	−12.8	−4.2
1960	661.29	1/12/60	660.43	566.05	−14.3	−6.7	−9.3	−7.1
1962	720.10	1/5/62	714.84	535.76	−25.1	−8.8	−10.8	−3.8
1966	939.53	3/1/66	938.19	744.32	−20.7	−16.3	−18.9	0.5[1]
1968	879.16	1/22/68	871.71	825.13	−5.3	8.3	4.3	−4.4[1, 2, 3]
1969	943.75	1/6/69	936.66	769.93	−17.8	−14.6	−15.2	−0.8
1970	769.93	1/26/70	768.88	631.16	−17.9	9.1	4.8	−7.6[2, 3]
1973	1000.00	1/29/73	996.46	788.31	−20.9	−14.6	−16.6	−1.7
1977	946.64	2/7/77	946.31	800.85	−15.4	−12.2	−17.3	−5.1
1978	806.22	1/5/78	804.92	742.12	−7.8	0.01	−3.1	−6.2[3]
1980	819.62	3/10/80	818.94	759.13	−7.3	17.7	14.9	5.8[2]
1982	868.25	1/5/82	865.30	776.92	−10.2	20.9	19.6	−1.8[1, 2]
1984	1236.79	1/25/84	1231.89	1086.57	−11.8	−1.6	−3.7	−0.9[3]
1990	2687.93	1/15/90	2669.37	2365.10	−11.4	−1.3	−4.3	−6.9[3]
1991	2565.59	1/7/91	2522.77	2470.30	−2.1	25.6	20.3	4.2[2]
1993	3255.18	1/8/93	3251.67	3241.95	−0.3	15.5	13.7	0.7[2]
1994	3697.08	3/30/94	3626.75	3593.35	−0.9	5.7	2.1	3.3[2, 3]
1996	5059.32	1/10/96	5032.94	5032.94	NC	28.1	26.0	3.3[2]
1998	7660.13	1/9/98	7580.42	7539.07	−0.5	21.1	16.1	1.0[2]
2000	10998.39	1/4/00	10997.93	9796.03	−10.9	−1.9	−6.2	−5.1
2001	10318.93	3/12/01	10208.25	8235.81	−19.3	−1.8	−7.1	3.5[1]
2002	9763.96	1/16/02	9712.27	7286.27	−25.0	−14.1	−16.8	−1.6
2003	8303.78	1/24/03	8131.01	7524.06	−7.5	28.6	25.3	−2.7[1, 2]
2005	10440.58	1/21/05	10392.99	10012.36	−3.7	3.1	−0.6	−2.5[3]
2006	10717.50	1/20/06	10667.39	10667.39	NC	16.8	16.3	2.5
2007	12194.13	3/2/07	12114.10	12050.41	−0.5	9.5	6.4	1.4[2]
2008	1316702	1/2/08	13043.96	7552.29	−42.1	−32.7	−33.8	−6.1
2009	8149.09	1/20/09	7949.09	6547.05	−17.6	31.2	18.8	−8.6[1, 2]
2010	10285.97	1/22/10	10172.98	9686.48	−4.8	13.8	11.0	−3.7[1, 2]
2014	15739.43	1/31/14	15698.85	15372.80	−2.1	??	??	−3.6
				Average Drop	**−10.9%**			

[1]January Barometer wrong [2]December Low Indicator wrong [3]Year Flat

44

MONDAY

D 52.4
S 52.4
N 47.6

20

Never will a man penetrate deeper into error than when he is continuing on a road that has led him to great success.
— Friedrich von Hayek (*Counterrevolution of Science,* 1899–1992)

TUESDAY

D 66.7
S 61.9
N 61.9

21

Patriotism is when love of your own people comes first. Nationalism is when hate for people other that your own comes first.
— Charles de Gaulle (French president and WWII General, 1890–1970)

April 1999 First Month Ever to Gain 1000 Dow Points

WEDNESDAY

D 61.9
S 66.7
N 61.9

22

When you're one step ahead of the crowd, you're a genius. When you're two steps ahead, you're a crackpot.
— Shlomo Riskin (Rabbi, author, b. 1940)

THURSDAY

D 57.1
S 52.4
N 57.1

23

That's the American way. If little kids don't aspire to make money like I did, what the hell good is this country?
— Lee Iacocca (American industrialist, Former Chrysler CEO, b. 1924)

FRIDAY

D 42.9
S 33.3
N 52.4

24

Government is like fire—useful when used legitimately, but dangerous when not.
— David Brooks (*NY Times* columnist, 10/5/07, b. 1961)

SATURDAY

25

May Almanac Investor Seasonalities: See Pages 94, 96 and 98

SUNDAY

26

MAY ALMANAC

MAY						
S	M	T	W	T	F	S
					1	2
3	4	5	6	7	8	9
10	11	12	13	14	15	16
17	18	19	20	21	22	23
24	25	26	27	28	29	30
31						

JUNE						
S	M	T	W	T	F	S
	1	2	3	4	5	6
7	8	9	10	11	12	13
14	15	16	17	18	19	20
21	22	23	24	25	26	27
28	29	30				

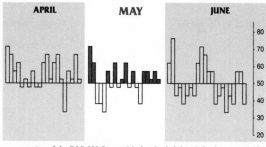

Market Probability Chart above is a graphic representation of the S&P 500 Recent Market Probability Calendar on page 124.

◆ "May/June disaster area" between 1965 and 1984 with S&P down 15 out of 20 Mays ◆ Between 1985 and 1997 May was the best month with 13 straight gains, gaining 3.3% per year on average, up 8, down 8 since ◆ Worst six months of the year begin with May (page 52) ◆ A $10,000 investment compounded to $816,984 for November–April in 64 years compared to a $678 loss for May–October ◆ Dow Memorial Day week record: up 12 years in a row (1984–1995), down 11 of the last 18 years ◆ Since 1950, pre-presidential election Mays rank poorly: #10 Dow and S&P, and #7 NASDAQ.

May Vital Statistics

	DJIA		S&P 500		NASDAQ		Russell 1K		Russell 2K	
Rank	9		8		6		6		5	
Up	32		36		25		23		22	
Down	32		28		18		12		13	
Average % Change	−0.1%		0.2%		0.8%		0.9%		1.3%	
Pre-Election Year	0.02%		0.2%		1.8%		1.2%		2.7%	
Best & Worst May										
	% Change		% Change		% Change		% Change		% Change	
Best	1990	8.3	1990	9.2	1997	11.1	1990	8.9	1997	11.0
Worst	2010	−7.9	1962	−8.6	2000	−11.9	2010	−8.1	2010	−7.7
Best & Worst May Weeks										
Best	5/29/70	5.8	5/2/97	6.2	5/17/02	8.8	5/2/97	6.4	5/14/10	6.3
Worst	5/25/62	−6.0	5/25/62	−6.8	5/7/10	−8.0	5/7/10	−6.6	5/7/10	−8.9
Best & Worst May Days										
Best	5/27/70	5.1	5/27/70	5.0	5/30/00	7.9	5/10/10	4.4	5/10/10	5.6
Worst	5/28/62	−5.7	5/28/62	−6.7	5/23/00	−5.9	5/20/10	−3.9	5/20/10	−5.1
First Trading Day of Expiration Week: 1980–2013										
Record (#Up–#Down)	22–13		23–12		19–16		21–14		17–18	
Current streak	U1		U2		U2		U1		U1	
Avg % Change	0.18		0.17		0.15		0.15		−0.01	
Options Expiration Day: 1980–2013										
Record (#Up–#Down)	16–19		19–16		17–18		19–16		17–18	
Current streak	U2		U2		U2		U2		U2	
Avg % Change	0.11		−0.11		−0.12		−0.10		−0.02	
Options Expiration Week: 1980–2013										
Record (#Up–#Down)	18–17		17–18		18–17		16–19		18–17	
Current streak	D1		D1		U2		D1		D1	
Avg % Change	0.06		0.02		0.16		0.02		−0.17	
Week After Options Expiration: 1980–2013										
Record (#Up–#Down)	18–16		20–14		22–12		20–14		24–10	
Current streak	D1		D1		D1		D1		D1	
Avg % Change	−0.06		0.07		0.08		0.10		0.23	
First Trading Day Performance										
% of Time Up	56.9		56.9		61.4		55.6		58.3	
Avg % Change	0.20		0.22		0.30		0.24		0.24	
Last Trading Day Performance										
% of Time Up	60.9		62.5		69.8		57.1		68.6	
Avg % Change	0.20		0.28		0.22		0.24		0.37	

Dow & S&P 1950–April 2014, NASDAQ 1971–April 2014, Russell 1K & 2K 1979–April 2014.

May's new pattern, a smile or a frown,
Odd years UP and even years DOWN.

MONDAY
D 61.9
S 57.1
N 52.4
27

The greatest good you can do for another is not just to share your riches, but to reveal to him his own.
— Benjamin Disraeli (British prime minister, 1804–1881)

TUESDAY
D 57.1
S 52.4
N 66.7
28

A weak currency is the sign of a weak economy, and a weak economy leads to a weak nation.
— H. Ross Perot (American businessman, *The Dollar Crisis*, 2-time 3rd-party presidential candidate 1992 & 1996, b. 1930)

WEDNESDAY
D 71.4
S 66.7
N 76.2
29

Corporate guidance has become something of an art. The CFO has refined and perfected his art, gracefully leading on the bulls with the calculating grace and cunning of a great matador.
— Joe Kalinowski (I/B/E/S)

End of"Best Six Months"of the Year (Pages 50, 52, 54 and 147)

THURSDAY
D 42.9
S 52.4
N 66.7
30

Never overpay for a stock. More money is lost than in any other way by projecting above-average growth and paying an extra multiple for it.
— Charles Neuhauser (Reich & Tang Asset Management)

First Trading Day in May, Dow Up 12 of Last 17

FRIDAY
D 71.4
S 71.4
N 71.4
1

"Sell in May and go away." However, no one ever said it was the beginning of the month.
— John L. Person (CTA, professional trader, author, speaker, nationalfutures.com, 6/19/2009, b. 1961)

SATURDAY
2

SUNDAY
3

DOWN JANUARYS: A REMARKABLE RECORD

In the first third of the twentieth century, there was no correlation between January markets and the year as a whole. Then, in 1972 Yale Hirsch discovered that the 1933 "lame duck" Amendment to the Constitution changed the political calendar, and the January Barometer (page 16) was born. Visit *http://tinyurl.com/STALameDuck* to see the history.

Down Januarys are harbingers of trouble ahead, in the economic, political, or military arenas. Eisenhower's heart attack in 1955 cast doubt on whether he could run in 1956—a flat year. Two other election years with down Januarys were also flat (1984 and 1992). Twelve bear markets began, and ten continued into second years with poor Januarys. 1968 started down, as we were mired in Vietnam, but Johnson's "bombing halt" changed the climate. Imminent military action in Iraq held January 2003 down before the market triple-bottomed in March. After Baghdad fell, pre-election and recovery forces fueled 2003 into a banner year. 2005 was flat, registering the narrowest Dow trading range on record. 2008 was the worst January on record and preceded the worst bear market since the Great Depression. A negative reading in 2010 preceded a 16% April–July correction, which was quickly reversed by QE2.

Unfortunately, bull and bear markets do not start conveniently at the beginnings and ends of months or years. Though some years ended higher, **every down January since 1950 was followed by a new or continuing bear market, a 10% correction or a flat year**. Down Januarys were followed by substantial declines averaging *minus* **13.9%**, providing excellent buying opportunities later in most years.

FROM DOWN JANUARY S&P CLOSES TO LOW NEXT 11 MONTHS

Year	January Close	% Change	11-Month Low	Date of Low	Jan Close to Low %	% Feb to Dec	Year % Change	
1953	26.38	−0.7%	22.71	14-Sep	−13.9%	−6.0%	−6.6%	bear
1956	43.82	−3.6	43.42	14-Feb	−0.9	6.5	2.6	FLAT/bear
1957	44.72	−4.2	38.98	22-Oct	−12.8	−10.6	−14.3	Cont. bear
1960	55.61	−7.1	52.30	25-Oct	−6.0	4.5	−3.0	bear
1962	68.84	−3.8	52.32	26-Jun	−24.0	−8.3	−11.8	bear
1968	92.24	−4.4	87.72	5-Mar	−4.9	12.6	7.7	−10%/bear
1969	103.01	−0.8	89.20	17-Dec	−13.4	−10.6	−11.4	Cont. bear
1970	85.02	−7.6	69.20	26-May	−18.6	8.4	0.1	Cont. bear/FLAT
1973	116.03	−1.7	92.16	5-Dec	−20.6	−15.9	−17.4	bear
1974	96.57	−1.0	62.28	3-Oct	−35.5	−29.0	−29.7	Cont. bear
1977	102.03	−5.1	90.71	2-Nov	−11.1	−6.8	−11.5	bear
1978	89.25	−6.2	86.90	6-Mar	−2.6	7.7	1.1	Cont. bear/bear
1981	129.55	−4.6	112.77	25-Sep	−13.0	−5.4	−9.7	bear
1982	120.40	−1.8	102.42	12-Aug	−14.9	16.8	14.8	Cont. bear
1984	163.42	−0.9	147.82	24-Jul	−9.5	2.3	1.4	Cont. bear/FLAT
1990	329.07	−6.9	295.46	11-Oct	−10.2	0.4	−6.6	bear
1992	408.79	−2.0	394.50	8-Apr	−3.5	6.6	4.5	FLAT
2000	1394.46	−5.1	1264.74	20-Dec	−9.3	−5.3	−10.1	bear
2002	1130.20	−1.6	776.76	9-Oct	−31.3	−22.2	−23.4	bear
2003	855.70	−2.7	800.73	11-Mar	−6.4	29.9	26.4	Cont. bear
2005	1181.27	−2.5	1137.50	20-Apr	−3.7	5.7	3.0	FLAT
2008	1378.55	−6.1	752.44	20-Nov	−45.4	−34.5	−38.5	Cont. bear
2009	825.88	−8.6	676.53	9-Mar	−18.1	35.0	23.5	Cont. bear
2010	1073.87	−3.7	1022.58	2-Jul	−4.8	17.1	12.8	−10%/no bear
2014	1782.59	−3.6	1741.89	3-Feb	−2.3	—	—	At Press time
				Totals	−334.4%	−1.1%	−96.2%	
				Average	−13.9%	−0.05%	−4.0%	

MAY

Most periodicals and trade journals are deadly dull, and indeed full of fluff provided by public relations agents.
— Jim Rogers (Financier, b. 1942)

[A contrarian's opportunity] If everybody is thinking alike, then somebody isn't thinking.
— General George S. Patton, Jr. (U.S. Army field commander WWII, 1885–1945)

There is a habitual nature to society and human activity. People's behavior and what they do with their money and time bears upon economics and the stock market.
— Jeffrey A. Hirsch (Editor *Stock Trader's Almanac*, b. 1966)

Markets are constantly in a state of uncertainty and flux and money is made by discounting the obvious and betting on the unexpected.
— George Soros (Financier, philanthropist, political activist, author, and philosopher, b. 1930)

Friday Before Mother's Day, Dow Up 13 of Last 20

We're not believers that the government is bigger than the business cycle.
— David Rosenberg (Economist, Gluskin Sheff & Associates, *Barron's* 4/21/2008)

Mother's Day

TOP PERFORMING MONTHS PAST 64⅓ YEARS: STANDARD & POOR'S 500 AND DOW JONES INDUSTRIALS

Monthly performance of the S&P and the Dow are ranked over the past 64⅓ years. NASDAQ monthly performance is shown on page 58.

April, November, and December still hold the top three positions in both the Dow and the S&P. March has reclaimed the fourth spot on the S&P. Two disastrous Januarys in 2008 and 2009 knocked January into fifth. This, in part, led to our discovery in 1986 of the market's most consistent seasonal pattern. You can divide the year into two sections and have practically all the gains in one six-month section and very little in the other. September is the worst month on both lists. (See "Best Six Months" on page 52.)

MONTHLY % CHANGES (JANUARY 1950 TO APRIL 2014)

Standard & Poor's 500

Month	Total % Change	Avg. % Change	# Up	# Down
Jan	71.0%	1.1%	40	25
Feb	−2.0	−0.03	36	29
Mar	78.5	1.2	43	22
Apr	97.6	1.5	45	20
May	9.9	0.2	36	28
Jun	−2.0	−0.03	33	31
Jul	64.0	1.0	35	29
Aug	−3.5	−0.06	35	29
Sep*	−30.0	−0.5	29	34
Oct	51.7	0.8	38	26
Nov	96.4	1.5	42	22
Dec	108.9	1.7	49	15

% Rank				
Dec	108.9%	1.7%	49	15
Apr	97.6	1.5	45	20
Nov	96.4	1.5	42	22
Mar	78.5	1.2	43	22
Jan	71.0	1.1	40	25
Jul	64.0	1.0	35	29
Oct	51.7	0.8	38	26
May	9.9	0.2	36	28
Feb	−2.0	−0.03	36	29
Jun	−2.0	−0.03	33	31
Aug	−3.5	−0.1	35	29
Sep*	−30.0	−0.5	29	34
Totals	**540.5%**	**8.4%**		
Average		**0.70%**		

*No change 1979

Dow Jones Industrials

Month	Total % Change	Avg. % Change	# Up	# Down
Jan	66.9%	1.0%	42	23
Feb	8.2	0.1	38	27
Mar	72.6	1.1	43	22
Apr	126.7	1.9	43	22
May	−3.3	−0.1	32	32
Jun	−20.4	−0.3	29	35
Jul	77.1	1.2	40	24
Aug	−8.6	−0.1	36	28
Sep	−48.3	−0.8	26	38
Oct	32.8	0.5	38	26
Nov	96.3	1.5	42	22
Dec	109.5	1.7	46	18

% Rank				
Apr	126.7%	1.9%	43	22
Dec	109.5	1.7	46	18
Nov	96.3	1.5	42	22
Jul	77.1	1.2	40	24
Mar	72.6	1.1	43	22
Jan	66.9	1.0	42	23
Oct	32.8	0.5	38	26
Feb	8.2	0.1	38	27
May	−3.3	−0.1	32	32
Aug	−8.6	−0.1	36	28
Jun	−20.4	−0.3	29	35
Sep*	−48.3	−0.8	26	38
Totals	**509.5%**	**7.7%**		
Average		**0.64%**		

Anticipators, shifts in cultural behavior, and faster information flow have altered seasonality in recent years. Here is how the months ranked over the past 15⅓ years (184 months) using total percentage gains on the S&P 500: April 32.3, March 31.6, October 24.1, December 22.7, November 13.0, July 2.7, August −3.0, May −3.0, January −9.0, June −14.1, February −16.2, September −19.4.

During the last 15⅓ years front-runners of our Best Six Months may have helped push October into the number-three spot. January has declined in 8 of the last 16 years. Sizeable turnarounds in "bear killing" October were a common occurrence from 1999 to 2007. Recent big Dow losses in the period were: September 2001 (9/11 attack), off 11.1%; September 2002 (Iraq war drums), off 12.4%; June 2008, off 10.2%; October 2008, off 14.1%; and February 2009 (financial crisis), off 11.7%.

MAY

Monday After Mother's Day, Dow Up 15 of Last 20
Monday Before May Expiration, Dow Up 21 of Last 27, Average Gain 0.4%

MONDAY
D 57.1
S 47.6
N 47.6
11

Financial markets will find and exploit hidden flaws, particularly in untested new innovations—and do so at a time that will inflict the most damage to the most people.
— Raymond F. DeVoe, Jr. (Market strategist, *The DeVoe Report*, 3/30/07)

TUESDAY
D 71.4
S 61.9
N 42.9
12

The men who can manage men manage the men who manage only things, and the men who can manage money manage all.
— Will Durant (*The Story of Civilization*, 1885–1981)

WEDNESDAY
D 42.9
S 47.6
N 57.1
13

A statistician is someone who can draw a straight line from an unwarranted assumption to a foregone conclusion.
— Anonymous

THURSDAY
D 57.1
S 52.4
N 47.6
14

Entrepreneurs who believe they're in business to vanquish the competition are less successful than those who believe their goal is to maximize profits or increase their company's value.
— Kaihan Krippendorff (Business consultant, strategist, author, *The Art of the Advantage*, The Strategic Learning Center, b. 1971)

May Expiration Day, Dow Down 14 of Last 25

FRIDAY
D 61.9
S 61.9
N 57.1
15

Experience is helpful, but it is judgment that matters.
— General Colin Powell (Chairman Joint Chiefs 1989–93, Secretary of State 2001–05, *NY Times* 10/22/2008, b. 1937)

SATURDAY
16

SUNDAY
17

"BEST SIX MONTHS": STILL AN EYE-POPPING STRATEGY

Our Best Six Months Switching Strategy consistently delivers. Investing in the Dow Jones Industrial Average between November 1st and April 30th each year and then switching into fixed income for the other six months has produced reliable returns with reduced risk since 1950.

The chart on page 147 shows November, December, January, March, and April to be the top months since 1950. Add February, and an excellent strategy is born! These six consecutive months gained 17432.70 Dow points in 64 years, while the remaining May-through-October months lost 1066.19 points. The S&P gained 1790.37 points in the same best six months versus 75.51 points in the worst six.

Percentage changes are shown along with a compounding $10,000 investment. The November–April $816,984 gain overshadows May–October's $678 loss. (S&P results were $607,883 to $6,891.) Just three November–April losses were double-digit: April 1970 (Cambodian invasion), 1973 (OPEC oil embargo), and 2008 (financial crisis). Similarly, Iraq muted the Best Six and inflated the Worst Six in 2003. When we discovered this strategy in 1986, November–April outperformed May–October by $88,163 to minus $1,522. Results improved substantially these past 28 years, $728,821 to $844. A simple timing indicator triples results (page 54).

	SIX-MONTH SWITCHING STRATEGY			
	DJIA % Change May 1–Oct 31	Investing $10,000	DJIA % Change Nov 1–Apr 30	Investing $10,000
1950	5.0%	$10,500	15.2%	$11,520
1951	1.2	10,626	−1.8	11,313
1952	4.5	11,104	2.1	11,551
1953	0.4	11,148	15.8	13,376
1954	10.3	12,296	20.9	16,172
1955	6.9	13,144	13.5	18,355
1956	−7.0	12,224	3.0	18,906
1957	−10.8	10,904	3.4	19,549
1958	19.2	12,998	14.8	22,442
1959	3.7	13,479	−6.9	20,894
1960	−3.5	13,007	16.9	24,425
1961	3.7	13,488	−5.5	23,082
1962	−11.4	11,950	21.7	28,091
1963	5.2	12,571	7.4	30,170
1964	7.7	13,539	5.6	31,860
1965	4.2	14,108	−2.8	30,968
1966	−13.6	12,189	11.1	34,405
1967	−1.9	11,957	3.7	35,678
1968	4.4	12,483	−0.2	35,607
1969	−9.9	11,247	−14.0	30,622
1970	2.7	11,551	24.6	38,155
1971	−10.9	10,292	13.7	43,382
1972	0.1	10,302	−3.6	41,820
1973	3.8	10,693	−12.5	36,593
1974	−20.5	8,501	23.4	45,156
1975	1.8	8,654	19.2	53,826
1976	−3.2	8,377	−3.9	51,727
1977	−11.7	7,397	2.3	52,917
1978	−5.4	6,998	7.9	57,097
1979	−4.6	6,676	0.2	57,211
1980	13.1	7,551	7.9	61,731
1981	−14.6	6,449	−0.5	61,422
1982	16.9	7,539	23.6	75,918
1983	−0.1	7,531	−4.4	72,578
1984	3.1	7,764	4.2	75,626
1985	9.2	8,478	29.8	98,163
1986	5.3	8,927	21.8	119,563
1987	−12.8	7,784	1.9	121,835
1988	5.7	8,228	12.6	137,186
1989	9.4	9,001	0.4	137,735
1990	−8.1	8,272	18.2	162,803
1991	6.3	8,793	9.4	178,106
1992	−4.0	8,441	6.2	189,149
1993	7.4	9,066	0.03	189,206
1994	6.2	9,628	10.6	209,262
1995	10.0	10,591	17.1	245,046
1996	8.3	11,470	16.2	284,743
1997	6.2	12,181	21.8	346,817
1998	−5.2	11,548	25.6	435,602
1999	−0.5	11,490	0.04	435,776
2000	2.2	11,743	−2.2	426,189
2001	−15.5	9,923	9.6	467,103
2002	−15.6	8,375	1.0	471,774
2003	15.6	9,682	4.3	492,060
2004	−1.9	9,498	1.6	499,933
2005	2.4	9,726	8.9	544,427
2006	6.3	10,339	8.1	588,526
2007	6.6	11,021	−8.0	541,444
2008	−27.3	8,012	−12.4	474,305
2009	18.9	9,526	13.3	537,388
2010	1.0	9,621	15.2	619,071
2011	−6.7	8,976	10.5	684,073
2012	−0.9	8,895	13.3	775,055
2013	4.8	9,322	6.7	826,984
Average/Gain	0.3%	($678)	7.6%	$816,894
# Up/Down	38/26		50/14	

MONDAY

D 42.9
S 47.6
N 52.4

18

Get inside information from the president and you will probably lose half your money. If you get it from the chairman of the board, you will lose all your money.
— Jim Rogers (Financier, b. 1942)

TUESDAY

D 57.1
S 57.1
N 66.7

19

To succeed in the markets, it is essential to make your own decisions. Numerous traders cited listening to others as their worst blunder.
— Jack D. Schwager (Investment manager, author, *Stock Market Wizards: Interviews with America's Top Stock Traders*, b. 1948)

WEDNESDAY

D 47.6
S 47.6
N 38.1

20

When an old man dies, a library burns down.
— African proverb

THURSDAY

D 33.3
S 38.1
N 42.9

21

You have to keep digging, keep asking questions, because otherwise you'll be seduced or brainwashed into the idea that it's somehow a great privilege, an honor, to report the lies they've been feeding you.
— David Halberstam (Amercian writer, war reporter, 1964 Pulitzer Prize, 1934–2007)

Friday Before Memorial Day Tends to Be Lackluster with Light Trading, Dow Down 8 of Last 14, Average –0.3%

FRIDAY

D 52.4
S 57.1
N 42.9

22

There is only one corner of the universe you can be certain of improving, and that's yourself.
— Aldous Huxley (English author, *Brave New World*, 1894–1963)

SATURDAY

23

June Almanac Investor Seasonalities: See Pages 94, 96 and 98

SUNDAY

24

MACD-TIMING TRIPLES "BEST SIX MONTHS" RESULTS

Using the simple MACD (Moving Average Convergence Divergence) indicator developed by our friend Gerald Appel to better time entries and exits into and out of the Best Six Months (page 52) period nearly triples the results. Several years ago, Sy Harding enhanced our Best Six Months Switching Strategy with MACD triggers, dubbing it the "best mechanical system ever." In 2006, we improved it even more, achieving similar results with just four trades every four years (page 62).

Our *Almanac Investor eNewsletter* (see insert) implements this system with quite a degree of success. Starting October 1, we look to catch the market's first hint of an uptrend after the summer doldrums, and beginning April 1, we prepare to exit these seasonal positions as soon as the market falters.

In up-trending markets, MACD signals get you in earlier and keep you in longer. But if the market is trending down, entries are delayed until the market turns up, and exit points can come a month earlier.

The results are astounding, applying the simple MACD signals. Instead of $10,000 gaining $816,984 over the 64 recent years when invested only during the Best Six Months (page 50), the gain nearly tripled to $2,214,909. The $678 loss during the Worst Six Months expanded to a loss of $6,578.

Impressive results for being invested during only 6.3 months of the year on average! For the rest of the year consider money markets, bonds, puts, bear funds, covered calls, or credit call spreads. See page 42 for more executable trades employing ETFs and mutual funds.

Updated signals are e-mailed to our *Almanac Investor eNewsletter* subscribers as soon as they are triggered. Visit *www.stocktradersalmanac.com,* or see the insert for details and a special offer for new subscribers.

BEST SIX-MONTH SWITCHING STRATEGY+TIMING

	DJIA % Change May 1–Oct 31*	DJIA Investing $10,000	DJIA % Change Nov 1–Apr 30*	DJIA Investing $10,000
1950	7.3%	$10,730	13.3%	$11,330
1951	0.1	10,741	1.9	11,545
1952	1.4	10,891	2.1	11,787
1953	0.2	10,913	17.1	13,803
1954	13.5	12,386	16.3	16,053
1955	7.7	13,340	13.1	18,156
1956	−6.8	12,433	2.8	18,664
1957	−12.3	10,904	4.9	19,579
1958	17.3	12,790	16.7	22,849
1959	1.6	12,995	−3.1	22,141
1960	−4.9	12,358	16.9	25,883
1961	2.9	12,716	−1.5	25,495
1962	−15.3	10,770	22.4	31,206
1963	4.3	11,233	9.6	34,202
1964	6.7	11,986	6.2	36,323
1965	2.6	12,298	−2.5	35,415
1966	−16.4	10,281	14.3	40,479
1967	−2.1	10,065	5.5	42,705
1968	3.4	10,407	0.2	42,790
1969	−11.9	9,169	−6.7	39,923
1970	−1.4	9,041	20.8	48,227
1971	−11.0	8,046	15.4	55,654
1972	−0.6	7,998	−1.4	54,875
1973	−11.0	7,118	0.1	54,930
1974	−22.4	5,524	28.2	70,420
1975	0.1	5,530	18.5	83,448
1976	−3.4	5,342	−3.0	80,945
1977	−11.4	4,733	0.5	81,350
1978	−4.5	4,520	9.3	88,916
1979	−5.3	4,280	7.0	95,140
1980	9.3	4,678	4.7	99,612
1981	−14.6	3,995	0.4	100,001
1982	15.5	4,614	23.5	123,512
1983	2.5	4,729	−7.3	114,496
1984	3.3	4,885	3.9	118,961
1985	7.0	5,227	38.1	164,285
1986	−2.8	5,081	28.2	210,613
1987	−14.9	4,324	3.0	216,931
1988	6.1	4,588	11.8	242,529
1989	9.8	5,038	3.3	250,532
1990	−6.7	4,700	15.8	290,116
1991	4.8	4,926	11.3	322,899
1992	−6.2	4,621	6.6	344,210
1993	5.5	4,875	5.6	363,486
1994	3.7	5,055	13.1	411,103
1995	7.2	5,419	16.7	479,757
1996	9.2	5,918	21.9	584,824
1997	3.6	6,131	18.5	693,016
1998	−12.4	5,371	39.9	969,529
1999	−6.4	5,027	5.1	1,018,975
2000	−6.0	4,725	5.4	1,074,000
2001	−17.3	3,908	15.8	1,243,692
2002	−25.2	2,923	6.0	1,318,314
2003	16.4	3,402	7.8	1,421,142
2004	−0.9	3,371	1.8	1,446,723
2005	−0.5	3,354	7.7	1,558,121
2006	4.7	3,512	14.4	1,782,490
2007	5.6	3,709	−12.7	1,556,114
2008	−24.7	2,793	−14.0	1,338,258
2009	23.8	3,458	10.8	1,482,790
2010	4.6	3,617	7.3	1,591,034
2011	−9.4	3,277	18.7	1,888,557
2012	0.3	3,287	10.0	2,077,413
2013	4.1	3,422	7.1	2,224,909
Average	**−1.1%**		**9.3%**	
# Up	**34**		**55**	
# Down	**30**		**9**	
64-Year Gain (Loss)		**($6,578)**		**$2,214,909**

*MACD generated entry and exit points (earlier or later) can lengthen or shorten six-month periods.

MAY

Memorial Day (*Market Closed*)

MONDAY
25

Being uneducated is sometimes beneficial. Then you don't know what can't be done.
— Michael Ott (Venture capitalist)

Day After Memorial Day, Dow Up 20 of Last 28

TUESDAY
D 52.4
S 57.1
N 52.4
26

Become more humble as the market goes your way.
— Bernard Baruch (Financier, speculator, statesman, presidential adviser, 1870–1965)

WEDNESDAY
D 47.6
S 52.4
N 57.1
27

You know you're right when the other side starts to shout.
— I. A. O'Shaughnessy (American oilman, 1885–1973)

Memorial Day Week Dow Down 11 of Last 18, Up 12 Straight 1984–1995

THURSDAY
D 66.7
S 57.1
N 71.4
28

To achieve satisfactory investment results is easier than most people realize. The typical individual investor has a great advantage over the large institutions.
— Benjamin Graham (Economist, investor, *Securities Analysis* 1934, *The Intelligent Investor* 1949, 1894–1976)

FRIDAY
D 47.6
S 52.4
N 57.1
29

I have but one lamp by which my feet (or "investments") are guided, and that is the lamp of experience. I know of no way of judging the future but by the past.
— Patrick Henry (U.S. Founding Father, twice Govenor of VA, 1736–1799, March 23, 1775 speech)

SATURDAY
30

SUNDAY
31

JUNE ALMANAC

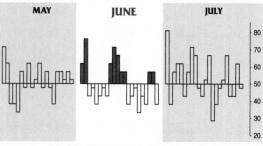

<table>
<tr><th colspan="2">JUNE</th></tr>
<tr><th>S M T W T F S</th><th>JULY
S M T W T F S</th></tr>
</table>

JUNE	JULY
S M T W T F S	S M T W T F S
1 2 3 4 5 6	1 2 3 4
7 8 9 10 11 12 13	5 6 7 8 9 10 11
14 15 16 17 18 19 20	12 13 14 15 16 17 18
21 22 23 24 25 26 27	19 20 21 22 23 24 25
28 29 30	26 27 28 29 30 31

Market Probability Chart above is a graphic representation of the S&P 500 Recent Market Probability Calendar on page 124.

◆ The "summer rally" in most years is the weakest rally of all four seasons (page 72) ◆ Week after June Triple-Witching Day Dow down 21 of last 24 (page 78) ◆ RECENT RECORD: S&P up 12, down 9, average loss 0.3%, ranks tenth ◆ Stronger for NASDAQ, average gain 0.9% last 21 years ◆ Watch out for end-of-quarter "portfolio pumping" on last day of June, Dow down 16 of last 23, NASDAQ down 6 of last 9 ◆ Pre-presidential election year Junes: #5 S&P, #6 NASDAQ, Dow ranks #8 ◆ June ends NASDAQ's Best Eight Months.

June Vital Statistics

	DJIA		S&P 500		NASDAQ		Russell 1K		Russell 2K	
Rank	11		10		7		11		8	
Up	29		33		24		20		21	
Down	35		31		19		15		14	
Average % Change	−0.3%		−0.03%		0.7%		0.2%		0.4%	
Pre-Election Year	1.0%		1.4%		2.3%		1.4%		1.4%	
	**Best & Worst June**									
	% Change		% Change		% Change		% Change		% Change	
Best	1955	6.2	1955	8.2	2000	16.6	1999	5.1	2000	8.6
Worst	2008	−10.2	2008	−8.6	2002	−9.4	2008	−8.5	2010	−7.9
	**Best & Worst June Weeks**									
Best	6/7/74	6.4	6/2/00	7.2	6/2/00	19.0	6/2/00	8.0	6/2/00	12.2
Worst	6/30/50	−6.8	6/30/50	−7.6	6/15/01	−8.4	6/15/01	−4.2	6/9/06	−4.9
	**Best & Worst June Days**									
Best	6/28/62	3.8	6/28/62	3.4	6/2/00	6.4	6/10/10	3.0	6/2/00	4.2
Worst	6/26/50	−4.7	6/26/50	−5.4	6/29/10	−3.9	6/4/10	−3.5	6/4/10	−5.0
	**First Trading Day of Expiration Week: 1980–2013**									
Record (#Up–#Down)	18–16		20–14		15–19		18–16		13–20	
Current streak	U1		U1		U1		U1		U1	
Avg % Change	0.001		−0.09		−0.26		−0.10		−0.35	
	**Options Expiration Day: 1980–2013**									
Record (#Up–#Down)	21–13		22–12		19–15		22–12		20–14	
Current streak	U4		U5		D1		U5		U5	
Avg % Change	−0.04		0.05		−0.001		0.01		0.01	
	**Options Expiration Week: 1980–2013**									
Record (#Up–#Down)	19–15		17–17		14–20		15–19		15–19	
Current streak	D14		D10		D1		D1		D1	
Avg % Change	−0.10		−0.15		−0.37		−0.21		−0.35	
	**Week After Options Expiration: 1980–2013**									
Record (#Up–#Down)	11–23		17–17		20–14		17–17		17–17	
Current streak	U1		U1		U3		U1		U3	
Avg % Change	−0.44		−0.15		0.16		−0.12		−0.07	
	**First Trading Day Performance**									
% of Time Up	53.1		51.6		58.1		57.1		62.9	
Avg % Change	0.14		0.11		0.11		0.05		0.12	
	**Last Trading Day Performance**									
% of Time Up	53.1		50.0		67.4		48.6		65.7	
Avg % Change	0.04		0.09		0.31		0.01		0.39	

Dow & S&P 1950–April 2014, NASDAQ 1971–April 2014, Russell 1K & 2K 1979–April 2014.

Last Day of June not hot for the Dow;
Down 16 of 23, WOW!

JUNE

First Trading Day in June, Dow Up 19 of Last 26,
Down 2008/2010 –1.1%, 2011/12 –2.2%

MONDAY
D 66.7
S 61.9
N 57.1

1

Bear markets don't act like a medicine ball rolling down a smooth hill. Instead, they behave like a basketball bouncing down a rock-strewn mountainside; there's lots of movement up and sideways before the bottom is reached.
— Daniel Turov (*Turov on Timing, Barron's* May 21, 2001, b. 1947)

TUESDAY
D 52.4
S 76.2
N 76.2

2

The way a young man spends his evenings is a part of that thin area between success and failure.
— Robert R. Young (U.S. financier and railroad tycoon, 1897–1958)

Start Looking for NASDAQ MACD SELL Signal on June 1 (Page 60)
Almanac Investor Subscribers Emailed When It Triggers (See Insert)

WEDNESDAY
D 47.6
S 42.9
N 52.4

3

Don't be the last bear or last bull standing, let history guide you, be contrary to the crowd, and let the tape tell you when to act.
— Jeffrey A. Hirsch (Editor *Stock Trader's Almanac*, b. 1966)

THURSDAY
D 57.1
S 47.6
N 52.4

4

Those that forget the past are condemned to repeat its mistakes, and those that mis-state the past should be condemned.
— Eugene D. Cohen (Letter to the Editor, *Financial Times* 10/30/06, b. 1946)

June Ends NASDAQ's "Best Eight Months" (Pages 60, 62 and 148)

FRIDAY
D 57.1
S 38.1
N 38.1

5

Laws are like sausages. It's better not to see them being made.
— Otto von Bismarck (German-Prussian politician, 1st Chancellor of Germany, 1815–1898)

SATURDAY

6

SUNDAY

7

TOP PERFORMING NASDAQ MONTHS PAST 43⅓ YEARS

NASDAQ stocks continue to run away during three consecutive months, November, December, and January, with an average gain of 6.5% despite the slaughter of November 2000, down 22.9%, December 2000, −4.9%, December 2002, −9.7%, November 2007, −6.9%, January 2008, −9.9%, November 2008, −10.8%, January 2009, −6.4%, and January 2010, −5.4%. Solid gains in November and December 2004 offset January 2005's 5.2% Iraq-turmoil-fueled drop.

You can see the months graphically on page 148. January by itself is impressive, up 2.9% on average. April, May, and June also shine, creating our NASDAQ Best Eight Months strategy. What appears as a Death Valley abyss occurs during NASDAQ's bleakest four months: July, August, September, and October. NASDAQ's Best Eight Months seasonal strategy using MACD timing is displayed on page 60.

MONTHLY % CHANGES (JANUARY 1971 TO APRIL 2014)

NASDAQ Composite*					Dow Jones Industrials				
Month	Total % Change	Avg. % Change	# Up	# Down	Month	Total % Change	Avg. % Change	# Up	# Down
Jan	125.6%	2.9%	29	15	Jan	57.2%	1.3%	28	16
Feb	24.7	0.6	24	20	Feb	13.8	0.3	26	18
Mar	35.7	0.8	28	16	Mar	51.4	1.2	30	14
Apr	63.0	1.4	28	16	Apr	95.7	2.2	28	16
May	34.1	0.8	25	18	May	10.1	0.2	22	21
Jun	30.9	0.7	24	19	Jun	−3.2	−0.07	21	22
Jul	7.6	0.2	22	21	Jul	33.6	0.8	24	19
Aug	6.5	0.2	23	20	Aug	−11.3	−0.3	24	19
Sep	−21.0	−0.5	24	19	Sep	−44.4	−1.0	16	27
Oct	24.2	0.6	23	20	Oct	21.4	0.5	26	17
Nov	67.3	1.6	28	15	Nov	52.3	1.2	28	15
Dec	86.9	2.0	26	17	Dec	73.2	1.7	31	12
% Rank					**% Rank**				
Jan	125.6%	2.9%	29	15	Apr	95.7%	2.2%	28	16
Dec	86.9	2.0	26	17	Dec	73.2	1.7	31	12
Nov	67.3	1.6	28	15	Jan	57.2	1.3	28	16
Apr	63.0	1.4	28	16	Nov	52.3	1.2	28	15
Mar	35.7	0.8	28	16	Mar	51.4	1.2	30	14
May	34.1	0.8	25	18	Jul	33.6	0.8	24	19
Jun	30.9	0.7	24	19	Oct	21.4	0.5	26	17
Feb	24.7	0.6	24	20	Feb	13.8	0.3	26	18
Oct	24.2	0.6	23	20	May	10.1	0.2	22	21
Jul	7.6	0.2	22	21	Jun	−3.2	−0.07	21	22
Aug	6.5	0.2	23	20	Aug	−11.3	−0.3	24	19
Sep	−21.0	−0.5	24	19	Sep	−44.4	−1.0	16	27
Totals	**485.5%**	**11.3%**			**Totals**	**349.8%**	**8.0%**		
Average		**0.94%**			**Average**		**0.67%**		

*Based on NASDAQ composite, prior to Feb. 5, 1971 based on National Quotation Bureau indices

For comparison, Dow figures are shown. During this period, NASDAQ averaged a 0.94% gain per month, 40 percent more than the Dow's 0.67% per month. Between January 1971 and January 1982, NASDAQ's composite index doubled in 12 years, while the Dow stayed flat. But while NASDAQ plummeted 77.9% from its 2000 highs to the 2002 bottom, the Dow only lost 37.8%. The Great Recession and bear market of 2007–2009 spread its carnage equally across Dow and NASDAQ. Recent market moves are increasingly more correlated.

JUNE

MONDAY

D 47.6
S 42.9
N 38.1

8

I don't know where speculation got such a bad name, since I know of no forward leap which was not fathered by speculation.
— John Steinbeck (Author, *Grapes of Wrath*, 1902–1968)

TUESDAY

D 38.1
S 47.6
N 42.9

9

Every successful enterprise requires three people—a dreamer, a businessman, and a son-of-a-bitch.
— Peter McArthur (1904)

2008 Second Worst June Ever, Dow –10.2%, S&P –8.6%, Only 1930 Was Worse, NASDAQ –9.1%, June 2002 –9.4%

WEDNESDAY

D 47.6
S 42.9
N 42.9

10

Drawing on my fine command of language, I said nothing.
— Robert Benchley (American writer, actor, and humorist, 1889–1945)

THURSDAY

D 61.9
S 61.9
N 52.4

11

In the stock market those who expect history to repeat itself exactly are doomed to failure.
— Yale Hirsch (Creator of *Stock Trader's Almanac*, b. 1923)

FRIDAY

D 71.4
S 71.4
N 61.9

12

The reasonable man adapts himself to the world; the unreasonable one persists in trying to adapt the world to himself. Therefore, all progress depends on the unreasonable man.
— George Bernard Shaw (Irish dramatist, 1856–1950)

SATURDAY

13

Father's Day

SUNDAY

14

GET MORE OUT OF NASDAQ'S "BEST EIGHT MONTHS" WITH MACD TIMING

NASDAQ's amazing eight-month run from November through June is hard to miss on pages 58 and 148. A $10,000 investment in these eight months since 1971 gained $475,624 versus a loss of $2,052 during the void that is the four-month period July–October (as of May 20, 2014).

Using the same MACD timing indicators on the NASDAQ as is done for the Dow (page 54) has enabled us to capture much of October's improved performance, pumping up NASDAQ's results considerably. Over the 43 years since NASDAQ began, the gain on the same $10,000 leaps to $1,138,732 while the $10,000 during the four-month void shrinks to $6,748. Only four sizeable losses occurred during the favorable period and the bulk of NASDAQ's bear markets were avoided including the worst of the 2000–2002 bear. See page 42 for more executable trades employing ETFs and mutual funds.

Updated signals are e-mailed to our monthly newsletter subscribers as soon as they are triggered. Visit *www.stocktradersalmanac.com,* or see insert for details and a special offer for new subscribers.

BEST EIGHT MONTHS STRATEGY + TIMING

MACD Signal Date	Worst 4 Months July 1–Oct 31* NASDAQ	% Change	Investing $10,000	MACD Signal Date	Best 8 Months Nov 1–June 30* NASDAQ	% Change	Investing $10,000
22-Jul-71	109.54	−3.6	$9,640	4-Nov-71	105.56	24.1	$12,410
7-Jun-72	131.00	−1.8	9,466	23-Oct-72	128.66	−22.7	9,593
25-Jun-73	99.43	−7.2	8,784	7-Dec-73	92.32	−20.2	7,655
3-Jul-74	73.66	−23.2	6,746	7-Oct-74	56.57	47.8	11,314
11-Jun-75	83.60	−9.2	6,125	7-Oct-75	75.88	20.8	13,667
22-Jun-76	91.66	−2.4	5,978	19-Oct-76	89.45	13.2	15,471
27-Jul-77	101.25	−4.0	5,739	4-Nov-77	97.21	26.6	19,586
7-Jun-78	123.10	−6.5	5,366	6-Nov-78	115.08	19.1	23,327
3-Jul-79	137.03	−1.1	5,307	30-Oct-79	135.48	15.5	26,943
20-Jun-80	156.51	26.2	6,697	9-Oct-80	197.53	11.2	29,961
4-Jun-81	219.68	−17.6	5,518	1-Oct-81	181.09	−4.0	28,763
7-Jun-82	173.84	12.5	6,208	7-Oct-82	195.59	57.4	45,273
1-Jun-83	307.95	−10.7	5,544	3-Nov-83	274.86	−14.2	38,844
1-Jun-84	235.90	5.0	5,821	15-Oct-84	247.67	17.3	45,564
3-Jun-85	290.59	−3.0	5,646	1-Oct-85	281.77	39.4	63,516
10-Jun-86	392.83	−10.3	5,064	1-Oct-86	352.34	20.5	76,537
30-Jun-87	424.67	−22.7	3,914	2-Nov-87	328.33	20.1	91,921
8-Jul-88	394.33	−6.6	3,656	29-Nov-88	368.15	22.4	112,511
13-Jun-89	450.73	0.7	3,682	9-Nov-89	454.07	1.9	114,649
11-Jun-90	462.79	−23.0	2,835	2-Oct-90	356.39	39.3	159,706
11-Jun-91	496.62	6.4	3,016	1-Oct-91	528.51	7.4	171,524
11-Jun-92	567.68	1.5	3,061	14-Oct-92	576.22	20.5	206,686
7-Jun-93	694.61	9.9	3,364	1-Oct-93	763.23	−4.4	197,592
17-Jun-94	729.35	5.0	3,532	11-Oct-94	765.57	13.5	224,267
1-Jun-95	868.82	17.2	4,140	13-Oct-95	1018.38	21.6	272,709
3-Jun-96	1238.73	1.0	4,181	7-Oct-96	1250.87	10.3	300,798
4-Jun-97	1379.67	24.4	5,201	3-Oct-97	1715.87	1.8	306,212
1-Jun-98	1746.82	−7.8	4,795	15-Oct-98	1611.01	49.7	458,399
1-Jun-99	2412.03	18.5	5,682	6-Oct-99	2857.21	35.7	622,047
29-Jun-00	3877.23	−18.2	4,648	18-Oct-00	3171.56	−32.2	421,748
1-Jun-01	2149.44	−31.1	3,202	1-Oct-01	1480.46	5.5	444,944
3-Jun-02	1562.56	−24.0	2,434	2-Oct-02	1187.30	38.5	616,247
20-Jun-03	1644.72	15.1	2,802	6-Oct-03	1893.46	4.3	642,746
21-Jun-04	1974.38	−1.6	2,757	1-Oct-04	1942.20	6.1	681,954
8-Jun-05	2060.18	1.5	2,798	19-Oct-05	2091.76	6.1	723,553
1-Jun-06	2219.86	3.9	2,907	5-Oct-06	2306.34	9.5	792,291
7-Jun-07	2541.38	7.9	3,137	1-Oct-07	2740.99	−9.1	724,796
2-Jun-08	2491.53	−31.3	2,155	17-Oct-08	1711.29	6.1	769,009
15-Jun-09	1816.38	17.8	2,539	9-Oct-09	2139.28	1.6	781,313
7-Jun-10	2173.90	18.6	3,011	4-Nov-10	2577.34	7.4	839,130
1-Jun-11	2769.19	−10.5	2,695	7-Oct-11	2479.35	10.8	929,756
1-Jun-12	2747.48	9.6	2,954	6-Nov-12	3011.93	16.2	1,080,376
4-Jun-13	3445.26	10.1	3,252	15-Oct-13	3794.01	8.0	1,148,732
20-May-14	4096.89	*As of 5/20/2014, MACD Sell Signal not triggered at press time*					
	43-Year Loss	**($6,748)**			**43-Year Gain $1,138,732**		

MACD-generated entry and exit points (earlier or later) can lengthen or shorten eight-month periods.

JUNE

Monday of Triple Witching Week, Dow Down 10 of Last 17

MONDAY
D 57.1
S 66.7
N 71.4
15

Six words that spell business success: create concept, communicate concept, sustain momentum.
— Yale Hirsch (Creator of *Stock Trader's Almanac*, b. 1923)

TUESDAY
D 57.1
S 57.1
N 47.6
16

If you spend more than 14 minutes a year worrying about the market, you've wasted 12 minutes.
— Peter Lynch (Fidelity Investments, *One Up on Wall Street*, b. 1944)

Triple Witching Week Often Up in Bull Markets and Down in Bears (Page 78)

WEDNESDAY
D 57.1
S 57.1
N 57.1
17

In an uptrend, if a higher high is made but fails to carry through, and prices dip below the previous high, the trend is apt to reverse. The converse is true for downtrends.
— Victor Sperandeo (*Trader Vic—Methods of a Wall Street Master*, b. 1945)

THURSDAY
D 42.9
S 38.1
N 42.9
18

Doubt is the father of invention.
— Galileo Galilei (Italian physicist and astronomer, 1564–1642)

June Triple Witching Day, Dow Up 9 of Last 15
However, Average Loss 0.2%

FRIDAY
D 38.1
S 42.9
N 52.4
19

As for it being different this time, it is different every time. The question is in what way, and to what extent.
— Tom McClellan (*The McClellan Market Report*)

SATURDAY
20

SUNDAY
21

TRIPLE RETURNS, LESS TRADES: BEST 6 + 4-YEAR CYCLE

We first introduced this strategy to *Almanac Investor* newsletter subscribers in October 2006. Recurring seasonal stock market patterns and the four-year Presidential Election/Stock Market Cycle (page 130) have been integral to our research since the first Almanac 48 years ago. Yale Hirsch discovered the Best Six Months in 1986 (page 52), and it has been a cornerstone of our seasonal investment analysis and strategies ever since.

Most of the market's gains have occurred during the Best Six Months, and the market generally hits a low point every four years in the first (post-election) or second (midterm) year and exhibits the greatest gains in the third (pre-election) year. This strategy combines the best of these two market phenomena, the Best Six Months and the four-year cycle, timing entries and exits with MACD (pages 54 and 60).

We've gone back to 1949 to include the full four-year cycle that began with post-election year 1949. Only four trades every four years are needed to nearly triple the results of the Best Six Months. Buy and sell during the post-election and midterm years and then hold from the mid-term MACD seasonal buy signal sometime after October 1 until the post-election MACD seasonal sell signal sometime after April 1, approximately 2.5 years: better returns, less effort, lower transaction fees, and fewer taxable events. See page 42 for more executable trades employing ETFs and mutual funds.

FOUR TRADES EVERY FOUR YEARS		
	Worst	Best
	Six Months	Six Months
Year	May–Oct	Nov–April
Post-election	Sell	Buy
Midterm	Sell	Buy
Pre-election	Hold	Hold
Election	Hold	Hold

BEST SIX MONTHS+TIMING+4-YEAR CYCLE STRATEGY

Year	DJIA % Change May 1–Oct 31*	Investing $10,000	DJIA % Change Nov 1–Apr 30*	Investing $10,000
1949	3.0%	$10,300	17.5%	$11,750
1950	7.3	11,052	19.7	14,065
1951		11,052		14,065
1952		11,052		14,065
1953	0.2	11,074	17.1	16,470
1954	13.5	12,569	35.7	22,350
1955		12,569		22,350
1956		12,569		22,350
1957	−12.3	11,023	4.9	23,445
1958	17.3	12,930	27.8	29,963
1959		12,930		29,963
1960		12,930		29,963
1961	2.9	13,305	−1.5	29,514
1962	−15.3	11,269	58.5	46,780
1963		11,269		46,780
1964		11,269		46,780
1965	2.6	11,562	−2.5	45,611
1966	−16.4	9,666	22.2	55,737
1967		9,666		55,737
1968		9,666		55,737
1969	−11.9	8,516	−6.7	52,003
1970	−1.4	8,397	21.5	63,184
1971		8,397		63,184
1972		8,397		63,184
1973	−11.0	7,473	0.1	63,247
1974	−22.4	5,799	42.5	90,127
1975		5,799		90,127
1976		5,799		90,127
1977	−11.4	5,138	0.5	90,578
1978	−4.5	4,907	26.8	114,853
1979		4,907		114,853
1980		4,907		114,853
1981	−14.6	4,191	0.4	115,312
1982	15.5	4,841	25.9	145,178
1983		4,841		145,178
1984		4,841		145,178
1985	7.0	5,180	38.1	200,491
1986	−2.8	5,035	33.2	267,054
1987		5,035		267,054
1988		5,035		267,054
1989	9.8	5,528	3.3	275,867
1990	−6.7	5,158	35.1	372,696
1991		5,158		372,696
1992		5,158		372,696
1993	5.5	5,442	5.6	393,455
1994	3.7	5,643	88.2	740,482
1995		5,643		740,482
1996		5,643		740,482
1997	3.6	5,846	18.5	877,471
1998	−12.4	5,121	36.3	1,195,993
1999		5,121		1,195,993
2000		5,121		1,195,993
2001	−17.3	4,235	15.8	1,384,960
2002	−25.2	3,168	34.2	1,858,616
2003		3,168		1,858,616
2004		3,168		1,858,616
2005	−0.5	3,152	7.7	2,001,729
2006	4.7	3,300	−31.7	1,367,181
2007		3,300		1,367,181
2008		3,300		1,367,181
2009	23.8	4,085	10.8	1,514,738
2010	4.6	4,273	27.4	1,929,777
2011		4,273		1,929,777
2012		4,273		1,929,777
2013	4.1	4,448	7.1	2,066,791
Average	−0.9%		9.8%	
# Up	17		29	
# Down	16		4	
65-Year Gain (Loss)		($5,552)		$2,056,791

* MACD and 2.5-year hold lengthen and shorten six-month periods

MONDAY
D 38.1
S 47.6
N 33.3
22

If you can ever buy with a P/E equivalent to growth, that's a good starting point.
— Alan Lowenstein (co-portfolio manager, John Hancock Technology Fund, *TheStreet.com* 3/12/2001)

TUESDAY
D 33.3
S 33.3
N 28.6
23

When everbody thinks alike, everyone is likely to be wrong.
— Humphrey B. Neill (Investor, analyst, author, *Art of Contrary Thinking* 1954, 1895–1977)

Week After June Triple Witching, Dow Down 21 of Last 24
Average Loss Since 1990, 1.1%

WEDNESDAY
D 38.1
S 42.9
N 42.9
24

There is no tool to change human nature...people are prone to recurring bouts of optimism and pessimism that manifest themselves from time to time in the buildup or cessation of speculative excesses.
— Alan Greenspan (Fed Chairman 1987–2006, July 18, 2001 monetary policy report to the Congress, b. 1926)

THURSDAY
D 47.6
S 38.1
N 47.6
25

Make it idiot-proof and someone will make a better idiot.
— Bumper sticker

FRIDAY
D 57.1
S 57.1
N 71.4
26

I'm not nearly so concerned about the return on my capital as I am the return of my capital.
— Will Rogers (American humorist and showman, 1879–1935)

SATURDAY
27

July Almanac Investor Seasonalities: See Pages 94, 96 and 98

SUNDAY
28

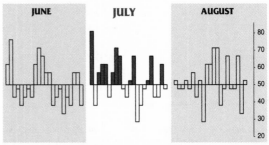

JUNE	JULY	AUGUST

◆ July is the best month of the third quarter except for NASDAQ (page 66) ◆ Start of 2nd half brings an inflow of retirement funds ◆ First trading day Dow up 20 of last 25 ◆ Graph above shows strength in the first half of July ◆ Huge gain in July usually provides better buying opportunity over next 4 months ◆ Start of NASDAQ's worst four months of the year (page 60) ◆ Pre-presidential election Julys are ranked #6 Dow (up 9, down 7), #8 S&P (up 9, down 7), and #10 NASDAQ (up 5, down 6).

July Vital Statistics

	DJIA		S&P 500		NASDAQ		Russell 1K		Russell 2K	
Rank	4		6		10		8		11	
Up	40		35		22		16		17	
Down	24		29		21		19		18	
Average % Change	1.2%		1.0%		0.2%		0.6%		−0.3%	
Pre-Election Year	1.1%		0.8%		0.8%		0.4%		0.5%	
Best & Worst July										
	% Change		% Change		% Change		% Change		% Change	
Best	1989	9.0	1989	8.8	1997	10.5	1989	8.2	1980	11.0
Worst	1969	−6.6	2002	−7.9	2002	−9.2	2002	−7.5	2002	−15.2
Best & Worst July Weeks										
Best	7/17/09	7.3	7/17/09	7.0	7/17/09	7.4	7/17/09	7.0	7/17/09	8.0
Worst	7/19/02	−7.7	7/19/02	−8.0	7/28/00	−10.5	7/19/02	−7.4	7/2/10	−7.2
Best & Worst July Days										
Best	7/24/02	6.4	7/24/02	5.7	7/29/02	5.8	7/24/02	5.6	7/29/02	4.9
Worst	7/19/02	−4.6	7/19/02	−3.8	7/28/00	−4.7	7/19/02	−3.6	7/23/02	−4.1
First Trading Day of Expiration Week: 1980–2013										
Record (#Up–#Down)	20–14		21–13		22–12		20–14		18–16	
Current streak	U1		U1		U1		U1		U1	
Avg % Change	0.07		0.01		0.001		−0.02		−0.10	
Options Expiration Day: 1980–2013										
Record (#Up–#Down)	15–17		17–17		14–20		17–17		13–21	
Current streak	D2		U1		D2		U1		U1	
Avg % Change	−0.28		−0.33		−0.51		−0.35		−0.52	
Options Expiration Week: 1980–2013										
Record (#Up–#Down)	21–13		18–16		17–17		18–16		18–16	
Current streak	U2		U2		D1		U2		U1	
Avg % Change	0.40		0.08		−0.04		0.03		−0.14	
Week After Options Expiration: 1980–2013										
Record (#Up–#Down)	18–16		16–18		15–19		17–17		13–21	
Current streak	U5		D1		U6		U5		D1	
Avg % Change	0.04		−0.14		−0.43		−0.15		−0.31	
First Trading Day Performance										
% of Time Up	64.1		70.3		60.5		71.4		62.9	
Avg % Change	0.25		0.25		0.10		0.30		0.06	
Last Trading Day Performance										
% of Time Up	51.6		62.5		51.2		60.0		65.7	
Avg % Change	0.06		0.10		0.01		0.03		0.03	

Dow & S&P 1950–April 2014, NASDAQ 1971–April 2014, Russell 1K & 2K 1979–April 2014.

When Dow and S&P in July are inferior,
NASDAQ days tend to be even drearier.

MONDAY

D 47.6
S 57.1
N 66.7

29

Women are expected to do twice as much as men in half the time and for no credit. Fortunately, this isn't difficult.
— Charlotte Whitton (Former Ottawa Mayor, feminist, 1896–1975)

Last Day of Q2 Bearish for Dow, Down 16 of Last 23
But Bullish for NASDAQ, Up 15 of 22, Although Down 6 of Last 9

TUESDAY

D 33.3
S 38.1
N 66.7

30

If you can buy more of your best idea, why put [the money] into your 10th-best idea or your 20th-best idea? The more positions you have, the more average you are.
— Bruce Berkowitz (Fairholme Fund, *Barron's* 3/17/08, b. 1961)

First Trading Day in July, Dow Up 20 of Last 25,
Average Gain 0.5%

WEDNESDAY

D 76.2
S 81.0
N 71.4

1

Never tell people how to do things. Tell them what to do and they will surprise you with their ingenuity.
— General George S. Patton, Jr. (U.S. Army field commander WWII, 1885–1945)

THURSDAY

D 38.1
S 38.1
N 42.9

2

The market can stay irrational longer than you can stay solvent.
— John Maynard Keynes (British economist, 1883–1946)

(Market Closed)

FRIDAY

3

What is conservatism? Is it not adherence to the old and tried, against the new and untried?
— Abraham Lincoln (16th U.S. President, 1809–1865)

Independence Day

SATURDAY

4

SUNDAY

5

FIRST MONTH OF QUARTERS IS THE MOST BULLISH

We have observed over the years that the investment calendar reflects the annual, semiannual, and quarterly operations of institutions during January, April, and July. The opening month of the first three quarters produces the greatest gains in the Dow Jones Industrials and the S&P 500. NASDAQ's record differs slightly.

The fourth quarter had behaved quite differently, since it is affected by year-end portfolio adjustments and presidential and congressional elections in even-numbered years. Since 1991, major turnarounds have helped October join the ranks of bullish first months of quarters. October transformed into a bear-killing-turnaround month, posting some mighty gains in 10 of the last 16 years, 2008 was a significant exception. (See pages 152–160.)

After experiencing the most powerful bull market of all time during the 1990s, followed by two ferocious bear markets early in the millennium, we divided the monthly average percentage changes into two groups: before 1991 and after. Comparing the month-by-month quarterly behavior of the three major U.S. averages in the table, you'll see that first months of the first three quarters perform best overall. Nasty sell-offs in April 2000, 2002, 2004, and 2005, and July 2000–2002 and 2004, hit the NASDAQ hardest. The bear market of October 2007–March 2009, which more than cut the markets in half, took a toll on every first month except April. October 2008 was the worst month in a decade. January was also a difficult month in 2008, 2009, and 2010. (See pages 152–160.)

Between 1950 and 1990, the S&P 500 gained 1.3% (Dow, 1.4%) on average in first months of the first three quarters. Second months barely eked out any gain, while third months, thanks to March, moved up 0.23% (Dow, 0.07%) on average. NASDAQ's first month of the first three quarters averages 1.67% from 1971–1990, with July being a negative drag.

DOW JONES INDUSTRIALS, S&P 500, AND NASDAQ
AVERAGE MONTHLY % CHANGES BY QUARTER

	DJIA 1950–1990			S&P 500 1950–1990			NASDAQ 1971–1990		
	1st Mo	2nd Mo	3rd Mo	1st Mo	2nd Mo	3rd Mo	1st Mo	2nd Mo	3rd Mo
1Q	1.5%	−0.01%	1.0%	1.5%	−0.1%	1.1%	3.8%	1.2%	0.9%
2Q	1.6	−0.4	0.1	1.3	−0.1	0.3	1.7	0.8	1.1
3Q	1.1	0.3	−0.9	1.1	0.3	−0.7	−0.5	0.1	−1.6
Tot	4.2%	−0.1%	0.2%	3.9%	0.1%	0.7%	5.0%	2.1%	0.4%
Avg	1.40%	−0.04%	0.07%	1.30%	0.03%	0.23%	1.67%	0.70%	0.13%
4Q	−0.1%	1.4%	1.7%	0.4%	1.7%	1.6%	−1.4%	1.6%	1.4%
	DJIA 1991–April 2014			S&P 500 1991–April 2014			NASDAQ 1991–April 2014		
1Q	0.3%	0.4%	1.2%	0.4%	0.1%	1.4%	2.1%	0.0%	0.7%
2Q	2.5	0.6	−1.0	1.9	0.6	−0.6	1.2	0.8	0.4
3Q	1.4	−0.9	−0.6	0.8	−0.6	−0.1	0.8	0.2	0.5
Tot	4.2%	0.1%	−0.4%	3.1%	0.1%	0.8%	4.1%	1.0%	1.6%
Avg	1.40%	0.02%	−0.13%	1.03%	0.03%	0.25%	1.37%	0.33%	0.53%
4Q	1.6%	1.6%	1.8%	1.6%	1.2%	1.9%	2.2%	1.6%	2.5%
	DJIA 1950–April 2014			S&P 500 1950–April 2014			NASDAQ 1971–April 2014		
1Q	1.0%	0.13%	1.1%	1.1%	0.0%	1.2%	2.9%	0.6%	0.8%
2Q	1.9	−0.05	−0.3	1.5	0.2	−0.03	1.4	0.8	0.7
3Q	1.2	−0.1	−0.8	1.0	−0.06	−0.5	0.2	0.2	−0.5
Tot	4.1%	−0.02%	0.0%	3.6%	0.14%	0.7%	4.5%	1.6%	1.0%
Avg	1.37%	−0.01%	0.00%	1.20%	0.05%	0.22%	1.49%	0.52%	0.33%
4Q	0.5%	1.5%	1.7%	0.8%	1.5%	1.7%	0.6%	1.6%	2.0%

Market Subject to Elevated Volatility After July 4th

MONDAY

D 52.4
S 57.1
N 52.4

6

We spend $500 million a year just in training our people. We've developed some technology that lets us do simulations. Think of Flight Simulation. What we've found is that the retention rate from simulation is about 75%, opposed to 25% from classroom work.
— Joe Forehand (CEO, Accenture, *Forbes*, 7/7/03)

TUESDAY

D 61.9
S 61.9
N 61.9

7

Those who cannot remember the past are condemned to repeat it.
— George Santayana (American philosopher, poet, 1863–1952)

July Begins NASDAQ's "Worst Four Months" (Pages 58, 60 and 148)

WEDNESDAY

D 66.7
S 61.9
N 66.7

8

People do not change when you tell them they should; they change when they tell themselves they must.
— Michael Mandelbaum (Johns Hopkins foreign policy specialist, *NY Times*, 6/24/2009, b. 1946)

THURSDAY

D 47.6
S 42.9
N 57.1

9

Today we deal with 65,000 more pieces of information each day than did our ancestors 100 years ago.
— Dr. Jean Houston (A founder of the Human Potential Movement, b. 1937)

July Is the Best Performing Dow and S&P Month of the Third Quarter

FRIDAY

D 57.1
S 57.1
N 61.9

10

Have not great merchants, great manufacturers, great inventors done more for the world than preachers and philanthropists. Can there be any doubt that cheapening the cost of necessities and conveniences of life is the most powerful agent of civilization and progress?
— Charles Elliott Perkins (Railroad magnate, 1888, 1840–1907)

SATURDAY

11

SUNDAY

12

2013 DAILY DOW POINT CHANGES (DOW JONES INDUSTRIAL AVERAGE)

Week #		Monday**	Tuesday	Wednsday	Thursday	Friday**	Weekly Dow Close	Net Point Change
						2012 Close	13104.14	
1		Holiday	308.41	−21.19		43.85	13435.21	331.07
2	J	−50.92	−55.44	61.66	80.71	17.21	13488.43	53.22
3	A	18.89	27.57	−23.66	84.79	53.68	13649.70	161.27
4	N	Holiday	62.51	67.12	46.00	70.65	13895.98	246.28
5		−14.05	72.49	−44.00	−49.84	149.21	14009.79	113.81
6	F	−129.71	99.22	7.22	−42.47	48.92	13992.97	−16.82
7	E	−21.73	47.46	−35.79	−9.52	8.37	13981.76	−11.21
8	B	Holiday	53.91	−108.13	−46.92	119.95	14000.57	18.81
9		−216.40	115.96	175.24	−20.88	35.17	14089.66	89.09
10	M	38.16	125.95	42.47	33.25	67.58	14397.07	307.41
11	A	50.22	2.77	5.22	83.86	−25.03	14514.11	117.04
12	R	−62.05	3.76	55.91	−90.24	90.54	14512.03	−2.08
13		−64.28	111.90	−33.49	52.38	Holiday	14578.54	66.51
14		−5.69	89.16	−111.66	55.76	−40.86	14565.25	−13.29
15	A	48.23	59.98	128.78	62.90	−0.08	14865.06	299.81
16	P	−265.86	157.58	−138.19	−81.45	10.37	14547.51	−317.55
17	R	19.66	152.29	−43.16	24.50	11.75	14712.55	165.04
18		106.20	21.05	−138.85	130.63	142.38	14973.96	261.41
19	M	−5.07	87.31	48.92	−22.50	35.87	15118.49	144.53
20	A	−26.81	123.57	60.44	−42.47	121.18	15354.40	235.91
21	Y	−19.12	52.30	−80.41	−12.67	8.60	15303.10	−51.30
22		Holiday	106.29	−106.59	21.73	−208.96	15115.57	−187.53
23	J	138.46	−76.49	−216.95	80.03	207.50	15248.12	132.55
24	U	−9.53	−116.57	−126.79	180.85	−105.90	15070.18	−177.94
25	N	109.67	138.38	−206.04	−353.87	41.08	14799.40	−270.78
26		−139.84	100.75	149.83	114.35	−114.89	14909.60	110.20
27		65.36	−42.55	56.14*	Holiday	147.29	15135.84	226.24
28	J	88.85	75.65	−8.68	169.26	3.38	15464.30	328.46
29	U	19.96	−32.41	18.67	78.02	−4.80	15543.74	79.44
30	L	1.81	22.19	−25.50	13.37	3.22	15558.83	15.09
31		−36.86	−1.38	−21.05	128.48	30.34	15658.36	99.53
32		−46.23	−93.39	−48.07	27.65	−72.81	15425.51	−232.85
33	A	−5.83	31.33	−113.35	−225.47	−30.72	15081.47	−344.04
34	U	−70.73	−7.75	−105.44	66.19	46.77	15010.51	−70.96
35	G	−64.05	−170.33	48.38	16.44	−30.64	14810.31	−200.20
36		Holiday	23.65	96.91	6.61	−14.98	14922.50	112.19
37	S	140.62	127.94	135.54	−25.96	75.42	15376.06	453.56
38	E	118.72	34.95	147.21	−40.39	−185.46	15451.09	75.03
39	P	−49.71	−66.79	−61.33	55.04	−70.06	15258.24	−192.85
40		−128.57	62.03	−58.56	−136.66	76.10	15072.58	−185.66
41		−136.34	−159.71	26.45	323.09	111.04	15237.11	164.53
42	O	64.15	−133.25	205.82	−2.18	28.00	15399.65	162.54
43	C	−7.45	75.46	−54.33	95.88	61.07	15570.28	170.63
44	T	−1.35	111.42	−61.59	−73.01	69.80	15615.55	45.27
45		23.57	−20.90	128.66	−152.90	167.80	15761.78	146.23
46	N	21.32	−32.43	70.96	54.59	85.48	15961.70	199.92
47	O	14.32	−8.99	−66.21	109.17	54.78	16064.77	103.07
48	V	7.77	0.26	24.53	Holiday	−10.92*	16086.41	21.64
49		−77.64	−94.15	−24.85	−68.26	198.69	16020.20	−66.21
50	D	5.33	−52.40	−129.60	−104.10	15.93	15755.36	−264.84
51	E	129.21	−9.31	292.71	11.11	42.06	16221.14	465.78
52	C	73.47	62.94*	Holiday	122.33	−1.47	16478.41	257.27
53		25.88	72.37			**Year's Close**	16576.66	98.25
TOTALS		**−79.63**	**1091.75**	**170.93**	**653.64**	**1635.83**		**3472.52**

Bold Color: Down Friday, Down Monday   * *Shortened trading day: Jul 3, Nov 29, Dec 24*

** *Monday denotes first trading day of week, Friday denotes last trading day of week*

JULY

Monday Before July Expiration, Dow Up 8 of Last 11

🐂 **MONDAY**

D 61.9
S 71.4
N 71.4

13

Throughout the centuries there were men who took first steps down new roads armed with nothing but their own vision.
— Ayn Rand (Russian-born American novelist and philosopher, *The Fountainhead*, 1957, 1905–1982)

🐂 **TUESDAY**

D 61.9
S 66.7
N 71.4

14

Anyone who believes that exponential growth can go on forever in a finite world is either a madman or an economist.
— Kenneth Ewart Boulding (Economist, activist, poet, scientist, philosopher, cofounder General Systems Theory, 1910–1993)

WEDNESDAY

D 52.4
S 47.6
N 57.1

15

In most admired companies, key priorities are teamwork, customer focus, fair treatment of employees, initiative, and innovation. In average companies the top priorities are minimizing risk, respecting the chain of command, supporting the boss, and making budget.
— Bruce Pfau (*Fortune*)

THURSDAY

D 52.4
S 42.9
N 47.6

16

At the age of 24, I began setting clear, written goals for each area of my life. I accomplished more in the following year than I had in the previous 24.
— Brian Tracy (Motivational speaker, b. 1944)

July Expiration Day, Dow Down 9 of Last 14, –4.6% in 2002 and –2.5% in 2010

🐻 **FRIDAY**

D 57.1
S 52.4
N 57.1

17

We will have to pay more and more attention to what the funds are doing. They are the ones who have been contributing to the activity, especially in the high-fliers.
— Humphrey B. Neill (Investor, analyst, author, *NY Times*, 6/11/1966, 1895–1977)

SATURDAY

18

SUNDAY

19

DON'T SELL STOCKS ON MONDAY OR FRIDAY

Since 1989, Monday,* Tuesday, and Wednesday have been the most consistently bullish days of the week for the Dow, Thursday and Friday* the most bearish, as traders have become reluctant to stay long going into the weekend. Since 1989 Mondays, Tuesdays, and Wednesdays gained 13747.11 Dow points, while Thursday and Friday combined for a total loss of 527.18 points. Also broken out are the last 13 and a third years to illustrate Monday's and Friday's poor performance in bear market years 2001–2002 and 2008–2009. During uncertain market times traders often sell before the weekend and are reluctant to jump in on Monday. See pages 68, 80, and 141–144 for more.

ANNUAL DOW POINT CHANGES FOR DAYS OF THE WEEK SINCE 1953

Year	Monday*	Tuesday	Wednesday	Thursday	Friday*	Year's DJIA Closing	Year's Point Change
1953	−36.16	−7.93	19.63	5.76	7.70	280.90	−11.00
1954	15.68	3.27	24.31	33.96	46.27	404.39	123.49
1955	−48.36	26.38	46.03	−0.66	60.62	488.40	84.01
1956	−27.15	−9.36	−15.41	8.43	64.56	499.47	11.07
1957	−109.50	−7.71	64.12	3.32	−14.01	435.69	−63.78
1958	17.50	23.59	29.10	22.67	55.10	583.65	147.96
1959	−44.48	29.04	4.11	13.60	93.44	679.36	95.71
1960	−111.04	−3.75	−5.62	6.74	50.20	615.89	−63.47
1961	−23.65	10.18	87.51	−5.96	47.17	731.14	115.25
1962	−101.60	26.19	9.97	−7.70	−5.90	652.10	−79.04
1963	−8.88	47.12	16.23	22.39	33.99	762.95	110.85
1964	−0.29	−17.94	39.84	5.52	84.05	874.13	111.18
1965	−73.23	39.65	57.03	3.20	68.48	969.26	95.13
1966	−153.24	−27.73	56.13	−46.19	−12.54	785.69	−183.57
1967	−68.65	31.50	25.42	92.25	38.90	905.11	119.42
1968†	6.41	34.94	25.16	−72.06	44.19	943.75	38.64
1969	−164.17	−36.70	18.33	23.79	15.36	800.36	−143.39
1970	−100.05	−46.09	116.07	−3.48	72.11	838.92	38.56
1971	−2.99	9.56	13.66	8.04	23.01	890.20	51.28
1972	−87.40	−1.23	65.24	8.46	144.75	1020.02	129.82
1973	−174.11	10.52	−5.94	36.67	−36.30	850.86	−169.16
1974	−149.37	47.51	−20.31	−13.70	−98.75	616.24	−234.62
1975	39.46	−109.62	56.93	124.00	125.40	852.41	236.17
1976	70.72	71.76	50.88	−33.70	−7.42	1004.65	152.24
1977	−65.15	−44.89	−79.61	−5.62	21.79	831.17	−173.48
1978	−31.29	−70.84	71.33	−64.67	69.31	805.01	−26.16
1979	−32.52	9.52	−18.84	75.18	0.39	838.74	33.73
1980	−86.51	135.13	137.67	−122.00	60.96	963.99	125.25
1981	−45.68	−49.51	−13.95	−14.67	34.82	875.00	−88.99
1982	5.71	86.20	28.37	−1.47	52.73	1046.54	171.54
1983	30.51	−30.92	149.68	61.16	1.67	1258.64	212.10
1984	−73.80	78.02	−139.24	92.79	−4.84	1211.57	−47.07
1985	80.36	52.70	51.26	46.32	104.46	1546.67	335.10
1986	−39.94	97.63	178.65	29.31	83.63	1895.95	349.28
1987	−559.15	235.83	392.03	139.73	−165.56	1938.83	42.88
1988	268.12	166.44	−60.48	−230.84	86.50	2168.57	229.74
1989	−53.31	143.33	233.25	90.25	171.11	2753.20	584.63
SubTotal	*−1937.20*	*941.79*	*1708.54*	*330.82*	*1417.35*		*2461.30*
1990	219.90	−25.22	47.96	−352.55	−9.63	2633.66	−119.54
1991	191.13	47.97	174.53	254.79	−133.25	3168.83	535.17
1992	237.80	−49.67	3.12	108.74	−167.71	3301.11	132.28
1993	322.82	−37.03	243.87	4.97	−81.65	3754.09	452.98
1994	206.41	−95.33	29.98	−168.87	108.16	3834.44	80.35
1995	262.97	210.06	357.02	140.07	312.56	5117.12	1282.68
1996	626.41	155.55	−34.24	268.52	314.91	6448.27	1331.15
1997	1136.04	1989.17	−590.17	−949.80	−125.26	7908.25	1459.98
1998	649.10	679.95	591.63	−1579.43	931.93	9181.43	1273.18
1999	980.49	−1587.23	826.68	735.94	1359.81	11497.12	2315.69
2000	2265.45	306.47	−1978.34	238.21	−1542.06	10786.85	−710.27
SubTotal	*7098.52*	*1594.69*	*−327.96*	*−1299.41*	*967.81*		*8033.65*
2001	−389.33	336.86	−396.53	976.41	−1292.76	10021.50	−765.35
2002	−1404.94	−823.76	1443.69	−428.12	−466.74	8341.63	−1679.87
2003	978.87	482.11	−425.46	566.22	510.55	10453.92	2112.29
2004	201.12	523.28	358.76	−409.72	−344.35	10783.01	329.09
2005	316.23	−305.62	27.67	−128.75	24.96	10717.50	−65.51
2006	95.74	573.98	1283.87	193.34	−401.28	12463.15	1745.65
2007	278.23	−157.93	1316.74	−766.63	131.26	13264.82	801.67
2008	−1387.20	1704.51	−3073.72	−940.88	−791.14	8776.39	−4488.43
2009	−45.22	161.76	617.56	932.68	−15.12	10428.05	1651.66
2010	1236.88	−421.80	1019.66	−76.73	−608.55	11577.51	1149.46
2011	−571.02	1423.66	−776.05	246.27	317.19	12217.56	640.05
2012	254.59	−49.28	−456.37	847.34	299.30	13104.14	886.58
2013	−79.63	1091.75	170.93	653.64	1635.83	16576.66	3472.52
2014 ‡	−208.06	1107.69	−125.18	−355.00	−504.80		
Subtotal	*−723.74*	*5647.21*	*985.57*	*1310.07*	*−1505.65*		*5789.81*
Totals	*4437.58*	*8183.69*	*2366.15*	*341.48*	*879.51*		*16284.76*

* Monday denotes first trading day of week, Friday denotes last trading day of week
† Most Wednesdays closed last 7 months of 1968 ‡ Partial year through May 16, 2014

MONDAY

D 66.7
S 66.7
N 66.7

20

A "tired businessman" is one whose business is usually not a successful one.
— Joseph R. Grundy (U.S. Senator Pennsylvania 1929–1930, businessman, 1863–1961)

Week After July Expiration Prone to Wild Swings, Dow Up 9 of Last 12
1998 –4.3%, 2002 +3.1%, 2006 +3.2%, 2007 –4.2%, 2009 +4.0%, 2010 +3.2

TUESDAY

D 28.6
S 28.6
N 23.8

21

Industrial capitalism has generated the greatest productive power in human history. To date, no other socioeconomic system has been able to generate comparable productive power.
— Peter L. Berger (*The Capitalist Revolution,* b. 1929)

WEDNESDAY

D 42.9
S 38.1
N 42.9

22

If you torture the data long enough, it will confess to anything.
— Darrell Huff (*How to Lie with Statistics,* 1954, 1913–2001)

Beware the "Summer Rally" Hype
Historically the Weakest Rally of All Seasons (Page 72)

THURSDAY

D 47.6
S 47.6
N 47.6

23

Buy when you are scared to death; sell when you are tickled to death.
— Market Maxim (*The Cabot Market Letter,* April 12, 2001)

FRIDAY

D 52.4
S 52.4
N 52.4

24

Let me end my talk by abusing slightly my status as an official representative of the Federal Reserve. I would like to say to Milton [Friedman]: Regarding the Great Depression, you're right; we did it. We're very sorry. But thanks to you, we won't do it again.
— Ben Bernanke (Fed Chairman 2006–2014, 11/8/02 speech as Fed Govenor, b. 1953)

SATURDAY

25

August Almanac Investor Seasonalities: See Pages 94, 96 and 98

SUNDAY

26

A RALLY FOR ALL SEASONS

Most years, especially when the market sells off during the first half, prospects for the perennial summer rally become the buzz on the street. Parameters for this "rally" were defined by the late Ralph Rotnem as the lowest close in the Dow Jones Industrials in May or June to the highest close in July, August, or September. Such a big deal is made of the "summer rally" that one might get the impression the market puts on its best performance in the summertime. Nothing could be further from the truth! Not only does the market "rally" in every season of the year, but it does so with more gusto in the winter, spring, and fall than in the summer.

Winters in 51 years averaged a 13.0% gain as measured from the low in November or December to the first quarter closing high. Spring rose 11.4% followed by fall with 10.9%. Last and least was the average 9.2% "summer rally." Even 2009's impressive 19.7% "summer rally" was outmatched by spring. Nevertheless, no matter how thick the gloom or grim the outlook, don't despair! There's always a rally for all seasons, statistically.

SEASONAL GAINS IN DOW JONES INDUSTRIALS

	WINTER RALLY Nov/Dec Low to Q1 High	SPRING RALLY Feb/Mar Low to Q2 High	SUMMER RALLY May/Jun Low to Q3 High	FALL RALLY Aug/Sep Low to Q4 High
1964	15.3%	6.2%	9.4%	8.3%
1965	5.7	6.6	11.6	10.3
1966	5.9	4.8	3.5	7.0
1967	11.6	8.7	11.2	4.4
1968	7.0	11.5	5.2	13.3
1969	0.9	7.7	1.9	6.7
1970	5.4	6.2	22.5	19.0
1971	21.6	9.4	5.5	7.4
1972	19.1	7.7	5.2	11.4
1973	8.6	4.8	9.7	15.9
1974	13.1	8.2	1.4	11.0
1975	36.2	24.2	8.2	8.7
1976	23.3	6.4	5.9	4.6
1977	8.2	3.1	2.8	2.1
1978	2.1	16.8	11.8	5.2
1979	11.0	8.9	8.9	6.1
1980	13.5	16.8	21.0	8.5
1981	11.8	9.9	0.4	8.3
1982	4.6	9.3	18.5	37.8
1983	15.7	17.8	6.3	10.7
1984	5.9	4.6	14.1	9.7
1985	11.7	7.1	9.5	19.7
1986	31.1	18.8	9.2	11.4
1987	30.6	13.6	22.9	5.9
1988	18.1	13.5	11.2	9.8
1989	15.1	12.9	16.1	5.7
1990	8.8	14.5	12.4	8.6
1991	21.8	11.2	6.6	9.3
1992	14.9	6.4	3.7	3.3
1993	8.9	7.7	6.3	7.3
1994	9.7	5.2	9.1	5.0
1995	13.6	19.3	11.3	13.9
1996	19.2	7.5	8.7	17.3
1997	17.7	18.4	18.4	7.3
1998	20.3	13.6	8.2	24.3
1999	15.1	21.6	8.2	12.6
2000	10.8	15.2	9.8	3.5
2001	6.4	20.8	1.7	23.1
2002	14.8	7.9	2.8	17.6
2003	6.5	23.9	14.3	15.7
2004	11.6	5.2	4.4	10.6
2005	9.0	2.1	5.6	5.3
2006	8.8	8.3	9.5	13.0
2007	6.7	13.5	6.6	10.3
2008	2.5	11.2	3.8	4.5
2009	19.6	34.4	19.7	15.5
2010	11.6	13.1	11.1	16.0
2011	12.6	10.3	7.0	14.7
2012	18.0	4.5	12.4	5.7
2013	16.2	11.8	6.9	12.2
2014	6.0	8.7*		
Totals	**664.2%**	**581.8%**	**462.4%**	**545.5%**
Average	**13.0%**	**11.4%**	**9.2%**	**10.9%**

As of 5/16/2014

MONDAY
D 71.4
S 66.7
N 71.4
27

I invest in people, not ideas; I want to see fire in the belly and intellect.
— Arthur Rock (First venture capitalist, b. 1926)

TUESDAY
D 42.9
S 42.9
N 52.4
28

I have always picked people's brains. That's the only way you can grow. Ninety percent of the information I throw out immediately; five percent I try and discard; and five percent I retain.
— Tiger Woods (Top-ranked golfer, on his swing, April 2004, b. 1975)

WEDNESDAY
D 38.1
S 42.9
N 42.9
29

I've continued to recognize the power individuals have to change virtually anything and everything in their lives in an instant. I've learned that the resources we need to turn our dreams into reality are within us, merely waiting for the day when we decide to wake up and claim our birthright.
— Anthony Robbins (Motivator, advisor, consultant, author, entrepreneur, philanthropist, b. 1960)

THURSDAY
D 52.4
S 61.9
N 66.7
30

It's a buy when the 10-week moving average crosses the 30-week moving average and the slope of both averages is up.
— Victor Sperandeo (*Trader Vic—Methods of a Wall Street Master*, b. 1945)

Last Trading Day in July, NASDAQ Down 7 of Last 9

FRIDAY
D 38.1
S 47.6
N 42.9
31

The game is lost only when we stop trying.
— Mario Cuomo (Former NY Governor, *C-Span*, b. 1932)

SATURDAY
1

SUNDAY
2

AUGUST ALMANAC

AUGUST						
S	M	T	W	T	F	S
						1
2	3	4	5	6	7	8
9	10	11	12	13	14	15
16	17	18	19	20	21	22
23	24	25	26	27	28	29
30	31					

SEPTEMBER						
S	M	T	W	T	F	S
		1	2	3	4	5
6	7	8	9	10	11	12
13	14	15	16	17	18	19
20	21	22	23	24	25	26
27	28	29	30			

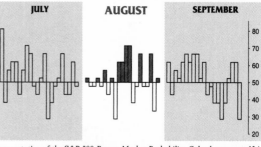

Market Probability Chart above is a graphic representation of the S&P 500 Recent Market Probability Calendar on page 124.

◆ Harvesting made August the best stock market month 1901–1951 ◆ Now that about 2% farm, August is the worst Dow, S&P, and NASDAQ (2000 up 11.7%, 2001 down 10.9) month since 1987 ◆ Shortest bear in history (45 days) caused by turmoil in Russia, currency crisis and hedge fund debacle ended here in 1998, 1344.22-point drop in the Dow, second worst behind October 2008, off 15.1% ◆ Saddam Hussein triggered a 10.0% slide in 1990 ◆ Best Dow gains: 1982 (11.5%) and 1984 (9.8%) as bear markets ended ◆ Next to last day S&P up only four times last 18 years ◆ Pre-presidential election year Augusts' rankings #6 S&P, # 5 Dow, and #8 NASDAQ.

August Vital Statistics

	DJIA	S&P 500	NASDAQ	Russell 1K	Russell 2K
Rank	10	11	11	9	9
Up	36	35	23	22	20
Down	28	29	20	13	15
Average % Change	−0.1%	−0.06%	0.2%	0.3%	0.3%
Pre-Election Year	1.4%	1.0%	1.4%	1.0%	0.7%
Best & Worst August					
	% Change	% Change	% Change	% Change	% Change
Best	1982 11.5	1982 11.6	2000 11.7	1982 11.3	1984 11.5
Worst	1998 −15.1	1998 −14.6	1998 −19.9	1998 −15.1	1998 −19.5
Best & Worst August Weeks					
Best	8/20/82 10.3	8/20/82 8.8	8/3/84 7.4	8/20/82 8.5	8/3/84 7.0
Worst	8/23/74 −6.1	8/5/11 −7.2	8/28/98 −8.8	8/5/11 −7.7	8/5/11 −10.3
Best & Worst August Days					
Best	8/17/82 4.9	8/17/82 4.8	8/9/11 5.3	8/9/11 5.0	8/9/11 6.9
Worst	8/31/98 −6.4	8/31/98 −6.8	8/31/98 −8.6	8/8/11 −6.9	8/8/11 −8.9
First Trading Day of Expiration Week: 1980–2013					
Record (#Up–#Down)	21–13	24–10	25–9	24–10	21–13
Current streak	D1	D2	U4	D2	U1
Avg % Change	0.27	0.28	0.30	0.25	0.24
Options Expiration Day: 1980–2013					
Record (#Up–#Down)	18–16	19–15	19–15	19–15	21–13
Current streak	D1	D1	D1	D1	D1
Avg % Change	−0.05	−0.003	−0.07	−0.002	0.12
Options Expiration Week: 1980–2013					
Record (#Up–#Down)	17–17	20–14	19–15	20–14	21–13
Current streak	D1	D1	D1	D1	D1
Avg % Change	0.18	0.36	0.53	0.38	0.60
Week After Options Expiration: 1980–2013					
Record (#Up–#Down)	20–14	22–12	21–13	21–12	21–13
Current streak	D2	U1	U1	U1	U1
Avg % Change	0.24	0.30	0.46	0.29	0.05
First Trading Day Performance					
% of Time Up	48.4	51.6	53.5	48.6	51.4
Avg % Change	0.04	0.06	−0.06	0.13	0.02
Last Trading Day Performance					
% of Time Up	60.9	64.1	67.4	60.0	71.4
Avg % Change	0.14	0.13	0.05	−0.04	0.04

Dow & S&P 1950–April 2014, NASDAQ 1971–April 2014, Russell 1K & 2K 1979–April 2014.

August's a good month to go on vacation;
Trading stocks will likely lead to frustration.

AUGUST

First Trading Day in August, Dow Down 11 of Last 17
Russell 2000 Up 7 of Last 10

MONDAY

D 42.9
S 52.4
N 52.4

3

I would rather be positioned as a petrified bull rather than a penniless bear.
— John L. Person (CTA, professional trader, author, speaker, nationalfutures.com, 11/3/2010, b. 1961)

TUESDAY

D 57.1
S 47.6
N 42.9

4

All there is to investing is picking good stocks at good times and staying with them as long as they remain good companies.
— Warren Buffett (CEO Berkshire Hathaway, investor & philanthropist, b. 1930)

First Nine Trading Days of August Are Historically Weak (Pages 74 and 124)

WEDNESDAY

D 47.6
S 47.6
N 47.6

5

To affect the quality of the day, that is the highest of the arts.
— Henry David Thoreau (American writer, naturalist, and philosopher, 1817–1862)

THURSDAY

D 47.6
S 52.4
N 52.4

6

News on stocks is not important. How the stock reacts to it is important.
— Michael L. Burke (*Investors Intelligence*)

August Worst Dow and S&P Month 1988–2014
Harvesting Made August Best Dow Month 1901–1951

FRIDAY

D 57.1
S 47.6
N 42.9

7

The first human who hurled an insult instead of a stone was the founder of civilization.
— Sigmund Freud (Austrian neurologist, psychiatrist, "father of psychoanalysis," 1856–1939)

SATURDAY

8

SUNDAY

9

BEST INVESTMENT BOOK OF THE YEAR

Profitable Day and Swing Trading: Using Price/Volume Surges and Pattern Recognition to Catch Big Moves in the Stock Market

By Harry Boxer

We only met Harry Boxer a few years ago during one of our annual pilgrimages to the Las Vegas Traders Expo, but we were immediately impressed with his trading style, techniques, and strategy. He also has a win-ning personality and is a fantastic speaker. In fact, we were so blown away by his track record, no-nonsense approach, and ability to teach others that we encouraged Wiley to do this book with him. However, the book is being chosen as the Best Investment Book of 2015 on its merits alone and not because we had anything to do with it.

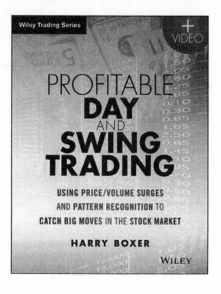

Bottom line, Harry's methods work, and they work especially well for short-term trad-ers. *Profitable Day and Swing Trading* is a breeze to read and it explains Harry's proven trading tactics that he uses himself and teaches subscribers and followers. A 45-year Wall Street veteran, Harry has worked as a chief technical analyst for three brokerage firms and AmericaInvest.com. He won the 1995 and 1996 worldwide Internet stock-market trading contest, "The Technical Analysis Challenge." He is widely syndicated and a featured guest on many financial programs and sites such as TheStreet.com, Forbes.com, MarketWatch.com, Yahoo! Finance, and CNBC.

In *Profitable Day and Swing Trading*, Harry explains his trading tactics that draw on price, volume, and pattern recognition. He shows you simply how to recognize chart patterns, identify trades, and execute entries and exits that will maximize profits and limit losses. He reveals his concept of price-volume surges as the key to identifying the most lucrative trades. This book trains you in Harry's own personal prep and trad-ing regimen for each and every trading day. How he selects stocks to monitor and how he keeps track of prices and executes trades. This book illustrates Harry's very own strategies for opening range gaps, breakouts, and other techniques that have generated massive profits for him over the past five decades—all explained clearly, thoroughly, and succinctly. To top it off, he reveals how to trade rising channels following an open-ing gap or high-volume breakout. He shows how his strategies can be applied for both day trading and swing trading.

After a brief journey through Harry's evolution as a trader, he walks you step-by-step through his process of preparing for the trading day, his favorite patterns, how to analyze trends, using moving averages, why trend lines are critical, targets and objec-tives, setting stops, using a series of technical indicators. And finally, you will learn proper position sizing and money management, as well as how to apply these tech-niques to swing trading.

If you are a day or swing trader, you should not be without this book!

Wiley, $70.00, www.thetechtrader.com. **2015 Best Investment Book of the Year.**

AUGUST

If the market does not rally, as it should during bullish seasonal periods, it is a sign that other forces are stronger and that when the seasonal period ends those forces will really have their say.
— Edson Gould (Stock market analyst, *Findings & Forecasts*, 1902–1987)

TUESDAY

D 42.9
S 42.9
N 42.9

11

My best shorts come from research reports where there are recommendations to buy stocks on weakness; also, where a brokerage firm changes its recommendation from a buy to a hold.
— Marc Howard (Hedge fund manager, *New York Magazine* 1976, b. 1941)

WEDNESDAY

D 52.4
S 52.4
N 52.4

12

When you get to the end of your rope, tie a knot and hang on.
— Franklin D. Roosevelt (32nd U.S. President, 1882–1945)

THURSDAY

D 28.6
S 28.6
N 42.9

13

The power to tax involves the power to destroy.
— John Marshall (U. S. Supreme Court, 1819, 1755–1835)

Mid-August Stronger Than Beginning and End

FRIDAY

D 66.7
S 61.9
N 61.9

14

What's going on... is the end of Silicon Valley as we know it. The next big thing ain't computers... it's biotechnology.
— Larry Ellison (Oracle CEO, quoted in the *Wall Street Journal*, April 8, 2003, b. 1944)

SATURDAY

15

SUNDAY

16

AURA OF THE TRIPLE WITCH—4TH QUARTER MOST BULLISH: DOWN WEEKS TRIGGER MORE WEAKNESS WEEK AFTER

Standard options expire the third Friday of every month, but in March, June, September, and December, a powerful coven gathers. Since the S&P index futures began trading on April 21, 1982, stock options, index options, as well as index futures all expire at the same time four times each year—known as Triple Witching. Traders have long sought to understand and master the magic of this quarterly phenomenon.

The market for single-stock and ETF futures and weekly options continues to grow. However, their impact on the market has thus far been subdued. As their availability continues to expand, trading volumes and market influence are also likely to broaden. Until such time, we do not believe the term "quadruple witching" is applicable just yet.

We have analyzed what the market does prior, during, and following Triple Witching expirations in search of consistent trading patterns. Here are some of our findings of how the Dow Jones Industrials perform around Triple-Witching Week (TWW).

- TWWs became more bullish since 1990, except in the second quarter.
- Following weeks became more bearish. Since Q1 2000, only 20 of 56 were up, and 9 occurred in December, 7 in March, 3 in September, 1 in June.
- TWWs have tended to be down in flat periods and dramatically so during bear markets.
- DOWN WEEKS TEND TO FOLLOW DOWN TWWs is a most interesting pattern. Since 1991, of 31 down TWWs, 22 following weeks were also down. This is surprising, inasmuch as the previous decade had an exactly opposite pattern: There were 13 down TWWs then, but 12 up weeks followed them.
- TWWs in the second and third quarter (Worst Six Months May through October) are much weaker, and the weeks following, horrendous. But in the first and fourth quarter (Best Six Months period November through April), only the week after Q1 expiration is negative.

Throughout the *Almanac* you will also see notations on the performance of Mondays and Fridays of TWW, as we place considerable significance on the beginnings and ends of weeks (pages 68, 70, and 141–144).

TRIPLE WITCHING WEEK AND WEEK AFTER DOW POINT CHANGES

	Expiration Week Q1	Week After	Expiration Week Q2	Week After	Expiration Week Q3	Week After	Expiration Week Q4	Week After
1991	−6.93	−89.36	−34.98	−58.81	33.54	−13.19	20.12	167.04
1992	40.48	−44.95	−69.01	−2.94	21.35	−76.73	9.19	12.97
1993	43.76	−31.60	−10.24	−3.88	−8.38	−70.14	10.90	6.15
1994	32.95	−120.92	3.33	−139.84	58.54	−101.60	116.08	26.24
1995	38.04	65.02	86.80	75.05	96.85	−33.42	19.87	−78.76
1996	114.52	51.67	55.78	−50.60	49.94	−15.54	179.53	76.51
1997	−130.67	−64.20	14.47	−108.79	174.30	4.91	−82.01	−76.98
1998	303.91	−110.35	−122.07	231.67	100.16	133.11	81.87	314.36
1999	27.20	−81.31	365.05	−303.00	−224.80	−524.30	32.73	148.33
2000	666.41	517.49	−164.76	−44.55	−293.65	−79.63	−277.95	200.60
2001	−821.21	−318.63	−353.36	−19.05	−1369.70	611.75	224.19	101.65
2002	34.74	−179.56	−220.42	−10.53	−326.67	−284.57	77.61	−207.54
2003	662.26	−376.20	83.63	−211.70	173.27	−331.74	236.06	46.45
2004	−53.48	26.37	6.31	−44.57	−28.61	−237.22	106.70	177.20
2005	−144.69	−186.80	110.44	−325.23	−36.62	−222.35	97.01	7.68
2006	203.31	0.32	122.63	−25.46	168.66	−52.67	138.03	−102.30
2007	−165.91	370.60	215.09	−279.22	377.67	75.44	110.80	−84.78
2008	410.23	−144.92	−464.66	−496.18	−33.55	−245.31	−50.57	−63.56
2009	54.40	497.80	−259.53	−101.34	214.79	−155.01	−142.61	191.21
2010	117.29	108.38	239.57	−306.83	145.08	252.41	81.59	81.58
2011	−185.88	362.07	52.45	−69.78	516.96	−737.61	−317.87	427.61
2012	310.60	−151.89	212.97	−126.39	−13.90	−142.34	55.83	−252.73
2013	117.04	−2.08	−270.78	110.20	75.03	−192.85	465.78	257.27
2014	237.10	20.29						
Up	17	10	13	3	14	5	18	16
Down	7	14	10	20	9	18	5	7

AUGUST

Monday Before August Expiration, Dow Up 12 of Last 19, Average Gain 0.4%

MONDAY
D 47.6
S 61.9
N 66.7

17

Let us have the courage to stop borrowing to meet the continuing deficits. Stop the deficits.
— Franklin D. Roosevelt (32nd U.S. President, 1882–1945)

TUESDAY
D 61.9
S 71.4
N 71.4

18

You don't learn to hold your own in the world by standing on guard, but by attacking and getting well hammered yourself.
— George Bernard Shaw (Irish dramatist, 1856–1950)

WEDNESDAY
D 66.7
S 71.4
N 66.7

19

The whole problem with the world is that fools and fanatics are always so certain of themselves, but wiser people so full of doubts.
— Bertrand Russell (British mathematician and philosopher, 1872–1970)

THURSDAY
D 42.9
S 38.1
N 38.1

20

A generation from now, Americans may marvel at the complacency that assumed the dollar's dominance would never end.
— Floyd Norris (Chief financial correspondent, *NY Times*, 2/2/07, b. 1947)

August Expiration Day Bullish Lately, Dow Up 8 of Last 11
Up 156 Points (1.7%) in 2009

FRIDAY
D 47.6
S 47.6
N 52.4

21

Every truth passes through three stages before it is recognized. In the first it is ridiculed; in the second it is opposed; in the third it is regarded as self-evident.
— Arthur Schopenhauer (German philosopher, 1788–1860)

SATURDAY

22

SUNDAY

23

TAKE ADVANTAGE OF DOWN FRIDAY/ DOWN MONDAY WARNING

Fridays and Mondays are the most important days of the week. Friday is the day for squaring positions—trimming longs or covering shorts before taking off for the weekend. Traders want to limit their exposure (particularly to stocks that are not acting well) since there could be unfavorable developments before trading resumes two or more days later.

Monday is important because the market then has the chance to reflect any weekend news, plus what traders think after digesting the previous week's action and the many Monday morning research and strategy comments.

For over 30 years, a down Friday followed by down Monday has frequently corresponded to important market inflection points that exhibit a clearly negative bias, often coinciding with market tops and, on a few climactic occasions, such as in October 2002 and March 2009, near major market bottoms.

One simple way to get a quick reading on which way the market may be heading is to keep track of the performance of the Dow Jones Industrial Average on Fridays and the following Mondays. Since 1995, there have been 196 occurrences of Down Friday/ Down Monday (DF/DM), with 57 falling in the bear market years of 2001, 2002, 2008, and 2011, producing an average decline of 12.8%.

To illustrate how Down Friday/ Down Monday can telegraph market inflection points we created the chart below of the Dow Jones Industrials from November 2012 to May 16, 2014 with arrows pointing to occurrences of DF/DM. Use DF/DM as a warning to examine market conditions carefully. Unprecedented central bank liquidity has tempered subsequent pullbacks, but has not eliminated them.

DOWN FRIDAY/DOWN MONDAY

Year	Total Number Down Friday/ Down Monday	Subsequent Average % Dow Loss*	Average Number of Days it took
1995	8	−1.2%	18
1996	9	−3.0%	28
1997	6	−5.1%	45
1998	9	−6.4%	47
1999	9	−6.4%	39
2000	11	−6.6%	32
2001	13	−13.5%	53
2002	18	−11.9%	54
2003	9	−3.0%	17
2004	9	−3.7%	51
2005	10	−3.0%	37
2006	11	−2.0%	14
2007	8	−6.0%	33
2008	15	−17.0%	53
2009	10	−8.7%	15
2010	7	−3.1%	10
2011	11	−9.0%	53
2012	11	−4.0%	38
2013	7	−2.4%	15
2014**	5	−2.9%	8
Average	10	−5.9%	33

* Over next 3 months, ** Ending May 16, 2014

DOW JONES INDUSTRIALS (NOVEMBER 2012–MAY 16, 2014)

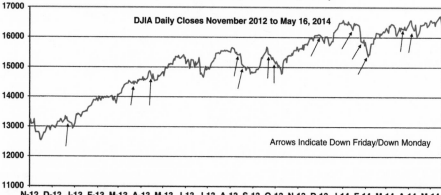

DJIA Daily Closes November 2012 to May 16, 2014

Arrows Indicate Down Friday/Down Monday

N-12 D-12 J-13 F-13 M-13 A-13 M-13 J-13 J-13 A-13 S-13 O-13 N-13 D-13 J-14 F-14 M-14 A-14 M-14

MONDAY

D 61.9
S 66.7
N 52.4

24

I'd be a bum on the street with a tin cup, if the markets were always efficient.
— Warren Buffett (CEO Berkshire Hathaway, investor & philanthropist, b. 1930)

TUESDAY

D 47.6
S 47.6
N 52.4

25

Based on my own personal experience—both as an investor in recent years and an expert witness in years past—rarely do more than three or four variables really count. Everything else is noise.
— Martin J. Whitman (Founder Third Avenue Funds, b. 1924)

WEDNESDAY

D 38.1
S 47.6
N 38.1

26

Civility is not a sign of weakness, and sincerity is always subject to proof. Let us never negotiate out of fear. But let us never fear to negotiate.
— John F. Kennedy (35th U.S. President, Inaugural Address 1/20/1961, 1917–1963)

THURSDAY

D 66.7
S 66.7
N 76.2

27

There are no secrets to success. Don't waste your time looking for them. Success is the result of perfection, hard work, learning from failure, loyalty to those for whom you work, and persistence.
— General Colin Powell (Chairman, Joint Chiefs 1989–1993, secretary of state 2001–2005, *N Y Times*, 10/22/2008, b. 1937)

August's Next-to-Last Trading Day, S&P Down 14 of Last 18 Years

FRIDAY

D 33.3
S 33.3
N 57.1

28

Sometimes the best investments are the ones you don't make.
— Donald Trump (Real estate mogul and entrepreneur, *Trump: How to Get Rich*, 2004, b. 1946)

SATURDAY

29

September Almanac Investor Seasonalities: See Pages 94, 96 and 98

SUNDAY

30

SEPTEMBER ALMANAC

SEPTEMBER							OCTOBER					
S	M	T	W	T	F	S	S	M	T	W	T	F	S
	1	2	3	4	5					1	2	3
6	7	8	9	10	11	12	4	5	6	7	8	9	10
13	14	15	16	17	18	19	11	12	13	14	15	16	17
20	21	22	23	24	25	26	18	19	20	21	22	23	24
27	28	29	30				25	26	27	28	29	30	31

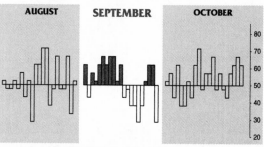

Market Probability Chart above is a graphic representation of the S&P 500 Recent Market Probability Calendar on page 124.

♦ Start of business year, end of vacations, and back to school made September a leading barometer month in first 60 years of 20th century, now portfolio managers back after Labor Day tend to clean house ♦ Biggest % loser on the S&P, Dow, and NASDAQ since 1950 (pages 50 & 58) ♦ Streak of four great Dow Septembers averaging 4.2% gains ended in 1999 with six losers in a row averaging –5.9% (see page 152), up three straight 2005–2007, down 6% in 2008 and 2011 ♦ Day after Labor Day Dow up 14 of last 20 ♦ S&P opened strong 13 of last 19 years but tends to close weak due to end-of-quarter mutual fund portfolio restructuring, last trading day: S&P down 15 of past 21 ♦ September Triple-Witching Week can be dangerous, week after is pitiful (see page 78).

September Vital Statistics

	DJIA		S&P 500		NASDAQ		Russell 1K		Russell 2K	
Rank	12		12		12		12		10	
Up	26		29		24		18		20	
Down	38		34		19		17		15	
Average % Change	–0.8%		–0.5%		–0.5%		–0.6%		–0.3%	
Pre-Election Year	–0.9%		–0.8%		–0.7%		–0.7%		–1.2%	
Best & Worst September										
	% Change		% Change		% Change		% Change		% Change	
Best	2010	7.7	2010	8.8	1998	13.0	2010	9.0	2010	12.3
Worst	2002	–12.4	1974	–11.9	2001	–17.0	2002	–10.9	2001	–13.6
Best & Worst September Weeks										
Best	9/28/01	7.4	9/28/01	7.8	9/16/11	6.3	9/28/01	7.6	9/28/01	6.9
Worst	9/21/01	–14.3	9/21/01	–11.6	9/21/01	–16.1	9/21/01	–11.7	9/21/01	–14.0
Best & Worst September Days										
Best	9/8/98	5.0	9/30/08	5.4	9/8/98	6.0	9/30/08	5.3	9/18/08	7.0
Worst	9/17/01	–7.1	9/29/08	–8.8	9/29/08	–9.1	9/29/08	–8.7	9/29/08	–6.7
First Trading Day of Expiration Week: 1980–2013										
Record (#Up–#Down)	22–12		19–15		13–21		19–15		14–20	
Current streak	U1		U1		D2		U1		U1	
Avg % Change	–0.09		–0.13		–0.32		–0.15		–0.22	
Options Expiration Day: 1980–2013										
Record (#Up–#Down)	17–17		19–15		23–11		20–14		23–11	
Current streak	D2		D2		D1		D1		D1	
Avg % Change	0.01		0.15		0.17		0.13		0.20	
Options Expiration Week: 1980–2013										
Record (#Up–#Down)	18–16		20–14		19–15		20–14		18–16	
Current streak	U1		U1		U1		U1		U1	
Avg % Change	–0.27		0.002		0.04		–0.01		0.15	
Week After Options Expiration: 1980–2013										
Record (#Up–#Down)	12–22		10–24		15–19		10–23		12–22	
Current streak	D3		D3		U1		D3		U1	
Avg % Change	–0.74		–0.77		–0.86		–0.78		–1.33	
First Trading Day Performance										
% of Time Up	60.9		62.5		55.8		51.4		51.4	
Avg % Change	0.04		0.03		0.01		–0.01		0.06	
Last Trading Day Performance										
% of Time Up	37.5		40.6		46.5		45.7		60.0	
Avg % Change	–0.15		–0.09		–0.06		–0.02		0.26	

Dow & S&P 1950–April 2014, NASDAQ 1971–April 2014, Russell 1K & 2K 1979–April 2014.

September is when leaves and stocks tend to fall;
On Wall Street it's the worst month of all.

AUGUST/SEPTEMBER

MONDAY
D 52.4
S 52.4
N 57.1
31

The four most expensive words in the English language, "This time it's different."
— Sir John Templeton (Founder Templeton Funds, philanthropist, 1912–2008)

First Trading Day in September, S&P Up 13 of Last 19, But Down 4 of Last 6

🐃 **TUESDAY**
D 57.1
S 61.9
N 61.9
1

Bankruptcy was designed to forgive stupidity, not reward criminality.
— William P. Barr (Verizon General Counsel, calling for government liquidation of MCI-WorldCom in Chap. 7, 4/14/2003, b. 1950)

WEDNESDAY
D 61.9
S 42.9
N 57.1
2

It isn't the incompetent who destroy an organization. It is those who have achieved something and want to rest upon their achievements who are forever clogging things up.
— Charles E. Sorenson (Danish-American engineer, officer, director of Ford Motor Co. 1907–1950, helped develop 1st auto assembly line, 1881–1968)

THURSDAY
D 57.1
S 57.1
N 57.1
3

But how do we know when irrational exuberance has unduly escalated asset values, which then become subject to unexpected and prolonged contractions as they have in Japan over the past decade?
— Alan Greenspan (Fed Chairman 1987–2006, 12/5/96 speech to American Enterprise Institute, b. 1926)

FRIDAY
D 38.1
S 52.4
N 57.1
4

Mankind is divided into three classes: Those that are immovable, those that are movable, and those that move.
— Arabian proverb (also attributed to Benjamin Franklin)

SATURDAY
5

SUNDAY
6

A CORRECTION FOR ALL SEASONS

While there's a rally for every season (page 72), almost always there's a decline or correction, too. Fortunately, corrections tend to be smaller than rallies, and that's what gives the stock market its long-term upward bias. In each season the average bounce outdoes the average setback. On average, the net gain between the rally and the correction is smallest in summer and fall.

The summer setback tends to be slightly outdone by the average correction in the fall. Tax selling and portfolio cleaning are the usual explanations—individuals sell to register a tax loss and institutions like to get rid of their losers before preparing year-end statements. The October jinx also plays a major part. Since 1964, there have been 18 fall declines of over 10%, and in 10 of them (1966, 1974, 1978, 1979, 1987, 1990, 1997, 2000, 2002, and 2008) much damage was done in October, where so many bear markets end. Recent October lows were also seen in 1998, 1999, 2004, 2005, and 2011. Most often, it has paid to buy after fourth quarter or late third quarter "waterfall declines" for a rally that may continue into January or even beyond. Anticipation of war in Iraq put the market down in 2003 Q1. Quick success rallied stocks through Q3. Financial crisis affected the pattern in 2008–2009, producing the worst winter decline since 1932. Easy monetary policy and strong corporate earnings spared Q1 2011 and 2012 from a seasonal slump.

SEASONAL CORRECTIONS IN DOW JONES INDUSTRIALS

	WINTER SLUMP Nov/Dec High to Q1 Low	SPRING SLUMP Feb/Mar High to Q2 Low	SUMMER SLUMP May/Jun High to Q3 Low	FALL SLUMP Aug/Sep High to Q4 Low
1964	−0.1%	−2.4%	−1.0%	−2.1%
1965	−2.5	−7.3	−8.3	−0.9
1966	−6.0	−13.2	−17.7	−12.7
1967	−4.2	−3.9	−5.5	−9.9
1968	−8.8	−0.3	−5.5	+0.4
1969	−8.7	−8.7	−17.2	−8.1
1970	−13.8	−20.2	−8.8	−2.5
1971	−1.4	−4.8	−10.7	−13.4
1972	−0.5	−2.6	−6.3	−5.3
1973	−11.0	−12.8	−10.9	−17.3
1974	−15.3	−10.8	−29.8	−27.6
1975	−6.3	−5.5	−9.9	−6.7
1976	−0.2	−5.1	−4.7	−8.9
1977	−8.5	−7.2	−11.5	−10.2
1978	−12.3	−4.0	−7.0	−13.5
1979	−2.5	−5.8	−3.7	−10.9
1980	−10.0	−16.0	−1.7	−6.8
1981	−6.9	−5.1	−18.6	−12.9
1982	−10.9	−7.5	−10.6	−3.3
1983	−4.1	−2.8	−6.8	−3.6
1984	−11.9	−10.5	−8.4	−6.2
1985	−4.8	−4.4	−2.8	−2.3
1986	−3.3	−4.7	−7.3	−7.6
1987	−1.4	−6.6	−1.7	−36.1
1988	−6.7	−7.0	−7.6	−4.5
1989	−1.7	−2.4	−3.1	−6.6
1990	−7.9	−4.0	−17.3	−18.4
1991	−6.3	−3.6	−4.5	−6.3
1992	+0.1	−3.3	−5.4	−7.6
1993	−2.7	−3.1	−3.0	−2.0
1994	−4.4	−9.6	−4.4	−7.1
1995	−0.8	−0.1	−0.2	−2.0
1996	−3.5	−4.6	−7.5	+0.2
1997	−1.8	−9.8	−2.2	−13.3
1998	−7.0	−3.1	−18.2	−13.1
1999	−2.7	−1.7	−8.0	−11.5
2000	−14.8	−7.4	−4.1	−11.8
2001	−14.5	−13.6	−27.4	−16.2
2002	−5.1	−14.2	−26.7	−19.5
2003	−15.8	−5.3	−3.1	−2.1
2004	−3.9	−7.7	−6.3	−5.7
2005	−4.5	−8.5	−3.3	−4.5
2006	−2.4	−5.4	−7.8	−0.4
2007	−3.7	−3.2	−6.1	−8.4
2008	−14.5	−11.0	−20.6	−35.9
2009	−32.0	−6.3	−7.4	−3.5
2010	−6.1	−10.4	−13.1	−1.0
2011	+0.2	−4.0	−16.3	−12.2
2012	+0.5	−8.7	−5.3	−7.8
2013	−0.2	−0.3	−4.1	−5.7
2014	−7.3	−2.6*		
Totals	−324.9%	−333.1%	−449.4%	−455.2%
Average	−6.4%	−6.5%	−9.0%	−9.1%

As of 5/16/2014

84

SEPTEMBER

Labor Day *(Market Closed)*

MONDAY

7

Take care of your employees and they'll take care of your customers.
— John W. Marriott (Founder Marriott International, 1900–1985)

Day After Labor Day, Dow Up 14 of Last 20, 1997 Up 3.4%, 1998 Up 5.0% TUESDAY

D 66.7
S 61.9
N 61.9

8

The universal line of distinction between the strong and the weak is that one persists, while the other hesitates, falters, trifles and at last collapses or caves in.
— Edwin Percy Whipple (American essayist, 1819–1886)

WEDNESDAY

D 57.1
S 66.7
N 66.7

9

The first panacea for a mismanaged nation is inflation of the currency; the second is war. Both bring a temporary prosperity; both bring a permanent ruin. But both are the refuge of political and economic opportunists.
— Ernest Hemingway (American writer, 1954 Nobel Prize, 1899–1961)

THURSDAY

D 61.9
S 61.9
N 52.4

10

No profession requires more hard work, intelligence, patience, and mental discipline than successful speculation.
— Robert Rhea (Economist, trader, *The Dow Theory*, 1887–1952)

2001 4-Day Market Closing, Longest Since
9-Day Banking Moratorium in March 1933

"In Memory"

FRIDAY

D 66.7
S 66.7
N 66.7

11

Knowing others is intelligence; knowing yourself is true wisdom. Mastering others is strength; mastering yourself is true power.
— Lau Tzu (Shaolin monk, founder of Taoism, circa 6th–4th century B.C.)

SATURDAY

12

SUNDAY

13

FIRST-TRADING-DAY-OF-THE-MONTH PHENOMENON: DOW GAINS MORE ONE DAY THAN ALL OTHER DAYS

Over the last 17 years the Dow Jones Industrial Average has gained more points on the first trading days of all months than all other days combined. While the Dow has gained 8868.89 points between September 2, 1997 (7622.42) and May 16, 2014 (16491.31), it is incredible that 5468.22 points were gained on the first trading days of these 201 months. The remaining 4003 trading days combined gained 3400.67 points during the period. This averages out to gains of 27.21 points on first days, in contrast to just 0.85 points on all others.

Note September 1997 through October 2000 racked up a total gain of 2632.39 Dow points on the first trading days of these 38 months (winners except for seven occasions). But between November 2000 and September 2002, when the 2000–2002 bear markets did the bulk of their damage, frightened investors switched from pouring money into the market on that day to pulling it out, fourteen months out of twenty-three, netting a 404.80 Dow point loss. The 2007–2009 bear market lopped off 964.14 Dow points on first days in 17 months November 2007–March 2009. First days had their worst year in 2011, declining seven times for a total loss of 644.45 Dow points.

First days of June have performed worst. Triple digit declines in four of the last six years have resulted in the biggest net loss. Due to persistent weakness, March and December are net losers as well. In rising market trends, first days perform much better, as institutions are likely anticipating strong performance at each month's outset. S&P 500 first days differ slightly from Dow's pattern as June is the sole loser. NASDAQ first days are not as strong with weakness in April, June, August, and October.

DOW POINTS GAINED FIRST DAY OF MONTH
SEPT 1997–MAY 16, 2014

	Jan	Feb	Mar	Apr	May	Jun	Jul	Aug	Sep	Oct	Nov	Dec	Totals
1997									257.36	70.24	232.31	189.98	749.89
1998	56.79	201.28	4.73	68.51	83.70	22.42	96.65	−96.55	288.36	−210.09	114.05	16.99	646.84
1999	2.84	−13.13	18.20	46.35	225.65	36.52	95.62	−9.19	108.60	−63.95	−81.35	120.58	486.74
2000	−139.61	100.52	9.62	300.01	77.87	129.87	112.78	84.97	23.68	49.21	−71.67	−40.95	636.30
2001	−140.70	96.27	−45.14	−100.85	163.37	78.47	91.32	−12.80	47.74	−10.73	188.76	−87.60	268.11
2002	51.90	−12.74	262.73	−41.24	113.41	−215.46	−133.47	−229.97	−355.45	346.86	120.61	−33.52	−126.34
2003	265.89	56.01	−53.22	77.73	−25.84	47.55	55.51	−79.83	107.45	194.14	57.34	116.59	819.32
2004	−44.07	11.11	94.22	15.63	88.43	14.20	−101.32	39.45	−5.46	112.38	26.92	162.20	413.69
2005	−53.58	62.00	63.77	−99.46	59.19	82.39	28.47	−17.76	−21.97	−33.22	−33.30	106.70	143.23
2006	129.91	89.09	60.12	35.62	−23.85	91.97	77.80	−59.95	83.00	−8.72	−49.71	−27.80	397.48
2007	11.37	51.99	−34.29	27.95	73.23	40.47	126.81	150.38	91.12	191.92	−362.14	−57.15	311.66
2008	−220.86	92.83	−7.49	391.47	189.87	−134.50	32.25	−51.70	−26.63	−19.59	−5.18	−679.95	−439.48
2009	258.30	−64.03	−299.64	152.68	44.29	221.11	57.06	114.95	−185.68	−203.00	76.71	126.74	299.49
2010	155.91	118.20	78.53	70.44	143.22	−112.61	−41.49	208.44	254.75	41.63	6.13	249.76	1172.91
2011	93.24	148.23	−168.32	56.99	−3.18	−279.65	168.43	−10.75	−119.96	−258.08	−297.05	−25.65	−695.75
2012	179.82	83.55	28.23	52.45	65.69	−274.88	−8.70	−37.62	−54.90	77.98	136.16	−59.98	187.80
2013	308.41	149.21	35.17	−5.69	−138.85	138.46	65.36	128.48	23.65	62.03	69.80	−77.64	758.39
2014	−135.31	−326.05	−153.68	74.95	−21.97								−562.06
Totals	780.25	844.34	−106.46	1123.54	1114.23	−113.67	723.08	120.55	515.66	339.01	128.39	−0.70	5468.22

SUMMARY FIRST DAYS VS. OTHER DAYS OF MONTH

	# of Days	Total Points Gained	Average Daily Point Gain
First days	201	5468.22	27.21
Other days	4003	3400.67	0.85

SEPTEMBER

Monday Before September Triple Witching, Russell 2000 Down 9 of Last 15
Rosh Hashanah

MONDAY

D 57.1
S 66.7
N 81.0

14

Taxes are what we pay for civilized society.
— Oliver Wendell Holmes Jr. (U.S. Supreme Court Justice 1902–1932, "The Great Dissenter," inscribed above IRS HQ entrance, 1841–1935)

TUESDAY

D 52.4
S 52.4
N 38.1

15

Don't compete. Create. Find out what everyone else is doing and then don't do it.
— Joel Weldon (Motivational speaker, b. 1941)

Expiration Week 2001, Dow Lost 1370 Points (14.3%)
2nd Worst Weekly Point Loss Ever, 5th Worst Week Overall

WEDNESDAY

D 61.9
S 61.9
N 71.4

16

We may face more inflation pressure than currently shows up in formal data.
— William Poole (Economist, president Federal Reserve Bank St. Louis 1998–2008, June 2006 speech, b. 1937)

THURSDAY

D 38.1
S 42.9
N 52.4

17

An economist is someone who sees something happen, and then wonders if it would work in theory.
— Ronald Reagan (40th U.S. President, 1911–2004)

September Triple Witching, Dow Up 9 of Last 12

FRIDAY

D 52.4
S 47.6
N 61.9

18

A president is elected and tries to get rid of the dirty stuff in the economy as quickly as possible, so that by the time the next election comes around, he looks like a hero. The stock market is reacting to what the politicians are doing.
— Yale Hirsch (Creator of *Stock Trader's Almanac*, NY Times 10/10/2010, b. 1923)

SATURDAY

19

SUNDAY

20

MARKET BEHAVIOR THREE DAYS BEFORE AND THREE DAYS AFTER HOLIDAYS

The *Stock Trader's Almanac* has tracked holiday seasonality annually since the first edition in 1968. Stocks used to rise on the day before holidays and sell off the day after, but nowadays, each holiday moves to its own rhythm. Eight holidays are separated into seven groups. Average percentage changes for the Dow, S&P 500, NASDAQ, and Russell 2000 are shown.

The Dow and S&P consist of blue chips and the largest cap stocks, whereas NASDAQ and the Russell 2000 would be more representative of smaller-cap stocks. This is evident on the last day of the year with NASDAQ and the Russell 2000 having a field day, while their larger brethren in the Dow and S&P are showing losses on average.

Thanks to the Santa Claus Rally, the three days before and after New Year's Day and Christmas are best. NASDAQ and the Russell 2000 average gains of 1.3% to 1.8% over the six-day spans. However, trading around the first day of the year has been mixed. Traders have been selling more the first trading day of the year recently, pushing gains and losses into the New Year.

Bullishness before Labor Day and after Memorial Day is affected by strength the first day of September and June. The second worst day after a holiday is the day after Easter. Surprisingly, the following day is one of the best second days after a holiday, right up there with the second day after New Year's Day.

Presidents' Day is the least bullish of all the holidays, bearish the day before and three days after. NASDAQ has dropped 19 of the last 25 days before Presidents' Day (Dow, 16 of 25; S&P, 18 of 25; Russell 2000, 14 of 25).

HOLIDAYS: 3 DAYS BEFORE, 3 DAYS AFTER (Average % change 1980–April 2014)

	−3	−2	−1		+1	+2	+3
S&P 500	0.02	0.25	−0.07	**New Year's**	0.23	0.34	0.05
DJIA	−0.02	0.19	−0.15	**Day**	0.35	0.35	0.17
NASDAQ	0.08	0.29	0.24	*1/1/15*	0.24	0.63	0.19
Russell 2K	0.07	0.41	0.49		0.08	0.24	0.14
S&P 500	0.35	0.03	−0.22	Negative Before & After	−0.22	−0.08	−0.12
DJIA	0.33	0.03	−0.14	**Presidents'**	−0.14	−0.12	−0.14
NASDAQ	0.54	0.28	−0.38	**Day**	−0.55	−0.09	−0.07
Russell 2K	0.43	0.19	−0.12	*2/16/15*	−0.41	−0.21	−0.04
S&P 500	0.22	−0.03	0.39	Positive Before &	−0.22	0.32	0.10
DJIA	0.19	−0.06	0.30	Negative After	−0.15	0.31	0.10
NASDAQ	0.44	0.26	0.50	**Good Friday**	−0.34	0.34	0.18
Russell 2K	0.23	0.12	0.53	*4/3/15*	−0.34	0.21	0.11
S&P 500	0.02	0.02	−0.01	Positive After	0.35	0.10	0.25
DJIA	−0.01	0.01	−0.07	**Memorial**	0.42	0.11	0.15
NASDAQ	0.07	0.23	0.01	**Day**	0.27	−0.05	0.49
Russell 2K	−0.07	0.31	0.08	*5/25/15*	0.28	0.01	0.42
S&P 500	0.13	0.08	0.06	Negative After	−0.13	0.06	0.07
DJIA	0.09	0.07	0.06	**Independence**	−0.07	0.09	0.05
NASDAQ	0.26	0.11	0.05	**Day**	−0.14	−0.08	0.22
Russell 2K	0.26	0.01	−0.03	*7/3/15*	−0.19	−0.003	0.04
S&P 500	0.17	−0.22	0.17	Positive Day Before	0.05	0.11	−0.08
DJIA	0.14	−0.27	0.18	**Labor**	0.08	0.17	−0.18
NASDAQ	0.38	0.01	0.17	**Day**	−0.04	−0.02	0.08
Russell 2K	0.53	0.06	0.10	*9/7/15*	0.05	0.17	0.05
S&P 500	0.14	0.01	0.26	Positive Before & After	0.20	−0.42	0.28
DJIA	0.15	0.02	0.28	**Thanksgiving**	0.16	−0.37	0.30
NASDAQ	0.07	−0.22	0.41	*11/26/15*	0.47	−0.42	0.10
Russell 2K	0.12	−0.10	0.38		0.35	−0.48	0.25
S&P 500	0.18	0.19	0.23	**Christmas**	0.14	−0.01	0.31
DJIA	0.25	0.22	0.28	*12/25/15*	0.19	−0.01	0.27
NASDAQ	−0.08	0.44	0.42		0.11	0.04	0.37
Russell 2K	0.24	0.37	0.36		0.19	0.05	0.50

SEPTEMBER

Week After September Triple Witching Dow Down 19 of Last 24,
Average Loss Since 1990, 1.2%

🐻 **MONDAY**

D 42.9
S 38.1
N 42.9

21

Every time everyone's talking about something, that's the time to sell.
— George Lindemann (Billionaire, *Forbes*, b. 1936)

🐻 **TUESDAY**

D 38.1
S 38.1
N 38.1

22

If you create an act, you create a habit. If you create a habit, you create a character. If you create a character, you create a destiny.
— André Maurois (Novelist, biographer, essayist, 1885–1967)

Yom Kippur

🐻 **WEDNESDAY**

D 28.6
S 28.6
N 42.9

23

It is better to be out wishing you were in, than in wishing you were out.
— Albert W. Thomas (Trader, investor, *Over My Shoulder*, mutualfundmagic.com, *If It Doesn't Go Up, Don't Buy It!*, b. 1927)

End of September Prone to Weakness
From End-of-Q3 Institutional Portfolio Restructuring

🐻 **THURSDAY**

D 42.9
S 38.1
N 42.9

24

Benjamin Graham was correct in suggesting that while the stock market in the short run may be a voting mechanism, in the long run it is a weighing mechanism. True value will win out in the end.
— Burton G. Malkiel (Economist, April 2003 Princeton Paper, *A Random Walk Down Wall Street*, b. 1932)

FRIDAY

D 57.1
S 52.4
N 47.6

25

The greatest safety lies in putting all your eggs in one basket and watching the basket.
— Gerald M. Loeb (E.F. Hutton, *The Battle for Investment Survival*, predicted 1929 Crash, 1900–1974)

SATURDAY

26

October Almanac Investor Seasonalities: See Pages 94, 96 and 98

SUNDAY

27

OCTOBER ALMANAC

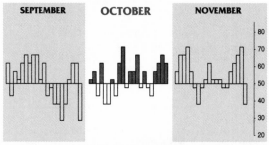

OCTOBER						
S	M	T	W	T	F	S
				1	2	3
4	5	6	7	8	9	10
11	12	13	14	15	16	17
18	19	20	21	22	23	24
25	26	27	28	29	30	31

NOVEMBER						
S	M	T	W	T	F	S
1	2	3	4	5	6	7
8	9	10	11	12	13	14
15	16	17	18	19	20	21
22	23	24	25	26	27	28
29	30					

Market Probability Chart above is a graphic representation of the S&P 500 Recent Market Probability Calendar on page 124.

◆ Known as the jinx month because of crashes in 1929 and 1987, the 554-point drop on October 27, 1997, back-to-back massacres in 1978 and 1979, Friday the 13th in 1989, and the meltdown in 2008 ◆ Yet October is a "bear killer" and turned the tide in 12 post–WWII bear markets: 1946, 1957, 1960, 1962, 1966, 1974, 1987, 1990, 1998, 2001, 2002, and 2011 ◆ First October Dow top in 2007, 20-year 1987 Crash anniversary −2.6% ◆ Worst six months of the year ends with October (page 52) ◆ No longer worst month (pages 50 & 58) ◆ Best Dow, S&P, and NASDAQ month from 1993 to 2007 ◆ Pre-presidential election year Octobers since 1950, #12 Dow (−1.0%), #11 S&P (−0.4%), and #12 NASDAQ (−0.8%) ◆ October is a great time to buy ◆ Big October gains five years 1999–2003 after atrocious Septembers ◆ Can get into Best Six Months earlier using MACD (page 52) ◆ October 2011, second month to gain 1000 Dow points.

October Vital Statistics

		DJIA		S&P 500		NASDAQ		Russell 1K		Russell 2K
Rank		7		7		9		7		12
Up		38		38		23		22		19
Down		26		26		20		13		16
Average % Change		0.5%		0.8%		0.6%		0.8%		−0.5%
Pre-Election Year		−1.0%		−0.4%		−0.8%		−0.6%		−2.7%
Best & Worst October										
		% Change		% Change		% Change		% Change		% Change
Best		1982	10.7	1974	16.3	1974	17.2	1982	11.3	2011	15.0
Worst		1987	−23.2	1987	−21.8	1987	−27.2	1987	−21.9	1987	−30.8
Best & Worst October Weeks										
Best	10/11/74	12.6	10/11/74	14.1	10/31/08	10.9	10/31/08	10.8	10/31/08	14.1
Worst	10/10/08	−18.2	10/10/08	−18.2	10/23/87	−19.2	10/10/08	−18.2	10/23/87	−20.4
Best & Worst October Days										
Best	10/13/08	11.1	10/13/08	11.6	10/13/08	11.8	10/13/08	11.7	10/13/08	9.3
Worst	10/19/87	−22.6	10/19/87	−20.5	10/19/87	−11.4	10/19/87	−19.0	10/19/87	−12.5
First Trading Day of Expiration Week: 1980–2013										
Record (#Up–#Down)		28–6		26–8		24–10		27–7		26–8
Current streak		U2		U2		U2		U2		U2
Avg % Change		0.81		0.79		0.63		0.76		0.44
Options Expiration Day: 1980–2013										
Record (#Up–#Down)		15–19		17–17		18–16		17–17		15–19
Current streak		U1		U1		U1		U1		U1
Avg % Change		−0.22		−0.28		−0.15		−0.27		−0.18
Options Expiration Week: 1980–2013										
Record (#Up–#Down)		24–10		24–10		19–15		24–10		20–14
Current streak		U6		U6		U1		U6		U1
Avg % Change		0.65		0.70		0.73		0.69		0.36
Week After Options Expiration: 1980–2013										
Record (#Up–#Down)		15–19		14–20		17–17		14–20		15–19
Current streak		U1		U1		U1		U1		U1
Avg % Change		−0.48		−0.51		−0.56		−0.53		−0.70
First Trading Day Performance										
% of Time Up		50.0		50.0		48.8		54.3		51.4
Avg % Change		0.08		0.07		−0.12		0.26		−0.22
Last Trading Day Performance										
% of Time Up		53.1		54.7		65.1		62.9		71.4
Avg % Change		0.06		0.14		0.49		0.34		0.60

Dow & S&P 1950–April 2014, NASDAQ 1971–April 2014, Russell 1K & 2K 1979–April 2014.

October has killed many a bear,
Buy techs and small caps and soon wear a grin ear to ear.

SEPTEMBER/OCTOBER

MONDAY
D 57.1
S 61.9
N 47.6
28

Companies which do well generally tend to report (their quarterly earnings) earlier than those which do poorly.
— Alan Abelson (Financial journalist and editor, *Barron's*, 1925–2013)

TUESDAY
D 61.9
S 61.9
N 47.6
29

There's no trick to being a humorist when you have the whole government working for you.
— Will Rogers (American humorist and showman, 1879–1935)

Last Day of Q3, Dow Down 13 of Last 17, Massive 4.7% Rally in 2008
WEDNESDAY
D 28.6
S 28.6
N 28.6
30

It's not what you say. It's what they hear.
— (A sign in an advertising office)

First Trading Day in October, Dow Down 5 of Last 9 Off 2.4% in 2011
THURSDAY
D 57.1
S 52.4
N 42.9
1

Anyone who has achieved excellence knows that it comes as a result of ceaseless concentration.
— Louise Brooks (Actress, 1906–1985)

Start Looking for MACD BUY Signals on October 1 (Pages 54, 60 and 62)
Almanac Investor Subscribers Emailed When It Triggers (See Insert)
FRIDAY
D 47.6
S 57.1
N 57.1
2

Innovation can't depend on trying to please the customer or the client. It is an elitist act by the inventor who acts alone and breaks rules.
— Dean Kamen (Inventor, President of DEKA R&D, *Business Week*, Feb. 12, 2001, b. 1951)

SATURDAY
3

SUNDAY
4

MARKET GAINS MORE ON SUPER-8 DAYS EACH MONTH THAN ON ALL 13 REMAINING DAYS COMBINED

For many years, the last day plus the first four days were the best days of the month. The market currently exhibits greater bullish bias from the last three trading days of the previous month through the first two days of the current month, and now shows significant bullishness during the middle three trading days, 9 to 11, due to 401(k) cash inflows (see pages 145 and 146). This pattern was not as pronounced during the boom years of the 1990s, with market strength all month long. It returned in 2000 with monthly bullishness at the ends, beginnings and middles of months versus weakness during the rest of the month. "Super Eight" performance in 2014, was on track as were other seasonal patterns and indicators.

SUPER-8 DAYS* DOW % CHANGES VS. REST OF MONTH

	Super 8 Days	Rest of Month		Super 8 Days	Rest of Month		Super 8 Days	Rest of Month
	2006			**2007**			**2008**	
Jan	−0.03%	0.34%		0.68%	−0.04%		−4.76%	−4.11%
Feb	1.67	0.71		3.02	−1.72		1.83	0.65
Mar	0.81	−0.03		−5.51	3.64		−4.85	2.92
Apr	1.69	−0.53		2.66	2.82		−0.27	4.09
May	−0.66	0.08		2.21	0.95		2.19	−4.81
Jun	2.39	−4.87		3.84	−5.00		0.37	−6.30
Jul	1.65	0.07		2.59	−1.47		−3.80	−1.99
Aug	1.83	0.41		−2.94	−0.26		1.53	1.06
Sep	1.13	1.64		4.36	1.18		−2.23	−1.19
Oct	1.58	2.59		1.28	−1.05		−3.39	−13.70
Nov	−0.01	−0.31		−0.59	−5.63		6.07	−11.90
Dec	2.40	−0.05		−0.04	4.62		−2.54	3.49
Totals	**14.45%**	**0.04%**		**11.56%**	**−1.96%**		**−9.85%**	**−31.79%**
Average	**1.20%**	**0.003%**		**0.96%**	**−0.163%**		**−0.82%**	**−2.65%**
	2009			**2010**			**2011**	
Jan	3.16%	−6.92%		0.66%	−3.92%		1.70%	1.80%
Feb	−6.05	−4.39		3.31	−2.38		0.45	0.57
Mar	−4.37	12.84		1.91	3.51		−1.40	2.21
Apr	1.52	−0.24		1.13	0.18		2.30	0.95
May	2.64	2.98		−3.08	−5.75		1.03	−2.61
Jun	1.71	−1.64		4.33	−3.26		−1.64	−1.19
Jul	2.30	5.03		−7.07	11.34		3.52	0.31
Aug	0.04	4.91		0.20	−5.49		2.04	−11.39
Sep	−0.81	2.21		3.83	4.22		3.24	−3.96
Oct	−0.05	2.40		−0.18	3.47		−4.47	10.71
Nov	0.00	5.57		−1.20	1.37		1.42	−6.66
Dec	0.62	0.46		1.98	1.45		5.74	3.58
Totals	**0.71%**	**23.21%**		**5.82%**	**4.74%**		**13.93%**	**−5.68%**
Average	**0.06%**	**1.93%**		**0.49%**	**0.40%**		**1.16%**	**−0.47%**
	2012			**2013**			**2014**	
Jan	1.90%	1.66%		2.28%	3.47%		0.92%	−4.26%
Feb	−0.39	2.33		−0.27	−0.41		−1.99	3.66
Mar	2.22	−0.55		2.93	1.82		0.77	−0.21
Apr	1.00	−1.80		0.11	1.65		2.44	−1.82
May	−0.38	−4.52		1.93	2.81			
Jun	−1.30	2.08		−0.27	−3.96			
Jul	5.11	−2.22		1.11	4.23			
Aug	−0.40	2.09		−1.35	−3.75			
Sep	−0.24	2.98		2.55	0.83			
Oct	0.77	−3.60		−0.64	2.60			
Nov	−2.01	0.55		1.79	1.41			
Dec	0.49	1.35		−0.72	3.30			
Totals	**6.77%**	**0.35%**		**9.45%**	**14.00%**		**2.14%**	**−2.63%**
Average	**0.56%**	**0.03%**		**0.79%**	**1.17%**		**0.54%**	**−0.66%**

	Super Eight Days		**Rest of Month (13 days)**	
100	Net % Changes	54.98%	Net % Changes	0.28%
Month	Average Period	0.55%	Average Period	0.003%
Totals	Average Day	0.07%	Average Day	0.0002%

* Super-8 Days = Last 3 + First 2 + Middle 3

OCTOBER

No other country can substitute for the U.S. The U.S. is still No. 1 in military, No. 1 in economy, No. 1 in promoting human rights and No. 1 in idealism. Only the U.S. can lead the world. No other country can.
— Senior Korean official (to Thomas L. Friedman *NY Times* Foreign Affairs columnist, 2/25/2009)

October Ends Dow and S&P "Worst Six Months" (Pages 50, 52, 54 and 147)
And NASDAQ "Worst Four Months" (Pages 58, 60 and 148)

TUESDAY

D 71.4
S 61.9
N 66.7

6

When you get into a tight place and everything goes against you, till it seems as though you could not hang on a minute longer, never give up then, for that is just the place and time that the tide will turn.
— Harriet Beecher Stowe (American writer and abolitionist, 1811–1896)

WEDNESDAY

D 38.1
S 38.1
N 47.6

7

The usual bull market successfully weathers a number of tests until it is considered invulnerable, whereupon it is ripe for a bust.
— George Soros (Financier, philanthropist, political activist, author, and philosopher, b. 1930)

Dow Lost 1874 Points (18.2%) on the Week Ending 10/10/08
Worst Dow Week in the History of Wall Street

THURSDAY

D 38.1
S 38.1
N 52.4

8

I'm not better than the next trader, just quicker at admitting my mistakes and moving on to the next opportunity.
— George Soros (Financier, philanthropist, political activist, author, and philosopher, b. 1930)

FRIDAY

D 52.4
S 52.4
N 57.1

9

Writing a book is an adventure. To begin with it is a toy, an amusement; then it is a mistress, and then a master, and then a tyrant.
— Winston Churchill (British statesman, 1874–1965)

SATURDAY

10

SUNDAY

11

SECTOR SEASONALITY: SELECTED PERCENTAGE PLAYS

Sector seasonality was featured in the first 1968 *Almanac*. A Merrill Lynch study showed that buying seven sectors around September or October and selling in the first few months of 1954–1964 tripled the gains of holding them for 10 years. Over the years we have honed this strategy significantly and now devote a large portion of our time and resources to investing and trading during positive and negative seasonal periods for different sectors with Exchange Traded Funds (ETFs).

Updated seasonalities appear in the table below. We specify whether the seasonality starts or finishes in the beginning third (B), middle third (M), or last third (E) of the month. These selected percentage plays are geared to take advantage of the bulk of seasonal sector strength or weakness.

By design, entry points are in advance of the major seasonal moves, providing traders ample opportunity to accumulate positions at favorable prices. Conversely, exit points have been selected to capture the majority of the move.

From the major seasonalities in the table below, we created the Sector Index Seasonality Strategy Calendar on pages 96 and 98. Note the concentration of bullish sector seasonalities during the Best Six Months, November to April, and bearish sector seasonalities during the Worst Six Months, May to October.

Almanac Investor newsletter subscribers receive specific entry and exit points for highly correlated ETFs and detailed analysis in our monthly ETF Scoreboard and ETF Trades. Visit *www.stocktradersalmanac.com,* or see the insert for additional details and a special offer for new subscribers.

SECTOR INDEX SEASONALITY TABLE

Ticker	Sector Index	Type	Seasonality Start		Finish		Average % Return[†] 15-Year	10-Year	5-Year
XCI	Computer Tech	Short	January	B	March	B	−7.0	−5.3	0.9
XNG	Natural Gas	Long	February	E	June	B	17.7	11.5	9.8
MSH	High-Tech	Long	March	M	July	B	8.3	6.7	6.8
UTY	Utilities	Long	March	M	October	B	9.4	8.2	9.8
XCI	Computer Tech	Long	April	M	July	M	8.4	5.4	5.9
BKX	Banking	Short	May	B	July	B	−8.0	−10.6	−11.1
CYC	Cyclical	Short	May	M	October	E	−6.6	−4.0	4.4
XAU	Gold & Silver	Short	May	M	June	E	−7.9	−6.9	−8.8
S5MATR	Materials	Short	May	M	October	M	−7.7	−3.8	2.5
XNG	Natural Gas	Short	June	M	July	E	−7.2	−3.0	−0.9
XAU	Gold & Silver	Long	July	E	December	E	14.6	11.8	10.2
DJT	Transports	Short	July	M	October	M	−7.4	−3.8	0.7
BTK	Biotech	Long	August	B	March	B	28.0	16.4	29.1
MSH	High-Tech	Long	August	M	January	M	15.1	11.3	19.3
SOX	Semiconductor	Short	August	M	October	M	−10.5	−6.6	−0.7
CMR	Consumer	Long	September	E	June	B	10.4	8.6	8.9
XOI	Oil	Short	September	B	November	E	−4.6	−3.0	2.2
BKX	Banking	Long	October	B	May	B	12.1	10.9	22.7
XBD	Broker/Dealer	Long	October	B	April	M	16.8	15.4	22.3
XCI	Computer Tech	Long	October	B	January	B	14.2	9.3	11.6
CYC	Cyclical	Long	October	B	May	M	19.6	18.7	27.0
HCX	Healthcare	Long	October	B	May	B	10.3*	10.1	17.1
S5MATR	Materials	Long	October	M	May	M	15.7	14.3	11.5
DRG	Pharmaceutical	Long	October	M	January	B	5.9	6.5	6.4
RMZ	Real Estate	Long	October	E	May	B	14.0	13.3	20.2
SOX	Semiconductor	Long	October	E	December	B	14.2	8.4	9.9
XTC	Telecom	Long	October	M	December	E	8.8	5.7	5.8
DJT	Transports	Long	October	B	May	B	18.8	20.4	27.4
XOI	Oil	Long	December	M	July	B	12.4	12.3	3.5

[†]*Average % Return based on full seasonality completion through May 23, 2014*

* Since 2002

OCTOBER

Columbus Day (*Bond Market Closed*)
Monday Before October Expiration, Dow Up 28 of 34

MONDAY
D 38.1
S 42.9
N 57.1
12

Interviewer: *How is it possible to fight an enemy willing and ready to die for his cause?*
Reply: *Accommodate him!*
— General Norman Schwarzkopf (Commander Allied Forces 1990–1991 Gulf War, Dec. 2001, 1934–2012)

🐃 TUESDAY
D 57.1
S 61.9
N 71.4
13

Love your enemies, for they tell you your faults.
— Benjamin Franklin (U.S. Founding Father, diplomat, inventor, 1706–1790)

October 2011, Second Dow Month to Gain 1000 Points

🐃 WEDNESDAY
D 81.0
S 71.4
N 71.4
14

People have difficulty cutting losses, admitting an error, and moving on. I am rather frequently—and on occasion, quite spectacularly—wrong. However, if we expect to be wrong, then there should be no ego tied up in admitting the error, honoring the stop loss, selling the loser—and preserving your capital.
— Barry L. Ritholtz (Founder/CIO Ritholtz Wealth Management, *Bailout Nation*, *The Big Picture* blog, 8/12/2010, b. 1961)

THURSDAY
D 52.4
S 47.6
N 47.6
15

Everything possible today was at one time impossible. Everything impossible today may at some time in the future be possible.
— Edward Lindaman (Apollo space project, president Whitworth College, 1920–1982)

October Expiration Day, Dow Down 6 Straight 2005–2010 and 8 of Last 11

🐻 FRIDAY
D 57.1
S 57.1
N 47.6
16

Politics ought to be the part-time profession of every citizen who would protect the rights and privileges of free people and who would preserve what is good and fruitful in our national heritage.
— Dwight D. Eisenhower (34th U.S. President, 1890–1969)

SATURDAY
17

SUNDAY
18

SECTOR INDEX SEASONALITY STRATEGY CALENDAR*

* Graphic representation of the Sector Index Seasonality Percentage Plays on page 94.
L = Long Trade, S = Short Trade, ⟶ = Start of Trade

(continued on page 98)

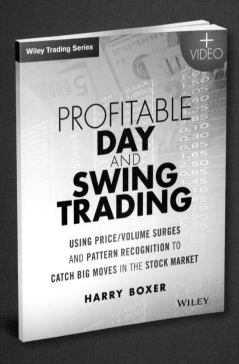

Follow Stock Trader's Almanac

@AlmanacTrader

Stock Trader's Almanac

Stock Trader's Almanac Group

STA Blog: http://blog.stocktradersalmanac.com/

Follow Wiley Trading

@Wiley_Trading

Wiley Trading

Wiley Trading Group

Website: WileyTrading.com

OCTOBER

Crash of October 19, 1987, Dow Down 22.6% in One Day

MONDAY
D 42.9
S 57.1
N 42.9
19

I went to a restaurant that serves "breakfast at any time." So I ordered French toast during the Renaissance.
— Steven Wright (Comedian, b. 1955)

TUESDAY
D 66.7
S 66.7
N 66.7
20

If investing is entertaining, if you're having fun, you're probably not making any money. Good investing is boring.
— George Soros (Financier, philanthropist, political activist, author, and philosopher, b. 1930)

Late October Is Time to Buy Depressed Stocks
Especially Techs and Small Caps

WEDNESDAY
D 42.9
S 47.6
N 42.9
21

Your chances for success in any undertaking can be measured by your belief in yourself.
— Robert Collier (Direct marketing copywriter & author, 1885–1950)

THURSDAY
D 47.6
S 57.1
N 57.1
22

Knowledge born from actual experience is the answer to why one profits; lack of it is the reason one loses.
— Gerald M. Loeb (E.F. Hutton, *The Battle for Investment Survival*, predicted 1929 Crash, 1900–1974)

FRIDAY
D 47.6
S 47.6
N 42.9
23

To know values is to know the meaning of the market.
— Charles Dow (Co-founder Dow Jones & Co, 1851–1902)

SATURDAY
24

SUNDAY
25

(continued from page 96)

SECTOR INDEX SEASONALITY STRATEGY CALENDAR*

* Graphic representation of the Sector Index Seasonality Percentage Plays on page 94.
L = Long Trade, S = Short Trade, ⟶ = Start of Trade

MONDAY

D 38.1
S 42.9
N 33.3

26

Your organization will never get better unless you are willing to admit that there is something wrong with it.
— General Norman Schwarzkopf (Commander Allied Forces 1990–1991 Gulf War, 1934–2012)

TUESDAY

D 52.4
S 57.1
N 47.6

27

You must automate, emigrate, or evaporate.
— James A. Baker (Executive VP General Electric, circa 1983, 1927–1999)

86th Anniversary of 1929 Crash, Dow Down 23.0% in Two Days, October 28 and 29

WEDNESDAY

D 66.7
S 61.9
N 61.9

28

A person's greatest virtue is his ability to correct his mistakes and continually make a new person of himself.
— Wang Yangming (Chinese philosopher, 1472–1529)

THURSDAY

D 66.7
S 66.7
N 66.7

29

I always keep these seasonal patterns in the back of my mind. My antennae start to purr at certain times of the year.
— Kenneth Ward (VP Hayden Stone, *General Technical Survey*, 1899–1976)

FRIDAY

D 52.4
S 61.9
N 66.7

30

Regardless of current economic conditions, it's always best to remember that the stock market is a barometer and not a thermometer.
— Yale Hirsch (Creator of *Stock Trader's Almanac*, b. 1923)

Halloween

SATURDAY

31

November Almanac Investor Seasonalities: See Pages 94, 96 and 98
Daylight Saving Time Ends

SUNDAY

1

NOVEMBER ALMANAC

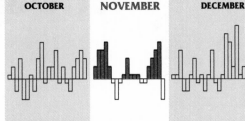

| OCTOBER | NOVEMBER | DECEMBER |

Market Probability Chart above is a graphic representation of the S&P 500 Recent Market Probability Calendar on page 124.

◆ #3 S&P and Dow month since 1950, #3 on NASDAQ since 1971 (pages 50 & 58) ◆ Start of the "Best Six Months" of the year (page 52), NASDAQ's Best Eight Months and Best Three (pages 147 & 148) ◆ Simple timing indicator almost triples "Best Six Months" strategy (page 54), doubles NASDAQ's Best Eight (page 60) ◆ Day before and after Thanksgiving Day combined, only 13 losses in 62 years (page 104) ◆ Week before Thanksgiving Dow up 16 of last 21 ◆ Pre-presidential election year Novembers rank #9 Dow, S&P, and NASDAQ.

November Vital Statistics

	DJIA	S&P 500	NASDAQ	Russell 1K	Russell 2K
Rank	3	3	3	2	3
Up	42	42	28	25	23
Down	22	22	15	10	12
Average % Change	1.5%	1.5%	1.6%	1.7%	1.8%
Pre-Election Year	0.3%	0.3%	0.9%	−0.3%	1.0%

						Best & Worst November				
	% Change		% Change		% Change		% Change		% Change	
Best	1962	10.1	1980	10.2	2001	14.2	1980	10.1	2002	8.8
Worst	1973	−14.0	1973	−11.4	2000	−22.9	2000	−9.3	2008	−12.0
					Best & Worst November Weeks					
Best	11/28/08	9.7	11/28/08	12.0	11/28/08	10.9	11/28/08	12.5	11/28/08	16.4
Worst	11/21/08	−5.3	11/21/08	−8.4	11/10/00	−12.2	11/21/08	−8.8	11/21/08	−11.0
					Best & Worst November Days					
Best	11/13/08	6.7	11/13/08	6.9	11/13/08	6.5	11/13/08	7.0	11/13/08	8.5
Worst	11/20/08	−5.6	11/20/08	−6.7	11/19/08	−6.5	11/20/08	−6.9	11/19/08	−7.9

First Trading Day of Expiration Week: 1980–2013					
Record (#Up–#Down)	17–17	15–19	13–21	16–18	15–19
Current streak	U1	U2	U1	U2	U1
Avg % Change	−0.05	−0.09	−0.15	−0.10	−0.10
Options Expiration Day: 1980–2013					
Record (#Up–#Down)	22–12	20–14	18–16	20–14	17–16
Current streak	U4	U2	U2	U2	U4
Avg % Change	0.24	0.17	0.02	0.16	0.12
Options Expiration Week: 1980–2013					
Record (#Up–#Down)	22–12	20–14	17–17	19–15	17–17
Current streak	U1	U1	U1	U1	U1
Avg % Change	0.25	−0.01	−0.06	−0.03	−0.31
Week After Options Expiration: 1980–2013					
Record (#Up–#Down)	20–14	21–13	22–12	21–13	20–14
Current streak	U2	U2	U2	U2	U2
Avg % Change	0.71	0.69	0.76	0.69	0.78
First Trading Day Performance					
% of Time Up	64.1	64.1	65.1	71.4	62.9
Avg % Change	0.28	0.30	0.28	0.39	0.19
Last Trading Day Performance					
% of Time Up	54.7	54.7	65.1	48.6	71.4
Avg % Change	0.11	0.14	−0.07	0.03	0.21

Dow & S&P 1950–April 2014, NASDAQ 1971–April 2014, Russell 1K & 2K 1979–April 2014.

Astute investors always smile and remember,
When stocks seasonally start soaring, and salute November.

NOVEMBER

First Trading Day in November, Dow Up 4 of Last 5

MONDAY

D 57.1
S 57.1
N 66.7

2

All you need to succeed is a yellow pad and a pencil.
— Andre Meyer (Top deal maker at Lazard Freres, 1898–1979)

Election Day

TUESDAY

D 57.1
S 66.7
N 66.7

3

In the course of evolution and a higher civilization we might be able to get along comfortably without Congress, but without Wall Street, never.
— Henry Clews (*Fifty Years in Wall Street*, 1836–1923)

WEDNESDAY

D 66.7
S 66.7
N 76.2

4

At a time of war, we need you to work for peace. At a time of inequality, we need you to work for opportunity. At a time of so much cynicism and so much doubt, we need you to make us believe again.
— Barack H. Obama (44th U.S. President, Commencement Wesleyan University 5/28/2008, b. 1961)

November Begins Dow and S&P "Best Six Months" (Pages 50, 52, 54 and 147)
And NASDAQ "Best Eight Months" (Pages 58, 60 and 148)

THURSDAY

D 71.4
S 71.4
N 61.9

5

Your emotions are often a reverse indicator of what you ought to be doing.
— John F. Hindelong (Dillon, Reed, b. 1946)

FRIDAY

D 57.1
S 57.1
N 57.1

6

History must repeat itself because we pay such little attention to it the first time.
— Blackie Sherrod (Sportswriter, b. 1919)

SATURDAY

7

SUNDAY

8

FOURTH QUARTER MARKET MAGIC

Examining market performance on a quarterly basis reveals several intriguing and helpful patterns. Fourth-quarter market gains have been magical, providing the greatest and most consistent gains over the years. First-quarter performance runs a respectable second. This should not be surprising, as cash inflows, trading volume, and buying bias are generally elevated during these two quarters.

Positive market psychology hits a fever pitch as the holiday season approaches, and does not begin to wane until spring. Professionals drive the market higher, as they make portfolio adjustments to maximize year-end numbers. Bonuses are paid and invested around the turn of the year.

The market's sweet spot of the four-year cycle begins in the fourth quarter of the midterm year. The best two-quarter span runs from the fourth quarter of the midterm year through the first quarter of the pre-election year, averaging 15.3% for the Dow, 16.0% for the S&P 500, and an amazing 23.3% for NASDAQ. Pre-election Q2 is smoking, too, the third best quarter of the cycle, creating a three-quarter sweet spot from midterm Q4 to pre-election Q2.

Quarterly strength fades in the latter half of the pre-election year, but stays impressively positive through the election year. Losses dominate the first quarter of post-election years and the second and third quarters of midterm years.

QUARTERLY % CHANGES

	Q1	Q2	Q3	Q4	Year	Q2–Q3	Q4–Q1
Dow Jones Industrials (1949–March 2014)							
Average	2.3%	1.5%	0.5%	3.8%	8.5%	2.1%	6.4%
Post Election	−0.4%	1.6%	0.3%	3.8%	5.7%	2.0%	5.4%
Midterm	1.4%	−1.8%	−0.5%	7.3%	6.7%	−2.2%	15.3%
Pre-Election	7.5%	5.3%	1.6%	2.3%	16.9%	6.8%	3.2%
Election	0.8%	1.0%	0.6%	2.0%	4.8%	1.7%	1.7%
S&P 500 (1949–March 2014)							
Average	2.3%	1.6%	0.7%	4.1%	9.0%	2.3%	6.7%
Post Election	−0.6%	2.2%	0.7%	3.5%	6.2%	3.0%	4.7%
Midterm	1.0%	−2.8%	0.1%	8.0%	6.4%	−2.7%	16.0%
Pre-Election	7.5%	5.2%	1.1%	3.0%	17.1%	6.3%	4.6%
Election	1.4%	1.8%	0.9%	1.9%	6.6%	2.8%	1.6%
NASDAQ Composite (1971–March 2014)							
Average	4.4%	3.1%	0.1%	4.4%	12.6%	3.4%	9.0%
Post Election	−2.2%	6.6%	2.2%	4.8%	11.1%	8.7%	6.7%
Midterm	2.0%	−3.4%	−5.2%	8.9%	1.7%	−8.1%	23.3%
Pre-Election	13.8%	8.0%	1.7%	5.1%	30.9%	9.8%	9.7%
Election	3.9%	0.8%	1.1%	−0.8%	5.8%	2.2%	−2.4%

NOVEMBER

MONDAY
9

D 52.4
S 47.6
N 57.1

When a falling stock becomes a screaming buy because it cannot conceivably drop further, try to buy it 30 percent lower.
— Al Rizzo (1986)

TUESDAY
10

D 42.9
S 38.1
N 42.9

Those who cast the votes decide nothing. Those who count the votes decide everything.
— Joseph Stalin (Ruler USSR 1929–1953, 1879–1953)

Veterans' Day (*Bond Market Closed*)

WEDNESDAY
11

D 47.6
S 47.6
N 52.4

People somehow think you must buy at the bottom and sell at the top. That's nonsense. The idea is to buy when the probability is greatest that the market is going to advance.
— Martin Zweig (Fund manager, *Winning on Wall Street*, 1943–2013)

THURSDAY
12

D 61.9
S 52.4
N 61.9

There is no great mystery to satisfying your customers. Build them a quality product and treat them with respect. It's that simple.
— Lee Iacocca (American industrialist, Former Chrysler CEO, b. 1924)

FRIDAY
13

D 66.7
S 61.9
N 57.1

The heights by great men reached and kept, were not attained by sudden flight, but they, while their companions slept, were toiling upward in the night.
— Henry Wadsworth Longfellow (American poet, 1807–1882)

SATURDAY
14

SUNDAY
15

TRADING THE THANKSGIVING MARKET

For 35 years, the "holiday spirit" gave the Wednesday before Thanksgiving and the Friday after a great track record, except for two occasions. Publishing it in the 1987 *Almanac* was the "kiss of death." Wednesday, Friday, and Monday were all crushed, down 6.6% over the three days in 1987. Since 1988, Wednesday–Friday gained 16 of 26 times, with a total Dow point-gain of 658.98 versus Monday's total Dow point-loss of 739.02, down 11 of 16 since 1998. The best strategy appears to be coming into the week long and exiting into strength Friday. Greece's debt crisis cancelled Thanksgiving on Wall Street in 2011.

DOW JONES INDUSTRIALS BEFORE AND AFTER THANKSGIVING

	Tuesday Before	Wednesday Before		Friday After	Total Gain Dow Points	Dow Close	Next Monday
1952	-0.18	1.54		1.22	2.76	283.66	0.04
1953	1.71	0.65		2.45	3.10	280.23	1.14
1954	3.27	1.89		3.16	5.05	387.79	0.72
1955	4.61	0.71		0.26	0.97	482.88	-1.92
1956	-4.49	-2.16		4.65	2.49	472.56	-2.27
1957	-9.04	10.69		3.84	14.53	449.87	-2.96
1958	-4.37	8.63		8.31	16.94	557.46	2.61
1959	2.94	1.41		1.42	2.83	652.52	6.66
1960	-3.44	1.37		4.00	5.37	606.47	-1.04
1961	-0.77	1.10		2.18	3.28	732.60	-0.61
1962	6.73	4.31		7.62	11.93	644.87	-2.81
1963	32.03	-2.52	T	9.52	7.00	750.52	1.39
1964	-1.68	-5.21		-0.28	-5.49	882.12	-6.69
1965	2.56	N/C	H	-0.78	-0.78	948.16	-1.23
1966	-3.18	1.84		6.52	8.36	803.34	-2.18
1967	13.17	3.07	A	3.58	6.65	877.60	4.51
1968	8.14	-3.17		8.76	5.59	985.08	-1.74
1969	-5.61	3.23	N	1.78	5.01	812.30	-7.26
1970	5.21	1.98		6.64	8.62	781.35	12.74
1971	-5.18	0.66	K	17.96	18.62	816.59	13.14
1972	8.21	7.29		4.67	11.96	1025.21	-7.45
1973	-17.76	10.08	S	-0.98	9.10	854.00	-29.05
1974	5.32	2.03		-0.63	1.40	618.66	-15.64
1975	9.76	3.15		2.12	5.27	860.67	-4.33
1976	-6.57	1.66	G	5.66	7.32	956.62	-6.57
1977	6.41	0.78		1.12	1.90	844.42	-4.85
1978	-1.56	2.95	I	3.12	6.07	810.12	3.72
1979	-6.05	-1.80		4.35	2.55	811.77	16.98
1980	3.93	7.00	V	3.66	10.66	993.34	-23.89
1981	18.45	7.90		7.80	15.70	885.94	3.04
1982	-9.01	9.01		7.36	16.37	1007.36	-4.51
1983	7.01	-0.20	I	1.83	1.63	1277.44	-7.62
1984	9.83	6.40		18.78	25.18	1220.30	-7.95
1985	0.12	18.92	N	-3.56	15.36	1472.13	-14.22
1986	6.05	4.64		-2.53	2.11	1914.23	-1.55
1987	40.45	-16.58	G	-36.47	-53.05	1910.48	-76.93
1988	11.73	14.58		-17.60	-3.02	2074.68	6.76
1989	7.25	17.49		18.77	36.26	2675.55	19.42
1990	-35.15	9.16		-12.13	-2.97	2527.23	5.94
1991	14.08	-16.10		-5.36	-21.46	2894.68	40.70
1992	25.66	17.56		15.94	33.50	3282.20	22.96
1993	3.92	13.41		-3.63	9.78	3683.95	-6.15
1994	-91.52	-3.36		33.64	30.28	3708.27	31.29
1995	40.46	18.06	D	7.23*	25.29	5048.84	22.04
1996	-19.38	-29.07		22.36*	-6.71	6521.70	N/C
1997	41.03	-14.17	A	28.35*	14.18	7823.13	189.98
1998	-73.12	13.13		18.80*	31.93	9333.08	-216.53
1999	-93.89	12.54	Y	-19.26*	-6.72	10988.91	-40.99
2000	31.85	-95.18		70.91*	-24.27	10470.23	75.84
2001	-75.08	-66.70		125.03*	58.33	9959.71	23.04
2002	-172.98	255.26		-35.59*	219.67	8896.09	-33.52
2003	16.15	15.63		2.89*	18.52	9782.46	116.59
2004	3.18	27.71		1.92*	29.63	10522.23	-46.33
2005	51.15	44.66		15.53*	60.19	10931.62	-40.90
2006	5.05	5.36		-46.78*	-41.42	12280.17	-158.46
2007	51.70	-211.10		181.84*	-29.26	12980.88	-237.44
2008	36.08	247.14		102.43*	349.57	8829.04	-679.95
2009	-17.24	30.69		-154.48*	-123.79	10309.92	34.92
2010	-142.21	150.91		-95.28*	55.63	11092.00	-39.51
2011	-53.59	-236.17		-25.77*	-261.94	11231.78	291.23
2012	-7.45	48.38		172.79*	221.17	13009.68	-42.31
2013	0.26	24.53		-10.92*	13.61	16086.41	-77.64

NOVEMBER

Monday Before November Expiration, Dow Down 9 of Last 15

MONDAY
D 61.9
S 52.4
N 47.6
16

The political problem of mankind is to combine three things: economic efficiency, social justice, and individual liberty.
— John Maynard Keynes (British economist, 1883–1946)

TUESDAY
D 47.6
S 52.4
N 47.6
17

The test of success is not what you do when you are on top. Success is how high you bounce when you hit bottom.
— General George S. Patton, Jr. (U.S. Army field commander WWII, 1885–1945)

Week Before Thanksgiving, Dow Up 16 of Last 21,
2003 –1.4%, 2004 –0.8%, 2008 –5.3%, 2011 –2.9%, 2012 –1.8%

WEDNESDAY
D 47.6
S 52.4
N 47.6
18

The most dangerous thing that takes place [in companies] is that success breeds arrogance, and arrogance seems to make people stop listening to their customers and to their employees. And that is the beginning of the end. The challenge is not to be a great company; the challenge is to remain a great company.
— George Fisher (Former CEO Eastman Kodak, Motorola, b. 1940)

THURSDAY
D 47.6
S 47.6
N 52.4
19

We prefer to cut back exposure on what's going against us and add exposure where it's more favorable to our portfolio. This way, we're always attempting to tilt the odds in our favor. This is the exact opposite of a long investor that would average down. Averaging down is a very dangerous practice.
— John Del Vecchio & Brad Lamensdorf (Portfolio managers Ranger Equity Bear ETF, 5/10/12 Almanac Investor)

November Expiration Day, Dow Up 10 of Last 12
Dow Surged in 2008, Up 494 Points (6.5%)

FRIDAY
D 57.1
S 47.6
N 57.1
20

I hate to be wrong. That has aborted many a tempting error, but not all of them. But I hate much more to stay wrong.
— Paul A. Samuelson (American economist, 12/23/03 University of Kansas interview, 1915–2009)

SATURDAY
21

SUNDAY
22

MOST OF THE SO-CALLED "JANUARY EFFECT" TAKES PLACE IN THE LAST HALF OF DECEMBER

Over the years we reported annually on the fascinating January Effect, showing that small-cap stocks handily outperformed large-cap stocks during January 40 out of 43 years between 1953 and 1995. Readers saw that "Cats and Dogs" on average quadrupled the returns of blue chips in this period. Then, the January Effect disappeared over the next four years.

Looking at the graph on page 110, comparing the Russell 1000 index of large-capitalization stocks to the Russell 2000 smaller-capitalization stocks, shows small-cap stocks beginning to outperform the blue chips in mid-December. Narrowing the comparison down to half-month segments was an inspiration and proved to be quite revealing, as you can see in the table below.

27-YEAR AVERAGE RATES OF RETURN (DEC 1987 – FEB 2014)

From mid-Dec*	Russell 1000 Change	Annualized	Russell 2000 Change	Annualized
12/15–12/31	1.8%	50.5%	3.4%	115.1%
12/15–01/15	2.3	29.8	4.1	58.4
12/15–01/31	2.4	21.3	4.2	39.7
12/15–02/15	3.4	22.2	5.8	40.3
12/15–02/28	2.7	14.4	5.6	31.6
end-Dec*				
12/31–01/15	0.5	11.0	0.6	13.4
12/31–01/31	0.6	7.4	0.8	10.0
12/31–02/15	1.5	12.4	2.3	19.6
12/31–02/28	0.9	5.8	2.1	14.0

35-YEAR AVERAGE RATES OF RETURN (DEC 1979 – FEB 2014)

From mid-Dec*	Russell 1000 Change	Annualized	Russell 2000 Change	Annualized
12/15–12/31	1.7%	47.1%	3.0%	96.8%
12/15–01/15	2.5	32.7	4.4	63.8
12/15–01/31	2.7	24.2	4.7	45.3
12/15–02/15	3.5	22.9	6.2	43.5
12/15–02/28	3.1	16.3	6.1	34.0
end-Dec*				
12/31–01/15	0.8	18.2	1.3	31.2
12/31–01/31	1.1	14.0	1.6	21.0
12/31–02/15	1.9	16.0	3.1	27.2
12/31–02/28	1.4	9.2	3.0	20.5

* Mid-month dates are the 11th trading day of the month, month end dates are monthly closes

Small-cap strength in the last half of December became even more magnified after the 1987 market crash. Note the dramatic shift in gains in the last half of December during the 27-year period starting in 1987, versus the 35 years from 1979 to 2014. With all the beaten-down small stocks being dumped for tax loss purposes, it generally pays to get a head start on the January Effect in mid-December. You don't have to wait until December either; the small-cap sector often begins to turn around toward the end of October and November.

NOVEMBER

Trading Thanksgiving Market: Long into Weakness Prior,
Exit into Strength After (Page 104)

MONDAY

D 61.9
S 57.1
N 61.9

23

Of a stock's move, 31% can be attributed to the general stock market, 12% to the industry influence, 37% to the influence of other groupings, and the remaining 20% is peculiar to the one stock.
— Benjamin F. King (*Market and Industry Factors in Stock Price Behavior, Journal of Business*, January 1966)

TUESDAY

D 66.7
S 61.9
N 57.1

24

In this age of instant information, investors can experience both fear and greed at the exact same moment.
— Sam Stovall (Chief Investment Strategist Standard & Poor's, October 2003)

WEDNESDAY

D 61.9
S 66.7
N 61.9

25

If you don't know who you are, the stock market is an expensive place to find out.
— George Goodman (*Institutional Investor, New York*, "Adam Smith," *The Money Game*, b. 1930)

Thanksgiving (*Market Closed*)

THURSDAY

26

Self-discipline is a form of freedom. Freedom from laziness and lethargy, freedom from expectations and demands of others, freedom from weakness and fear—and doubt.
— Harvey A. Dorfman (Sports psychologist, *The Mental ABC's of Pitching*, b. 1935)

(Shortened Trading Day)
Last Trading Day of November, S&P Up 6 of Last 8

FRIDAY

D 57.1
S 71.4
N 66.7

27

In my experience, selling a put is much safer than buying a stock.
— Kyle Rosen (Rosen Capital Advisors, *Barron's* 8/23/04, b. 1970)

SATURDAY

28

December Almanac Investor Seasonalities: See Pages 94, 96 and 98

SUNDAY

29

DECEMBER ALMANAC

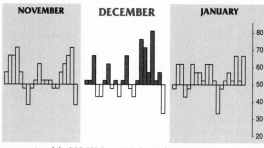

DECEMBER						
S	M	T	W	T	F	S
		1	2	3	4	5
6	7	8	9	10	11	12
13	14	15	16	17	18	19
20	21	22	23	24	25	26
27	28	29	30	31		

JANUARY						
S	M	T	W	T	F	S
					1	2
3	4	5	6	7	8	9
10	11	12	13	14	15	16
17	18	19	20	21	22	23
24	25	26	27	28	29	30
31						

Market Probability Chart above is a graphic representation of the S&P 500 Recent Market Probability Calendar on page 124.

◆ #1 S&P (+1.7%) and #2 Dow (+1.7%) month since 1950 (page 50), #2 NASDAQ 2.0% since 1971 ◆ 2002 worst December since 1931, down over 6% Dow and S&P, –9.7% on NASDAQ (pages 152, 155, & 157) ◆ "Free lunch" served on Wall Street before Christmas (page 112) ◆ Small caps start to outperform larger caps near middle of month (pages 106 & 110) ◆ "Santa Claus Rally" visible in graph above and on page 114 ◆ In 1998 was part of best fourth quarter since 1928 (page 167) ◆ Fourth quarter expiration week most bullish triple witching week, Dow up 18 of last 23 (page 78) ◆ Pre-presidential election years Decembers rankings: #3 Dow and S&P, #2 NASDAQ.

December Vital Statistics

	DJIA	S&P 500	NASDAQ	Russell 1K	Russell 2K
Rank	2	1	2	1	1
Up	46	49	26	28	28
Down	18	15	17	7	7
Average % Change	1.7%	1.7%	2.0%	1.7%	2.8%
Pre-Election Year	3.0%	3.2%	4.9%	3.5%	4.0%
Best & Worst December					
	% Change	% Change	% Change	% Change	% Change
Best	1991 9.5	1991 11.2	1999 22.0	1991 11.2	1999 11.2
Worst	2002 –6.2	2002 –6.0	2002 –9.7	2002 –5.8	2002 –5.7
Best & Worst December Weeks					
Best	12/2/11 7.0	12/2/11 7.4	12/8/00 10.3	12/2/11 7.4	12/2/11 10.3
Worst	12/4/87 –7.5	12/6/74 –7.1	12/15/00 –9.1	12/4/87 –7.0	12/12/80 –6.5
Best & Worst December Days					
Best	12/16/08 4.2	12/16/08 5.1	12/5/00 10.5	12/16/08 5.2	12/16/08 6.7
Worst	12/1/08 –7.7	12/1/08 –8.9	12/1/08 –9.0	12/1/08 –9.1	12/1/08 –11.9
First Trading Day of Expiration Week: 1980–2013					
Record (#Up–#Down)	20–14	21–13	15–19	21–13	16–18
Current streak	U2	U2	U2	U2	U2
Avg % Change	0.19	0.15	–0.03	0.12	–0.13
Options Expiration Day: 1980–2013					
Record (#Up–#Down)	22–12	25–9	24–10	25–9	22–12
Current streak	U1	U1	U1	U1	U1
Avg % Change	0.33	0.39	0.37	0.37	0.46
Options Expiration Week: 1980–2013					
Record (#Up–#Down)	26–8	25–9	20–14	24–10	18–16
Current streak	U2	U2	U2	U2	U2
Avg % Change	0.72	0.73	0.24	0.67	0.61
Week After Options Expiration: 1980–2013					
Record (#Up–#Down)	23–10	20–14	21–13	20–14	23–11
Current streak	U1	U1	U1	U1	U1
Avg % Change	0.73	0.47	0.64	0.50	0.80
First Trading Day Performance					
% of Time Up	46.9	50.0	60.5	51.4	51.4
Avg % Change	–0.06	–0.04	0.15	–0.05	–0.11
Last Trading Day Performance					
% of Time Up	54.7	62.5	74.4	54.3	71.4
Avg % Change	0.09	0.13	0.38	–0.03	0.49

Dow & S&P 1950–April 2014, NASDAQ 1971–April 2014, Russell 1K & 2K 1979–April 2014.

If Santa Claus should fail to call,
Bears may come to Broad and Wall.

MONDAY

D 52.4
S 38.1
N 47.6

30

If there is something you really want to do, make your plan and do it. Otherwise, you'll just regret it forever.
— Richard Rocco (PostNet franchisee, *Entrepreneur* magazine 12/2006, b. 1946)

First Trading Day in December, NASDAQ Up 19 of 27
Down 5 of Last 8

TUESDAY

D 47.6
S 52.4
N 61.9

1

Pullbacks near the 30-week moving average are often good times to take action.
— Michael L. Burke (*Investors Intelligence*)

WEDNESDAY

D 47.6
S 52.4
N 61.9

2

Never mind telling me what stocks to buy; tell me when to buy them.
— Humphrey B. Neill (Investor, analyst, author, *Neill Letters of Contrary Opinion*, 1895–1977)

THURSDAY

D 66.7
S 66.7
N 61.9

3

Amongst democratic nations, each generation is a new people.
— Alexis de Tocqueville (Author, *Democracy in America*, 1840, 1805–1859)

FRIDAY

D 57.1
S 42.9
N 52.4

4

What investors really get paid for is holding dogs. Small stocks tend to have higher average returns than big stocks, and value stocks tend to have higher average returns than growth stocks.
— Kenneth R. French (Economist, Dartmouth, NBER, b. 1954)

SATURDAY

5

SUNDAY

6

JANUARY EFFECT NOW STARTS IN MID-DECEMBER

Small-cap stocks tend to outperform big caps in January. Known as the "January Effect," the tendency is clearly revealed by the graph below. Thirty-six years of daily data for the Russell 2000 index of smaller companies are divided by the Russell 1000 index of largest companies, and then compressed into a single year to show an idealized yearly pattern. When the graph is descending, big blue chips are outperforming smaller companies; when the graph is rising, smaller companies are moving up faster than their larger brethren.

In a typical year, the smaller fry stay on the sidelines while the big boys are on the field. Then, around late November, small stocks begin to wake up, and in mid-December, they take off. Anticipated year-end dividends, payouts, and bonuses could be a factor. Other major moves are quite evident just before Labor Day—possibly because individual investors are back from vacations—and off the low points in late October. Small caps hold the lead through the beginning of May, though the bulk of the move is complete by early March.

RUSSELL 2000/RUSSELL 1000 ONE-YEAR SEASONAL PATTERN

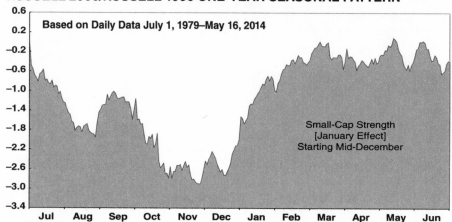

The bottom graph shows the actual ratio of the Russell 2000 divided by the Russell 1000 from 1979. Smaller companies had the upper hand for five years into 1983, as the last major bear trend wound to a close and the nascent bull market logged its first year. After falling behind for about eight years, they came back after the Persian Gulf War bottom in 1990, moving up until 1994, when big caps ruled the latter stages of the millennial bull. For six years, the picture was bleak for small fry, as the blue chips and tech stocks moved to stratospheric PE ratios. Small caps spiked in late 1999 and early 2000 and reached a peak in early 2006, as the four-year-old bull entered its final year. Note how the small-cap advantage has waned during major bull moves and intensified during weak market times.

RUSSELL 2000/RUSSELL 1000 (1979–APRIL 2014)

DECEMBER

Chanukah

MONDAY

D 47.6
S 42.9
N 33.3

7

People with a sense of fulfillment think the world is good, while the frustrated blame the world for their failure.
— Eric Hoffer (*The True Believer*, 1951, 1902–1983)

TUESDAY

D 52.4
S 52.4
N 57.1

8

It is tact that is golden, not silence.
— Samuel Butler (English writer, 1600–1680)

Small Cap Strength Starts in Mid-December (Page 106)

WEDNESDAY

D 57.1
S 61.9
N 57.1

9

Resentment is like taking poison and waiting for the other person to die.
— Malachy McCourt (*A Monk Swimming: A Memoir*, b. 1931)

THURSDAY

D 47.6
S 47.6
N 42.9

10

A government which robs Peter to pay Paul can always depend on the support of Paul.
— George Bernard Shaw (Irish dramatist, 1856–1950)

FRIDAY

D 47.6
S 52.4
N 42.9

11

The authority of a thousand is not worth the humble reasoning of a single individual.
— Galileo Galilei (Italian physicist and astronomer, 1564–1642)

SATURDAY

12

SUNDAY

13

WALL STREET'S ONLY "FREE LUNCH" SERVED BEFORE CHRISTMAS

Investors tend to get rid of their losers near year-end for tax purposes, often hammering these stocks down to bargain levels. Over the years, the *Almanac* has shown that NYSE stocks selling at their lows on December 15 will usually outperform the market by February 15 in the following year. Preferred stocks, closed-end funds, splits, and new issues are eliminated. When there are a huge number of new lows, stocks down the most are selected, even though there are usually good reasons why some stocks have been battered.

BARGAIN STOCKS VS. THE MARKET*

Short Span* Late Dec–Jan/Feb	New Lows Late Dec	% Change Jan/Feb	% Change NYSE Composite	Bargain Stocks Advantage
1974–75	112	48.9%	22.1%	26.8%
1975–76	21	34.9	14.9	20.0
1976–77	2	1.3	−3.3	4.6
1977–78	15	2.8	−4.5	7.3
1978–79	43	11.8	3.9	7.9
1979–80	5	9.3	6.1	3.2
1980–81	14	7.1	−2.0	9.1
1981–82	21	−2.6	−7.4	4.8
1982–83	4	33.0	9.7	23.3
1983–84	13	−3.2	−3.8	0.6
1984–85	32	19.0	12.1	6.9
1985–86	4	−22.5	3.9	−26.4
1986–87	22	9.3	12.5	−3.2
1987–88	23	13.2	6.8	6.4
1988–89	14	30.0	6.4	23.6
1989–90	25	−3.1	−4.8	1.7
1990–91	18	18.8	12.6	6.2
1991–92	23	51.1	7.7	43.4
1992–93	9	8.7	0.6	8.1
1993–94	10	−1.4	2.0	−3.4
1994–95	25	14.6	5.7	8.9
1995–96	5	−11.3	4.5	−15.8
1996–97	16	13.9	11.2	2.7
1997–98	29	9.9	5.7	4.2
1998–99	40	−2.8	4.3	−7.1
1999–00	26	8.9	−5.4	14.3
2000–01	51	44.4	0.1	44.3
2001–02	12	31.4	−2.3	33.7
2002–03	33	28.7	3.9	24.8
2003–04	15	16.7	2.3	14.4
2004–05	36	6.8	−2.8	9.6
2005–06	71	12.0	2.6	9.4
2006–07	43	5.1	−0.5	5.6
2007–08	71	−3.2	−9.4	6.2
2008–09	88	11.4	−2.4	13.8
2009–10	25	1.8	−3.0	4.8
2010–11	20	8.3	3.4	4.9
2011–12	65	18.1	6.1	12.0
2012–13	17	20.9	3.4	17.5
2013–14	18	25.7	1.7	24.0
40-Year Totals		**527.7%**	**124.6%**	**403.1%**
Average		**13.2%**	**3.1%**	**10.1%**

* Dec 15–Feb 15 (1974–1999), Dec 1999–2014 based on actual newsletter advice

In response to changing market conditions, we tweaked the strategy the last 15 years, adding selections from NASDAQ and AMEX, and selling in mid-January some years. We e-mail the list of stocks to our *Almanac Investor* newsletter subscribers. Visit *www.stocktradersalmanac.com,* or see the insert for additional details and a special offer for new subscribers.

We have come to the conclusion that the most prudent course of action is to compile our list from the stocks making new lows on Triple-Witching Friday before Christmas, capitalizing on the Santa Claus Rally (page 114). This also gives us the weekend to evaluate the issues in greater depth and weed out any glaringly problematic stocks. Subscribers will receive the list of stocks selected from the new lows made on December 19, 2014 and December 18, 2015 via e-mail.

This "Free Lunch" strategy is an extremely short-term strategy reserved for the nimblest traders. It has performed better after market corrections and when there are more new lows to choose from. The object is to buy bargain stocks near their 52-week lows and sell any quick, generous gains, as these issues can often be real dogs.

DECEMBER

Monday Before December Triple Witching S&P Up 10 of Last 14

MONDAY
D 52.4
S 42.9
N 42.9
14

There is a perfect inverse correlation between inflation rates and price/earnings ratios... When inflation has been very high... P/E has been [low].
— Liz Ann Sonders (Chief Investment Strategist Charles Schwab, June 2006, b. 1965)

TUESDAY
D 52.4
S 52.4
N 52.4
15

Whenever a well-known bearish analyst is interviewed [Cover story] in the financial press, it usually coincides with an important near-term market bottom.
— Clif Droke (Clifdroke.com, 11/15/04, b. 1972)

December Triple Witching Week, S&P Up 24 of Last 30

WEDNESDAY
D 61.9
S 66.7
N 57.1
16

Lack of money is the root of all evil.
— George Bernard Shaw (Irish dramatist, 1856–1950)

THURSDAY
D 42.9
S 47.6
N 38.1
17

You try to be greedy when others are fearful, and fearful when others are greedy.
— Warren Buffett (CEO Berkshire Hathaway, investor and philanthropist, b. 1930)

December Triple Witching, S&P Up 23 of 32, Average Gain 0.4%

FRIDAY
D 47.6
S 42.9
N 52.4
18

Inflation is the modern way that governments default on their debt.
— Mike Epstein (MTA, MIT/Sloan Lab for Financial Engineering)

SATURDAY
19

SUNDAY
20

IF SANTA CLAUS SHOULD FAIL TO CALL, BEARS MAY COME TO BROAD AND WALL

Santa Claus tends to come to Wall Street nearly every year, bringing a short, sweet, respectable rally within the last five days of the year and the first two in January. This has been good for an average 1.5% gain since 1969 (1.5% since 1950). Santa's failure to show tends to precede bear markets, or times stocks could be purchased later in the year at much lower prices. We discovered this phenomenon in 1972.

DAILY % CHANGE IN S&P 500 AT YEAR END

	Trading Days Before Year End						First Days in January			Rally % Change
	6	5	4	3	2	1	1	2	3	
1969	−0.4	1.1	0.8	−0.7	0.4	0.5	1.0	0.5	−0.7	3.6
1970	0.1	0.6	0.5	1.1	0.2	−0.1	−1.1	0.7	0.6	1.9
1971	−0.4	0.2	1.0	0.3	−0.4	0.3	−0.4	0.4	1.0	1.3
1972	−0.3	−0.7	0.6	0.4	0.5	1.0	0.9	0.4	−0.1	3.1
1973	−1.1	−0.7	3.1	2.1	−0.2	0.01	0.1	2.2	−0.9	6.7
1974	−1.4	1.4	0.8	−0.4	0.03	2.1	2.4	0.7	0.5	7.2
1975	0.7	0.8	0.9	−0.1	−0.4	0.5	0.8	1.8	1.0	4.3
1976	0.1	1.2	0.7	−0.4	0.5	0.5	−0.4	−1.2	−0.9	0.8
1977	0.8	0.9	N/C	0.1	0.2	0.2	−1.3	−0.3	−0.8	−0.3
1978	0.03	1.7	1.3	−0.9	−0.4	−0.2	0.6	1.1	0.8	3.3
1979	−0.6	0.1	0.1	0.2	−0.1	0.1	−2.0	−0.5	1.2	−2.2
1980	−0.4	0.4	0.5	−1.1	0.2	0.3	0.4	1.2	0.1	2.0
1981	−0.5	0.2	−0.2	−0.5	0.5	0.2	0.2	−2.2	−0.7	−1.8
1982	0.6	1.8	−1.0	0.3	−0.7	0.2	−1.6	2.2	0.4	1.2
1983	−0.2	−0.03	0.9	0.3	−0.2	0.05	−0.5	1.7	1.2	2.1
1984	−0.5	0.8	−0.2	−0.4	0.3	0.6	−1.1	−0.5	−0.5	−0.6
1985	−1.1	−0.7	0.2	0.9	0.5	0.3	−0.8	0.6	−0.1	1.1
1986	−1.0	0.2	0.1	−0.9	−0.5	−0.5	1.8	2.3	0.2	2.4
1987	1.3	−0.5	−2.6	−0.4	1.3	−0.3	3.6	1.1	0.1	2.2
1988	−0.2	0.3	−0.4	0.1	0.8	−0.6	−0.9	1.5	0.2	0.9
1989	0.6	0.8	−0.2	0.6	0.5	0.8	1.8	−0.3	−0.9	4.1
1990	0.5	−0.6	0.3	−0.8	0.1	0.5	−1.1	−1.4	−0.3	−3.0
1991	2.5	0.6	1.4	0.4	2.1	0.5	0.04	0.5	−0.3	5.7
1992	−0.3	0.2	−0.1	−0.3	0.2	−0.7	−0.1	−0.2	0.04	−1.1
1993	0.01	0.7	0.1	−0.1	−0.4	−0.5	−0.2	0.3	0.1	−0.1
1994	0.01	0.2	0.4	−0.3	0.1	−0.4	−0.03	0.3	−0.1	0.2
1995	0.8	0.2	0.4	0.04	−0.1	0.3	0.8	0.1	−0.6	1.8
1996	−0.3	0.5	0.6	0.1	−0.4	−1.7	−0.5	1.5	−0.1	0.1
1997	−1.5	−0.7	0.4	1.8	1.8	−0.04	0.5	0.2	−1.1	4.0
1998	2.1	−0.2	−0.1	1.3	−0.8	−0.2	−0.1	1.4	2.2	1.3
1999	1.6	−0.1	0.04	0.4	0.1	0.3	−1.0	−3.8	0.2	−4.0
2000	0.8	2.4	0.7	1.0	0.4	−1.0	−2.8	5.0	−1.1	5.7
2001	0.4	−0.02	0.4	0.7	0.3	−1.1	0.6	0.9	0.6	1.8
2002	0.2	−0.5	−0.3	−1.6	0.5	0.05	3.3	−0.05	2.2	1.2
2003	0.3	−0.2	0.2	1.2	0.01	0.2	−0.3	1.2	0.1	2.4
2004	0.1	−0.4	0.7	−0.01	0.01	−0.1	−0.8	−1.2	−0.4	−1.8
2005	0.4	0.04	−1.0	0.1	−0.3	−0.5	1.6	0.4	0.002	0.4
2006	−0.4	−0.5	0.4	0.7	−0.1	−0.5	−0.1	0.1	−0.6	0.003
2007	1.7	0.8	0.1	−1.4	0.1	−0.7	−1.4	N/C	−2.5	−2.5
2008	−1.0	0.6	0.5	−0.4	2.4	1.4	3.2	−0.5	0.8	7.4
2009	0.2	0.5	0.1	−0.1	0.02	−1.0	1.6	0.3	0.05	1.4
2010	−0.2	0.1	0.1	0.1	−0.2	−0.02	1.1	−0.1	0.5	1.1
2011	0.8	0.9	0.01	−1.3	1.1	−0.4	1.6	0.02	0.3	1.9
2012	−0.9	−0.2	−0.5	−0.1	−1.1	1.7	2.5	−0.2	0.5	2.0
2013	0.5	0.3	0.5	−0.03	−0.02	0.4	−0.9	−0.03	−0.3	0.2
Avg	0.10	0.32	0.27	0.04	0.20	0.05	0.25	0.40	0.04	1.5

The couplet above was certainly on the mark in 1999, as the period suffered a horrendous 4.0% loss. On January 14, 2000, the Dow started its 33-month 37.8% slide to the October 2002 midterm election year bottom. NASDAQ cracked eight weeks later, falling 37.3% in 10 weeks, eventually dropping 77.9% by October 2002. Saddam Hussein cancelled Christmas by invading Kuwait in 1990. Energy prices and Middle East terror woes may have grounded Santa in 2004. In 2007, the third worst reading since 1950 was recorded, as sub-prime mortgages and their derivatives led to a full-blown financial crisis and the second worst bear market in history. In 2012, a last-minute tax deal was reached and Christmas was saved.

DECEMBER

The Only FREE LUNCH on Wall Street Is Served (Page 112)
Almanac Investors Emailed Alert Before the Open, Monday (See Insert)

MONDAY
D 57.1
S 52.4
N 57.1
21

Change is the law of life. And those who look only to the past or present are certain to miss the future.
— John F. Kennedy (35th U.S. President, 1917–1963)

TUESDAY
D 76.2
S 76.2
N 61.9
22

People's spending habits depend more on how wealthy they feel than with the actual amount of their current income.
— A.C. Pigou (English economist, The Theory of Unemployment, 1877–1959)

Watch for the Santa Claus Rally (Page 112)

WEDNESDAY
D 71.4
S 71.4
N 71.4
23

Small volume is usually accompanied by a fall in price; large volume by a rise in price.
— Charles C. Ying ("Stock Market Prices and Volumes of Sales," Econometrica, July 1966)

(Shortened Trading Day)
Last Trading Day Before Christmas, Dow Up 6 of Last 7 Years

THURSDAY
D 52.4
S 57.1
N 61.9
24

We are nowhere near a capitulation point because it's at that point where it's despair, not hope, that reigns supreme, and there was scant evidence of any despair at any of the meetings I gave.
— David Rosenberg (Economist, Merrill Lynch, Barron's 4/21/2008)

Christmas Day (*Market Closed*)

FRIDAY
25

Don't worry about people stealing your ideas. If the ideas are any good, you'll have to ram them down people's throats.
— Howard Aiken (U.S. computer scientist, 1900–1973)

SATURDAY
26

SUNDAY
27

YEAR'S TOP INVESTMENT BOOKS

Profitable Day and Swing Trading: Using Price/Volume Surges and Pattern Recognition to Catch Big Moves in the Stock Market, Harry Boxer, Wiley, $70.00, www.thetechtrader.com/. <u>2015 Best Investment Book of the Year. See page 76.</u>

Clash of the Financial Pundits: How the Media Influences Your Investment Decisions for Better or Worse, Joshua M. Brown and Jeff Macke, McGraw-Hill, $25.00. Two of our favorite financial media mavens team up to help save you from the vagaries of investing and trading on what you hear, see, and read on TV, radio, and in all forms of financial broadcasting and commentary. "The Reformed Broker" and Yahoo! Finance Commentator—two Wall Street vets—give you a front-row seat to the making of financial news and the skinny on all the talking heads and how to cut through the baloney and zero in on the usable information in the media, including insightful interviews with the most sagacious and candid commentators in finance.

Trading Options: Using Technical Analysis to Design Winning Trades, Greg Harmon, Wiley, $75.00. We recently got to know Greg at Traders Expo New York and he impressed us so much that we sought out his new book. Harmon meticulously and comprehensively turns the dark arts of technical analysis and options trading into second nature. In this easy read, Harmon takes you on an easy ride, simplifying major trend recognition, sector analysis, high-level technical analysis, and effective options trading.

Panic, Prosperity, and Progress: Five Centuries of History and the Markets, Timothy Knight, Wiley, $60.00. How could we resist a book like this? As the title promises Tim Knight delivers. From the Tulipmania to the 2007–2009 Financial Crisis and Great Recession, Knight takes us on an insightful and whirlwind tour of the history of economic booms, busts, and panics that reads like a classic novel, packed with insightful tales and wisdom about previously unseen linkages.

Millennial Money: How Young Investors Can Build a Fortune, Hardcover, Patrick O'Shaughnessy, Palgrave Macmillan, $25.00. Portfolio manager and principal at O'Shaughnessy Asset Management, classically trained, a CFA, and mentored by his illustrious father, Jim, O'Shaughnessy exposes the most common mistakes that hurt long-term returns and why investments in hot stocks or industries yield underwhelming results. The book introduces a strategy that can help us overcome our shortcomings as investors.

Money: How the Destruction of the Dollar Threatens the Global Economy—and What We Can Do About It, Steve Forbes, Elizabeth Ames, McGraw-Hill, $28.00. The legend lives! Forbes understands money, economics, and politics—a rare combination. Once again, his iconic thinking provides us with a roadmap to a more stable economic future. Policymakers read carefully.

The Dao of Capital: Austrian Investing in a Distorted World, Mark Spitznagel, Wiley, $29.95. With a foreword by Ron Paul and endorsements from a who's-who of finance and riches, this book does not disappoint. Trader and hedge fund manager extraordinaire Mark Spitznagel takes you on a whirlwind, around-the-world tour from the trading pits of Chicago to 19th-century Austria and shows us the harmony of the markets. Plus, he is donating all personal book profits to charity.

Visual Guide to Elliott Wave Trading, Wayne Gorman, Jeffrey Kennedy, Bloomberg Press, $60.00. From the Elliot Wave pros, with a foreword from the master, Robert R. Prechter Jr. We had the pleasure of reading this book at the Wiley bookstore at the Orlando MoneyShow. This is a must-have for all wavers. Gorman is head of Elliot Wave International's Education Resources and we've had the pleasure of learning from Kennedy directly, EWI's chief commodity analyst. A picture is worth 1,000 words and this visual guide is worth a lot more.

Short Sellers: How Wall Street's Most Reviled Traders Beat the Odds, Exploit Fraud and Rack up Billions, Richard Teitelbaum, Bloomberg Press, $45.00. Come on over to the dark side. Bloomberg journalist profiles more than a dozen short sellers to reveal how they employ the tactics, strategies, and various styles to zero in on their target, get the needed financing, and see their investment through to its ultimate conclusion. Learn how traders profit from financial failure and ruin with tales from the short-sellers crypt.

The 17.6 Year Stock Market Cycle: Connecting the Panics of 1929, 1987, 2000 and 2007, Kerry Balenthiran, Harriman House, $32.99. This British-chartered accountant with a math and engineering background has a knack for grasping the cyclical nature of stock market booms and busts. Balenthiran studied stock market data going back 100 years and discovered a regular 17.6-year stock market cycle consisting of increments of 2.2 years. He has also extrapolated the cycle forward to provide investors with a market roadmap stretching out to 2053.

DECEMBER/JANUARY 2016

MONDAY
D 81.0
S 81.0
N 71.4
28

We go to the movies to be entertained, not see rape, ransacking, pillage and looting. We can get all that in the stock market.
— Kennedy Gammage (*The Richland Report*, 1926–2006)

TUESDAY
D 52.4
S 52.4
N 47.6
29

It was never my thinking that made the big money for me. It was always my sitting. Got that? My sitting tight!
— Jesse Livermore (Early 20th-century stock trader & speculator, *How to Trade in Stocks*, 1877–1940)

WEDNESDAY
D 42.9
S 57.1
N 47.6
30

Short-term volatility is greatest at turning points and diminishes as a trend becomes established.
— George Soros (Financier, philanthropist, political activist, author, and philosopher, b. 1930)

Last Trading Day of the Year, NASDAQ Down 11 of last 14
NASDAQ Was Up 29 Years in a Row 1971–1999

THURSDAY
D 42.9
S 33.3
N 47.6
31

What the superior man seeks, is in himself. What the inferior man seeks, is in others.
— Confucius (Chinese philosopher, 551–478 B.C.)

New Years Day (*Market Closed*)

FRIDAY
1

Brilliant men are often strikingly ineffectual; they fail to realize that the brilliant insight is not by itself achievement. They never have learned that insights become effectiveness only through hard systematic work.
— Peter Drucker (Austrian-born pioneer management theorist, 1909–2005)

SATURDAY
2

January Almanac Investor Seasonalities: See Pages 94, 96 and 98

SUNDAY
3

2016 STRATEGY CALENDAR

(Option expiration dates circled)

	MONDAY	TUESDAY	WEDNESDAY	THURSDAY	FRIDAY	SATURDAY	SUNDAY
JANUARY	28	29	30	31	1 JANUARY New Year's Day	2	3
	4	5	6	7	8	9	10
	11	12	13	14	(15)	16	17
	18 Martin Luther King Day	19	20	21	22	23	24
	25	26	27	28	29	30	31
FEBRUARY	1 FEBRUARY	2	3	4	5	6	7
	8	9	10 Ash Wednesday	11	12	13	14 ♥
	15 President's Day	16	17	18	(19)	20	21
	22	23	24	25	26	27	28
MARCH	29	1 MARCH	2	3	4	5	6
	7	8	9	10	11	12	13
	14	15	16	17 ♣ St. Patrick's Day	(18)	19	20
	21	22	23	24	25 Good Friday	26	27 Easter
	28	29	30	31	1 APRIL	2	3
APRIL	4	5	6	7	8	9	10
	11	12	13	14	(15)	16	17
	18	19	20	21	22	23 Passover	24
	25	26	27	28	29	30	1 MAY
MAY	2	3	4	5	6	7	8 Mother's Day
	9	10	11	12	13	14	15
	16	17	18	19	(20)	21	22
	23	24	25	26	27	28	29
JUNE	30 Memorial Day	31	1 JUNE	2	3	4	5
	6	7	8	9	10	11	12
	13	14	15	16	(17)	18	19 Father's Day
	20	21	22	23	24	25	26

Market closed on shaded weekdays; closes early when half-shaded.

2016 STRATEGY CALENDAR

(Option expiration dates circled)

MONDAY	TUESDAY	WEDNESDAY	THURSDAY	FRIDAY	SATURDAY	SUNDAY	
27	28	29	30	1 JULY	2	3	JULY
4 Independence Day	5	6	7	8	9	10	
11	12	13	14	(15)	16	17	
18	19	20	21	22	23	24	
25	26	27	28	29	30	31	
1 AUGUST	2	3	4	5	6	7	AUGUST
8	9	10	11	(12)	13	14	
15	16	17	18	19	20	21	
22	23	24	25	26	27	28	
29	30	31	1 SEPTEMBER	2	3	4	SEPTEMBER
5 Labor Day	6	7	8	9	10	11	
12	13	14	15	(16)	17	18	
19	20	21	22	23	24	25	
26	27	28	29	30	1 OCTOBER	2	OCTOBER
3 Rosh Hashanah	4	5	6	7	8	9	
10 Columbus Day	11	12 Yom Kippur	13	14	15	16	
17	18	19	20	(21)	22	23	
24	25	26	27	28	29	30	
31	1 NOVEMBER	2	3	4	5	6	NOVEMBER
7	8 Election Day	9	10	11 Veterans' Day	12	13	
14	15	16	17	(18)	19	20	
21	22	23	24 Thanksgiving Day	25	26	27	
28	29	30	1 DECEMBER	2	3	4	DECEMBER
5	6	7	8	9	10	11	
12	13	14	15	(16)	17	18	
19	20	21	22	23	24	25 Christmas Chanukah	
26	27	28	29	30	31	1 JANUARY New Year's Day	

DIRECTORY OF TRADING PATTERNS AND DATABANK

CONTENTS

121   Dow Jones Industrials Market Probability Calendar 2015
122   Recent Dow Jones Industrials Market Probability Calendar 2015
123   S&P 500 Market Probability Calendar 2015
124   Recent S&P 500 Market Probability Calendar 2015
125   NASDAQ Market Probability Calendar 2015
126   Recent NASDAQ Market Probability Calendar 2015
127   Russell 1000 Index Market Probability Calendar 2015
128   Russell 2000 Index Market Probability Calendar 2015
129   Decennial Cycle: A Market Phenomenon
130   Presidential Election/Stock Market Cycle: The 181-Year Saga Continues
131   Dow Jones Industrials Bull and Bear Markets Since 1900
132   Standard & Poor's 500 Bull and Bear Markets Since 1929/NASDAQ Composite Since 1971
133   Dow Jones Industrials 10-Year Daily Point Changes: January and February
134   Dow Jones Industrials 10-Year Daily Point Changes: March and April
135   Dow Jones Industrials 10-Year Daily Point Changes: May and June
136   Dow Jones Industrials 10-Year Daily Point Changes: July and August
137   Dow Jones Industrials 10-Year Daily Point Changes: September and October
138   Dow Jones Industrials 10-Year Daily Point Changes: November and December
139   A Typical Day in the Market
140   Through the Week on a Half-Hourly Basis
141   Tuesday Most Profitable Day of Week
142   NASDAQ Strongest Last 3 Days of Week
143   S&P Daily Performance Each Year Since 1952
144   NASDAQ Daily Performance Each Year Since 1971
145   Monthly Cash Inflows into S&P Stocks
146   Monthly Cash Inflows into NASDAQ Stocks
147   November, December, and January: Year's Best Three-Month Span
148   November Through June: NASDAQ's Eight-Month Run
149   Dow Jones Industrials Annual Highs, Lows, and Closes Since 1901
150   S&P 500 Annual Highs, Lows, and Closes Since 1930
151   NASDAQ, Russell 1000 and 2000 Annual Highs, Lows, and Closes Since 1971
152   Dow Jones Industrials Monthly Percent Changes Since 1950
153   Dow Jones Industrials Monthly Point Changes Since 1950
154   Dow Jones Industrials Monthly Closing Prices Since 1950
155   Standard & Poor's 500 Monthly Percent Changes Since 1950
156   Standard & Poor's 500 Monthly Closing Prices Since 1950
157   NASDAQ Composite Monthly Percent Changes Since 1971
158   NASDAQ Composite Monthly Closing Prices Since 1971
159   Russell 1000 Monthly Percent Changes and Closing Prices Since 1979
160   Russell 2000 Monthly Percent Changes and Closing Prices Since 1979
161   10 Best Days by Percent and Point
162   10 Worst Days by Percent and Point
163   10 Best Weeks by Percent and Point
164   10 Worst Weeks by Percent and Point
165   10 Best Months by Percent and Point
166   10 Worst Months by Percent and Point
167   10 Best Quarters by Percent and Point
168   10 Worst Quarters by Percent and Point
169   10 Best Years by Percent and Point
170   10 Worst Years by Percent and Point
171   Dow Jones Industrials One-Year Seasonal Pattern Charts Since 1901
172   S&P 500 One-Year Seasonal Pattern Charts Since 1930
173   NASDAQ, Russell 1000 & 2000 One-Year Seasonal Pattern Charts Since 1971

DOW JONES INDUSTRIALS MARKET PROBABILITY CALENDAR 2015

THE % CHANCE OF THE MARKET RISING ON ANY TRADING DAY OF THE YEAR*

(Based on the number of times the DJIA rose on a particular trading day during January 1953-December 2013)

Date	Jan	Feb	Mar	Apr	May	Jun	Jul	Aug	Sep	Oct	Nov	Dec
1	H	S	S	60.7	57.4	55.7	63.9	S	59.0	49.2	S	44.3
2	59.0	60.7	65.6	59.0	S	52.5	59.0	S	59.0	57.4	62.3	52.5
3	S	54.1	63.9	H	S	50.8	H	45.9	59.0	S	52.5	63.9
4	S	39.3	59.0	S	65.6	57.4	S	45.9	45.9	S	67.2	57.4
5	72.1	54.1	49.2	S	49.2	52.5	S	49.2	S	50.8	59.0	S
6	49.2	47.5	47.5	52.5	47.5	S	60.7	50.8	S	62.3	45.9	S
7	54.1	S	S	59.0	44.3	S	57.4	54.1	H	45.9	S	47.5
8	45.9	S	S	52.5	52.5	44.3	63.9	S	49.2	50.8	S	45.9
9	49.2	42.6	55.7	57.4	S	36.1	55.7	S	45.9	44.3	59.0	54.1
10	S	45.9	60.7	62.3	S	55.7	49.2	45.9	57.4	S	52.5	55.7
11	S	60.7	55.7	S	49.2	60.7	S	45.9	59.0	S	59.0	44.3
12	47.5	45.9	55.7	S	52.5	59.0	S	49.2	S	39.3	47.5	S
13	50.8	47.5	54.1	63.9	44.3	S	41.0	45.9	S	54.1	49.2	S
14	57.4	S	S	55.7	54.1	S	63.9	62.3	47.5	60.7	S	52.5
15	57.4	S	S	70.5	54.1	50.8	49.2	S	54.1	52.5	S	47.5
16	59.0	H	59.0	63.9	S	47.5	45.9	S	55.7	52.5	57.4	57.4
17	S	54.1	60.7	55.7	S	50.8	52.5	55.7	41.0	S	50.8	47.5
18	S	41.0	59.0	S	42.6	44.3	S	50.8	49.2	S	49.2	55.7
19	H	49.2	52.5	S	52.5	49.2	S	47.5	S	42.6	49.2	S
20	39.3	50.8	39.3	55.7	44.3	S	52.5	54.1	S	60.7	65.6	S
21	37.7	S	S	54.1	32.8	S	41.0	49.2	44.3	47.5	S	55.7
22	41.0	S	S	50.8	50.8	45.9	47.5	S	42.6	42.6	S	59.0
23	47.5	37.7	50.8	52.5	S	42.6	49.2	S	39.3	49.2	57.4	50.8
24	S	44.3	39.3	52.5	S	36.1	45.9	54.1	50.8	S	63.9	60.7
25	S	59.0	49.2	S	H	49.2	S	47.5	54.1	S	60.7	H
26	57.4	47.5	44.3	S	44.3	47.5	S	44.3	S	27.9	H	S
27	57.4	50.8	55.7	59.0	45.9	S	60.7	59.0	S	52.5	54.1	S
28	52.5	S	S	55.7	55.7	S	52.5	42.6	52.5	55.7	S	70.5
29	57.4		S	50.8	59.0	54.1	45.9	S	49.2	60.7	S	47.5
30	59.0		42.6	50.8	S	52.5	60.7	S	37.7	52.5	52.5	57.4
31	S		42.6		S		50.8	60.7		S		55.7

*See new trends developing on pages 70, 92, 141–146

121

RECENT DOW JONES INDUSTRIALS MARKET PROBABILITY CALENDAR 2015

THE % CHANCE OF THE MARKET RISING ON ANY TRADING DAY OF THE YEAR*
(Based on the number of times the DJIA rose on a particular trading day during January 1993-December 2013**)

Date	Jan	Feb	Mar	Apr	May	Jun	Jul	Aug	Sep	Oct	Nov	Dec
1	H	S	S	76.2	71.4	66.7	76.2	S	57.1	57.1	S	47.6
2	71.4	76.2	57.1	66.7	S	52.4	38.1	S	61.9	47.6	57.1	47.6
3	S	42.9	47.6	H	S	47.6	H	42.9	57.1	S	57.1	66.7
4	S	47.6	61.9	S	66.7	57.1	S	57.1	38.1	S	66.7	57.1
5	66.7	52.4	42.9	S	33.3	57.1	S	47.6	S	47.6	71.4	S
6	52.4	57.1	66.7	47.6	33.3	S	52.4	47.6	S	71.4	57.1	S
7	47.6	S	S	66.7	38.1	S	61.9	57.1	H	38.1	S	47.6
8	38.1	S	S	42.9	66.7	47.6	66.7	S	66.7	38.1	S	52.4
9	57.1	42.9	52.4	47.6	S	38.1	47.6	S	57.1	52.4	52.4	57.1
10	S	52.4	66.7	52.4	S	47.6	57.1	47.6	61.9	S	42.9	47.6
11	S	57.1	66.7	S	57.1	61.9	S	42.9	66.7	S	47.6	47.6
12	52.4	61.9	52.4	S	71.4	71.4	S	52.4	S	38.1	61.9	S
13	57.1	42.9	66.7	66.7	42.9	S	61.9	28.6	S	57.1	66.7	S
14	52.4	S	S	57.1	57.1	S	61.9	66.7	57.1	81.0	S	52.4
15	61.9	S	S	66.7	61.9	57.1	52.4	S	52.4	52.4	S	52.4
16	57.1	H	61.9	66.7	S	57.1	52.4	S	61.9	57.1	61.9	61.9
17	S	66.7	52.4	57.1	S	57.1	57.1	47.6	38.1	S	47.6	42.9
18	S	52.4	66.7	S	42.9	42.9	S	61.9	52.4	S	47.6	47.6
19	H	33.3	61.9	S	57.1	38.1	S	66.7	S	42.9	47.6	S
20	33.3	52.4	38.1	52.4	47.6	S	66.7	42.9	S	66.7	57.1	S
21	33.3	S	S	66.7	33.3	S	28.6	47.6	42.9	42.9	S	57.1
22	38.1	S	S	61.9	52.4	38.1	42.9	S	38.1	47.6	S	76.2
23	38.1	57.1	47.6	57.1	S	33.3	47.6	S	28.6	47.6	61.9	71.4
24	S	33.3	42.9	42.9	S	38.1	52.4	61.9	42.9	S	66.7	52.4
25	S	42.9	61.9	S	H	47.6	S	47.6	57.1	S	61.9	H
26	61.9	47.6	23.8	S	52.4	57.1	S	38.1	S	38.1	H	S
27	61.9	42.9	52.4	61.9	47.6	S	71.4	66.7	S	52.4	57.1	S
28	61.9	S	S	57.1	66.7	S	42.9	33.3	57.1	66.7	S	81.0
29	47.6		S	71.4	47.6	47.6	38.1	S	61.9	66.7	S	52.4
30	61.9		52.4	42.9	S	33.3	52.4	S	28.6	52.4	52.4	42.9
31	S		38.1		S		38.1	52.4		S		42.9

* See new trends developing on pages 70, 92, 141–146 ** Based on most recent 21-year period

S&P 500 MARKET PROBABILITY CALENDAR 2015

THE % CHANCE OF THE MARKET RISING ON ANY TRADING DAY OF THE YEAR*
(Based on the number of times the S&P 500 rose on a particular trading day during January 1953-December 2013)

Date	Jan	Feb	Mar	Apr	May	Jun	Jul	Aug	Sep	Oct	Nov	Dec
1	H	S	S	63.9	57.4	54.1	70.5	S	62.3	49.2	S	47.5
2	49.2	62.3	62.3	59.0	S	62.3	55.7	S	54.1	65.6	62.3	52.5
3	S	57.4	59.0	H	S	50.8	H	49.2	59.0	S	57.4	62.3
4	S	47.5	62.3	S	68.9	55.7	S	44.3	47.5	S	68.9	57.4
5	70.5	49.2	47.5	S	55.7	45.9	S	49.2	S	52.5	55.7	S
6	54.1	50.8	49.2	54.1	44.3	S	55.7	50.8	S	62.3	47.5	S
7	49.2	S	S	55.7	42.6	S	60.7	54.1	H	47.5	S	42.6
8	44.3	S	S	54.1	52.5	42.6	62.3	S	50.8	49.2	S	50.8
9	50.8	44.3	57.4	59.0	S	41.0	54.1	S	54.1	42.6	57.4	55.7
10	S	39.3	60.7	62.3	S	55.7	50.8	45.9	57.4	S	59.0	49.2
11	S	63.9	50.8	S	47.5	63.9	S	52.5	62.3	S	59.0	47.5
12	52.5	54.1	63.9	S	52.5	59.0	S	47.5	S	44.3	47.5	S
13	55.7	44.3	47.5	55.7	44.3	S	49.2	45.9	S	54.1	49.2	S
14	59.0	S	S	50.8	50.8	S	68.9	62.3	52.5	54.1	S	44.3
15	63.9	S	S	60.7	54.1	57.4	54.1	S	54.1	52.5	S	47.5
16	55.7	H	60.7	62.3	S	45.9	42.6	S	55.7	55.7	49.2	59.0
17	S	52.5	62.3	59.0	S	55.7	47.5	62.3	47.5	S	50.8	44.3
18	S	37.7	57.4	S	47.5	39.3	S	54.1	50.8	S	54.1	47.5
19	H	52.5	49.2	S	54.1	49.2	S	54.1	S	42.6	52.5	S
20	50.8	44.3	42.6	52.5	41.0	S	52.5	50.8	S	67.2	63.9	S
21	45.9	S	S	54.1	42.6	S	41.0	47.5	47.5	50.8	S	49.2
22	45.9	S	S	54.1	50.8	50.8	41.0	S	47.5	42.6	S	55.7
23	60.7	42.6	44.3	45.9	S	44.3	47.5	S	37.7	44.3	57.4	47.5
24	S	39.3	54.1	47.5	S	36.1	44.3	52.5	49.2	S	65.6	62.3
25	S	57.4	44.3	S	H	42.6	S	45.9	50.8	S	62.3	H
26	54.1	52.5	45.9	S	49.2	52.5	S	44.3	S	32.8	H	S
27	52.5	57.4	55.7	59.0	47.5	S	57.4	59.0	S	59.0	59.0	S
28	49.2	S	S	49.2	55.7	S	52.5	44.3	59.0	59.0	S	72.1
29	60.7		S	47.5	60.7	57.4	49.2	S	50.8	60.7	S	50.8
30	63.9		36.1	57.4	S	49.2	63.9	S	41.0	54.1	52.5	63.9
31	S		41.0		S		62.3	63.9		S		63.9

* See new trends developing on pages 70, 92, 141–146

RECENT S&P 500 MARKET PROBABILITY CALENDAR 2015

THE % CHANCE OF THE MARKET RISING ON ANY TRADING DAY OF THE YEAR*

(Based on the number of times the S&P 500 rose on a particular trading day during January 1993-December 2013**)

Date	Jan	Feb	Mar	Apr	May	Jun	Jul	Aug	Sep	Oct	Nov	Dec
1	H	S	S	71.4	71.4	61.9	81.0	S	61.9	52.4	S	52.4
2	47.6	76.2	57.1	66.7	S	76.2	38.1	S	42.9	57.1	57.1	52.4
3	S	52.4	42.9	H	S	42.9	H	52.4	57.1	S	66.7	66.7
4	S	47.6	71.4	S	61.9	47.6	S	47.6	52.4	S	66.7	42.9
5	61.9	52.4	47.6	S	38.1	38.1	S	47.6	S	42.9	71.4	S
6	61.9	52.4	61.9	57.1	38.1	S	57.1	52.4	S	61.9	57.1	S
7	42.9	S	S	61.9	33.3	S	61.9	47.6	H	38.1	S	42.9
8	47.6	S	S	47.6	57.1	42.9	61.9	S	61.9	38.1	S	52.4
9	61.9	57.1	57.1	52.4	S	47.6	42.9	S	66.7	52.4	47.6	61.9
10	S	42.9	57.1	47.6	S	42.9	57.1	57.1	61.9	S	38.1	47.6
11	S	71.4	52.4	S	47.6	61.9	S	42.9	66.7	S	47.6	52.4
12	57.1	71.4	66.7	S	61.9	71.4	S	52.4	S	42.9	52.4	S
13	57.1	42.9	52.4	57.1	47.6	S	71.4	28.6	S	61.9	61.9	S
14	52.4	S	S	47.6	52.4	S	66.7	61.9	66.7	71.4	S	42.9
15	61.9	S	S	47.6	61.9	66.7	47.6	S	52.4	47.6	S	52.4
16	61.9	H	61.9	61.9	S	57.1	42.9	S	61.9	57.1	52.4	66.7
17	S	66.7	57.1	66.7	S	57.1	52.4	61.9	42.9	S	52.4	47.6
18	S	42.9	71.4	S	47.6	38.1	S	71.4	47.6	S	52.4	42.9
19	H	38.1	47.6	S	57.1	42.9	S	71.4	S	57.1	47.6	S
20	52.4	47.6	42.9	52.4	47.6	S	66.7	38.1	S	66.7	47.6	S
21	33.3	S	S	61.9	38.1	S	28.6	47.6	38.1	47.6	S	52.4
22	47.6	S	S	66.7	57.1	47.6	38.1	S	38.1	57.1	S	76.2
23	52.4	61.9	38.1	52.4	S	33.3	47.6	S	28.6	47.6	57.1	71.4
24	S	38.1	66.7	33.3	S	42.9	52.4	66.7	38.1	S	61.9	57.1
25	S	47.6	61.9	S	H	38.1	S	47.6	52.4	S	66.7	H
26	57.1	57.1	28.6	S	57.1	57.1	S	47.6	S	42.9	H	S
27	52.4	47.6	47.6	57.1	52.4	S	66.7	66.7	S	57.1	71.4	S
28	66.7	S	S	52.4	57.1	S	42.9	33.3	61.9	61.9	S	81.0
29	52.4		S	66.7	52.4	57.1	42.9	S	61.9	66.7	S	52.4
30	66.7		38.1	52.4	S	38.1	61.9	S	28.6	61.9	38.1	57.1
31	S		42.9		S		47.6	52.4		S		33.3

*See new trends developing on pages 70, 92, 141–146 ** Based on most recent 21-year period*

NASDAQ COMPOSITE MARKET PROBABILITY CALENDAR 2015

THE % CHANCE OF THE MARKET RISING ON ANY TRADING DAY OF THE YEAR*

(Based on the number of times the NASDAQ rose on a particular trading day during January 1971-December 2013)

Date	Jan	Feb	Mar	Apr	May	Jun	Jul	Aug	Sep	Oct	Nov	Dec
1	H	S	S	46.5	60.5	58.1	60.5	S	55.8	48.8	S	60.5
2	58.1	72.1	62.8	62.8	S	74.4	48.8	S	60.5	60.5	65.1	62.8
3	S	67.4	55.8	H	S	55.8	H	53.5	60.5	S	55.8	65.1
4	S	58.1	67.4	S	72.1	60.5	S	41.9	58.1	S	72.1	58.1
5	67.4	62.8	51.2	S	58.1	48.8	S	51.2	S	55.8	58.1	S
6	60.5	55.8	53.5	65.1	53.5	S	46.5	55.8	S	65.1	48.8	S
7	62.8	S	S	55.8	53.5	S	53.5	55.8	H	58.1	S	41.9
8	53.5	S	S	46.5	62.8	44.2	62.8	S	55.8	58.1	S	55.8
9	62.8	53.5	58.1	60.5	S	41.9	62.8	S	51.2	48.8	53.5	48.8
10	S	46.5	58.1	62.8	S	53.5	60.5	39.5	51.2	S	58.1	44.2
11	S	60.5	48.8	S	53.5	62.8	S	51.2	60.5	S	62.8	41.9
12	58.1	60.5	72.1	S	41.9	65.1	S	51.2	S	51.2	53.5	S
13	62.8	62.8	53.5	62.8	58.1	S	69.8	55.8	S	74.4	53.5	S
14	60.5	S	S	53.5	55.8	S	72.1	58.1	62.8	62.8	S	41.9
15	65.1	S	S	58.1	55.8	58.1	65.1	S	37.2	51.2	S	46.5
16	69.8	H	51.2	53.5	S	46.5	46.5	S	51.2	51.2	41.9	58.1
17	S	58.1	60.5	60.5	S	51.2	55.8	58.1	53.5	S	46.5	48.8
18	S	48.8	58.1	S	53.5	46.5	S	51.2	62.8	S	51.2	53.5
19	H	53.5	62.8	S	51.2	60.5	S	58.1	S	39.5	53.5	S
20	60.5	37.2	39.5	53.5	41.9	S	58.1	51.2	S	69.8	67.4	S
21	39.5	S	S	53.5	48.8	S	39.5	53.5	51.2	58.1	S	53.5
22	46.5	S	S	58.1	51.2	44.2	41.9	S	48.8	46.5	S	60.5
23	58.1	48.8	58.1	55.8	S	46.5	48.8	S	46.5	44.2	58.1	65.1
24	S	53.5	55.8	51.2	S	44.2	53.5	53.5	53.5	S	58.1	67.4
25	S	62.8	48.8	S	H	48.8	S	53.5	44.2	S	67.4	H
26	48.8	55.8	44.2	S	53.5	60.5	S	53.5	S	32.6	H	S
27	67.4	53.5	53.5	48.8	60.5	S	58.1	65.1	S	44.2	65.1	S
28	62.8	S	S	69.8	58.1	S	48.8	60.5	48.8	58.1	S	72.1
29	51.2		S	65.1	69.8	67.4	44.2	S	48.8	60.5	S	48.8
30	65.1		53.5	67.4	S	67.4	55.8	S	46.5	65.1	65.1	65.1
31	S		65.1		S		51.2	67.4		S		74.4

* See new trends developing on pages 70, 92, 141–146
Based on NASDAQ composite, prior to Feb. 5, 1971 based on National Quotation Bureau indices

RECENT NASDAQ COMPOSITE MARKET PROBABILITY CALENDAR 2015

THE % CHANCE OF THE MARKET RISING ON ANY TRADING DAY OF THE YEAR*
(Based on the number of times the NASDAQ rose on a particular trading day during January 1993-December 2013**)

Date	Jan	Feb	Mar	Apr	May	Jun	Jul	Aug	Sep	Oct	Nov	Dec
1	H	S	S	61.9	71.4	57.1	71.4	S	61.9	42.9	S	61.9
2	66.7	81.0	52.4	57.1	S	76.2	42.9	S	57.1	57.1	66.7	61.9
3	S	57.1	38.1	H	S	52.4	H	52.4	57.1	S	66.7	61.9
4	S	47.6	71.4	S	61.9	52.4	S	42.9	57.1	S	76.2	52.4
5	61.9	52.4	38.1	S	52.4	38.1	S	47.6	S	52.4	61.9	S
6	57.1	57.1	52.4	71.4	47.6	S	52.4	52.4	S	66.7	57.1	S
7	52.4	S	S	57.1	38.1	S	61.9	42.9	H	47.6	S	33.3
8	52.4	S	S	38.1	76.2	38.1	66.7	S	61.9	52.4	S	57.1
9	71.4	61.9	52.4	57.1	S	42.9	57.1	S	66.7	57.1	57.1	57.1
10	S	42.9	52.4	47.6	S	42.9	61.9	38.1	52.4	S	42.9	42.9
11	S	52.4	47.6	S	47.6	52.4	S	42.9	66.7	S	52.4	42.9
12	57.1	61.9	71.4	S	42.9	61.9	S	52.4	S	57.1	61.9	S
13	61.9	61.9	52.4	66.7	57.1	S	71.4	42.9	S	71.4	57.1	S
14	52.4	S	S	47.6	47.6	S	71.4	61.9	81.0	71.4	S	42.9
15	47.6	S	S	47.6	57.1	71.4	57.1	S	38.1	47.6	S	52.4
16	71.4	H	47.6	42.9	S	47.6	47.6	S	71.4	47.6	47.6	57.1
17	S	52.4	57.1	52.4	S	57.1	57.1	66.7	52.4	S	47.6	38.1
18	S	42.9	61.9	S	52.4	42.9	S	71.4	61.9	S	47.6	52.4
19	H	42.9	61.9	S	66.7	52.4	S	66.7	S	42.9	52.4	S
20	66.7	38.1	33.3	47.6	38.1	S	66.7	38.1	S	66.7	57.1	S
21	28.6	S	S	61.9	42.9	S	23.8	52.4	42.9	42.9	S	57.1
22	38.1	S	S	61.9	42.9	33.3	42.9	S	38.1	57.1	S	61.9
23	57.1	61.9	57.1	57.1	S	28.6	47.6	S	42.9	42.9	61.9	71.4
24	S	52.4	61.9	52.4	S	42.9	52.4	52.4	42.9	S	57.1	61.9
25	S	52.4	66.7	S	H	47.6	S	52.4	47.6	S	61.9	H
26	47.6	52.4	38.1	S	52.4	71.4	S	38.1	S	33.3	H	S
27	76.2	38.1	42.9	52.4	57.1	S	71.4	76.2	S	47.6	66.7	S
28	71.4	S	S	66.7	71.4	S	52.4	57.1	47.6	61.9	S	71.4
29	42.9		S	76.2	57.1	66.7	42.9	S	47.6	66.7	S	47.6
30	61.9		47.6	66.7	S	66.7	66.7	S	28.6	66.7	47.6	47.6
31	S		57.1		S		42.9	57.1		S		47.6

*See new trends developing on pages 70, 92, 141–146 ** Based on most recent 21-year period*

RUSSELL 1000 INDEX MARKET PROBABILITY CALENDAR 2015

THE % CHANCE OF THE MARKET RISING ON ANY TRADING DAY OF THE YEAR*

(Based on the number of times the RUSSELL 1000 rose on a particular trading day during January 1979-December 2013)

Date	Jan	Feb	Mar	Apr	May	Jun	Jul	Aug	Sep	Oct	Nov	Dec
1	H	S	S	60.0	54.3	57.1	71.4	S	51.4	54.3	S	51.4
2	45.7	68.6	60.0	62.9	S	60.0	42.9	S	48.6	57.1	71.4	54.3
3	S	57.1	48.6	H	S	48.6	H	48.6	54.3	S	57.1	62.9
4	S	57.1	62.9	S	65.7	57.1	S	42.9	42.9	S	60.0	42.9
5	60.0	51.4	40.0	S	54.3	34.3	S	48.6	S	51.4	60.0	S
6	62.9	60.0	45.7	54.3	40.0	S	45.7	48.6	S	62.9	45.7	S
7	51.4	S	S	57.1	40.0	S	60.0	54.3	H	42.9	S	42.9
8	48.6	S	S	45.7	57.1	40.0	60.0	S	51.4	51.4	S	51.4
9	62.9	51.4	60.0	62.9	S	42.9	48.6	S	57.1	37.1	54.3	54.3
10	S	40.0	57.1	57.1	S	51.4	57.1	57.1	62.9	S	48.6	45.7
11	S	68.6	45.7	S	57.1	57.1	S	45.7	65.7	S	60.0	45.7
12	54.3	65.7	62.9	S	51.4	60.0	S	48.6	S	40.0	57.1	S
13	60.0	42.9	45.7	54.3	54.3	S	65.7	42.9	S	65.7	54.3	S
14	57.1	S	S	45.7	51.4	S	77.1	60.0	62.9	65.7	S	45.7
15	71.4	S	S	54.3	57.1	62.9	51.4	S	51.4	57.1	S	54.3
16	65.7	H	57.1	65.7	S	48.6	48.6	S	48.6	51.4	48.6	60.0
17	S	60.0	60.0	60.0	S	62.9	48.6	62.9	45.7	S	45.7	48.6
18	S	37.1	60.0	S	54.3	37.1	S	60.0	48.6	S	62.9	45.7
19	H	45.7	48.6	S	57.1	48.6	S	65.7	S	42.9	48.6	S
20	42.9	40.0	42.9	45.7	48.6	S	60.0	62.9	S	74.3	62.9	S
21	34.3	S	S	54.3	40.0	S	40.0	48.6	40.0	54.3	S	48.6
22	45.7	S	S	54.3	60.0	51.4	37.1	S	45.7	45.7	S	71.4
23	51.4	45.7	48.6	57.1	S	42.9	45.7	S	37.1	40.0	60.0	57.1
24	S	42.9	48.6	45.7	S	34.3	40.0	60.0	40.0	S	62.9	62.9
25	S	57.1	54.3	S	H	40.0	S	42.9	48.6	S	74.3	H
26	54.3	57.1	37.1	S	62.9	54.3	S	51.4	S	34.3	H	S
27	62.9	57.1	48.6	57.1	57.1	S	77.1	57.1	S	57.1	65.7	S
28	60.0	S	S	54.3	54.3	S	54.3	48.6	65.7	57.1	S	71.4
29	54.3		S	54.3	57.1	60.0	45.7	S	57.1	65.7	S	57.1
30	60.0		40.0	57.1	S	48.6	65.7	S	45.7	62.9	48.6	68.6
31	S		48.6		S		60.0	60.0		S		54.3

* See new trends developing on pages 70, 92, 141–146

RUSSELL 2000 INDEX MARKET PROBABILITY CALENDAR 2015

THE % CHANCE OF THE MARKET RISING ON ANY TRADING DAY OF THE YEAR*

(Based on the number of times the RUSSELL 2000 rose on a particular trading day during January 1979-December 2013)

Date	Jan	Feb	Mar	Apr	May	Jun	Jul	Aug	Sep	Oct	Nov	Dec
1	H	S	S	48.6	60.0	62.9	62.9	S	51.4	51.4	S	51.4
2	48.6	68.6	65.7	60.0	S	68.6	51.4	S	60.0	48.6	62.9	62.9
3	S	62.9	60.0	H	S	51.4	H	51.4	57.1	S	71.4	65.7
4	S	54.3	68.6	S	65.7	57.1	S	45.7	65.7	S	65.7	62.9
5	62.9	65.7	54.3	S	62.9	54.3	S	51.4	S	48.6	57.1	S
6	62.9	62.9	62.9	48.6	57.1	S	42.9	48.6	S	71.4	51.4	S
7	60.0	S	S	54.3	51.4	S	54.3	48.6	H	42.9	S	45.7
8	57.1	S	S	42.9	54.3	37.1	54.3	S	54.3	45.7	S	57.1
9	65.7	62.9	54.3	57.1	S	48.6	57.1	S	60.0	45.7	54.3	48.6
10	S	42.9	57.1	60.0	S	54.3	51.4	45.7	60.0	S	51.4	48.6
11	S	71.4	40.0	S	60.0	60.0	S	57.1	65.7	S	68.6	40.0
12	54.3	62.9	62.9	S	48.6	65.7	S	51.4	S	54.3	51.4	S
13	68.6	62.9	54.3	62.9	57.1	S	62.9	45.7	S	71.4	51.4	S
14	62.9	S	S	51.4	48.6	S	62.9	71.4	60.0	62.9	S	45.7
15	68.6	S	S	54.3	48.6	60.0	57.1	S	34.3	57.1	S	40.0
16	68.6	H	48.6	60.0	S	48.6	48.6	S	48.6	42.9	48.6	57.1
17	S	54.3	57.1	57.1	S	42.9	51.4	62.9	42.9	S	20.0	60.0
18	S	54.3	68.6	S	54.3	40.0	S	60.0	42.9	S	60.0	60.0
19	H	42.9	54.3	S	54.3	51.4	S	60.0	S	48.6	45.7	S
20	71.4	34.3	48.6	45.7	54.3	S	51.4	51.4	S	71.4	62.9	S
21	34.3	S	S	60.0	54.3	S	40.0	48.6	48.6	54.3	S	60.0
22	48.6	S	S	65.7	57.1	42.9	42.9	S	51.4	45.7	S	65.7
23	57.1	51.4	62.9	54.3	S	48.6	40.0	S	42.9	42.9	60.0	65.7
24	S	54.3	51.4	54.3	S	40.0	48.6	60.0	45.7	S	60.0	77.1
25	S	57.1	54.3	S	H	48.6	S	57.1	31.4	S	65.7	H
26	48.6	62.9	42.9	S	54.3	60.0	S	57.1	S	34.3	H	S
27	68.6	60.0	51.4	62.9	68.6	S	65.7	65.7	S	40.0	68.6	S
28	62.9	S	S	62.9	65.7	S	62.9	62.9	54.3	57.1	S	68.6
29	51.4		S	60.0	68.6	71.4	45.7	S	60.0	57.1	S	54.3
30	77.1		51.4	68.6	S	65.7	57.1	S	60.0	71.4	71.4	62.9
31	S		82.9		S		65.7	71.4		S		71.4

* See new trends developing on pages 70, 92, 141–146

DECENNIAL CYCLE: A MARKET PHENOMENON

By arranging each year's market gain or loss so the first and succeeding years of each decade fall into the same column, certain interesting patterns emerge—strong fifth and eighth years; weak first, seventh, and zero years.

This fascinating phenomenon was first presented by Edgar Lawrence Smith in *Common Stocks and Business Cycles* (William-Frederick Press, 1959). Anthony Gaubis co-pioneered the decennial pattern with Smith.

When Smith first cut graphs of market prices into 10-year segments and placed them above one another, he observed that each decade tended to have three bull market cycles and that the longest and strongest bull markets seem to favor the middle years of a decade.

Don't place too much emphasis on the decennial cycle nowadays, other than the extraordinary fifth and zero years, as the stock market is more influenced by the quadrennial presidential election cycle, shown on page 130. Also, the last half-century, which has been the most prosperous in U.S. history, has distributed the returns among most years of the decade. Interestingly, NASDAQ suffered its worst bear market ever in a zero year.

Fifth years are the strongest and had a 12 and zero record until post-election-year 2005. Not only is this year a "fifth" year, it is also a pre-election year, which is the best performing year of the 4-year cycle. (See pre-election years on page 130.) As historical patterns continue to assert themselves, the probability of a solid 2015 is improving.

THE 10-YEAR STOCK MARKET CYCLE
Annual % Change in Dow Jones Industrial Average
Year of Decade

DECADES	1st	2nd	3rd	4th	5th	6th	7th	8th	9th	10th
1881–1890	3.0%	−2.9%	−8.5%	−18.8%	20.1%	12.4%	−8.4%	4.8%	5.5%	−14.1%
1891–1900	17.6	−6.6	−24.6	−0.6	2.3	−1.7	21.3	22.5	9.2	7.0
1901–1910	−8.7	−0.4	−23.6	41.7	38.2	−1.9	−37.7	46.6	15.0	−17.9
1911–1920	0.4	7.6	−10.3	−5.4	81.7	−4.2	−21.7	10.5	30.5	−32.9
1921–1930	12.7	21.7	−3.3	26.2	30.0	0.3	28.8	48.2	−17.2	−33.8
1931–1940	−52.7	−23.1	66.7	4.1	38.5	24.8	−32.8	28.1	−2.9	−12.7
1941–1950	−15.4	7.6	13.8	12.1	26.6	−8.1	2.2	−2.1	12.9	17.6
1951–1960	14.4	8.4	−3.8	44.0	20.8	2.3	−12.8	34.0	16.4	−9.3
1961–1970	18.7	−10.8	17.0	14.6	10.9	−18.9	15.2	4.3	−15.2	4.8
1971–1980	6.1	14.6	−16.6	−27.6	38.3	17.9	−17.3	−3.1	4.2	14.9
1981–1990	−9.2	19.6	20.3	−3.7	27.7	22.6	2.3	11.8	27.0	−4.3
1991–2000	20.3	4.2	13.7	2.1	33.5	26.0	22.6	16.1	25.2	−6.2
2001–2010	−7.1	−16.8	25.3	3.1	−0.6	16.3	6.4	−33.8	18.8	11.0
2011–2020	5.5	7.3	26.5							
Total % Change	5.6%	30.4%	92.6%	91.8%	368.0%	87.3%	−31.9%	187.9%	129.4%	−75.9%
Avg % Change	0.4%	2.2%	6.6%	7.1%	28.3%	6.8%	−2.5%	14.5%	10.0%	−5.8%
Up Years	9	8	7	8	12	8	7	10	10	5
Down Years	5	6	7	5	1	5	6	3	3	8

Based on annual close; Cowles indices 1881–1885; 12 Mixed Stocks, 10 Rails, 2 Inds 1886–1889;

20 Mixed Stocks, 18 Rails, 2 Inds 1890–1896; Railroad average 1897 (First industrial average published May 26, 1896).

PRESIDENTIAL ELECTION/STOCK MARKET CYCLE: THE 181-YEAR SAGA CONTINUES

It is no mere coincidence that the last two years (pre-election year and election year) of the 45 administrations since 1833 produced a total net market gain of 731.3%, dwarfing the 299.6% gain of the first two years of these administrations.

Presidential elections every four years have a profound impact on the economy and the stock market. Wars, recessions, and bear markets tend to start or occur in the first half of the term; prosperous times and bull markets, in the latter half. After nine straight annual Dow gains during the millennial bull, the four-year election cycle reasserted its overarching domination of market behavior until 2008. Recovery from the worst recession since the Great Depression has produced five straight annual gains.

STOCK MARKET ACTION SINCE 1833
Annual % Change In Dow Jones Industrial Average[1]

4-Year Cycle Beginning	Elected President	Post-Election Year	Mid-Term Year	Pre-Election Year	Election Year
1833	Jackson (D)	−0.9	13.0	3.1	−11.7
1837	Van Buren (D)	−11.5	1.6	−12.3	5.5
1841*	W.H. Harrison (W)**	−13.3	−18.1	45.0	15.5
1845*	Polk (D)	8.1	−14.5	1.2	−3.6
1849*	Taylor (W)	N/C	18.7	−3.2	19.6
1853*	Pierce (D)	−12.7	−30.2	1.5	4.4
1857	Buchanan (D)	−31.0	14.3	−10.7	14.0
1861*	Lincoln (R)	−1.8	55.4	38.0	6.4
1865	Lincoln (R)**	−8.5	3.6	1.6	10.8
1869	Grant (R)	1.7	5.6	7.3	6.8
1873	Grant (R)	−12.7	2.8	−4.1	−17.9
1877	Hayes (R)	−9.4	6.1	43.0	18.7
1881	Garfield (R)**	3.0	−2.9	−8.5	−18.8
1885*	Cleveland (D)	20.1	12.4	−8.4	4.8
1889*	B. Harrison (R)	5.5	−14.1	17.6	−6.6
1893*	Cleveland (D)	−24.6	−0.6	2.3	−1.7
1897*	McKinley (R)	21.3	22.5	9.2	7.0
1901	McKinley (R)**	−8.7	−0.4	−23.6	41.7
1905	T. Roosevelt (R)	38.2	−1.9	−37.7	46.6
1909	Taft (R)	15.0	−17.9	0.4	7.6
1913*	Wilson (D)	−10.3	−5.4	81.7	−4.2
1917	Wilson (D)	−21.7	10.5	30.5	−32.9
1921*	Harding (R)**	12.7	21.7	−3.3	26.2
1925	Coolidge (R)	30.0	0.3	28.8	48.2
1929	Hoover (R)	−17.2	−33.8	−52.7	−23.1
1933*	F. Roosevelt (D)	66.7	4.1	38.5	24.8
1937	F. Roosevelt (D)	−32.8	28.1	−2.9	−12.7
1941	F. Roosevelt (D)	−15.4	7.6	13.8	12.1
1945	F. Roosevelt (D)**	26.6	−8.1	2.2	−2.1
1949	Truman (D)	12.9	17.6	14.4	8.4
1953*	Eisenhower (R)	−3.8	44.0	20.8	2.3
1957	Eisenhower (R)	−12.8	34.0	16.4	−9.3
1961*	Kennedy (D)**	18.7	−10.8	17.0	14.6
1965	Johnson (D)	10.9	−18.9	15.2	4.3
1969*	Nixon (R)	−15.2	4.8	6.1	14.6
1973	Nixon (R)***	−16.6	−27.6	38.3	17.9
1977*	Carter (D)	−17.3	−3.1	4.2	14.9
1981*	Reagan (R)	−9.2	19.6	20.3	−3.7
1985	Reagan (R)	27.7	22.6	2.3	11.8
1989	G. H. W. Bush (R)	27.0	−4.3	20.3	4.2
1993*	Clinton (D)	13.7	2.1	33.5	26.0
1997	Clinton (D)	22.6	16.1	25.2	−6.2
2001*	G. W. Bush (R)	−7.1	−16.8	25.3	3.1
2005	G. W. Bush (R)	−0.6	16.3	6.4	−33.8
2009*	Obama (D)	18.8	11.0	5.5	7.3
2013	Obama (D)	26.5			
Total % Gain		**112.6%**	**187.0%**	**469.5%**	**261.8%**
Average % Gain		**2.5%**	**4.2%**	**10.4%**	**5.8%**
# Up		21	27	34	30
# Down		24	18	11	15

*Party in power ousted   **Death in office   ***Resigned   **D**–Democrat, **W**–Whig, **R**–Republican

[1] Based on annual close; Prior to 1886 based on Cowles and other indices; 12 Mixed Stocks, 10 Rails, 2 Inds 1886–1889; 20 Mixed Stocks, 18 Rails, 2 Inds 1890–1896; Railroad average 1897 (First industrial average published May 26, 1896).

DOW JONES INDUSTRIALS BULL AND BEAR MARKETS SINCE 1900

Bear markets begin at the end of one bull market and end at the start of the next bull market (7/17/90 to 10/11/90 as an example). The high at Dow 3978.36 on 1/31/94, was followed by a 9.7 percent correction. A 10.3 percent correction occurred between the 5/22/96 closing high of 5778 and the intraday low on 7/16/96. The longest bull market on record ended on 7/17/98, and the shortest bear market on record ended on 8/31/98, when the new bull market began. The greatest bull super cycle in history that began 8/12/82 ended in 2000 after the Dow gained 1409% and NASDAQ climbed 3072%. The Dow gained only 497% in the eight-year super bull from 1921 to the top in 1929. NASDAQ suffered its worst loss ever from the 2000 top to the 2002 bottom, down 77.9%, nearly as much as the 89.2% drop in the Dow from the 1929 top to the 1932 bottom. The third longest Dow bull since 1900 that began 10/9/02 ended on its fifth anniversary. The ensuing bear market was the second worst bear market since 1900, slashing the Dow 53.8%. European debt concerns in 2011 triggered a 16.8% Dow slide, ending the recovery bull shortly after its second anniversary. At press time, the current bull market was alive and well, making new all-time Dow highs. (See page 132 for S&P 500 and NASDAQ bulls and bears.)

DOW JONES INDUSTRIALS BULL AND BEAR MARKETS SINCE 1900

— Beginning —		— Ending —		Bull		Bear	
Date	DJIA	Date	DJIA	% Gain	Days	% Change	Days
9/24/00	38.80	6/17/01	57.33	47.8%	266	−46.1%	875
11/9/03	30.88	1/19/06	75.45	144.3	802	−48.5	665
11/15/07	38.83	11/19/09	73.64	89.6	735	−27.4	675
9/25/11	53.43	9/30/12	68.97	29.1	371	−24.1	668
7/30/14	52.32	11/21/16	110.15	110.5	845	−40.1	393
12/19/17	65.95	11/3/19	119.62	81.4	684	−46.6	660
8/24/21	63.90	3/20/23	105.38	64.9	573	−18.6	221
10/27/23	85.76	9/3/29	381.17	344.5	2138	−47.9	71
11/13/29	198.69	4/17/30	294.07	48.0	155	−86.0	813
7/8/32	41.22	9/7/32	79.93	93.9	61	−37.2	173
2/27/33	50.16	2/5/34	110.74	120.8	343	−22.8	171
7/26/34	85.51	3/10/37	194.40	127.3	958	−49.1	386
3/31/38	98.95	11/12/38	158.41	60.1	226	−23.3	147
4/8/39	121.44	9/12/39	155.92	28.4	157	−40.4	959
4/28/42	92.92	5/29/46	212.50	128.7	1492	−23.2	353
5/17/47	163.21	6/15/48	193.16	18.4	395	−16.3	363
6/13/49	161.60	1/5/53	293.79	81.8	1302	−13.0	252
9/14/53	255.49	4/6/56	521.05	103.9	935	−19.4	564
10/22/57	419.79	1/5/60	685.47	63.3	805	−17.4	294
10/25/60	566.05	12/13/61	734.91	29.8	414	−27.1	195
6/26/62	535.76	2/9/66	995.15	85.7	1324	−25.2	240
10/7/66	744.32	12/3/68	985.21	32.4	788	−35.9	539
5/26/70	631.16	4/28/71	950.82	50.6	337	−16.1	209
11/23/71	797.97	1/11/73	1051.70	31.8	415	−45.1	694
12/6/74	577.60	9/21/76	1014.79	75.7	655	−26.9	525
2/28/78	742.12	9/8/78	907.74	22.3	192	−16.4	591
4/21/80	759.13	4/27/81	1024.05	34.9	371	−24.1	472
8/12/82	776.92	11/29/83	1287.20	65.7	474	−15.6	238
7/24/84	1086.57	8/25/87	2722.42	150.6	1127	−36.1	55
10/19/87	1738.74	7/17/90	2999.75	72.5	1002	−21.2	86
10/11/90	2365.10	7/17/98	9337.97	294.8	2836	−19.3	45
8/31/98	7539.07	1/14/00	11722.98	55.5	501	−29.7	616
9/21/01	8235.81	3/19/02	10635.25	29.1	179	−31.5	204
10/9/02	7286.27	10/9/07	14164.53	94.4	1826	−53.8	517
3/9/09	6547.05	4/29/11	12810.54	95.7	781	−16.8	157
10/3/11	10655.30	4/30/14	16580.84	55.6*	940*	*As of May 9, 2014 – not in averages	
		Average		**86.0%**	**756**	**−31.1%**	**402**

Based on Dow Jones Industrial Average.
1900–2000 Data: Ned Davis Research
The NYSE was closed from 7/31/1914 to 12/11/1914 due to World War I.
DJIA figures were then adjusted back to reflect the composition change from 12 to 20 stocks in September 1916.

131

STANDARD & POOR'S 500 BULL AND BEAR MARKETS SINCE 1929 NASDAQ COMPOSITE SINCE 1971

A constant debate of the definition and timing of bull and bear markets permeates Wall Street like the bell that signals the open and close of every trading day. We have relied on the Ned Davis Research parameters for years to track bulls and bears on the Dow (see page 131). Standard & Poor's 500 index has been a stalwart indicator for decades and at times marched to a different beat than the Dow. The moves of the S&P 500 and NASDAQ have been correlated to the bull and bear dates on page 131. Many dates line up for the three indices, but you will notice quite a lag or lead on several occasions, including NASDAQ's independent cadence from 1975 to 1980.

STANDARD & POOR'S 500 BULL AND BEAR MARKETS

— Beginning —		— Ending —		Bull		Bear	
Date	S&P 500	Date	S&P 500	% Gain	Days	% Change	Days
11/13/29	17.66	4/10/30	25.92	46.8%	148	−83.0%	783
6/1/32	4.40	9/7/32	9.31	111.6	98	−40.6	173
2/27/33	5.53	2/6/34	11.82	113.7	344	−31.8	401
3/14/35	8.06	3/6/37	18.68	131.8	723	−49.0	390
3/31/38	8.50	11/9/38	13.79	62.2	223	−26.2	150
4/8/39	10.18	10/25/39	13.21	29.8	200	−43.5	916
4/28/42	7.47	5/29/46	19.25	157.7	1492	−28.8	353
5/17/47	13.71	6/15/48	17.06	24.4	395	−20.6	363
6/13/49	13.55	1/5/53	26.66	96.8	1302	−14.8	252
9/14/53	22.71	8/2/56	49.74	119.0	1053	−21.6	446
10/22/57	38.98	8/3/59	60.71	55.7	650	−13.9	449
10/25/60	52.30	12/12/61	72.64	38.9	413	−28.0	196
6/26/62	52.32	2/9/66	94.06	79.8	1324	−22.2	240
10/7/66	73.20	11/29/68	108.37	48.0	784	−36.1	543
5/26/70	69.29	4/28/71	104.77	51.2	337	−13.9	209
11/23/71	90.16	1/11/73	120.24	33.4	415	−48.2	630
10/3/74	62.28	9/21/76	107.83	73.1	719	−19.4	531
3/6/78	86.90	9/12/78	106.99	23.1	190	−8.2	562
3/27/80	98.22	11/28/80	140.52	43.1	246	−27.1	622
8/12/82	102.42	10/10/83	172.65	68.6	424	−14.4	288
7/24/84	147.82	8/25/87	336.77	127.8	1127	−33.5	101
12/4/87	223.92	7/16/90	368.95	64.8	955	−19.9	87
10/11/90	295.46	7/17/98	1186.75	301.7	2836	−19.3	45
8/31/98	957.28	3/24/00	1527.46	59.6	571	−36.8	546
9/21/01	965.80	1/4/02	1172.51	21.4	105	−33.8	278
10/9/02	776.76	10/9/07	1565.15	101.5	1826	−56.8	517
3/9/09	676.53	4/29/11	1363.61	101.6	781	−19.4	157
10/3/11	1099.23	4/2/14	1890.90	72.0*	912*	*As of May 9, 2014 – not in averages	
		Average		**81.0%**	**729**	**−30.2%**	**379**

NASDAQ COMPOSITE BULL AND BEAR MARKETS

— Beginning —		— Ending —		Bull		Bear	
Date	NASDAQ	Date	NASDAQ	% Gain	Days	% Change	Days
11/23/71	100.31	1/11/73	136.84	36.4%	415	−59.9%	630
10/3/74	54.87	7/15/75	88.00	60.4	285	−16.2	63
9/16/75	73.78	9/13/78	139.25	88.7	1093	−20.4	62
11/14/78	110.88	2/8/80	165.25	49.0	451	−24.9	48
3/27/80	124.09	5/29/81	223.47	80.1	428	−28.8	441
8/13/82	159.14	6/24/83	328.91	106.7	315	−31.5	397
7/25/84	225.30	8/26/87	455.26	102.1	1127	−35.9	63
10/28/87	291.88	10/9/89	485.73	66.4	712	−33.0	372
10/16/90	325.44	7/20/98	2014.25	518.9	2834	−29.5	80
10/8/98	1419.12	3/10/00	5048.62	255.8	519	−71.8	560
9/21/01	1423.19	1/4/02	2059.38	44.7	105	−45.9	278
10/9/02	1114.11	10/31/07	2859.12	156.6	1848	−55.6	495
3/9/09	1268.64	4/29/11	2873.54	126.5	781	−18.7	157
10/3/11	2335.83	3/5/14	4357.97	86.6*	884*	*As of May 9, 2014 – not in averages	
		Average		**130.2%**	**839**	**−36.3%**	**280**

JANUARY DAILY POINT CHANGES DOW JONES INDUSTRIALS

	2005	2006	2007	2008	2009	2010	2011	2012	2013	2014
Previous Month Close	10783.01	10717.50	12463.15	13264.82	8776.39	10428.05	11577.51	12217.56	13104.14	16576.66
1	S	S	H	H	H	H	S	S	H	H
2	S	H	H*	−220.86	258.30	S	S	H	308.41	−135.31
3	−53.58	129.91	11.37	12.76	S	S	93.24	179.82	−21.19	28.64
4	−98.65	32.74	6.17	−256.54	S	155.91	20.43	21.04	43.85	S
5	−32.95	2.00	−82.68	S	−81.80	−11.94	31.71	−2.72	S	S
6	25.05	77.16	S	S	62.21	1.66	−25.58	−55.78	S	−44.89
7	−18.92	S	S	27.31	−245.40	33.18	−22.55	S	−50.92	105.84
8	S	S	25.48	−238.42	−27.24	11.33	S	S	−55.44	−68.20
9	S	52.59	−6.89	146.24	−143.28	S	S	32.77	61.66	−17.98
10	17.07	−0.32	25.56	117.78	S	S	−37.31	69.78	80.71	−7.71
11	−64.81	31.86	72.82	−246.79	S	45.80	34.43	−13.02	17.21	S
12	61.56	−81.08	41.10	S	−125.21	−36.73	83.56	21.57	S	S
13	−111.95	−2.49	S	S	−25.41	53.51	−23.54	−48.96	S	−179.11
14	52.17	S	S	171.85	−248.42	29.78	55.48	S	18.89	115.92
15	S	S	H	−277.04	12.35	−100.90	S	S	27.57	108.08
16	S	H	26.51	−34.95	68.73	S	S	H	−23.66	−64.93
17	H	−63.55	−5.44	−306.95	S	S	H	60.01	84.79	41.55
18	70.79	−41.46	−9.22	−59.91	S	H	50.55	96.88	53.68	S
19	−88.82	25.85	−2.40	S	H	115.78	−12.64	45.03	S	S
20	−68.50	−213.32	S	S	−332.13	−122.28	−2.49	96.50	S	H
21	−78.48	S	S	H	279.01	−213.27	49.04	S	H	−44.12
22	S	S	−88.37	−128.11	−105.30	−216.90	S	S	62.51	−41.10
23	S	21.38	56.64	298.98	−45.24	S	S	−11.66	67.12	−175.99
24	−24.38	23.45	87.97	108.44	S	S	108.68	−33.07	46.00	−318.24
25	92.95	−2.48	−119.21	−171.44	S	23.88	−3.33	81.21	70.65	S
26	37.03	99.73	−15.54	S	38.47	−2.57	8.25	−22.33	S	S
27	−31.19	97.74	S	S	58.70	41.87	4.39	−74.17	S	−41.23
28	−40.20	S	S	176.72	200.72	−115.70	−166.13	S	−14.05	90.68
29	S	S	3.76	96.41	−226.44	−53.13	S	S	72.49	−189.77
30	S	−7.29	32.53	−37.47	−148.15	S	S	−6.74	−44.00	109.82
31	62.74	−35.06	98.38	207.53	S	S	68.23	−20.81	−49.84	−149.76
Close	10489.94	10864.86	12621.69	12650.36	8000.86	10067.33	11891.93	12632.91	13860.58	15698.85
Change	−293.07	147.36	158.54	−614.46	−775.53	−360.72	314.42	415.35	756.44	−877.81

* Ford funeral

FEBRUARY DAILY POINT CHANGES DOW JONES INDUSTRIALS

	2005	2006	2007	2008	2009	2010	2011	2012	2013	2014
Previous Month Close	10489.94	10864.86	12621.69	12650.36	8000.86	10067.33	11891.93	12632.91	13860.58	15698.85
1	62.00	89.09	51.99	92.83	S	118.20	148.23	83.55	149.21	S
2	44.85	−101.97	−20.19	S	−64.03	111.32	1.81	−11.05	S	S
3	−3.69	−58.36	S	S	141.53	−26.30	20.29	156.82	S	−326.05
4	123.03	S	S	−108.03	−121.70	−268.37	29.89	S	−129.71	72.44
5	S	S	8.25	−370.03	106.41	10.05	S	−17.10	99.22	−5.01
6	S	4.65	4.57	−65.03	217.52	S	S	−17.10	7.22	188.30
7	−0.37	−48.51	0.56	46.90	S	S	69.48	33.07	−42.47	165.55
8	8.87	108.86	−29.24	−64.87	S	−103.84	71.52	5.75	48.92	S
9	−60.52	24.73	−56.80	S	−9.72	150.25	6.74	6.51	S	S
10	85.50	35.70	S	S	−381.99	−20.26	−10.60	−89.23	S	7.71
11	46.40	S	S	57.88	50.65	105.81	43.97	S	−21.73	192.98
12	S	S	−28.28	133.40	−6.77	−45.05	S	S	47.46	−30.83
13	S	−26.73	102.30	178.83	−82.35	S	S	72.81	−35.79	63.65
14	−4.88	136.07	87.01	−175.26	S	S	−5.07	4.24	−9.52	126.80
15	46.19	30.58	23.15	−28.77	S	H	−41.55	−97.33	8.37	S
16	−2.44	61.71	2.56	S	H	169.67	61.53	123.13	S	S
17	−80.62	−5.36	S	S	−297.81	40.43	29.97	45.79	S	H
18	30.96	S	S	H	3.03	83.66	73.11	S	H	−23.99
19	S	S	H	−10.99	−89.68	9.45	S	S	53.91	−89.84
20	S	H	19.07	90.04	−100.28	S	S	H	−108.13	92.67
21	H	−46.26	−48.23	−142.96	S	S	H	15.82	−46.92	−29.93
22	−174.02	68.11	−52.39	96.72	S	−18.97	−178.46	−27.02	119.95	S
23	62.59	−67.95	−38.54	S	−250.89	−100.97	−107.01	46.02	S	S
24	75.00	−7.37	S	S	236.16	91.75	−37.28	−1.74	S	103.84
25	92.81	S	S	189.20	−80.05	−53.13	61.95	S	−216.40	−27.48
26	S	S	−15.22	114.70	−88.81	4.23	S	S	115.96	18.75
27	S	35.70	−416.02	9.36	−119.15	S	S	−1.44	175.24	74.24
28	−75.37	−104.14	52.39	−112.10	S	S	95.89	23.61	−20.88	49.06
29	—	—	—	−315.79	—	—	—	−53.05	—	—
Close	10766.23	10993.41	12268.63	12266.39	7062.93	10325.26	12226.34	12952.07	14054.49	16321.71
Change	276.29	128.55	−353.06	−383.97	−937.93	257.93	334.41	319.16	193.91	622.86

MARCH DAILY POINT CHANGES DOW JONES INDUSTRIALS

Previous Month	2005	2006	2007	2008	2009	2010	2011	2012	2013	2014
Close	10766.23	10993.41	12268.63	12266.39	7062.93	10325.26	12226.34	12952.07	14054.49	16321.71
1	63.77	60.12	−34.29	S	S	78.53	−168.32	28.23	35.17	S
2	−18.03	−28.02	−120.24	S	−299.64	2.19	8.78	−2.73	S	S
3	21.06	−3.92	S	−7.49	−37.27	−9.22	191.40	S	S	−153.68
4	107.52	S	S	−45.10	149.82	47.38	−88.32	S	38.16	227.85
5	S	S	−63.69	41.19	−281.40	122.06	S	−14.76	125.95	−35.70
6	S	−63.00	157.18	−214.60	32.50	S	S	−203.66	42.47	61.71
7	−3.69	22.10	−15.14	−146.70	S	S	−79.85	78.18	33.25	30.83
8	−24.24	25.05	68.25	S	S	−13.68	124.35	70.61	67.58	S
9	−107.00	−33.46	15.62	S	−79.89	11.86	−1.29	14.08	S	S
10	45.89	104.06	S	−153.54	379.44	2.95	−228.48	S	S	−34.04
11	−77.15	S	S	416.66	3.91	44.51	59.79	S	50.22	−67.43
12	S	S	42.30	−46.57	239.66	12.85	S	37.69	2.77	−11.17
13	S	−0.32	−242.66	35.50	53.92	S	S	217.97	5.22	−231.19
14	30.15	75.32	57.44	−194.65	S	S	−51.24	16.42	83.86	−43.22
15	−59.41	58.43	26.28	S	S	17.46	−137.74	58.66	−25.03	S
16	−112.03	43.47	−49.27	S	−7.01	43.83	−242.12	−20.14	S	S
17	−6.72	26.41	S	21.16	178.73	47.69	161.29	S	S	181.55
18	3.32	S	S	420.41	90.88	45.50	83.93	S	−62.05	88.97
19	S	S	115.76	−293.00	−85.78	−37.19	S	6.51	3.76	−114.02
20	S	−5.12	61.93	261.66	−122.42	S	S	−68.94	55.91	108.88
21	−64.28	−39.06	159.42	H	S	S	178.01	−45.57	−90.24	−28.28
22	−94.88	81.96	13.62	S	S	43.91	−17.90	−78.48	90.54	S
23	−14.49	−47.14	19.87	S	497.48	102.94	67.39	34.59	S	S
24	−13.15	9.68	S	187.32	−115.89	−52.68	84.54	S	S	−26.08
25	H	S	S	−16.04	89.84	5.06	50.03	S	−64.28	91.19
26	S	S	−11.94	−109.74	174.75	9.15	S	160.90	111.90	−98.89
27	S	−29.86	−71.78	−120.40	−148.38	S	S	−43.90	−33.49	−4.76
28	42.78	−95.57	−96.93	−86.06	S	S	−22.71	−71.52	52.38	58.83
29	−79.95	61.16	48.39	S	S	45.50	81.13	19.61	H	S
30	135.23	−65.00	5.60	S	−254.16	11.56	71.60	66.22	S	S
31	−37.17	−41.38	S	46.49	86.90	−50.79	−30.88	S	S	134.60
Close	10503.76	11109.32	12354.35	12262.89	7608.92	10856.63	12319.73	13212.04	14578.54	16457.66
Change	−262.47	115.91	85.72	−3.50	545.99	531.37	93.39	259.97	524.05	135.95

APRIL DAILY POINT CHANGES DOW JONES INDUSTRIALS

Previous Month	2005	2006	2007	2008	2009	2010	2011	2012	2013	2014
Close	10503.76	11109.32	12354.35	12262.89	7608.92	10856.63	12319.73	13212.04	14578.54	16457.66
1	−99.46	S	S	391.47	152.68	70.44	56.99	S	−5.69	74.95
2	S	S	27.95	−48.53	216.48	H	S	52.45	89.16	40.39
3	S	35.62	128.00	20.20	39.51	S	S	−64.94	−111.66	−0.45
4	16.84	58.91	19.75	−16.61	S	S	23.31	−124.80	55.76	−159.84
5	37.32	35.70	30.15	S	S	46.48	−6.13	−14.61	−40.86	S
6	27.56	−23.05	H	S	−41.74	−3.56	32.85	H	S	S
7	60.30	−96.46	S	3.01	−186.29	−72.47	−17.26	S	S	−166.84
8	−84.98	S	S	−35.99	47.55	29.55	−29.44	S	48.23	10.27
9	S	S	8.94	−49.18	246.27	70.28	S	−130.55	59.98	181.04
10	S	21.29	4.71	54.72	H	S	S	−213.66	128.78	−266.96
11	−12.78	−51.70	−89.23	−256.56	S	S	1.06	89.46	62.90	−143.47
12	59.41	40.34	68.34	S	S	8.62	−117.53	181.19	−0.08	S
13	−104.04	7.68	59.17	S	−25.57	13.45	7.41	−136.99	S	S
14	−125.18	H	S	−23.36	−137.63	103.69	14.16	S	S	146.49
15	−191.24	S	S	60.41	109.44	21.46	56.68	S	−265.86	89.32
16	S	S	108.33	256.80	95.81	−125.91	S	71.82	157.58	162.29
17	S	−63.87	52.58	1.22	5.90	S	S	194.13	−138.19	−16.31
18	−16.26	194.99	30.80	228.87	S	S	−140.24	−82.79	−81.45	H
19	56.16	10.00	4.79	S	S	73.39	65.16	−68.65	10.37	S
20	−115.05	64.12	153.35	S	−289.60	25.01	186.79	65.16	S	S
21	206.24	4.56	S	−24.34	127.83	7.86	52.45	S	S	40.71
22	−60.89	S	S	−104.79	−82.99	9.37	H	S	19.66	65.12
23	S	S	−42.58	42.99	70.49	69.99	S	−102.09	152.29	−12.72
24	S	−11.13	34.54	85.73	119.23	S	S	74.39	−43.16	0.00
25	84.76	−53.07	135.95	42.91	S	S	−26.11	89.16	24.50	−140.19
26	−91.34	71.24	15.61	S	S	0.75	115.49	113.90	11.75	S
27	47.67	28.02	15.44	S	−51.29	−213.04	95.59	23.69	S	S
28	−128.43	−15.37	S	−20.11	−8.05	53.28	72.35	S	S	87.28
29	122.14	S	S	−39.81	168.78	122.05	47.23	S	106.20	86.63
30	S	S	−58.03	−11.81	−17.61	−158.71	S	−14.68	21.05	45.47
Close	10192.51	11367.14	13062.91	12820.13	8168.12	11008.61	12810.54	13213.63	14839.80	16580.84
Change	−311.25	257.82	708.56	557.24	559.20	151.98	490.81	1.59	261.26	123.18

MAY DAILY POINT CHANGES DOW JONES INDUSTRIALS

	2004	2005	2006	2007	2008	2009	2010	2011	2012	2013
Previous Month Close	10225.57	10192.51	11367.14	13062.91	12820.13	8168.12	11008.61	12810.54	13213.63	14839.80
1	S	S	-23.85	73.23	189.87	44.29	S	S	65.69	-138.85
2	S	59.19	73.16	75.74	48.20	S	S	-3.18	-10.75	130.63
3	88.43	5.25	-16.17	29.50	S	S	143.22	0.15	-61.98	142.38
4	3.20	127.69	38.58	23.24	S	214.33	-225.06	-83.93	-168.32	S
5	-6.25	-44.26	138.88	S	-88.66	-16.09	-58.65	-139.41	S	S
6	-69.69	5.02	S	S	51.29	101.63	-347.80	54.57	S	-5.07
7	-123.92	S	S	48.35	-206.48	-102.43	-139.89	S	-29.74	87.31
8	S	S	6.80	-3.90	52.43	164.80	S	S	-76.44	48.92
9	S	38.94	55.23	53.80	-120.90	S	S	45.94	-97.03	-22.50
10	-127.32	-103.23	2.88	-147.74	S	S	404.71	75.68	19.98	35.87
11	29.45	19.14	-141.92	111.09	S	-155.88	-36.88	-130.33	-34.44	S
12	25.69	-110.77	-119.74	S	130.43	50.34	148.65	65.89	S	S
13	-34.42	-49.36	S	S	-44.13	-184.22	-113.96	-100.17	S	-26.81
14	2.13	S	S	20.56	66.20	46.43	-162.79	S	-125.25	123.57
15	S	S	47.78	37.06	94.28	-62.68	S	S	-63.35	60.44
16	S	112.17	-8.88	103.69	-5.86	S	S	-47.38	-33.45	-42.47
17	-105.96	79.59	-214.28	-10.81	S	S	5.67	-68.79	-156.06	121.18
18	61.60	132.57	-77.32	79.81	S	235.44	-114.88	80.60	-73.11	S
19	-30.80	28.74	15.77	S	41.36	-29.23	-66.58	45.14	S	S
20	-0.07	-21.28	S	S	-199.48	-52.81	-376.36	-93.28	S	-19.12
21	29.10	S	S	-13.65	-227.49	-129.91	125.38	S	135.10	52.30
22	S	S	-18.73	-2.93	24.43	-14.81	S	S	-1.67	-80.41
23	S	51.65	-26.98	-14.30	-145.99	S	S	-130.78	-6.66	-12.67
24	-8.31	-19.88	18.97	-84.52	S	S	-126.82	-25.05	33.60	8.60
25	159.19	-45.88	93.73	66.15	S	H	-22.82	38.45	-74.92	S
26	-7.73	79.80	67.56	S	H	196.17	-69.30	8.10	S	S
27	95.31	4.95	S	S	68.72	-173.47	284.54	38.82	S	H
28	-16.75	S	S	H	45.68	103.78	-122.36	S	H	106.29
29	S	S	H	14.06	52.19	96.53	S	S	125.86	-106.59
30	S	H	-184.18	111.74	-7.90	S	S	H	-160.83	21.73
31	H	-75.07	73.88	-5.44	S	S	H	128.21	-26.41	-208.96
Close	10188.45	10467.48	11168.31	13627.64	12638.32	8500.33	10136.63	12569.79	12393.45	15115.57
Change	-37.12	274.97	-198.83	564.73	-181.81	332.21	-871.98	-240.75	-820.18	275.77

JUNE DAILY POINT CHANGES DOW JONES INDUSTRIALS

	2004	2005	2006	2007	2008	2009	2010	2011	2012	2013
Previous Month Close	10188.45	10467.48	11168.31	13627.64	12638.32	8500.33	10136.63	12569.79	12393.45	15115.57
1	14.20	82.39	91.97	40.47	S	221.11	-112.61	-279.65	-274.88	S
2	60.32	3.62	-12.41	S	-134.50	19.43	225.52	-41.59	S	S
3	-67.06	-92.52	S	S	-100.97	-65.59	5.74	-97.29	S	138.46
4	46.91	S	S	8.21	-12.37	74.96	-323.31	S	-17.11	-76.49
5	S	S	-199.15	-80.86	213.97	12.89	S	S	26.49	-216.95
6	S	6.06	-46.58	-129.79	-394.64	S	S	-61.30	286.84	80.03
7	148.26	16.04	-71.24	-198.94	S	S	-115.48	-19.15	46.17	207.50
8	41.44	-6.21	7.92	157.66	S	1.36	123.49	-21.87	93.24	S
9	-64.08	26.16	-46.90	S	70.51	-1.43	-40.73	75.42	S	S
10	41.66	9.61	S	S	9.44	-24.04	273.28	-172.45	S	-9.53
11	H*	S	S	0.57	-205.99	31.90	38.54	S	-142.97	-116.57
12	S	S	-99.34	-129.95	57.81	28.34	S	S	162.57	-126.79
13	S	9.93	-86.44	187.34	165.77	S	S	1.06	-77.42	180.85
14	-75.37	25.01	110.78	71.37	S	S	-20.18	123.14	155.53	-105.90
15	45.70	18.80	198.27	85.76	S	-187.13	213.88	-178.84	115.26	S
16	-0.85	12.28	-0.64	S	-38.27	-107.46	4.69	64.25	S	S
17	-2.06	44.42	S	S	-108.78	-7.49	24.71	42.84	S	109.67
18	38.89	S	S	-26.50	-131.24	58.42	16.47	S	-25.35	138.38
19	S	S	-72.44	22.44	34.03	-15.87	S	S	95.51	-206.04
20	S	-13.96	32.73	-146.00	-220.40	S	S	76.02	-12.94	-353.87
21	-44.94	-9.44	104.62	56.42	S	S	-8.23	109.63	-250.82	41.08
22	23.60	-11.74	-60.35	-185.58	S	-200.72	-148.89	-80.34	67.21	S
23	84.50	-166.49	-30.02	S	-0.33	-16.10	4.92	-59.67	S	S
24	-35.76	-123.60	S	S	-34.93	-23.05	-145.64	-115.42	S	-139.84
25	-71.97	S	S	-8.21	4.40	172.54	-8.99	S	-138.12	100.75
26	S	S	56.19	-14.39	-358.41	-34.01	S	S	32.01	149.83
27	S	-7.06	-120.54	90.07	-106.91	S	S	108.98	92.34	114.35
28	-14.75	114.85	48.82	-5.45	S	S	-5.29	145.13	-24.75	-114.89
29	56.34	-31.15	217.24	-13.66	S	90.99	-268.22	72.73	277.83	S
30	22.05	-99.51	-40.58	S	3.50	-82.38	-96.28	152.92	S	S
Close	10435.48	10274.97	11150.22	13408.62	11350.01	8447.00	9774.02	12414.34	12880.09	14909.60
Change	247.03	-192.51	-18.09	-219.02	-1288.31	-53.33	-362.61	-155.45	486.64	-205.97

* Reagan funeral

135

JULY DAILY POINT CHANGES DOW JONES INDUSTRIALS

Previous Month Close	2004	2005	2006	2007	2008	2009	2010	2011	2012	2013
	10435.48	10274.97	11150.22	13408.62	11350.01	8447.00	9774.02	12414.34	12880.09	14909.60
1	−101.32	28.47	S	S	32.25	57.06	−41.49	168.43	S	65.36
2	−51.33	S	S	126.81	−166.75	−223.32	−46.05	S	−8.70	−42.55
3	S	S	77.8*	41.87*	73.03*	H	S	S	72.43*	56.14*
4	S	H	H	H	H	S	S	H	H	H
5	H	68.36	−76.20	−11.46	S	S	H	−12.90	−47.15	147.29
6	−63.49	−101.12	73.48	45.84	S	44.13	57.14	56.15	−124.20	S
7	20.95	31.61	−134.63	S	−56.58	−161.27	274.66	93.47	S	S
8	−68.73	146.85	S	S	152.25	14.81	120.71	−62.29	S	88.85
9	41.66	S	S	38.29	−236.77	4.76	59.04	S	−36.18	75.65
10	S	S	12.88	−148.27	81.58	−36.65	S	S	−83.17	−8.68
11	S	70.58	31.22	76.17	−128.48	S	S	−151.44	−48.59	169.26
12	25.00	−5.83	−121.59	283.86	S	S	18.24	−58.88	−31.26	3.38
13	9.37	43.50	−166.89	45.52	S	185.16	146.75	44.73	203.82	S
14	−38.79	71.50	−106.94	S	−45.35	27.81	3.70	−54.49	S	S
15	−45.64	11.94	S	43.73	−92.65	256.72	−7.41	42.61	S	19.96
16	−23.38	S	S	8.01	276.74	95.61	−261.41	S	−49.88	−32.41
17	S	S	8.01	20.57	207.38	32.12	S	S	78.33	18.67
18	S	−65.84	51.87	−53.33	49.91	S	S	−94.57	103.16	78.02
19	−45.72	71.57	212.19	82.19	S	S	56.53	202.26	34.66	−4.80
20	55.01	42.59	−83.32	−149.33	S	104.21	75.53	−15.51	−120.79	S
21	−102.94	−61.38	−59.72	S	−29.23	67.79	−109.43	152.50	S	S
22	4.20	23.41	S	S	135.16	−34.68	201.77	−43.25	S	1.81
23	−88.11	S	S	92.34	29.88	188.03	102.32	S	−101.11	22.19
24	S	S	182.67	−226.47	−283.10	23.95	S	S	−104.14	−25.50
25	S	−54.70	52.66	68.12	21.41	S	S	−88.36	58.73	13.37
26	−0.30	−16.71	−1.20	−311.50	S	S	100.81	−91.50	211.88	3.22
27	123.22	57.32	−2.08	−208.10	S	15.27	12.26	−198.75	187.73	S
28	31.93	68.46	119.27	S	−239.61	−11.79	−39.81	−62.44	S	S
29	12.17	−64.64	S	S	266.48	−26.00	−30.72	−96.87	S	−36.86
30	10.47	S	S	92.84	186.13	83.74	−1.22	S	−2.65	−1.38
31	S	S	−34.02	−146.32	−205.67	17.15	S	S	−64.33	−21.05
Close	10139.71	10640.91	11185.68	13211.99	11378.02	9171.61	10465.94	12143.24	13008.68	15499.54
Change	−295.77	365.94	35.46	−196.63	28.01	724.61	691.92	−271.10	128.59	589.94

* Shortened trading day

AUGUST DAILY POINT CHANGES DOW JONES INDUSTRIALS

Previous Month Close	2004	2005	2006	2007	2008	2009	2010	2011	2012	2013
	10139.71	10640.91	11185.68	13211.99	11378.02	9171.61	10465.94	12143.24	13008.68	15499.54
1	S	−17.76	−59.95	150.38	−51.70	S	S	−10.75	−37.62	128.48
2	39.45	60.59	74.20	100.96	S	S	208.44	−265.87	−92.18	30.34
3	−58.92	13.85	42.66	−281.42	S	114.95	−38.00	29.82	217.29	S
4	6.27	−87.49	−2.24	S	−42.17	33.63	44.05	−512.76	S	S
5	−163.48	−52.07	S	S	331.62	−39.22	−5.45	60.93	S	−46.23
6	−147.70	S	S	286.87	40.30	−24.71	−21.42	S	21.34	−93.39
7	S	S	−20.97	35.52	−224.64	113.81	S	S	51.09	−48.07
8	S	−21.10	−45.79	153.56	302.89	S	S	−634.76	7.04	27.65
9	−0.67	78.74	−97.41	−387.18	S	S	45.19	429.92	−10.45	−72.81
10	130.01	−21.26	48.19	−31.14	S	−32.12	−54.50	−519.83	42.76	S
11	−6.35	91.48	−36.34	S	−96.50	−265.42	423.37	S	S	S
12	−123.73	−85.58	S	S	−139.88	120.16	−58.88	125.71	S	−5.83
13	10.76	S	S	−3.01	−109.51	36.58	−16.80	S	−38.52	31.33
14	S	S	9.84	−207.61	82.97	−76.79	S	S	2.71	−113.35
15	S	34.07	132.39	−167.45	43.97	S	S	213.88	−7.36	−225.47
16	129.20	−120.93	96.86	−15.69	S	−1.14	−76.97	85.33	−30.72
17	18.28	37.26	7.84	233.30	S	−186.06	103.84	4.28	25.09	S
18	110.32	4.22	46.51	S	−180.51	82.60	9.69	−419.63	S	S
19	−42.33	4.30	S	S	−130.84	61.22	−144.33	−172.93	S	−70.73
20	69.32	S	42.27	68.88	70.89	−57.59	S	−3.56	−7.75
21	S	S	−36.42	−30.49	12.78	155.91	S	S	−68.06	−105.44
22	S	10.66	−5.21	145.27	197.85	S	S	37.00	−30.82	66.19
23	−37.09	−50.31	−41.94	−0.25	S	S	−39.21	322.11	−115.30	46.77
24	25.58	−84.71	6.56	142.99	S	3.32	−133.96	143.95	100.51	S
25	83.11	15.76	−20.41	S	−241.81	30.01	19.61	−170.89	S	S
26	−8.33	−53.34	S	S	26.62	4.23	−74.25	134.72	S	−64.05
27	21.60	S	S	−56.74	89.64	37.11	164.84	S	−33.30	−170.33
28	S	S	67.96	−280.28	212.67	−36.43	S	S	−21.68	48.38
29	S	65.76	17.93	247.44	−171.63	S	S	254.71	4.49	16.44
30	−72.49	−50.23	12.97	−50.56	S	S	−140.92	20.70	−106.77	−30.64
31	51.40	68.78	−1.76	119.01	S	−47.92	4.99	53.58	90.13	S
Close	10173.92	10481.60	11381.15	13357.74	11543.55	9496.28	10014.72	11613.53	13090.84	14810.31
Change	34.21	−159.31	195.47	145.75	165.53	324.67	−451.22	−529.71	82.16	−689.23

136

SEPTEMBER DAILY POINT CHANGES DOW JONES INDUSTRIALS

Previous Month Close	2004	2005	2006	2007	2008	2009	2010	2011	2012	2013
	10173.92	10481.60	11381.15	13357.74	11543.55	9496.28	10014.72	11613.53	13090.84	14810.31
1	−5.46	−21.97	83.00	S	H	−185.68	254.75	−119.96	S	S
2	121.82	−12.26	S	S	−26.63	−29.93	50.63	−253.31	S	H
3	−30.08	S	S	S	15.96	63.94	157.83	S	H	23.65
4	S	S	H	91.12	−344.65	96.66	S	S	S	96.91
5	S	H	5.13	−143.39	32.73	S	S	H	11.54	6.61
6	H	141.87	−63.08	57.88	S	S	H	−100.96	244.52	−14.98
7	82.59	44.26	−74.76	−249.97	S	H	−137.24	275.56	14.64	S
8	−29.43	−37.57	60.67	S	289.78	56.07	46.32	−119.05	S	S
9	−24.26	82.63	S	S	−280.01	49.88	28.23	−303.68	S	140.62
10	23.97	S	S	14.47	38.19	80.26	47.53	S	−52.35	127.94
11	S	S	4.73	180.54	164.79	−22.07	S	S	69.07	135.54
12	S	4.38	101.25	−16.74	−11.72	S	S	68.99	9.99	−25.96
13	1.69	−85.50	45.23	133.23	S	S	81.36	44.73	206.51	75.42
14	3.40	−52.54	−15.93	17.64	S	21.39	−17.64	140.88	53.51	S
15	−86.80	13.85	33.38	S	−504.48	56.61	46.24	186.45	S	S
16	13.13	83.19	S	S	141.51	108.30	22.10	75.91	S	118.72
17	39.97	S	S	−39.10	−449.36	−7.79	13.02	S	−40.27	34.95
18	S	S	−5.77	335.97	410.03	36.28	S	S	11.54	147.21
19	S	−84.31	−14.09	76.17	368.75	S	S	−108.08	13.32	−40.39
20	−79.57	−76.11	72.28	−48.86	S	S	145.77	7.65	18.97	−185.46
21	40.04	−103.49	−79.96	53.49	S	−41.34	7.41	−283.82	−17.46	S
22	−135.75	44.02	−25.13	S	−372.75	51.01	−21.72	−391.01	S	S
23	−70.28	−2.46	S	S	−161.52	−81.32	−76.89	37.65	S	−49.71
24	8.34	S	S	−61.13	−29.00	−41.11	197.84	S	−20.55	−66.79
25	S	S	67.71	19.59	196.89	−42.25	S	S	−101.37	−61.33
26	S	24.04	93.58	99.50	121.07	S	S	272.38	−44.04	55.04
27	−58.70	12.58	19.85	34.79	S	S	−48.22	146.83	72.46	−70.06
28	88.86	16.88	29.21	−17.31	S	124.17	46.10	−179.79	−48.84	S
29	58.84	79.69	−39.38	S	−777.68	−47.16	−22.86	143.08	S	S
30	−55.97	15.92	S	S	485.21	−29.92	−47.23	−240.60	S	−128.57
Close	10080.27	10568.70	11679.07	13895.63	10850.66	9712.28	10788.05	10913.38	13437.13	15129.67
Change	−93.65	87.10	297.92	537.89	−692.89	216.00	773.33	−700.15	346.29	319.36

OCTOBER DAILY POINT CHANGES DOW JONES INDUSTRIALS

Previous Month Close	2004	2005	2006	2007	2008	2009	2010	2011	2012	2013
	10080.27	10568.70	11679.07	13895.63	10850.66	9712.28	10788.05	10913.38	13437.13	15129.67
1	112.38	S	S	191.92	−19.59	−203.00	41.63	S	77.98	62.03
2	S	S	−8.72	−40.24	−348.22	−21.61	S	S	−32.75	−58.56
3	S	−33.22	56.99	−79.26	−157.47	S	S	−258.08	12.25	−136.66
4	23.89	−94.37	123.27	6.26	S	S	−78.41	153.41	80.75	76.10
5	−38.86	−123.75	16.08	91.70	S	112.08	193.45	131.24	34.79	S
6	62.24	−30.26	−16.48	S	−369.88	131.50	22.93	183.38	S	S
7	−114.52	5.21	S	S	−508.39	−5.67	−19.07	−20.21	S	−136.34
8	−70.20	S	S	−22.28	−189.01	61.29	57.90	S	−26.50	−159.71
9	S	S	7.60	120.80	−678.91	78.07	S	S	−110.12	26.45
10	S	−53.55	9.36	−85.84	−128.00	S	S	330.06	−128.56	323.09
11	26.77	14.41	−15.04	−63.57	S	S	3.86	−16.88	−18.58	111.04
12	−4.79	−36.26	95.57	77.96	S	20.86	10.06	102.55	2.46	S
13	−74.85	−0.32	12.81	S	936.42	−14.74	75.68	−40.72	S	S
14	−107.88	70.75	S	S	−76.62	144.80	−1.51	166.36	S	64.15
15	38.93	S	S	−108.28	−733.08	47.08	−31.79	S	95.38	−133.25
16	S	S	20.09	−71.86	401.35	−67.03	S	S	127.55	205.82
17	S	60.76	−30.58	−20.40	−127.04	S	S	−247.49	5.22	−2.18
18	22.94	−62.84	42.66	−3.58	S	S	80.91	180.05	−8.06	28.00
19	−58.70	128.87	19.05	−366.94	S	96.28	−165.07	−72.43	−205.43	S
20	−10.69	−133.03	−9.36	S	413.21	−50.71	129.35	37.16	S	S
21	−21.17	−65.88	S	S	−231.77	−92.12	38.60	267.01	S	−7.45
22	−107.95	S	S	44.95	−514.45	131.95	−14.01	S	2.38	75.46
23	S	S	114.54	109.26	172.04	−109.13	S	S	−243.36	−54.33
24	S	169.78	10.97	−0.98	−312.30	S	S	104.83	−25.19	95.88
25	−7.82	−7.13	6.80	−3.33	S	S	31.49	−207.00	26.34	61.07
26	138.49	−32.89	28.98	134.78	S	−104.22	5.41	162.42	3.53	S
27	113.55	−115.03	−73.40	S	−203.18	14.21	−43.18	339.51	S	S
28	2.51	172.82	S	S	889.35	−119.48	−12.33	22.56	S	−1.35
29	22.93	S	S	63.56	−74.16	199.89	4.54	S	H*	111.42
30	S	S	−3.76	−77.79	189.73	−249.85	S	S	H*	−61.59
31	S	37.30	−5.77	137.54	144.32	S	S	−276.10	S	−73.01
Close	10027.47	10440.07	12080.73	13930.01	9325.01	9712.73	11118.49	11955.01	13096.46	15545.75
Change	−52.80	−128.63	401.66	34.38	−1525.65	0.45	330.44	1041.63	−340.67	416.08

* Hurricane Sandy

NOVEMBER DAILY POINT CHANGES DOW JONES INDUSTRIALS

	2004	2005	2006	2007	2008	2009	2010	2011	2012	2013
Previous Month Close	10027.47	10440.07	12080.73	13930.01	9325.01	9712.73	11118.49	11955.01	13096.46	15545.75
1	26.92	−33.30	−49.71	−362.14	S	S	6.13	−297.05	136.16	69.80
2	−18.66	65.96	−12.48	27.23	S	76.71	64.10	178.08	−139.46	S
3	101.32	49.86	−32.50	S	−5.18	−17.53	26.41	208.43	S	S
4	177.71	8.17	S	S	305.45	30.23	219.71	−61.23	S	23.57
5	72.78	S	S	−51.70	−486.01	203.82	9.24	S	19.28	−20.90
6	S	S	119.51	117.54	−443.48	17.46	S	S	133.24	128.66
7	S	55.47	51.22	−360.92	248.02	S	S	85.15	−312.95	−152.90
8	3.77	−46.51	19.77	−33.73	S	S	−37.24	101.79	−121.41	167.80
9	−4.94	6.49	−73.24	−223.55	S	203.52	−60.09	−389.24	4.07	S
10	−0.89	93.89	5.13	S	−73.27	20.03	10.29	112.85	S	S
11	84.36	45.94	S	S	−176.58	44.29	−73.94	259.89	S	21.32
12	69.17	S	S	−55.19	−411.30	−93.79	−90.52	S	−0.31	−32.43
13	S	S	23.45	319.54	552.59	73.00	S	S	−58.90	70.96
14	S	11.13	86.13	−76.08	−337.94	S	S	−74.70	−185.23	54.59
15	11.23	−10.73	33.70	−120.96	S	S	9.39	17.18	−28.57	85.48
16	−62.59	−11.68	54.11	66.74	S	136.49	−178.47	−190.57	45.93	S
17	61.92	45.46	36.74	S	−223.73	30.46	−15.62	−134.86	S	S
18	22.98	46.11	S	S	151.17	−11.11	173.35	25.43	S	14.32
19	−115.64	S	S	−218.35	−427.47	−93.87	22.32	S	207.65	−8.99
20	S	S	−26.02	51.70	−444.99	−14.28	S	S	−7.45	−66.21
21	S	53.95	5.05	−211.10	494.13	S	S	−248.85	48.38	109.17
22	32.51	51.15	5.36	H	S	S	−24.97	−53.59	H	54.78
23	3.18	44.66	H	181.84*	S	132.79	−142.21	−236.17	172.79*	S
24	27.71	H	−46.78*	S	396.97	−17.24	150.91	H	S	S
25	H	15.53*	S	S	36.08	30.69	H	−25.77*	H	7.77
26	1.92*	S	S	−237.44	247.14	H	−95.28*	S	−42.31	0.26
27	S	S	−158.46	215.00	H	−154.48*	S	S	−89.24	24.53
28	S	−40.90	14.74	331.01	102.43*	S	S	291.23	106.98	H
29	−46.33	−2.56	90.28	22.28	S	S	−39.51	32.62	36.71	−10.92*
30	−47.88	−82.29	−4.80	59.99	S	34.92	−46.47	490.05	3.76	S
Close	10428.02	10805.87	12221.93	13371.72	8829.04	10344.84	11006.02	12045.68	13025.58	16086.41
Change	400.55	365.80	141.20	−558.29	−495.97	632.11	−112.47	90.67	−70.88	540.66

* Shortened trading day

DECEMBER DAILY POINT CHANGES DOW JONES INDUSTRIALS

	2004	2005	2006	2007	2008	2009	2010	2011	2012	2013
Previous Month Close	10428.02	10805.87	12221.93	13371.72	8829.04	10344.84	11006.02	12045.68	13025.58	16086.41
1	162.20	106.70	−27.80	S	−679.95	126.74	249.76	−25.65	S	S
2	−5.10	−35.06	S	S	270.00	−18.90	106.63	−0.61	S	−77.64
3	7.09	S	S	−57.15	172.60	−86.53	19.68	S	−59.98	−94.15
4	S	S	89.72	−65.84	−215.45	22.75	S	S	−13.82	−24.85
5	S	−42.50	47.75	196.23	259.18	S	S	78.41	82.71	−68.26
6	−45.15	21.85	−22.35	174.93	S	S	−19.90	52.30	39.55	198.69
7	−106.48	−45.95	−30.84	5.69	S	1.21	−3.03	46.24	81.09	S
8	53.65	−55.79	29.08	S	298.76	−104.14	13.32	−198.67	S	S
9	58.59	23.46	S	S	−242.85	51.08	−2.42	186.56	S	5.33
10	−9.60	S	S	101.45	70.09	68.78	40.26	S	14.75	−52.40
11	S	S	20.99	−294.26	−196.33	65.67	S	S	78.56	−129.60
12	S	−10.81	−12.90	41.13	64.59	S	S	−162.87	−2.99	−104.10
13	95.10	55.95	1.92	44.06	S	29.55	18.24	−66.45	−74.73	15.93
14	38.13	59.79	99.26	−178.11	S	29.55	47.98	−131.46	−35.71	S
15	15.00	−1.84	28.76	S	−65.15	−49.05	−19.07	45.33	S	S
16	14.19	−6.08	S	S	359.61	−10.88	41.78	−2.42	S	129.21
17	−55.72	S	S	−172.65	−99.80	−132.63	−7.34	S	100.38	−9.31
18	S	S	−4.25	65.27	−219.35	20.63	S	S	115.57	292.71
19	S	−39.06	30.05	−25.20	−25.88	S	S	−100.13	−98.99	11.11
20	11.68	−30.98	−7.45	38.37	S	S	−13.78	337.32	59.75	42.06
21	97.83	28.18	−42.62	205.01	S	85.25	55.03	4.16	−120.88	S
22	56.46	55.71	−78.03	S	−59.34	50.79	26.33	61.91	S	73.47
23	11.23	−6.17	S	S	−100.28	1.51	14.00	124.35	S	73.47
24	H	S	S	98.68*	48.99*	53.66*	H	S	−51.76*	62.94*
25	S	H	H	H	H	H	S	S	H	H
26	S	H	64.41	2.36	47.07	S	S	H	−24.49	122.33
27	−50.99	−105.50	102.94	−192.08	S	S	−18.46	−2.65	−18.28	−1.47
28	78.41	18.49	−9.05	6.26	S	26.98	20.51	−139.94	−158.20	S
29	−25.35	−11.44	−38.37	S	−31.62	−1.67	9.84	135.63	S	S
30	−28.89	−67.32	S	S	184.46	3.10	−15.67	−69.48	S	25.88
31	−17.29	S	S	−101.05	108.00	−120.46	7.80	S	166.03	72.37
Close	10783.01	10717.50	12463.15	13264.82	8776.39	10428.05	11577.51	12217.56	13104.14	16576.66
Change	354.99	−88.37	241.22	−106.90	−52.65	83.21	571.49	171.88	78.56	490.25

* Shortened trading day

A TYPICAL DAY IN THE MARKET

Half-hourly data became available for the Dow Jones Industrial Average starting in January 1987. The NYSE switched 10:00 a.m. openings to 9:30 a.m. in October 1985. Below is the comparison between half-hourly performance from January 1987 to May 2, 2014, and hourly performance from November 1963 to June 1985. Stronger openings and closings in a more bullish climate are evident. Morning and afternoon weaknesses appear an hour earlier.

MARKET % PERFORMANCE EACH HALF-HOUR OF THE DAY
(January 1987 to May 2, 2014)

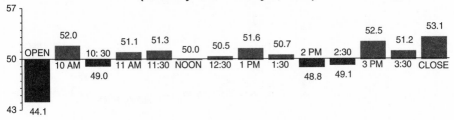

Based on the number of times the Dow Jones Industrial Average increased over previous half-hour.

MARKET % PERFORMANCE EACH HOUR OF THE DAY
(November 1963 to June 1985)

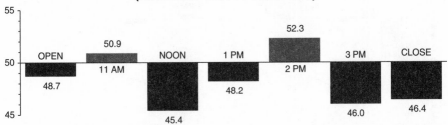

Based on the number of times the Dow Jones Industrial Average increased over previous hour.

On the next page, half-hourly movements since January 1987 are separated by day of the week. From 1953 to 1989, Monday was the worst day of the week, especially during long bear markets, but times changed. Monday reversed positions and became the best day of the week and on the plus side eleven years in a row from 1990 to 2000.

During the last 14 years (2001–May 2, 2014) Monday and Friday are net losers. Tuesday through Thursday are solid gainers, Tuesday the best (page 70). On all days stocks do tend to firm up near the close with weakness early morning and from 2 to 2:30 frequently.

THROUGH THE WEEK ON A HALF-HOURLY BASIS

From the chart showing the percentage of times the Dow Jones Industrial Average rose over the preceding half-hour (January 1987 to May 2, 2014*), the typical week unfolds.

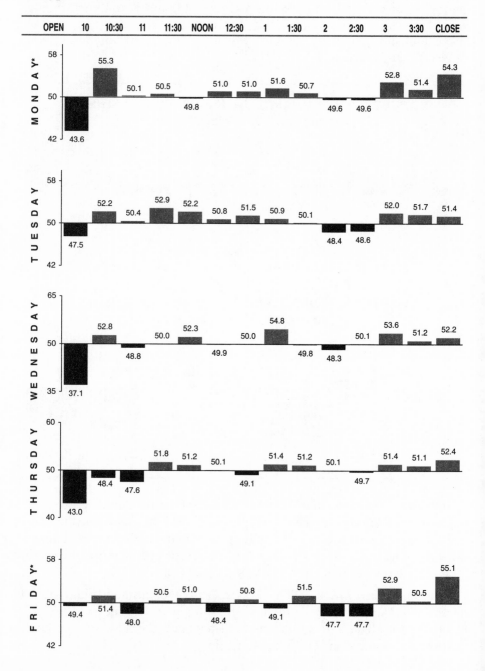

*Monday denotes first trading day of the week, Friday denotes last trading day of the week.

TUESDAY MOST PROFITABLE DAY OF WEEK

Between 1952 and 1989, Monday was the worst trading day of the week. The first trading day of the week (including Tuesday, when Monday is a holiday) rose only 44.3% of the time, while the other trading days closed higher 54.8% of the time. (NYSE Saturday trading was discontinued June 1952.)

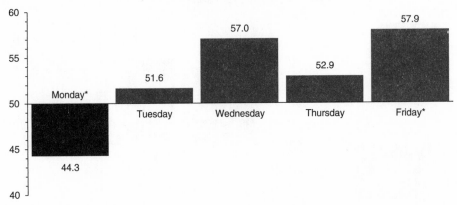

MARKET % PERFORMANCE EACH DAY OF THE WEEK
(June 1952 to December 1989)

A dramatic reversal occurred in 1990—Monday became the most powerful day of the week. However, during the last 13 and a third years, Tuesday has produced the most gains. Since the top in 2000, traders have not been inclined to stay long over the weekend nor buy up equities at the outset of the week. This is not uncommon during uncertain market times. Monday was the worst day during the 2007–2009 bear, and only Tuesday was a net gainer. Since the March 2009 bottom, Tuesday and Thursday are best. See pages 70 and 143.

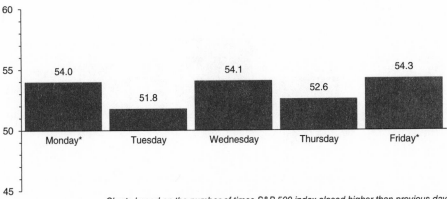

MARKET % PERFORMANCE EACH DAY OF THE WEEK
(January 1990 to May 2, 2014)

Charts based on the number of times S&P 500 index closed higher than previous day.
*Monday denotes first trading day of the week, Friday denotes last trading day of the week.

NASDAQ STRONGEST LAST 3 DAYS OF WEEK

Despite 20 years less data, daily trading patterns on NASDAQ through 1989 appear to be fairly similar to the S&P on page 141, except for more bullishness on Thursdays. During the mostly flat markets of the 1970s and early 1980s, it would appear that apprehensive investors decided to throw in the towel over weekends and sell on Mondays and Tuesdays.

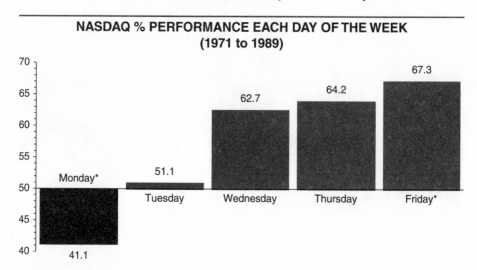

NASDAQ % PERFORMANCE EACH DAY OF THE WEEK
(1971 to 1989)

Notice the vast difference in the daily trading pattern between NASDAQ and S&P from January 1, 1990, to recent times. The reason for so much more bullishness is that NASDAQ moved up 1010%, over three times as much during the 1990 to 2000 period. The gain for the S&P was 332% and for the Dow Jones industrials, 326%. NASDAQ's weekly patterns are beginning to move in step with the rest of the market. Notice the similarities to the S&P since 2001 on pages 143 and 144—Monday and Friday weakness, midweek strength.

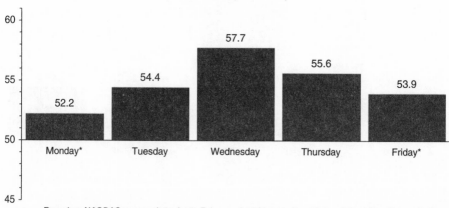

NASDAQ % PERFORMANCE EACH DAY OF THE WEEK
(1990 to May 2, 2014)

Based on NASDAQ composite, prior to February 5, 1971, based on National Quotation Bureau indices.
*Monday denotes first trading day of the week, Friday denotes last trading day of the week.

S&P DAILY PERFORMANCE EACH YEAR SINCE 1952

To determine if market trend alters performance of different days of the week, we separated 22 bear years—1953, '56, '57, '60, '62, '66, '69, '70, '73, '74, '77, '78, '81, '84, '87, '90, '94, 2000, 2001, 2002, 2008, and 2011—from 40 bull market years. While Tuesday and Thursday did not vary much between bull and bear years, Mondays and Fridays were sharply affected. There was a swing of 10.6 percentage points in Monday's and 9.5 in Friday's performance. Tuesday is the best day of the week based upon total points gained. See page 70.

PERCENTAGE OF TIMES MARKET CLOSED HIGHER THAN PREVIOUS DAY
(June 1952 to May 2, 2014)

	Monday*	Tuesday	Wednesday	Thursday	Friday*
1952	48.4%	55.6%	58.1%	51.9%	66.7%
1953	32.7	50.0	54.9	57.5	56.6
1954	50.0	57.5	63.5	59.2	73.1
1955	50.0	45.7	63.5	60.0	78.9
1956	36.5	39.6	46.9	50.0	59.6
1957	25.0	54.0	66.7	48.9	44.2
1958	59.6	52.0	59.6	68.1	72.6
1959	42.3	53.1	55.8	48.9	69.8
1960	34.6	50.0	44.2	54.0	59.6
1961	52.9	54.4	64.7	56.0	67.3
1962	28.3	52.1	54.0	51.0	50.0
1963	46.2	63.3	51.0	57.5	69.2
1964	40.4	48.0	61.5	58.7	77.4
1965	44.2	57.5	55.8	51.0	71.2
1966	36.5	47.8	53.9	42.0	57.7
1967	38.5	50.0	60.8	64.0	69.2
1968†	49.1	57.5	64.3	42.6	54.9
1969	30.8	45.8	50.0	67.4	50.0
1970	38.5	46.0	63.5	48.9	52.8
1971	44.2	64.6	57.7	55.1	51.9
1972	38.5	60.9	57.7	51.0	67.3
1973	32.1	51.1	52.9	44.9	44.2
1974	32.7	57.1	51.0	36.7	30.8
1975	53.9	38.8	61.5	56.3	55.8
1976	55.8	55.3	55.8	40.8	58.5
1977	40.4	40.4	46.2	53.1	53.9
1978	51.9	43.5	59.6	54.0	48.1
1979	54.7	53.2	58.8	66.0	44.2
1980	55.8	54.2	71.7	35.4	59.6
1981	44.2	38.8	55.8	53.2	47.2
1982	46.2	39.6	44.2	44.9	50.0
1983	55.8	46.8	61.5	52.0	55.8
1984	39.6	63.8	31.4	46.0	44.2
1985	44.2	61.2	54.9	56.3	53.9
1986	51.9	44.9	67.3	58.3	55.8
1987	51.9	57.1	63.5	61.7	49.1
1988	51.9	61.7	51.9	48.0	59.6
1989	51.9	47.8	69.2	58.0	69.2
1990	67.9	53.2	52.9	40.0	51.9
1991	44.2	46.9	52.9	49.0	51.9
1992	51.9	49.0	53.9	56.3	45.3
1993	65.4	41.7	55.8	44.9	48.1
1994	55.8	46.8	52.9	48.0	59.6
1995	63.5	56.5	63.5	62.0	63.5
1996	54.7	44.9	51.0	57.1	63.5
1997	67.3	67.4	42.3	41.7	57.7
1998	57.7	62.5	57.7	38.3	60.4
1999	46.2	29.8	67.3	53.1	57.7
2000	51.9	43.5	40.4	56.0	46.2
2001	45.3	51.1	44.0	59.2	43.1
2002	40.4	37.5	56.9	38.8	48.1
2003	59.6	62.5	42.3	58.3	50.0
2004	51.9	61.7	59.6	52.1	52.8
2005	59.6	47.8	59.6	56.0	55.8
2006	55.8	55.6	67.3	52.0	48.1
2007	47.2	50.0	64.0	50.0	61.5
2008	42.3	50.0	41.5	60.4	55.8
2009	53.9	50.0	57.7	63.8	52.8
2010	61.5	57.5	55.8	53.1	57.7
2011	48.1	56.5	55.8	56.0	57.7
2012	52.8	48.9	50.0	58.0	53.9
2013	51.9	60.4	54.9	59.2	65.4
2014‡	52.9	86.7	47.1	52.9	38.9
Average	**48.0%**	**51.5%**	**55.9%**	**52.8%**	**56.6%**
40 Bull Years	**51.8%**	**52.9%**	**58.2%**	**53.6%**	**60.0%**
22 Bear Years	**41.2%**	**48.9%**	**51.8%**	**51.3%**	**50.5%**

Based on S&P 500

† Most Wednesdays closed last 7 months of 1968 ‡ Through 5/2/2014 only, not included in averages
*Monday denotes first trading day of the week, Friday denotes last trading day of the week.

NASDAQ DAILY PERFORMANCE EACH YEAR SINCE 1971

After dropping a hefty 77.9% from its 2000 high (versus –37.8% on the Dow and –49.1% on the S&P 500), NASDAQ tech stocks still outpace the blue chips and big caps—but not by nearly as much as they did. From January 1, 1971 through May 2, 2014, NASDAQ, moved up an impressive 4502%. The Dow (up 1868%) and the S&P (up 1941%) gained less than half as much.

Monday's performance on NASDAQ was lackluster during the three-year bear market of 2000–2002. As NASDAQ rebounded (up 50% in 2003), strength returned to Monday during 2003–2006. During the bear market from late 2007 to early 2009, weakness was most consistent on Monday and Friday.

PERCENTAGE OF TIMES NASDAQ CLOSED HIGHER THAN PREVIOUS DAY
(1971 to May 2, 2014)

	Monday*	Tuesday	Wednesday	Thursday	Friday*
1971	51.9%	52.1%	59.6%	65.3%	71.2%
1972	30.8	60.9	63.5	57.1	78.9
1973	34.0	48.9	52.9	53.1	48.1
1974	30.8	44.9	52.9	51.0	42.3
1975	44.2	42.9	63.5	64.6	63.5
1976	50.0	63.8	67.3	59.2	58.5
1977	51.9	40.4	53.9	63.3	73.1
1978	48.1	47.8	73.1	72.0	84.6
1979	45.3	53.2	64.7	86.0	82.7
1980	46.2	64.6	84.9	52.1	73.1
1981	42.3	32.7	67.3	76.6	69.8
1982	34.6	47.9	59.6	51.0	63.5
1983	42.3	44.7	67.3	68.0	73.1
1984	22.6	53.2	35.3	52.0	51.9
1985	36.5	59.2	62.8	68.8	66.0
1986	38.5	55.1	65.4	72.9	75.0
1987	42.3	49.0	65.4	68.1	66.0
1988	50.0	55.3	61.5	66.0	63.5
1989	38.5	54.4	71.2	72.0	75.0
1990	54.7	42.6	60.8	46.0	55.8
1991	51.9	59.2	66.7	65.3	51.9
1992	44.2	53.1	59.6	60.4	45.3
1993	55.8	56.3	69.2	57.1	67.3
1994	51.9	46.8	54.9	52.0	55.8
1995	50.0	52.2	63.5	64.0	63.5
1996	50.9	57.1	64.7	61.2	63.5
1997	65.4	59.2	53.9	52.1	55.8
1998	59.6	58.3	65.4	44.7	58.5
1999	61.5	40.4	63.5	57.1	65.4
2000	40.4	41.3	42.3	60.0	57.7
2001	41.5	57.8	52.0	55.1	47.1
2002	44.2	37.5	56.9	46.9	46.2
2003	57.7	60.4	40.4	60.4	46.2
2004	57.7	59.6	53.9	50.0	50.9
2005	61.5	47.8	51.9	48.0	59.6
2006	55.8	51.1	65.4	50.0	44.2
2007	47.2	63.0	66.0	56.0	57.7
2008	34.6	52.1	49.1	54.2	42.3
2009	51.9	54.2	63.5	63.8	50.9
2010	61.5	53.2	61.5	55.1	61.5
2011	50.0	56.5	50.0	64.0	53.9
2012	49.1	53.3	50.0	54.0	51.9
2013	57.7	60.4	52.9	59.2	67.3
2014†	47.1	86.7	64.7	52.9	27.8
Average	**47.4%**	**52.2%**	**59.8%**	**59.4%**	**60.5%**
31 Bull Years	**49.9%**	**54.2%**	**62.3%**	**60.5%**	**63.3%**
12 Bear Years	**40.8%**	**46.9%**	**53.3%**	**56.6%**	**53.1%**

Based on NASDAQ composite; prior to February 5, 1971, based on National Quotation Bureau indices.
† Through 5/2/2014 only, not included in averages
*Monday denotes first trading day of the week, Friday denotes last trading day of the week.

MONTHLY CASH INFLOWS INTO S&P STOCKS

For many years, the last trading day of the month, plus the first four of the following month, were the best market days of the month. This pattern is quite clear in the first chart, showing these five consecutive trading days towering above the other 16 trading days of the average month in the 1953–1981 period. The rationale was that individuals and institutions tended to operate similarly, causing a massive flow of cash into stocks near beginnings of months.

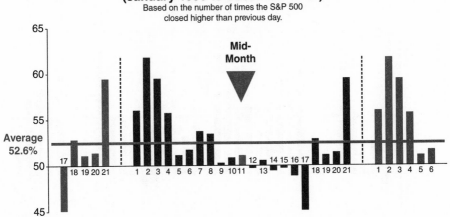

MARKET % PERFORMANCE EACH DAY OF THE MONTH
(January 1953 to December 1981)
Based on the number of times the S&P 500 closed higher than previous day.

Clearly, "front-running" traders took advantage of this phenomenon, drastically altering the previous pattern. The second chart from 1982 onward shows the trading shift caused by these "anticipators" to the last three trading days of the month, plus the first two. Another astonishing development shows the ninth, tenth, and eleventh trading days rising strongly as well. Growth of 401(k) retirement plans, IRAs, and similar plans (participants' salaries are usually paid twice monthly) is responsible for this mid-month bulge. First trading days of the month have produced the greatest gains in recent years (see page 86).

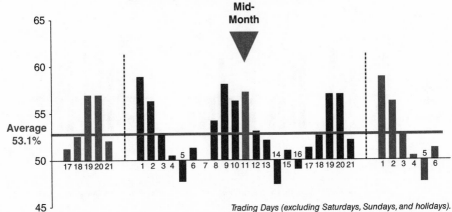

MARKET % PERFORMANCE EACH DAY OF THE MONTH
(January 1982 to December 2013)

Trading Days (excluding Saturdays, Sundays, and holidays).

MONTHLY CASH INFLOWS INTO NASDAQ STOCKS

NASDAQ stocks moved up 58.1% of the time through 1981 compared to 52.6% for the S&P on page 145. Ends and beginnings of the month are fairly similar, specifically the last plus the first four trading days. But notice how investors piled into NASDAQ stocks until mid-month. NASDAQ rose 118.6% from January 1, 1971, to December 31, 1981, compared to 33.0% for the S&P.

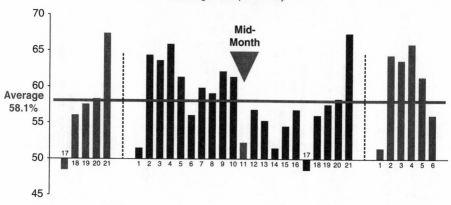

NASDAQ % PERFORMANCE EACH DAY OF THE MONTH
(January 1971 to December 1981)
Based on the number of times the NASDAQ composite
closed higher than previous day.

After the air was let out of the tech market 2000–2002, S&P's 1408% gain over the last 32 years is more evenly matched with NASDAQ's 2033% gain. Last three, first four, and middle ninth and tenth days rose the most. Where the S&P has three days of the month that go down more often than up, NASDAQ has none. NASDAQ exhibits the most strength on the last trading day of the month; however, over the past 17 years, last days have weakened considerably, down more often then not.

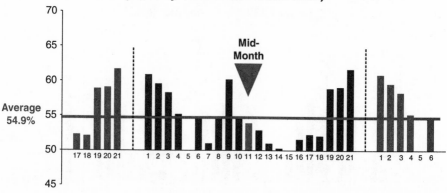

NASDAQ % PERFORMANCE EACH DAY OF THE MONTH
(January 1982 to December 2013)

Trading Days (excluding Saturdays, Sundays, and holidays).
Based on NASDAQ composite, prior to February 5, 1971, based on National Quotation Bureau indices.

NOVEMBER, DECEMBER, AND JANUARY: YEAR'S BEST THREE-MONTH SPAN

The most important observation to be made from a chart showing the average monthly percent change in market prices since 1950 is that institutions (mutual funds, pension funds, banks, etc.) determine the trading patterns in today's market.

The "investment calendar" reflects the annual, semi-annual and quarterly operations of institutions during January, April and July. October, besides being the last campaign month before elections, is also the time when most bear markets seem to end, as in 1946, 1957, 1960, 1966, 1974, 1987, 1990, 1998 and 2002. (August and September tend to combine to make the worst consecutive two-month period.)

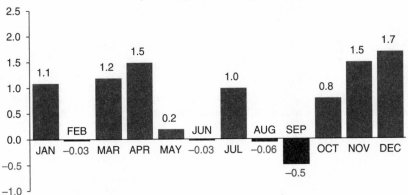

S&P 500 MONTHLY % PERFORMANCE
(January 1950 to April 2014)

Average month-to-month % change in S&P 500
(Based on monthly closing prices.)

Unusual year-end strength comes from corporate and private pension funds, producing a 4.3% gain on average between November 1 and January 31. In 2007–2008, these three months were all down for the fourth time since 1930; previously in 1931–1932, 1940–1941, and 1969–1970, also bear markets. September's dismal performance makes it the worst month of the year. However, in the last 19 years, it has been up 12 times—down five in a row 1999–2003.

In pre-presidential election years since 1950, the best three months are January +4.3% (15–1), April +3.6% (15–1), and December +3.2% (12–4). February, March, May, June, July, August, and November are gainers while September and October are losers. September is worst, –0.8% (5–11).

See page 50 for monthly performance tables for the S&P 500 and the Dow Jones industrials. See pages 52, 54, and 62 for unique switching strategies.

On page 66, you can see how the first month of the first three quarters far outperforms the second and the third months since 1950, and note the improvement in May's and October's performance since 1991.

NOVEMBER THROUGH JUNE:
NASDAQ'S EIGHT-MONTH RUN

The two-and-a-half-year plunge of 77.9% in NASDAQ stocks, between March 10, 2000, and October 9, 2002, brought several horrendous monthly losses (the two greatest were November 2000, –22.9%, and February 2001, –22.4%), which trimmed average monthly performance over the 43$\frac{1}{3}$-year period. Ample Octobers in 11 of the last 16 years, including three huge turnarounds in 2001 (+12.8%), 2002 (+13.5%), and 2011 (+11.1%) have put bear-killing October in the number one spot since 1998. January's 2.9% average gain is still awesome, and twice S&P's 1.4% January average since 1971.

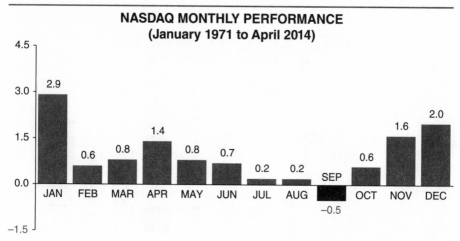

NASDAQ MONTHLY PERFORMANCE
(January 1971 to April 2014)

Average month-to-month % change in NASDAQ composite, prior to February 5, 1971, based on National Quotation Bureau indices. (Based on monthly closing prices.)

Bear in mind, when comparing NASDAQ to the S&P on page 147, that there are 22 fewer years of data here. During this 43$\frac{1}{3}$-year (1971–April 2014) period, NASDAQ gained 4492%, while the S&P and the Dow rose only 1944% and 1876%, respectively. On page 58 you can see a statistical monthly comparison between NASDAQ and the Dow.

Year-end strength is even more pronounced in NASDAQ, producing a 6.5% gain on average between November 1 and January 31—1.5 times greater than that of the S&P 500 on page 147. September is the worst month of the year for the over-the-counter index as well, posting an average loss of –0.5%. These extremes underscore NASDAQ's higher volatility—and moves of greater magnitude.

In pre-presidential election years since 1971, the best three months are January +7.3% (10–1), December +4.9% (6–5), and April +3.7% (10–1). February, March, May, June, July, August, and December also provide gains. September and October are net losers with October the worst, averaging –0.8% (6–5).

DOW JONES INDUSTRIALS ANNUAL HIGHS, LOWS, & CLOSES SINCE 1901

YEAR	HIGH DATE	HIGH CLOSE	LOW DATE	LOW CLOSE	YEAR CLOSE	YEAR	HIGH DATE	HIGH CLOSE	LOW DATE	LOW CLOSE	YEAR CLOSE
1901	6/17	57.33	12/24	45.07	47.29	1958	12/31	583.65	2/25	436.89	583.65
1902	4/24	50.14	12/15	43.64	47.10	1959	12/31	679.36	2/9	574.46	679.36
1903	2/16	49.59	11/9	30.88	35.98	1960	1/5	685.47	10/25	566.05	615.89
1904	12/5	53.65	3/12	34.00	50.99	1961	12/13	734.91	1/3	610.25	731.14
1905	12/29	70.74	1/25	50.37	70.47	1962	1/3	726.01	6/26	535.76	652.10
1906	1/19	75.45	7/13	62.40	69.12	1963	12/18	767.21	1/2	646.79	762.95
1907	1/7	70.60	11/15	38.83	43.04	1964	11/18	891.71	1/2	766.08	874.13
1908	11/13	64.74	2/13	42.94	63.11	1965	12/31	969.26	6/28	840.59	969.26
1909	11/19	73.64	2/23	58.54	72.56	1966	2/9	995.15	10/7	744.32	785.69
1910	1/3	72.04	7/26	53.93	59.60	1967	9/25	943.08	1/3	786.41	905.11
1911	6/19	63.78	9/25	53.43	59.84	1968	12/3	985.21	3/21	825.13	943.75
1912	9/30	68.97	2/10	58.72	64.37	1969	5/14	968.85	12/17	769.93	800.36
1913	1/9	64.88	6/11	52.83	57.71	1970	12/29	842.00	5/26	631.16	838.92
1914	3/20	61.12	7/30	52.32	54.58	1971	4/28	950.82	11/23	797.97	890.20
1915	12/27	99.21	2/24	54.22	99.15	1972	12/11	1036.27	1/26	889.15	1020.02
1916	11/21	110.15	4/22	84.96	95.00	1973	1/11	1051.70	12/5	788.31	850.86
1917	1/3	99.18	12/19	65.95	74.38	1974	3/13	891.66	12/6	577.60	616.24
1918	10/18	89.07	1/15	73.38	82.20	1975	7/15	881.81	1/2	632.04	852.41
1919	11/3	119.62	2/8	79.15	107.23	1976	9/21	1014.79	1/2	858.71	1004.65
1920	1/3	109.88	12/21	66.75	71.95	1977	1/3	999.75	11/2	800.85	831.17
1921	12/15	81.50	8/24	63.90	81.10	1978	9/8	907.74	2/28	742.12	805.01
1922	10/14	103.43	1/10	78.59	98.73	1979	10/5	897.61	11/7	796.67	838.74
1923	3/20	105.38	10/27	85.76	95.52	1980	11/20	1000.17	4/21	759.13	963.99
1924	12/31	120.51	5/20	88.33	120.51	1981	4/27	1024.05	9/25	824.01	875.00
1925	11/6	159.39	3/30	115.00	156.66	1982	12/27	1070.55	8/12	776.92	1046.54
1926	8/14	166.64	3/30	135.20	157.20	1983	11/29	1287.20	1/3	1027.04	1258.64
1927	12/31	202.40	1/25	152.73	202.40	1984	1/6	1286.64	7/24	1086.57	1211.57
1928	12/31	300.00	2/20	191.33	300.00	1985	12/16	1553.10	1/4	1184.96	1546.67
1929	9/3	381.17	11/13	198.69	248.48	1986	12/2	1955.57	1/22	1502.29	1895.95
1930	4/17	294.07	12/16	157.51	164.58	1987	8/25	2722.42	10/19	1738.74	1938.83
1931	2/24	194.36	12/17	73.79	77.90	1988	10/21	2183.50	1/20	1879.14	2168.57
1932	3/8	88.78	7/8	41.22	59.93	1989	10/9	2791.41	1/3	2144.64	2753.20
1933	7/18	108.67	2/27	50.16	99.90	1990	7/17	2999.75	10/11	2365.10	2633.66
1934	2/5	110.74	7/26	85.51	104.04	1991	12/31	3168.83	1/9	2470.30	3168.83
1935	11/19	148.44	3/14	96.71	144.13	1992	6/1	3413.21	10/9	3136.58	3301.11
1936	11/17	184.90	1/6	143.11	179.90	1993	12/29	3794.33	1/20	3241.95	3754.09
1937	3/10	194.40	11/24	113.64	120.85	1994	1/31	3978.36	4/4	3593.35	3834.44
1938	11/12	158.41	3/31	98.95	154.76	1995	12/13	5216.47	1/30	3832.08	5117.12
1939	9/12	155.92	4/8	121.44	150.24	1996	12/27	6560.91	1/10	5032.94	6448.27
1940	1/3	152.80	6/10	111.84	131.13	1997	8/6	8259.31	4/11	6391.69	7908.25
1941	1/10	133.59	12/23	106.34	110.96	1998	11/23	9374.27	8/31	7539.07	9181.43
1942	12/26	119.71	4/28	92.92	119.40	1999	12/31	11497.12	1/22	9120.67	11497.12
1943	7/14	145.82	1/8	119.26	135.89	2000	1/14	11722.98	3/7	9796.03	10786.85
1944	12/16	152.53	2/7	134.22	152.32	2001	5/21	11337.92	9/21	8235.81	10021.50
1945	12/11	195.82	1/24	151.35	192.91	2002	3/19	10635.25	10/9	7286.27	8341.63
1946	5/29	212.50	10/9	163.12	177.20	2003	12/31	10453.92	3/11	7524.06	10453.92
1947	7/24	186.85	5/17	163.21	181.16	2004	12/28	10854.54	10/25	9749.99	10783.01
1948	6/15	193.16	3/16	165.39	177.30	2005	3/4	10940.55	4/20	10012.36	10717.50
1949	12/30	200.52	6/13	161.60	200.13	2006	12/27	12510.57	1/20	10667.39	12463.15
1950	11/24	235.47	1/13	196.81	235.41	2007	10/9	14164.53	3/5	12050.41	13264.82
1951	9/13	276.37	1/3	238.99	269.23	2008	5/2	13058.20	11/20	7552.29	8776.39
1952	12/30	292.00	5/1	256.35	291.90	2009	12/30	10548.51	3/9	6547.05	10428.05
1953	1/5	293.79	9/14	255.49	280.90	2010	12/29	11585.38	7/2	9686.48	11577.51
1954	12/31	404.39	1/11	279.87	404.39	2011	4/29	12810.54	10/3	10655.30	12217.56
1955	12/30	488.40	1/17	388.20	488.40	2012	10/5	13610.15	6/4	12101.46	13104.14
1956	4/6	521.05	1/23	462.35	499.47	2013	12/31	16576.66	1/8	13328.85	16576.66
1957	7/12	520.77	10/22	419.79	435.69	2014*	4/30	16580.84	2/3	15372.80	At Press Time

*Through May 2, 2014

S&P 500 ANNUAL HIGHS, LOWS, & CLOSES SINCE 1930

YEAR	HIGH DATE	HIGH CLOSE	LOW DATE	LOW CLOSE	YEAR CLOSE	YEAR	HIGH DATE	HIGH CLOSE	LOW DATE	LOW CLOSE	YEAR CLOSE
1930	4/10	25.92	12/16	14.44	15.34	1973	1/11	120.24	12/5	92.16	97.55
1931	2/24	18.17	12/17	7.72	8.12	1974	1/3	99.80	10/3	62.28	68.56
1932	9/7	9.31	6/1	4.40	6.89	1975	7/15	95.61	1/8	70.04	90.19
1933	7/18	12.20	2/27	5.53	10.10	1976	9/21	107.83	1/2	90.90	107.46
1934	2/6	11.82	7/26	8.36	9.50	1977	1/3	107.00	11/2	90.71	95.10
1935	11/19	13.46	3/14	8.06	13.43	1978	9/12	106.99	3/6	86.90	96.11
1936	11/9	17.69	1/2	13.40	17.18	1979	10/5	111.27	2/27	96.13	107.94
1937	3/6	18.68	11/24	10.17	10.55	1980	11/28	140.52	3/27	98.22	135.76
1938	11/9	13.79	3/31	8.50	13.21	1981	1/6	138.12	9/25	112.77	122.55
1939	1/4	13.23	4/8	10.18	12.49	1982	11/9	143.02	8/12	102.42	140.64
1940	1/3	12.77	6/10	8.99	10.58	1983	10/10	172.65	1/3	138.34	164.93
1941	1/10	10.86	12/29	8.37	8.69	1984	11/6	170.41	7/24	147.82	167.24
1942	12/31	9.77	4/28	7.47	9.77	1985	12/16	212.02	1/4	163.68	211.28
1943	7/14	12.64	1/2	9.84	11.67	1986	12/2	254.00	1/22	203.49	242.17
1944	12/16	13.29	2/7	11.56	13.28	1987	8/25	336.77	12/4	223.92	247.08
1945	12/10	17.68	1/23	13.21	17.36	1988	10/21	283.66	1/20	242.63	277.72
1946	5/29	19.25	10/9	14.12	15.30	1989	10/9	359.80	1/3	275.31	353.40
1947	2/8	16.20	5/17	13.71	15.30	1990	7/16	368.95	10/11	295.46	330.22
1948	6/15	17.06	2/14	13.84	15.20	1991	12/31	417.09	1/9	311.49	417.09
1949	12/30	16.79	6/13	13.55	16.76	1992	12/18	441.28	4/8	394.50	435.71
1950	12/29	20.43	1/14	16.65	20.41	1993	12/28	470.94	1/8	429.05	466.45
1951	10/15	23.85	1/3	20.69	23.77	1994	2/2	482.00	4/4	438.92	459.27
1952	12/30	26.59	2/20	23.09	26.57	1995	12/13	621.69	1/3	459.11	615.93
1953	1/5	26.66	9/14	22.71	24.81	1996	11/25	757.03	1/10	598.48	740.74
1954	12/31	35.98	1/11	24.80	35.98	1997	12/5	983.79	1/2	737.01	970.43
1955	11/14	46.41	1/17	34.58	45.48	1998	12/29	1241.81	1/9	927.69	1229.23
1956	8/2	49.74	1/23	43.11	46.67	1999	12/31	1469.25	1/14	1212.19	1469.25
1957	7/15	49.13	10/22	38.98	39.99	2000	3/24	1527.46	12/20	1264.74	1320.28
1958	12/31	55.21	1/2	40.33	55.21	2001	2/1	1373.47	9/21	965.80	1148.08
1959	8/3	60.71	2/9	53.58	59.89	2002	1/4	1172.51	10/9	776.76	879.82
1960	1/5	60.39	10/25	52.30	58.11	2003	12/31	1111.92	3/11	800.73	1111.92
1961	12/12	72.64	1/3	57.57	71.55	2004	12/30	1213.55	8/12	1063.23	1211.92
1962	1/3	71.13	6/26	52.32	63.10	2005	12/14	1272.74	4/20	1137.50	1248.29
1963	12/31	75.02	1/2	62.69	75.02	2006	12/15	1427.09	6/13	1223.69	1418.30
1964	11/20	86.28	1/2	75.43	84.75	2007	10/9	1565.15	3/5	1374.12	1468.36
1965	11/15	92.63	6/28	81.60	92.43	2008	1/2	1447.16	11/20	752.44	903.25
1966	2/9	94.06	10/7	73.20	80.33	2009	12/28	1127.78	3/9	676.53	1115.10
1967	9/25	97.59	1/3	80.38	96.47	2010	12/29	1259.78	7/2	1022.58	1257.64
1968	11/29	108.37	3/5	87.72	103.86	2011	4/29	1363.61	10/3	1099.23	1257.60
1969	5/14	106.16	12/17	89.20	92.06	2012	9/14	1465.77	1/3	1277.06	1426.19
1970	1/5	93.46	5/26	69.29	92.15	2013	12/31	1848.36	1/8	1457.15	1848.36
1971	4/28	104.77	11/23	90.16	102.09	2014*	4/2	1890.90	2/3	1741.89	At Press Time
1972	12/11	119.12	1/3	101.67	118.05						

*Through May 2, 2014

NASDAQ ANNUAL HIGHS, LOWS, & CLOSES SINCE 1971

YEAR	HIGH DATE	HIGH CLOSE	LOW DATE	LOW CLOSE	YEAR CLOSE	YEAR	HIGH DATE	HIGH CLOSE	LOW DATE	LOW CLOSE	YEAR CLOSE
1971	12/31	114.12	1/5	89.06	114.12	1993	10/15	787.42	4/26	645.87	776.80
1972	12/8	135.15	1/3	113.65	133.73	1994	3/18	803.93	6/24	693.79	751.96
1973	1/11	136.84	12/24	88.67	92.19	1995	12/4	1069.79	1/3	743.58	1052.13
1974	3/15	96.53	10/3	54.87	59.82	1996	12/9	1316.27	1/15	988.57	1291.03
1975	7/15	88.00	1/2	60.70	77.62	1997	10/9	1745.85	4/2	1201.00	1570.35
1976	12/31	97.88	1/2	78.06	97.88	1998	12/31	2192.69	10/8	1419.12	2192.69
1977	12/30	105.05	4/5	93.66	105.05	1999	12/31	4069.31	1/4	2208.05	4069.31
1978	9/13	139.25	1/11	99.09	117.98	2000	3/10	5048.62	12/20	2332.78	2470.52
1979	10/5	152.29	1/2	117.84	151.14	2001	1/24	2859.15	9/21	1423.19	1950.40
1980	11/28	208.15	3/27	124.09	202.34	2002	1/4	2059.38	10/9	1114.11	1335.51
1981	5/29	223.47	9/28	175.03	195.84	2003	12/30	2009.88	3/11	1271.47	2003.37
1982	12/8	240.70	8/13	159.14	232.41	2004	12/30	2178.34	8/12	1752.49	2175.44
1983	6/24	328.91	1/3	230.59	278.60	2005	12/2	2273.37	4/28	1904.18	2205.32
1984	1/6	287.90	7/25	225.30	247.35	2006	11/22	2465.98	7/21	2020.39	2415.29
1985	12/16	325.16	1/2	245.91	324.93	2007	10/31	2859.12	3/5	2340.68	2652.28
1986	7/3	411.16	1/9	323.01	349.33	2008	1/2	2609.63	11/20	1316.12	1577.03
1987	8/26	455.26	10/28	291.88	330.47	2009	12/30	2291.28	3/9	1268.64	2269.15
1988	7/5	396.11	1/12	331.97	381.38	2010	12/22	2671.48	7/2	2091.79	2652.87
1989	10/9	485.73	1/3	378.56	454.82	2011	4/29	2873.54	10/3	2335.83	2605.15
1990	7/16	469.60	10/16	325.44	373.84	2012	9/14	3183.95	1/4	2648.36	3019.51
1991	12/31	586.34	1/14	355.75	586.34	2013	12/31	4176.59	1/8	3091.81	4176.59
1992	12/31	676.95	6/26	547.84	676.95	2014*	3/5	4357.97	2/3	3996.96	At Press Time

RUSSELL 1000 ANNUAL HIGHS, LOWS, & CLOSES SINCE 1979

YEAR	HIGH DATE	HIGH CLOSE	LOW DATE	LOW CLOSE	YEAR CLOSE	YEAR	HIGH DATE	HIGH CLOSE	LOW DATE	LOW CLOSE	YEAR CLOSE
1979	10/5	61.18	2/27	51.83	59.87	1997	12/5	519.72	4/11	389.03	513.79
1980	11/28	78.26	3/27	53.68	75.20	1998	12/29	645.36	1/9	490.26	642.87
1981	1/6	76.34	9/25	62.03	67.93	1999	12/31	767.97	2/9	632.53	767.97
1982	11/9	78.47	8/12	55.98	77.24	2000	9/1	813.71	12/20	668.75	700.09
1983	10/10	95.07	1/3	76.04	90.38	2001	1/30	727.35	9/21	507.98	604.94
1984	1/6	92.80	7/24	79.49	90.31	2002	3/19	618.74	10/9	410.52	466.18
1985	12/16	114.97	1/4	88.61	114.39	2003	12/31	594.56	3/11	425.31	594.56
1986	7/2	137.87	1/22	111.14	130.00	2004	12/30	651.76	8/13	566.06	650.99
1987	8/25	176.22	12/4	117.65	130.02	2005	12/14	692.09	4/20	613.37	679.42
1988	10/21	149.94	1/20	128.35	146.99	2006	12/15	775.08	6/13	665.81	770.08
1989	10/9	189.93	1/3	145.78	185.11	2007	10/9	852.32	3/5	749.85	799.82
1990	7/16	191.56	10/11	152.36	171.22	2008	1/2	788.62	11/20	402.91	487.77
1991	12/31	220.61	1/9	161.94	220.61	2009	12/28	619.22	3/9	367.55	612.01
1992	12/18	235.06	4/8	208.87	233.59	2010	12/29	698.11	7/2	562.58	696.90
1993	10/15	252.77	1/8	229.91	250.71	2011	4/29	758.45	10/3	604.42	693.36
1994	2/1	258.31	4/4	235.38	244.65	2012	9/14	809.01	1/4	703.72	789.90
1995	12/13	331.18	1/3	244.41	328.89	2013	12/31	1030.36	1/8	807.95	1030.36
1996	12/2	401.21	1/10	318.24	393.75	2014*	4/2	1057.29	2/3	972.95	At Press Time

RUSSELL 2000 ANNUAL HIGHS, LOWS, & CLOSES SINCE 1979

YEAR	HIGH DATE	HIGH CLOSE	LOW DATE	LOW CLOSE	YEAR CLOSE	YEAR	HIGH DATE	HIGH CLOSE	LOW DATE	LOW CLOSE	YEAR CLOSE
1979	12/31	55.91	1/2	40.81	55.91	1997	10/13	465.21	4/25	335.85	437.02
1980	11/28	77.70	3/27	45.36	74.80	1998	4/21	491.41	10/8	310.28	421.96
1981	6/15	85.16	9/25	65.37	73.67	1999	12/31	504.75	3/23	383.37	504.75
1982	12/8	91.01	8/12	60.33	88.90	2000	3/9	606.05	12/20	443.80	483.53
1983	6/24	126.99	1/3	88.29	112.27	2001	5/22	517.23	9/21	378.89	488.50
1984	1/12	116.69	7/25	93.95	101.49	2002	4/16	522.95	10/9	327.04	383.09
1985	12/31	129.87	1/2	101.21	129.87	2003	12/30	565.47	3/12	345.94	556.91
1986	7/3	155.30	1/9	128.23	135.00	2004	12/28	654.57	8/12	517.10	651.57
1987	8/25	174.44	10/28	106.08	120.42	2005	12/2	690.57	4/28	575.02	673.22
1988	7/15	151.42	1/12	121.23	147.37	2006	12/27	797.73	7/21	671.94	787.66
1989	10/9	180.78	1/3	146.79	168.30	2007	7/13	855.77	11/26	735.07	766.03
1990	6/15	170.90	10/30	118.82	132.16	2008	6/5	763.27	11/20	385.31	499.45
1991	12/31	189.94	1/15	125.25	189.94	2009	12/24	634.07	3/9	343.26	625.39
1992	12/31	221.01	7/8	185.81	221.01	2010	12/27	792.35	2/8	586.49	783.65
1993	11/2	260.17	2/23	217.55	258.59	2011	4/29	865.29	10/3	609.49	740.92
1994	3/18	271.08	12/9	235.16	250.36	2012	9/14	864.70	6/4	737.24	849.35
1995	9/14	316.12	1/30	246.56	315.97	2013	12/31	1163.64	1/3	872.60	1163.64
1996	5/22	364.61	1/16	301.75	362.61	2014*	3/4	1208.65	2/5	1093.59	At Press Time

*Through May 2, 2014

DOW JONES INDUSTRIALS MONTHLY PERCENT CHANGES SINCE 1950

	Jan	Feb	Mar	Apr	May	Jun	Jul	Aug	Sep	Oct	Nov	Dec	Year's Change
1950	0.8	0.8	1.3	4.0	4.2	-6.4	0.1	3.6	4.4	-0.6	1.2	3.4	17.6
1951	5.7	1.3	-1.6	4.5	-3.7	-2.8	6.3	4.8	0.3	-3.2	-0.4	3.0	14.4
1952	0.5	-3.9	3.6	-4.4	2.1	4.3	1.9	-1.6	-1.6	-0.5	5.4	2.9	8.4
1953	-0.7	-1.9	-1.5	-1.8	-0.9	-1.5	2.7	-5.1	1.1	4.5	2.0	-0.2	-3.8
1954	4.1	0.7	3.0	5.2	2.6	1.8	4.3	-3.5	7.3	-2.3	9.8	4.6	44.0
1955	1.1	0.7	-0.5	3.9	-0.2	6.2	3.2	0.5	-0.3	-2.5	6.2	1.1	20.8
1956	-3.6	2.7	5.8	0.8	-7.4	3.1	5.1	-3.0	-5.3	1.0	-1.5	5.6	2.3
1957	-4.1	-3.0	2.2	4.1	2.1	-0.3	1.0	-4.8	-5.8	-3.3	2.0	-3.2	-12.8
1958	3.3	-2.2	1.6	2.0	1.5	3.3	5.2	1.1	4.6	2.1	2.6	4.7	34.0
1959	1.8	1.6	-0.3	3.7	3.2	-0.03	4.9	-1.6	-4.9	2.4	1.9	3.1	16.4
1960	-8.4	1.2	-2.1	-2.4	4.0	2.4	-3.7	1.5	-7.3	0.04	2.9	3.1	-9.3
1961	5.2	2.1	2.2	0.3	2.7	-1.8	3.1	2.1	-2.6	0.4	2.5	1.3	18.7
1962	-4.3	1.1	-0.2	-5.9	-7.8	-8.5	6.5	1.9	-5.0	1.9	10.1	0.4	-10.8
1963	4.7	-2.9	3.0	5.2	1.3	-2.8	-1.6	4.9	0.5	3.1	-0.6	1.7	17.0
1964	2.9	1.9	1.6	-0.3	1.2	1.3	1.2	-0.3	4.4	-0.3	0.3	-0.1	14.6
1965	3.3	0.1	-1.6	3.7	-0.5	-5.4	1.6	1.3	4.2	3.2	-1.5	2.4	10.9
1966	1.5	-3.2	-2.8	1.0	-5.3	-1.6	-2.6	-7.0	-1.8	4.2	-1.9	-0.7	-18.9
1967	8.2	-1.2	3.2	3.6	-5.0	0.9	5.1	-0.3	2.8	-5.1	-0.4	3.3	15.2
1968	-5.5	-1.7	0.02	8.5	-1.4	-0.1	-1.6	1.5	4.4	1.8	3.4	-4.2	4.3
1969	0.2	-4.3	3.3	1.6	-1.3	-6.9	-6.6	2.6	-2.8	5.3	-5.1	-1.5	-15.2
1970	-7.0	4.5	1.0	-6.3	-4.8	-2.4	7.4	4.1	-0.5	-0.7	5.1	5.6	4.8
1971	3.5	1.2	2.9	4.1	-3.6	-1.8	-3.7	4.6	-1.2	-5.4	-0.9	7.1	6.1
1972	1.3	2.9	1.4	1.4	0.7	-3.3	-0.5	4.2	-1.1	0.2	6.6	0.2	14.6
1973	-2.1	-4.4	-0.4	-3.1	-2.2	-1.1	3.9	-4.2	6.7	1.0	-14.0	3.5	-16.6
1974	0.6	0.6	-1.6	-1.2	-4.1	0.03	-5.6	-10.4	-10.4	9.5	-7.0	-0.4	-27.6
1975	14.2	5.0	3.9	6.9	1.3	5.6	-5.4	0.5	-5.0	5.3	2.9	-1.0	38.3
1976	14.4	-0.3	2.8	-0.3	-2.2	2.8	-1.8	-1.1	1.7	-2.6	-1.8	6.1	17.9
1977	-5.0	-1.9	-1.8	0.8	-3.0	2.0	-2.9	-3.2	-1.7	-3.4	1.4	0.2	-17.3
1978	-7.4	-3.6	2.1	10.6	0.4	-2.6	5.3	1.7	-1.3	-8.5	0.8	0.7	-3.1
1979	4.2	-3.6	6.6	-0.8	-3.8	2.4	0.5	4.9	-1.0	-7.2	0.8	2.0	4.2
1980	4.4	-1.5	-9.0	4.0	4.1	2.0	7.8	-0.3	-0.02	-0.9	7.4	-3.0	14.9
1981	-1.7	2.9	3.0	-0.6	-0.6	-1.5	-2.5	-7.4	-3.6	0.3	4.3	-1.6	-9.2
1982	-0.4	-5.4	-0.2	3.1	-3.4	-0.9	-0.4	11.5	-0.6	10.7	4.8	0.7	19.6
1983	2.8	3.4	1.6	8.5	-2.1	1.8	-1.9	1.4	1.4	-0.6	4.1	-1.4	20.3
1984	-3.0	-5.4	0.9	0.5	-5.6	2.5	-1.5	9.8	-1.4	0.1	-1.5	1.9	-3.7
1985	6.2	-0.2	-1.3	-0.7	4.6	1.5	0.9	-1.0	-0.4	3.4	7.1	5.1	27.7
1986	1.6	8.8	6.4	-1.9	5.2	0.9	-6.2	6.9	-6.9	6.2	1.9	-1.0	22.6
1987	13.8	3.1	3.6	-0.8	0.2	5.5	6.3	3.5	-2.5	-23.2	-8.0	5.7	2.3
1988	1.0	5.8	-4.0	2.2	-0.1	5.4	-0.6	-4.6	4.0	1.7	-1.6	2.6	11.8
1989	8.0	-3.6	1.6	5.5	2.5	-1.6	9.0	2.9	-1.6	-1.8	2.3	1.7	27.0
1990	-5.9	1.4	3.0	-1.9	8.3	0.1	0.9	-10.0	-6.2	-0.4	4.8	2.9	-4.3
1991	3.9	5.3	1.1	-0.9	4.8	-4.0	4.1	0.6	-0.9	1.7	-5.7	9.5	20.3
1992	1.7	1.4	-1.0	3.8	1.1	-2.3	2.3	-4.0	0.4	-1.4	2.4	-0.1	4.2
1993	0.3	1.8	1.9	-0.2	2.9	-0.3	0.7	3.2	-2.6	3.5	0.1	1.9	13.7
1994	6.0	-3.7	-5.1	1.3	2.1	-3.5	3.8	4.0	-1.8	1.7	-4.3	2.5	2.1
1995	0.2	4.3	3.7	3.9	3.3	2.0	3.3	-2.1	3.9	-0.7	6.7	0.8	33.5
1996	5.4	1.7	1.9	-0.3	1.3	0.2	-2.2	1.6	4.7	2.5	8.2	-1.1	26.0
1997	5.7	0.9	-4.3	6.5	4.6	4.7	7.2	-7.3	4.2	-6.3	5.1	1.1	22.6
1998	-0.02	8.1	3.0	3.0	-1.8	0.6	-0.8	-15.1	4.0	9.6	6.1	0.7	16.1
1999	1.9	-0.6	5.2	10.2	-2.1	3.9	-2.9	1.6	-4.5	3.8	1.4	5.7	25.2
2000	-4.8	-7.4	7.8	-1.7	-2.0	-0.7	0.7	6.6	-5.0	3.0	-5.1	3.6	-6.2
2001	0.9	-3.6	-5.9	8.7	1.6	-3.8	0.2	-5.4	-11.1	2.6	8.6	1.7	-7.1
2002	-1.0	1.9	2.9	-4.4	-0.2	-6.9	-5.5	-0.8	-12.4	10.6	5.9	-6.2	-16.8
2003	-3.5	-2.0	1.3	6.1	4.4	1.5	2.8	2.0	-1.5	5.7	-0.2	6.9	25.3
2004	0.3	0.9	-2.1	-1.3	-0.4	2.4	-2.8	0.3	-0.9	-0.5	4.0	3.4	3.1
2005	-2.7	2.6	-2.4	-3.0	2.7	-1.8	3.6	-1.5	0.8	-1.2	3.5	-0.8	-0.6
2006	1.4	1.2	1.1	2.3	-1.7	-0.2	0.3	1.7	2.6	3.4	1.2	2.0	16.3
2007	1.3	-2.8	0.7	5.7	4.3	-1.6	-1.5	1.1	4.0	0.2	-4.0	-0.8	6.4
2008	-4.6	-3.0	-0.03	4.5	-1.4	-10.2	0.2	1.5	-6.0	-14.1	-5.3	-0.6	-33.8
2009	-8.8	-11.7	7.7	7.3	4.1	-0.6	8.6	3.5	2.3	0.005	6.5	0.8	18.8
2010	-3.5	2.6	5.1	1.4	-7.9	-3.6	7.1	-4.3	7.7	3.1	-1.0	5.2	11.0
2011	2.7	2.8	0.8	4.0	-1.9	-1.2	-2.2	-4.4	-6.0	9.5	0.8	1.4	5.5
2012	3.4	2.5	2.0	0.01	-6.2	3.9	1.0	0.6	2.6	-2.5	-0.5	0.6	7.3
2013	5.8	1.4	3.7	1.8	1.9	-1.4	4.0	-4.4	2.2	2.8	3.5	3.0	26.5
2014	-5.3	4.0	0.8	0.7									
TOTALS	66.9	8.2	72.6	126.7	-3.3	-20.4	77.1	-8.6	-48.3	32.8	96.3	109.5	
AVG.	1.0	0.1	1.1	1.9	-0.1	-0.3	1.2	-0.1	-0.8	0.5	1.5	1.7	
# Up	42	38	43	43	32	29	40	36	26	38	42	46	
# Down	23	27	22	22	32	35	24	28	38	26	22	18	

DOW JONES INDUSTRIALS MONTHLY POINT CHANGES SINCE 1950

	Jan	Feb	Mar	Apr	May	Jun	Jul	Aug	Sep	Oct	Nov	Dec	Year's Close
1950	1.66	1.65	2.61	8.28	9.09	-14.31	0.29	7.47	9.49	-1.35	2.59	7.81	235.41
1951	13.42	3.22	-4.11	11.19	-9.48	-7.01	15.22	12.39	0.91	-8.81	-1.08	7.96	269.23
1952	1.46	-10.61	9.38	-11.83	5.31	11.32	5.30	-4.52	-4.43	-1.38	14.43	8.24	291.90
1953	-2.13	-5.50	-4.40	-5.12	-2.47	-4.02	7.12	-14.16	2.82	11.77	5.56	-0.47	280.90
1954	11.49	2.15	8.97	15.82	8.16	6.04	14.39	-12.12	24.66	-8.32	34.63	17.62	404.39
1955	4.44	3.04	-2.17	15.95	-0.79	26.52	14.47	2.33	-1.56	-11.75	28.39	5.14	488.40
1956	-17.66	12.91	28.14	4.33	-38.07	14.73	25.03	-15.77	-26.79	4.60	-7.07	26.69	499.47
1957	-20.31	-14.54	10.19	19.55	10.57	-1.64	5.23	-24.17	-28.05	-15.26	8.83	-14.18	435.69
1958	14.33	-10.10	6.84	9.10	6.84	15.48	24.81	5.64	23.46	11.13	14.24	26.19	583.65
1959	10.31	9.54	-1.79	22.04	20.04	-0.19	31.28	-10.47	-32.73	14.92	12.58	20.18	679.36
1960	-56.74	7.50	-13.53	-14.89	23.80	15.12	-23.89	9.26	-45.85	0.22	16.86	18.67	615.89
1961	32.31	13.88	14.55	2.08	18.01	-12.76	21.41	14.57	-18.73	2.71	17.68	9.54	731.14
1962	-31.14	8.05	-1.10	-41.62	-51.97	-52.08	36.65	11.25	-30.20	10.79	59.53	2.80	652.10
1963	30.75	-19.91	19.58	35.18	9.26	-20.08	-11.45	33.89	3.47	22.44	-4.71	12.43	762.95
1964	22.39	14.80	13.15	-2.52	9.79	10.94	9.60	-2.62	36.89	-2.29	2.35	-1.30	874.13
1965	28.73	0.62	-14.43	33.26	-4.27	-50.01	13.71	11.36	37.48	30.24	-14.11	22.55	969.26
1966	14.25	-31.62	-27.12	8.91	-49.61	-13.97	-22.72	-58.97	-14.19	32.85	-15.48	-5.90	785.69
1967	64.20	-10.52	26.61	31.07	-44.49	7.70	43.98	-2.95	25.37	-46.92	-3.93	29.30	905.11
1968	-49.64	-14.97	0.17	71.55	-13.22	-1.20	-14.80	13.01	39.78	16.60	32.69	-41.33	943.75
1969	2.30	-40.84	30.27	14.70	-12.62	-64.37	-57.72	21.25	-23.63	42.90	-43.69	-11.94	800.36
1970	-56.30	33.53	7.98	-49.50	-35.63	-16.91	50.59	30.46	-3.90	-5.07	38.48	44.83	838.92
1971	29.58	10.33	25.54	37.38	-33.94	-16.67	-32.71	39.64	-10.88	-48.19	-7.66	58.86	890.20
1972	11.97	25.96	12.57	13.47	6.55	-31.69	-4.29	38.99	-10.46	2.25	62.69	1.81	1020.02
1973	-21.00	-43.95	-4.06	-29.58	-20.02	-9.70	34.69	-38.83	59.53	9.48	-134.33	28.61	850.86
1974	4.69	4.98	-13.85	-9.93	-34.58	0.24	-44.98	-78.85	-70.71	57.65	-46.86	-2.42	616.24
1975	87.45	35.36	29.10	53.19	10.95	46.70	-47.48	3.83	-41.46	42.16	24.63	-8.26	852.41
1976	122.87	-2.67	26.84	-2.60	-21.62	27.55	-18.14	-10.90	16.45	-25.26	-17.71	57.43	1004.65
1977	-50.28	-17.95	-17.29	7.77	-28.24	17.64	-26.23	-28.58	-14.38	-28.76	11.35	1.47	831.17
1978	-61.25	-27.80	15.24	79.96	3.29	-21.66	43.32	14.55	-11.00	-73.37	6.58	5.98	805.01
1979	34.21	-30.40	53.36	-7.28	-32.57	19.65	4.44	41.21	-9.05	-62.88	6.65	16.39	838.74
1980	37.11	-12.71	-77.39	31.31	33.79	17.07	67.40	-2.73	-0.17	-7.93	68.85	-29.35	963.99
1981	-16.72	27.31	29.29	-6.12	-6.00	-14.87	-24.54	-70.87	-31.49	2.57	36.43	-13.98	875.00
1982	-3.90	-46.71	-1.62	25.59	-28.82	-7.61	-3.33	92.71	-5.06	95.47	47.56	7.26	1046.54
1983	29.16	36.92	17.41	96.17	-26.22	21.98	-22.74	16.94	16.97	-7.93	50.82	-17.38	1258.64
1984	-38.06	-65.95	10.26	5.86	-65.90	27.55	-17.12	109.10	-17.67	0.67	-18.44	22.63	1211.57
1985	75.20	-2.76	-17.23	-8.72	57.35	20.05	11.99	-13.44	-5.38	45.68	97.82	74.54	1546.67
1986	24.32	138.07	109.55	-34.63	92.73	16.01	-117.41	123.03	-130.76	110.23	36.42	-18.28	1895.95
1987	262.09	65.95	80.70	-18.33	5.21	126.96	153.54	90.88	-66.67	-602.75	-159.98	105.28	1938.83
1988	19.39	113.40	-83.56	44.27	-1.21	110.59	-12.98	-97.08	81.26	35.74	-34.14	54.06	2168.57
1989	173.75	-83.93	35.23	125.18	61.35	-40.09	220.60	76.61	-44.45	-47.74	61.19	46.93	2753.20
1990	-162.66	36.71	79.96	-50.45	219.90	4.03	24.51	-290.84	-161.88	-10.15	117.32	74.01	2633.66
1991	102.73	145.79	31.68	-25.99	139.63	-120.75	118.07	18.78	-26.83	52.33	-174.42	274.15	3168.83
1992	54.56	44.28	-32.20	123.65	37.76	-78.36	75.26	-136.43	14.31	-45.38	78.88	-4.05	3301.11
1993	8.92	60.78	64.30	-7.56	99.88	-11.35	23.39	111.78	-96.13	125.47	3.36	70.14	3754.09
1994	224.27	-146.34	-196.06	45.73	76.68	-133.41	139.54	148.92	-70.23	64.93	-168.89	95.21	3834.44
1995	9.42	167.19	146.64	163.58	143.87	90.96	152.37	-97.91	178.52	-33.60	319.01	42.63	5117.12
1996	278.18	90.32	101.52	-18.06	74.10	11.45	-125.72	87.30	265.96	147.21	492.32	-73.43	6448.27
1997	364.82	64.65	-294.26	425.51	322.05	341.75	549.82	-600.19	322.84	-503.18	381.05	85.12	7908.25
1998	-1.75	639.22	254.09	263.56	-163.42	52.07	-68.73	-1344.22	303.55	749.48	524.45	64.88	9181.43
1999	177.40	-52.25	479.58	1002.88	-229.30	411.06	-315.65	174.13	-492.33	392.91	147.95	619.31	11497.12
2000	-556.59	-812.22	793.61	-188.01	-211.58	-74.44	74.09	693.12	-564.18	320.22	-556.65	372.36	10786.85
2001	100.51	-392.08	-616.50	856.19	176.97	-409.54	20.41	-573.06	-1102.19	227.58	776.42	169.94	10021.50
2002	-101.50	186.13	297.81	-457.72	-20.97	-681.99	-506.67	-73.09	-1071.57	805.10	499.06	-554.46	8341.63
2003	-287.82	-162.73	101.05	487.96	370.17	135.18	248.36	182.02	-140.76	526.06	-18.66	671.46	10453.92
2004	34.15	95.85	-226.22	-132.13	-37.12	247.03	-295.77	34.21	-93.65	-52.80	400.55	354.99	10783.01
2005	-293.07	276.29	-262.47	-311.25	274.97	-192.51	365.94	-159.31	87.10	-128.63	365.80	-88.37	10717.50
2006	147.36	128.55	115.91	257.82	-198.83	-18.09	35.46	195.47	297.92	401.66	141.20	241.22	12463.15
2007	158.54	-353.06	85.72	708.56	564.73	-219.02	-196.63	145.75	537.89	34.38	-558.29	-106.90	13264.82
2008	-614.46	-383.97	-3.50	557.24	-181.81	-1288.31	28.01	165.53	-692.89	-1525.65	-495.97	-52.65	8776.39
2009	-775.53	-937.93	545.99	559.20	332.21	-53.33	724.61	324.67	216.00	0.45	632.11	83.21	10428.05
2010	-360.72	257.93	531.37	151.98	-871.98	-362.61	691.92	-451.22	773.33	330.44	-112.47	571.49	11577.51
2011	314.42	334.41	93.39	490.81	-240.75	-155.45	-271.10	-529.71	-700.15	1041.63	90.67	171.88	12217.56
2012	415.35	319.16	259.97	1.59	-820.18	486.64	128.59	82.16	346.29	-340.67	-70.88	78.56	13104.14
2013	756.44	193.91	524.05	261.26	275.77	-205.97	589.94	-689.23	319.36	416.08	540.66	490.25	16576.66
2014	-877.81	622.86	135.95	123.18									
TOTALS	-146.14	499.18	3351.26	5870.02	-36.90	-2065.96	2562.55	-2248.03	-1870.83	2592.98	3645.22	4227.36	
# Up	42	38	43	43	32	29	40	36	26	38	42	46	
# Down	23	27	22	22	32	35	24	28	38	26	22	18	

DOW JONES INDUSTRIALS MONTHLY CLOSING PRICES SINCE 1950

	Jan	Feb	Mar	Apr	May	Jun	Jul	Aug	Sep	Oct	Nov	Dec
1950	201.79	203.44	206.05	214.33	223.42	209.11	209.40	216.87	226.36	225.01	227.60	235.41
1951	248.83	252.05	247.94	259.13	249.65	242.64	257.86	270.25	271.16	262.35	261.27	269.23
1952	270.69	260.08	269.46	257.63	262.94	274.26	279.56	275.04	270.61	269.23	283.66	291.90
1953	289.77	284.27	279.87	274.75	272.28	268.26	275.38	261.22	264.04	275.81	281.37	280.90
1954	292.39	294.54	303.51	319.33	327.49	333.53	347.92	335.80	360.46	352.14	386.77	404.39
1955	408.83	411.87	409.70	425.65	424.86	451.38	465.85	468.18	466.62	454.87	483.26	488.40
1956	470.74	483.65	511.79	516.12	478.05	492.78	517.81	502.04	475.25	479.85	472.78	499.47
1957	479.16	464.62	474.81	494.36	504.93	503.29	508.52	484.35	456.30	441.04	449.87	435.69
1958	450.02	439.92	446.76	455.86	462.70	478.18	502.99	508.63	532.09	543.22	557.46	583.65
1959	593.96	603.50	601.71	623.75	643.79	643.60	674.88	664.41	631.68	646.60	659.18	679.36
1960	622.62	630.12	616.59	601.70	625.50	640.62	616.73	625.99	580.14	580.36	597.22	615.89
1961	648.20	662.08	676.63	678.71	696.72	683.96	705.37	719.94	701.21	703.92	721.60	731.14
1962	700.00	708.05	706.95	665.33	613.36	561.28	597.93	609.18	578.98	589.77	649.30	652.10
1963	682.85	662.94	682.52	717.70	726.96	706.88	695.43	729.32	732.79	755.23	750.52	762.95
1964	785.34	800.14	813.29	810.77	820.56	831.50	841.10	838.48	875.37	873.08	875.43	874.13
1965	902.86	903.48	889.05	922.31	918.04	868.03	881.74	893.10	930.58	960.82	946.71	969.26
1966	983.51	951.89	924.77	933.68	884.07	870.10	847.38	788.41	774.22	807.07	791.59	785.69
1967	849.89	839.37	865.98	897.05	852.56	860.26	904.24	901.29	926.66	879.74	875.81	905.11
1968	855.47	840.50	840.67	912.22	899.00	897.80	883.00	896.01	935.79	952.39	985.08	943.75
1969	946.05	905.21	935.48	950.18	937.56	873.19	815.47	836.72	813.09	855.99	812.30	800.36
1970	744.06	777.59	785.57	736.07	700.44	683.53	734.12	764.58	760.68	755.61	794.09	838.92
1971	868.50	878.83	904.37	941.75	907.81	891.14	858.43	898.07	887.19	839.00	831.34	890.20
1972	902.17	928.13	940.70	954.17	960.72	929.03	924.74	963.73	953.27	955.52	1018.21	1020.02
1973	999.02	955.07	951.01	921.43	901.41	891.71	926.40	887.57	947.10	956.58	822.25	850.86
1974	855.55	860.53	846.68	836.75	802.17	802.41	757.43	678.58	607.87	665.52	618.66	616.24
1975	703.69	739.05	768.15	821.34	832.29	878.99	831.51	835.34	793.88	836.04	860.67	852.41
1976	975.28	972.61	999.45	996.85	975.23	1002.78	984.64	973.74	990.19	964.93	947.22	1004.65
1977	954.37	936.42	919.13	926.90	898.66	916.30	890.07	861.49	847.11	818.35	829.70	831.17
1978	769.92	742.12	757.36	837.32	840.61	818.95	862.27	876.82	865.82	792.45	799.03	805.01
1979	839.22	808.82	862.18	854.90	822.33	841.98	846.42	887.63	878.58	815.70	822.35	838.74
1980	875.85	863.14	785.75	817.06	850.85	867.92	935.32	932.59	932.42	924.49	993.34	963.99
1981	947.27	974.58	1003.87	997.75	991.75	976.88	952.34	881.47	849.98	852.55	888.98	875.00
1982	871.10	824.39	822.77	848.36	819.54	811.93	808.60	901.31	896.25	991.72	1039.28	1046.54
1983	1075.70	1112.62	1130.03	1226.20	1199.98	1221.96	1199.22	1216.16	1233.13	1225.20	1276.02	1258.64
1984	1220.58	1154.63	1164.89	1170.75	1104.85	1132.40	1115.28	1224.38	1206.71	1207.38	1188.94	1211.57
1985	1286.77	1284.01	1266.78	1258.06	1315.41	1335.46	1347.45	1334.01	1328.63	1374.31	1472.13	1546.67
1986	1570.99	1709.06	1818.61	1783.98	1876.71	1892.72	1775.31	1898.34	1767.58	1877.81	1914.23	1895.95
1987	2158.04	2223.99	2304.69	2286.36	2291.57	2418.53	2572.07	2662.95	2596.28	1993.53	1833.55	1938.83
1988	1958.22	2071.62	1988.06	2032.33	2031.12	2141.71	2128.73	2031.65	2112.91	2148.65	2114.51	2168.57
1989	2342.32	2258.39	2293.62	2418.80	2480.15	2440.06	2660.66	2737.27	2692.82	2645.08	2706.27	2753.20
1990	2590.54	2627.25	2707.21	2656.76	2876.66	2880.69	2905.20	2614.36	2452.48	2442.33	2559.65	2633.66
1991	2736.39	2882.18	2913.86	2887.87	3027.50	2906.75	3024.82	3043.60	3016.77	3069.10	2894.68	3168.83
1992	3223.39	3267.67	3235.47	3359.12	3396.88	3318.52	3393.78	3257.35	3271.66	3226.28	3305.16	3301.11
1993	3310.03	3370.81	3435.11	3427.55	3527.43	3516.08	3539.47	3651.25	3555.12	3680.59	3683.95	3754.09
1994	3978.36	3832.02	3635.96	3681.69	3758.37	3624.96	3764.50	3913.42	3843.19	3908.12	3739.23	3834.44
1995	3843.86	4011.05	4157.69	4321.27	4465.14	4556.10	4708.47	4610.56	4789.08	4755.48	5074.49	5117.12
1996	5395.30	5485.62	5587.14	5569.08	5643.18	5654.63	5528.91	5616.21	5882.17	6029.38	6521.70	6448.27
1997	6813.09	6877.74	6583.48	7008.99	7331.04	7672.79	8222.61	7622.42	7945.26	7442.08	7823.13	7908.25
1998	7906.50	8545.72	8799.81	9063.37	8899.95	8952.02	8883.29	7539.07	7842.62	8592.10	9116.55	9181.43
1999	9358.83	9306.58	9786.16	10789.04	10559.74	10970.80	10655.15	10829.28	10336.95	10729.86	10877.81	11497.12
2000	10940.53	10128.31	10921.92	10733.91	10522.33	10447.89	10521.98	11215.10	10650.92	10971.14	10414.49	10786.85
2001	10887.36	10495.28	9878.78	10734.97	10911.94	10502.40	10522.81	9949.75	8847.56	9075.14	9851.56	10021.50
2002	9920.00	10106.13	10403.94	9946.22	9925.25	9243.26	8736.59	8663.50	7591.93	8397.03	8896.09	8341.63
2003	8053.81	7891.08	7992.13	8480.09	8850.26	8985.44	9233.80	9415.82	9275.06	9801.12	9782.46	10453.92
2004	10488.07	10583.92	10357.70	10225.57	10188.45	10435.48	10139.71	10173.92	10080.27	10027.47	10428.02	10783.01
2005	10489.94	10766.23	10503.76	10192.51	10467.48	10274.97	10640.91	10481.60	10568.70	10440.07	10805.87	10717.50
2006	10864.86	10993.41	11109.32	11367.14	11168.31	11150.22	11185.68	11381.15	11679.07	12080.73	12221.93	12463.15
2007	12621.69	12268.63	12354.35	13062.91	13627.64	13408.62	13211.99	13357.74	13895.63	13930.01	13371.72	13264.82
2008	12650.36	12266.39	12262.89	12820.13	12638.32	11350.01	11378.02	11543.55	10850.66	9325.01	8829.04	8776.39
2009	8000.86	7062.93	7608.92	8168.12	8500.33	8447.00	9171.61	9496.28	9712.28	9712.73	10344.84	10428.05
2010	10067.33	10325.26	10856.63	11008.61	10136.63	9774.02	10465.94	10014.72	10788.05	11118.49	11006.02	11577.51
2011	11891.93	12226.34	12319.73	12810.54	12569.79	12414.34	12143.24	11613.53	10913.38	11955.01	12045.68	12217.56
2012	12632.91	12952.07	13212.04	13213.63	12393.45	12880.09	13008.68	13090.84	13437.13	13096.46	13025.58	13104.14
2013	13860.58	14054.49	14578.54	14839.80	15115.57	14909.60	15499.54	14810.31	15129.67	15545.75	16086.41	16576.66
2014	15698.85	16321.71	16457.66	16580.84								

154

	Jan	Feb	Mar	Apr	May	Jun	Jul	Aug	Sep	Oct	Nov	Dec	Year's Change
1950	1.7	1.0	0.4	4.5	3.9	−5.8	0.8	3.3	5.6	0.4	−0.1	4.6	21.8
1951	6.1	0.6	−1.8	4.8	−4.1	−2.6	6.9	3.9	−0.1	−1.4	−0.3	3.9	16.5
1952	1.6	−3.6	4.8	−4.3	2.3	4.6	1.8	−1.5	−2.0	−0.1	4.6	3.5	11.8
1953	−0.7	−1.8	−2.4	−2.6	−0.3	−1.6	2.5	−5.8	0.1	5.1	0.9	0.2	−6.6
1954	5.1	0.3	3.0	4.9	3.3	0.1	5.7	−3.4	8.3	−1.9	8.1	5.1	45.0
1955	1.8	0.4	−0.5	3.8	−0.1	8.2	6.1	−0.8	1.1	−3.0	7.5	−0.1	26.4
1956	−3.6	3.5	6.9	−0.2	−6.6	3.9	5.2	−3.8	−4.5	0.5	−1.1	3.5	2.6
1957	−4.2	−3.3	2.0	3.7	3.7	−0.1	1.1	−5.6	−6.2	−3.2	1.6	−4.1	−14.3
1958	4.3	−2.1	3.1	3.2	1.5	2.6	4.3	1.2	4.8	2.5	2.2	5.2	38.1
1959	0.4	−0.02	0.1	3.9	1.9	−0.4	3.5	−1.5	−4.6	1.1	1.3	2.8	8.5
1960	−7.1	0.9	−1.4	−1.8	2.7	2.0	−2.5	2.6	−6.0	−0.2	4.0	4.6	−3.0
1961	6.3	2.7	2.6	0.4	1.9	−2.9	3.3	2.0	−2.0	2.8	3.9	0.3	23.1
1962	−3.8	1.6	−0.6	−6.2	−8.6	−8.2	6.4	1.5	−4.8	0.4	10.2	1.3	−11.8
1963	4.9	−2.9	3.5	4.9	1.4	−2.0	−0.3	4.9	−1.1	3.2	−1.1	2.4	18.9
1964	2.7	1.0	1.5	0.6	1.1	1.6	1.8	−1.6	2.9	0.8	−0.5	0.4	13.0
1965	3.3	−0.1	−1.5	3.4	−0.8	−4.9	1.3	2.3	3.2	2.7	−0.9	0.9	9.1
1966	0.5	−1.8	−2.2	2.1	−5.4	−1.6	−1.3	−7.8	−0.7	4.8	0.3	−0.1	−13.1
1967	7.8	0.2	3.9	4.2	−5.2	1.8	4.5	−1.2	3.3	−2.9	0.1	2.6	20.1
1968	−4.4	−3.1	0.9	8.2	1.1	0.9	−1.8	1.1	3.9	0.7	4.8	−4.2	7.7
1969	−0.8	−4.7	3.4	2.1	−0.2	−5.6	−6.0	4.0	−2.5	4.4	−3.5	−1.9	−11.4
1970	−7.6	5.3	0.1	−9.0	−6.1	−5.0	7.3	4.4	3.3	−1.1	4.7	5.7	0.1
1971	4.0	0.9	3.7	3.6	−4.2	0.1	−4.1	3.6	−0.7	−4.2	−0.3	8.6	10.8
1972	1.8	2.5	0.6	0.4	1.7	−2.2	0.2	3.4	−0.5	0.9	4.6	1.2	15.6
1973	−1.7	−3.7	−0.1	−4.1	−1.9	−0.7	3.8	−3.7	4.0	−0.1	−11.4	1.7	−17.4
1974	−1.0	−0.4	−2.3	−3.9	−3.4	−1.5	−7.8	−9.0	−11.9	16.3	−5.3	−2.0	−29.7
1975	12.3	6.0	2.2	4.7	4.4	4.4	−6.8	−2.1	−3.5	6.2	2.5	−1.2	31.5
1976	11.8	−1.1	3.1	−1.1	−1.4	4.1	−0.8	−0.5	2.3	−2.2	−0.8	5.2	19.1
1977	−5.1	−2.2	−1.4	0.02	−2.4	4.5	−1.6	−2.1	−0.2	−4.3	2.7	0.3	−11.5
1978	−6.2	−2.5	2.5	8.5	0.4	−1.8	5.4	2.6	−0.7	−9.2	1.7	1.5	1.1
1979	4.0	−3.7	5.5	0.2	−2.6	3.9	0.9	5.3	N/C	−6.9	4.3	1.7	12.3
1980	5.8	−0.4	−10.2	4.1	4.7	2.7	6.5	0.6	2.5	1.6	10.2	−3.4	25.8
1981	−4.6	1.3	3.6	−2.3	−0.2	−1.0	−0.2	−6.2	−5.4	4.9	3.7	−3.0	−9.7
1982	−1.8	−6.1	−1.0	4.0	−3.9	−2.0	−2.3	11.6	0.8	11.0	3.6	1.5	14.8
1983	3.3	1.9	3.3	7.5	−1.2	3.5	−3.3	1.1	1.0	−1.5	1.7	−0.9	17.3
1984	−0.9	−3.9	1.3	0.5	−5.9	1.7	−1.6	10.6	−0.3	−0.01	−1.5	2.2	1.4
1985	7.4	0.9	−0.3	−0.5	5.4	1.2	−0.5	−1.2	−3.5	4.3	6.5	4.5	26.3
1986	0.2	7.1	5.3	−1.4	5.0	1.4	−5.9	7.1	−8.5	5.5	2.1	−2.8	14.6
1987	13.2	3.7	2.6	−1.1	0.6	4.8	4.8	3.5	−2.4	−21.8	−8.5	7.3	2.0
1988	4.0	4.2	−3.3	0.9	0.3	4.3	−0.5	−3.9	4.0	2.6	−1.9	1.5	12.4
1989	7.1	−2.9	2.1	5.0	3.5	−0.8	8.8	1.6	−0.7	−2.5	1.7	2.1	27.3
1990	−6.9	0.9	2.4	−2.7	9.2	−0.9	−0.5	−9.4	−5.1	−0.7	6.0	2.5	−6.6
1991	4.2	6.7	2.2	0.03	3.9	−4.8	4.5	2.0	−1.9	1.2	−4.4	11.2	26.3
1992	−2.0	1.0	−2.2	2.8	0.1	−1.7	3.9	−2.4	0.9	0.2	3.0	1.0	4.5
1993	0.7	1.0	1.9	−2.5	2.3	0.1	−0.5	3.4	−1.0	1.9	−1.3	1.0	7.1
1994	3.3	−3.0	−4.6	1.2	1.2	−2.7	3.1	3.8	−2.7	2.1	−4.0	1.2	−1.5
1995	2.4	3.6	2.7	2.8	3.6	2.1	3.2	−0.03	4.0	−0.5	4.1	1.7	34.1
1996	3.3	0.7	0.8	1.3	2.3	0.2	−4.6	1.9	5.4	2.6	7.3	−2.2	20.3
1997	6.1	0.6	−4.3	5.8	5.9	4.3	7.8	−5.7	5.3	−3.4	4.5	1.6	31.0
1998	1.0	7.0	5.0	0.9	−1.9	3.9	−1.2	−14.6	6.2	8.0	5.9	5.6	26.7
1999	4.1	−3.2	3.9	3.8	−2.5	5.4	−3.2	−0.6	−2.9	6.3	1.9	5.8	19.5
2000	−5.1	−2.0	9.7	−3.1	−2.2	2.4	−1.6	6.1	−5.3	−0.5	−8.0	0.4	−10.1
2001	3.5	−9.2	−6.4	7.7	0.5	−2.5	−1.1	−6.4	−8.2	1.8	7.5	0.8	−13.0
2002	−1.6	−2.1	3.7	−6.1	−0.9	−7.2	−7.9	0.5	−11.0	8.6	5.7	−6.0	−23.4
2003	−2.7	−1.7	1.0	8.0	5.1	1.1	1.6	1.8	−1.2	5.5	0.7	5.1	26.4
2004	1.7	1.2	−1.6	−1.7	1.2	1.8	−3.4	0.2	0.9	1.4	3.9	3.2	9.0
2005	−2.5	1.9	−1.9	−2.0	3.0	−0.01	3.6	−1.1	0.7	−1.8	3.5	−0.1	3.0
2006	2.5	0.05	1.1	1.2	−3.1	0.01	0.5	2.1	2.5	3.2	1.6	1.3	13.6
2007	1.4	−2.2	1.0	4.3	3.3	−1.8	−3.2	1.3	3.6	1.5	−4.4	−0.9	3.5
2008	−6.1	−3.5	−0.6	4.8	1.1	−8.6	−1.0	1.2	−9.1	−16.9	−7.5	0.8	−38.5
2009	−8.6	−11.0	8.5	9.4	5.3	0.02	7.4	3.4	3.6	−2.0	5.7	1.8	23.5
2010	−3.7	2.9	5.9	1.5	−8.2	−5.4	6.9	−4.7	8.8	3.7	−0.2	6.5	12.8
2011	2.3	3.2	−0.1	2.8	−1.4	−1.8	−2.1	−5.7	−7.2	10.8	−0.5	0.9	−0.003
2012	4.4	4.1	3.1	−0.7	−6.3	4.0	1.3	2.0	2.4	−2.0	0.3	0.7	13.4
2013	5.0	1.1	3.6	1.8	2.1	−1.5	4.9	−3.1	3.0	4.5	2.8	2.4	29.6
2014	−3.6	4.3	0.7	0.6									
TOTALS	71.0	−2.0	78.5	97.6	9.9	−2.0	64.0	−3.5	−30.0	51.7	96.4	108.9	
AVG.	1.1	−0.03	1.2	1.5	0.2	−0.03	1.0	−0.06	−0.5	0.8	1.5	1.7	
# Up	40	36	43	45	36	33	35	35	29	38	42	49	
# Down	25	29	22	20	28	31	29	29	34	26	22	15	

STANDARD & POOR'S 500 MONTHLY CLOSING PRICES SINCE 1950

	Jan	Feb	Mar	Apr	May	Jun	Jul	Aug	Sep	Oct	Nov	Dec
1950	17.05	17.22	17.29	18.07	18.78	17.69	17.84	18.42	19.45	19.53	19.51	20.41
1951	21.66	21.80	21.40	22.43	21.52	20.96	22.40	23.28	23.26	22.94	22.88	23.77
1952	24.14	23.26	24.37	23.32	23.86	24.96	25.40	25.03	24.54	24.52	25.66	26.57
1953	26.38	25.90	25.29	24.62	24.54	24.14	24.75	23.32	23.35	24.54	24.76	24.81
1954	26.08	26.15	26.94	28.26	29.19	29.21	30.88	29.83	32.31	31.68	34.24	35.98
1955	36.63	36.76	36.58	37.96	37.91	41.03	43.52	43.18	43.67	42.34	45.51	45.48
1956	43.82	45.34	48.48	48.38	45.20	46.97	49.39	47.51	45.35	45.58	45.08	46.67
1957	44.72	43.26	44.11	45.74	47.43	47.37	47.91	45.22	42.42	41.06	41.72	39.99
1958	41.70	40.84	42.10	43.44	44.09	45.24	47.19	47.75	50.06	51.33	52.48	55.21
1959	55.42	55.41	55.44	57.59	58.68	58.47	60.51	59.60	56.88	57.52	58.28	59.89
1960	55.61	56.12	55.34	54.37	55.83	56.92	55.51	56.96	53.52	53.39	55.54	58.11
1961	61.78	63.44	65.06	65.31	66.56	64.64	66.76	68.07	66.73	68.62	71.32	71.55
1962	68.84	69.96	69.55	65.24	59.63	54.75	58.23	59.12	56.27	56.52	62.26	63.10
1963	66.20	64.29	66.57	69.80	70.80	69.37	69.13	72.50	71.70	74.01	73.23	75.02
1964	77.04	77.80	78.98	79.46	80.37	81.69	83.18	81.83	84.18	84.86	84.42	84.75
1965	87.56	87.43	86.16	89.11	88.42	84.12	85.25	87.17	89.96	92.42	91.61	92.43
1966	92.88	91.22	89.23	91.06	86.13	84.74	83.60	77.10	76.56	80.20	80.45	80.33
1967	86.61	86.78	90.20	94.01	89.08	90.64	94.75	93.64	96.71	93.90	94.00	96.47
1968	92.24	89.36	90.20	97.59	98.68	99.58	97.74	98.86	102.67	103.41	108.37	103.86
1969	103.01	98.13	101.51	103.69	103.46	97.71	91.83	95.51	93.12	97.24	93.81	92.06
1970	85.02	89.50	89.63	81.52	76.55	72.72	78.05	81.52	84.21	83.25	87.20	92.15
1971	95.88	96.75	100.31	103.95	99.63	99.70	95.58	99.03	98.34	94.23	93.99	102.09
1972	103.94	106.57	107.20	107.67	109.53	107.14	107.39	111.09	110.55	111.58	116.67	118.05
1973	116.03	111.68	111.52	106.97	104.95	104.26	108.22	104.25	108.43	108.29	95.96	97.55
1974	96.57	96.22	93.98	90.31	87.28	86.00	79.31	72.15	63.54	73.90	69.97	68.56
1975	76.98	81.59	83.36	87.30	91.15	95.19	88.75	86.88	83.87	89.04	91.24	90.19
1976	100.86	99.71	102.77	101.64	100.18	104.28	103.44	102.91	105.24	102.90	102.10	107.46
1977	102.03	99.82	98.42	98.44	96.12	100.48	98.85	96.77	96.53	92.34	94.83	95.10
1978	89.25	87.04	89.21	96.83	97.24	95.53	100.68	103.29	102.54	93.15	94.70	96.11
1979	99.93	96.28	101.59	101.76	99.08	102.91	103.81	109.32	109.32	101.82	106.16	107.94
1980	114.16	113.66	102.09	106.29	111.24	114.24	121.67	122.38	125.46	127.47	140.52	135.76
1981	129.55	131.27	136.00	132.81	132.59	131.21	130.92	122.79	116.18	121.89	126.35	122.55
1982	120.40	113.11	111.96	116.44	111.88	109.61	107.09	119.51	120.42	133.71	138.54	140.64
1983	145.30	148.06	152.96	164.42	162.39	168.11	162.56	164.40	166.07	163.55	166.40	164.93
1984	163.41	157.06	159.18	160.05	150.55	153.18	150.66	166.68	166.10	166.09	163.58	167.24
1985	179.63	181.18	180.66	179.83	189.55	191.85	190.92	188.63	182.08	189.82	202.17	211.28
1986	211.78	226.92	238.90	235.52	247.35	250.84	236.12	252.93	231.32	243.98	249.22	242.17
1987	274.08	284.20	291.70	288.36	290.10	304.00	318.66	329.80	321.83	251.79	230.30	247.08
1988	257.07	267.82	258.89	261.33	262.16	273.50	272.02	261.52	271.91	278.97	273.70	277.72
1989	297.47	288.86	294.87	309.64	320.52	317.98	346.08	351.45	349.15	340.36	345.99	353.40
1990	329.08	331.89	339.94	330.80	361.23	358.02	356.15	322.56	306.05	304.00	322.22	330.22
1991	343.93	367.07	375.22	375.35	389.83	371.16	387.81	395.43	387.86	392.46	375.22	417.09
1992	408.79	412.70	403.69	414.95	415.35	408.14	424.21	414.03	417.80	418.68	431.35	435.71
1993	438.78	443.38	451.67	440.19	450.19	450.53	448.13	463.56	458.93	467.83	461.79	466.45
1994	481.61	467.14	445.77	450.91	456.50	444.27	458.26	475.49	462.69	472.35	453.69	459.27
1995	470.42	487.39	500.71	514.71	533.40	544.75	562.06	561.88	584.41	581.50	605.37	615.93
1996	636.02	640.43	645.50	654.17	669.12	670.63	639.95	651.99	687.31	705.27	757.02	740.74
1997	786.16	790.82	757.12	801.34	848.28	885.14	954.29	899.47	947.28	914.62	955.40	970.43
1998	980.28	1049.34	1101.75	1111.75	1090.82	1133.84	1120.67	957.28	1017.01	1098.67	1163.63	1229.23
1999	1279.64	1238.33	1286.37	1335.18	1301.84	1372.71	1328.72	1320.41	1282.71	1362.93	1388.91	1469.25
2000	1394.46	1366.42	1498.58	1452.43	1420.60	1454.60	1430.83	1517.68	1436.51	1429.40	1314.95	1320.28
2001	1366.01	1239.94	1160.33	1249.46	1255.82	1224.42	1211.23	1133.58	1040.94	1059.78	1139.45	1148.08
2002	1130.20	1106.73	1147.39	1076.92	1067.14	989.82	911.62	916.07	815.28	885.76	936.31	879.82
2003	855.70	841.15	849.18	916.92	963.59	974.50	990.31	1008.01	995.97	1050.71	1058.20	1111.92
2004	1131.13	1144.94	1126.21	1107.30	1120.68	1140.84	1101.72	1104.24	1114.58	1130.20	1173.82	1211.92
2005	1181.27	1203.60	1180.59	1156.85	1191.50	1191.33	1234.18	1220.33	1228.81	1207.01	1249.48	1248.29
2006	1280.08	1280.66	1294.83	1310.61	1270.09	1270.20	1276.66	1303.82	1335.85	1377.94	1400.63	1418.30
2007	1438.24	1406.82	1420.86	1482.37	1530.62	1503.35	1455.27	1473.99	1526.75	1549.38	1481.14	1468.36
2008	1378.55	1330.63	1322.70	1385.59	1400.38	1280.00	1267.38	1282.83	1166.36	968.75	896.24	903.25
2009	825.88	735.09	797.87	872.81	919.14	919.32	987.48	1020.62	1057.08	1036.19	1095.63	1115.10
2010	1073.87	1104.49	1169.43	1186.69	1089.41	1030.71	1101.60	1049.33	1141.20	1183.26	1180.55	1257.64
2011	1286.12	1327.22	1325.83	1363.61	1345.20	1320.64	1292.28	1218.89	1131.42	1253.30	1246.96	1257.60
2012	1312.41	1365.68	1408.47	1397.91	1310.33	1362.16	1379.32	1406.58	1440.67	1412.16	1416.18	1426.19
2013	1498.11	1514.68	1569.19	1597.57	1630.74	1606.28	1685.73	1632.97	1681.55	1756.54	1805.81	1848.36
2014	1782.59	1859.45	1872.34	1883.95								

NASDAQ COMPOSITE MONTHLY PERCENT CHANGES SINCE 1971

	Jan	Feb	Mar	Apr	May	Jun	Jul	Aug	Sep	Oct	Nov	Dec	Year's Change
1971	10.2	2.6	4.6	6.0	–3.6	–0.4	–2.3	3.0	0.6	–3.6	–1.1	9.8	27.4
1972	4.2	5.5	2.2	2.5	0.9	–1.8	–1.8	1.7	–0.3	0.5	2.1	0.6	17.2
1973	–4.0	–6.2	–2.4	–8.2	–4.8	–1.6	7.6	–3.5	6.0	–0.9	–15.1	–1.4	–31.1
1974	3.0	–0.6	–2.2	–5.9	–7.7	–5.3	–7.9	–10.9	–10.7	17.2	–3.5	–5.0	–35.1
1975	16.6	4.6	3.6	3.8	5.8	4.7	–4.4	–5.0	–5.9	3.6	2.4	–1.5	29.8
1976	12.1	3.7	0.4	–0.6	–2.3	2.6	1.1	–1.7	1.7	–1.0	0.9	7.4	26.1
1977	–2.4	–1.0	–0.5	1.4	0.1	4.3	0.9	–0.5	0.7	–3.3	5.8	1.8	7.3
1978	–4.0	0.6	4.7	8.5	4.4	0.05	5.0	6.9	–1.6	–16.4	3.2	2.9	12.3
1979	6.6	–2.6	7.5	1.6	–1.8	5.1	2.3	6.4	–0.3	–9.6	6.4	4.8	28.1
1980	7.0	–2.3	–17.1	6.9	7.5	4.9	8.9	5.7	3.4	2.7	8.0	–2.8	33.9
1981	–2.2	0.1	6.1	3.1	3.1	–3.5	–1.9	–7.5	–8.0	8.4	3.1	–2.7	–3.2
1982	–3.8	–4.8	–2.1	5.2	–3.3	–4.1	–2.3	6.2	5.6	13.3	9.3	0.04	18.7
1983	6.9	5.0	3.9	8.2	5.3	3.2	–4.6	–3.8	1.4	–7.4	4.1	–2.5	19.9
1984	–3.7	–5.9	–0.7	–1.3	–5.9	2.9	–4.2	10.9	–1.8	–1.2	–1.8	2.0	–11.2
1985	12.7	2.0	–1.7	0.5	3.6	1.9	1.7	–1.2	–5.8	4.4	7.3	3.5	31.4
1986	3.3	7.1	4.2	2.3	4.4	1.3	–8.4	3.1	–8.4	2.9	–0.3	–2.8	7.5
1987	12.2	8.4	1.2	–2.8	–0.3	2.0	2.4	4.6	–2.3	–27.2	–5.6	8.3	–5.4
1988	4.3	6.5	2.1	1.2	–2.3	6.6	–1.9	–2.8	3.0	–1.4	–2.9	2.7	15.4
1989	5.2	–0.4	1.8	5.1	4.4	–2.4	4.3	3.4	0.8	–3.7	0.1	–0.3	19.3
1990	–8.6	2.4	2.3	–3.6	9.3	0.7	–5.2	–13.0	–9.6	–4.3	8.9	4.1	–17.8
1991	10.8	9.4	6.5	0.5	4.4	–6.0	5.5	4.7	0.2	3.1	–3.5	11.9	56.8
1992	5.8	2.1	–4.7	–4.2	1.1	–3.7	3.1	–3.0	3.6	3.8	7.9	3.7	15.5
1993	2.9	–3.7	2.9	–4.2	5.9	0.5	0.1	5.4	2.7	2.2	–3.2	3.0	14.7
1994	3.0	–1.0	–6.2	–1.3	0.2	–4.0	2.3	6.0	–0.2	1.7	–3.5	0.2	–3.2
1995	0.4	5.1	3.0	3.3	2.4	8.0	7.3	1.9	2.3	–0.7	2.2	–0.7	39.9
1996	0.7	3.8	0.1	8.1	4.4	–4.7	–8.8	5.6	7.5	–0.4	5.8	–0.1	22.7
1997	6.9	–5.1	–6.7	3.2	11.1	3.0	10.5	–0.4	6.2	–5.5	0.4	–1.9	21.6
1998	3.1	9.3	3.7	1.8	–4.8	6.5	–1.2	–19.9	13.0	4.6	10.1	12.5	39.6
1999	14.3	–8.7	7.6	3.3	–2.8	8.7	–1.8	3.8	0.2	8.0	12.5	22.0	85.6
2000	–3.2	19.2	–2.6	–15.6	–11.9	16.6	–5.0	11.7	–12.7	–8.3	–22.9	–4.9	–39.3
2001	12.2	–22.4	–14.5	15.0	–0.3	2.4	–6.2	–10.9	–17.0	12.8	14.2	1.0	–21.1
2002	–0.8	–10.5	6.6	–8.5	–4.3	–9.4	–9.2	–1.0	–10.9	13.5	11.2	–9.7	–31.5
2003	–1.1	1.3	0.3	9.2	9.0	1.7	6.9	4.3	–1.3	8.1	1.5	2.2	50.0
2004	3.1	–1.8	–1.8	–3.7	3.5	3.1	–7.8	–2.6	3.2	4.1	6.2	3.7	8.6
2005	–5.2	–0.5	–2.6	–3.9	7.6	–0.5	6.2	–1.5	–0.02	–1.5	5.3	–1.2	1.4
2006	4.6	–1.1	2.6	–0.7	–6.2	–0.3	–3.7	4.4	3.4	4.8	2.7	–0.7	9.5
2007	2.0	–1.9	0.2	4.3	3.1	–0.05	–2.2	2.0	4.0	5.8	–6.9	–0.3	9.8
2008	–9.9	–5.0	0.3	5.9	4.6	–9.1	1.4	1.8	–11.6	–17.7	–10.8	2.7	–40.5
2009	–6.4	–6.7	10.9	12.3	3.3	3.4	7.8	1.5	5.6	–3.6	4.9	5.8	43.9
2010	–5.4	4.2	7.1	2.6	–8.3	–6.5	6.9	–6.2	12.0	5.9	–0.4	6.2	16.9
2011	1.8	3.0	–0.04	3.3	–1.3	–2.2	–0.6	–6.4	–6.4	11.1	–2.4	–0.6	–1.8
2012	8.0	5.4	4.2	–1.5	–7.2	3.8	0.2	4.3	1.6	–4.5	1.1	0.3	15.9
2013	4.1	0.6	3.4	1.9	3.8	–1.5	6.6	–1.0	5.1	3.9	3.6	2.9	38.3
2014	–1.7	5.0	–2.5	–2.0									
TOTALS	125.6	24.7	35.7	63.0	34.1	30.9	7.6	6.5	–21.0	24.2	67.3	86.9	
AVG.	2.9	0.6	0.8	1.4	0.8	0.7	0.2	0.2	–0.5	0.6	1.6	2.0	
# Up	29	24	28	28	25	24	22	23	24	23	28	26	
# Down	15	20	16	16	18	19	21	20	19	20	15	17	

Based on NASDAQ composite; prior to February 5, 1971, based on National Quotation Bureau indices.

NASDAQ COMPOSITE MONTHLY CLOSING PRICES SINCE 1971

	Jan	Feb	Mar	Apr	May	Jun	Jul	Aug	Sep	Oct	Nov	Dec
1971	98.77	101.34	105.97	112.30	108.25	107.80	105.27	108.42	109.03	105.10	103.97	114.12
1972	118.87	125.38	128.14	131.33	132.53	130.08	127.75	129.95	129.61	130.24	132.96	133.73
1973	128.40	120.41	117.46	107.85	102.64	100.98	108.64	104.87	111.20	110.17	93.51	92.19
1974	94.93	94.35	92.27	86.86	80.20	75.96	69.99	62.37	55.67	65.23	62.95	59.82
1975	69.78	73.00	75.66	78.54	83.10	87.02	83.19	79.01	74.33	76.99	78.80	77.62
1976	87.05	90.26	90.62	90.08	88.04	90.32	91.29	89.70	91.26	90.35	91.12	97.88
1977	95.54	94.57	94.13	95.48	95.59	99.73	100.65	100.10	100.85	97.52	103.15	105.05
1978	100.84	101.47	106.20	115.18	120.24	120.30	126.32	135.01	132.89	111.12	114.69	117.98
1979	125.82	122.56	131.76	133.82	131.42	138.13	141.33	150.44	149.98	135.53	144.26	151.14
1980	161.75	158.03	131.00	139.99	150.45	157.78	171.81	181.52	187.76	192.78	208.15	202.34
1981	197.81	198.01	210.18	216.74	223.47	215.75	211.63	195.75	180.03	195.24	201.37	195.84
1982	188.39	179.43	175.65	184.70	178.54	171.30	167.35	177.71	187.65	212.63	232.31	232.41
1983	248.35	260.67	270.80	293.06	308.73	318.70	303.96	292.42	296.65	274.55	285.67	278.60
1984	268.43	252.57	250.78	247.44	232.82	239.65	229.70	254.64	249.94	247.03	242.53	247.35
1985	278.70	284.17	279.20	280.56	290.80	296.20	301.29	297.71	280.33	292.54	313.95	324.93
1986	335.77	359.53	374.72	383.24	400.16	405.51	371.37	382.86	350.67	360.77	359.57	349.33
1987	392.06	424.97	430.05	417.81	416.54	424.67	434.93	454.97	444.29	323.30	305.16	330.47
1988	344.66	366.95	374.64	379.23	370.34	394.66	387.33	376.55	387.71	382.46	371.45	381.38
1989	401.30	399.71	406.73	427.55	446.17	435.29	453.84	469.33	472.92	455.63	456.09	454.82
1990	415.81	425.83	435.54	420.07	458.97	462.29	438.24	381.21	344.51	329.84	359.06	373.84
1991	414.20	453.05	482.30	484.72	506.11	475.92	502.04	525.68	526.88	542.98	523.90	586.34
1992	620.21	633.47	603.77	578.68	585.31	563.60	580.83	563.12	583.27	605.17	652.73	676.95
1993	696.34	670.77	690.13	661.42	700.53	703.95	704.70	742.84	762.78	779.26	754.39	776.80
1994	800.47	792.50	743.46	733.84	735.19	705.96	722.16	765.62	764.29	777.49	750.32	751.96
1995	755.20	793.73	817.21	843.98	864.58	933.45	1001.21	1020.11	1043.54	1036.06	1059.20	1052.13
1996	1059.79	1100.05	1101.40	1190.52	1243.43	1185.02	1080.59	1141.50	1226.92	1221.51	1292.61	1291.03
1997	1379.85	1309.00	1221.70	1260.76	1400.32	1442.07	1593.81	1587.32	1685.69	1593.61	1600.55	1570.35
1998	1619.36	1770.51	1835.68	1868.41	1778.87	1894.74	1872.39	1499.25	1693.84	1771.39	1949.54	2192.69
1999	2505.89	2288.03	2461.40	2542.85	2470.52	2686.12	2638.49	2739.35	2746.16	2966.43	3336.16	4069.31
2000	3940.35	4696.69	4572.83	3860.66	3400.91	3966.11	3766.99	4206.35	3672.82	3369.63	2597.93	2470.52
2001	2772.73	2151.83	1840.26	2116.24	2110.49	2160.54	2027.13	1805.43	1498.80	1690.20	1930.58	1950.40
2002	1934.03	1731.49	1845.35	1688.23	1615.73	1463.21	1328.26	1314.85	1172.06	1329.75	1478.78	1335.51
2003	1320.91	1337.52	1341.17	1464.31	1595.91	1622.80	1735.02	1810.45	1786.94	1932.21	1960.26	2003.37
2004	2066.15	2029.82	1994.22	1920.15	1986.74	2047.79	1887.36	1838.10	1896.84	1974.99	2096.81	2175.44
2005	2062.41	2051.72	1999.23	1921.65	2068.22	2056.96	2184.83	2152.09	2151.69	2120.30	2232.82	2205.32
2006	2305.82	2281.39	2339.79	2322.57	2178.88	2172.09	2091.47	2183.75	2258.43	2366.71	2431.77	2415.29
2007	2463.93	2416.15	2421.64	2525.09	2604.52	2603.23	2545.57	2596.36	2701.50	2859.12	2660.96	2652.28
2008	2389.86	2271.48	2279.10	2412.80	2522.66	2292.98	2325.55	2367.52	2091.88	1720.95	1535.57	1577.03
2009	1476.42	1377.84	1528.59	1717.30	1774.33	1835.04	1978.50	2009.06	2122.42	2045.11	2144.60	2269.15
2010	2147.35	2238.26	2397.96	2461.19	2257.04	2109.24	2254.70	2114.03	2368.62	2507.41	2498.23	2652.87
2011	2700.08	2782.27	2781.07	2873.54	2835.30	2773.52	2756.38	2579.46	2415.40	2684.41	2620.34	2605.15
2012	2813.84	2966.89	3091.57	3046.36	2827.34	2935.05	2939.52	3066.96	3116.23	2977.23	3010.24	3019.51
2013	3142.13	3160.19	3267.52	3328.79	3455.91	3403.25	3626.37	3589.87	3771.48	3919.71	4059.89	4176.59
2014	4103.88	4308.12	4198.99	4114.56								

Based on NASDAQ composite; prior to February 5, 1971, based on National Quotation Bureau indices.

RUSSELL 1000 INDEX MONTHLY PERCENT CHANGES SINCE 1979

	Jan	Feb	Mar	Apr	May	Jun	Jul	Aug	Sep	Oct	Nov	Dec	Year's Change
1979	4.2	-3.5	6.0	0.3	-2.2	4.3	1.1	5.6	0.02	-7.1	5.1	2.1	16.1
1980	5.9	-0.5	-11.5	4.6	5.0	3.2	6.4	1.1	2.6	1.8	10.1	-3.9	25.6
1981	-4.6	1.0	3.8	-1.9	0.2	-1.2	-0.1	-6.2	-6.4	5.4	4.0	-3.3	-9.7
1982	-2.7	-5.9	-1.3	3.9	-3.6	-2.6	-2.3	11.3	1.2	11.3	4.0	1.3	13.7
1983	3.2	2.1	3.2	7.1	-0.2	3.7	-3.2	0.5	1.3	-2.4	2.0	-1.2	17.0
1984	-1.9	-4.4	1.1	0.3	-5.9	2.1	-1.8	10.8	-0.2	-0.1	-1.4	2.2	-0.1
1985	7.8	1.1	-0.4	-0.3	5.4	1.6	-0.8	-1.0	-3.9	4.5	6.5	4.1	26.7
1986	0.9	7.2	5.1	-1.3	5.0	1.4	-5.9	6.8	-8.5	5.1	1.4	-3.0	13.6
1987	12.7	4.0	1.9	-1.8	0.4	4.5	4.2	3.8	-2.4	-21.9	-8.0	7.2	0.02
1988	4.3	4.4	-2.9	0.7	0.2	4.8	-0.9	-3.3	3.9	2.0	-2.0	1.7	13.1
1989	6.8	-2.5	2.0	4.9	3.8	-0.8	8.2	1.7	-0.5	-2.8	1.5	1.8	25.9
1990	-7.4	1.2	2.2	-2.8	8.9	-0.7	-1.1	-9.6	-5.3	-0.8	6.4	2.7	-7.5
1991	4.5	6.9	2.5	-0.1	3.8	-4.7	4.6	2.2	-1.5	1.4	-4.1	11.2	28.8
1992	-1.4	0.9	-2.4	2.3	0.3	-1.9	4.1	-2.5	1.0	0.7	3.5	1.4	5.9
1993	0.7	0.6	2.2	-2.8	2.4	0.4	-0.4	3.5	-0.5	1.2	-1.7	1.6	7.3
1994	2.9	-2.9	-4.5	1.1	1.0	-2.9	3.1	3.9	-2.6	1.7	-3.9	1.2	-2.4
1995	2.4	3.8	2.3	2.5	3.5	2.4	3.7	0.5	3.9	-0.6	4.2	1.4	34.4
1996	3.1	1.1	0.7	1.4	2.1	-0.1	-4.9	2.5	5.5	2.1	7.1	-1.8	19.7
1997	5.8	0.2	-4.6	5.3	6.2	4.0	8.0	-4.9	5.4	-3.4	4.2	1.9	30.5
1998	0.6	7.0	4.9	0.9	-2.3	3.6	-1.3	-15.1	6.5	7.8	6.1	6.2	25.1
1999	3.5	-3.3	3.7	4.2	-2.3	5.1	-3.2	-1.0	-2.8	6.5	2.5	6.0	19.5
2000	-4.2	-0.4	8.9	-3.3	-2.7	2.5	-1.8	7.4	-4.8	-1.2	-9.3	1.1	-8.8
2001	3.2	-9.5	-6.7	8.0	0.5	-2.4	-1.4	-6.2	-8.6	2.0	7.5	0.9	-13.6
2002	-1.4	-2.1	4.0	-5.8	-1.0	-7.5	-7.5	0.3	-10.9	8.1	5.7	-5.8	-22.9
2003	-2.5	-1.7	0.9	7.9	5.5	1.2	1.8	1.9	-1.2	5.7	1.0	4.6	27.5
2004	1.8	1.2	-1.5	-1.9	1.3	1.7	-3.6	0.3	1.1	1.5	4.1	3.5	9.5
2005	-2.6	2.0	-1.7	-2.0	3.4	0.3	3.8	-1.1	0.8	-1.9	3.5	0.01	4.4
2006	2.7	0.01	1.3	1.1	-3.2	0.003	0.1	2.2	2.3	3.3	1.9	1.1	13.3
2007	1.8	-1.9	0.9	4.1	3.4	-2.0	-3.2	1.2	3.7	1.6	-4.5	-0.8	3.9
2008	-6.1	-3.3	-0.8	5.0	1.6	-8.5	-1.3	1.2	-9.7	-17.6	-7.9	1.3	-39.0
2009	-8.3	-10.7	8.5	10.0	5.3	0.1	7.5	3.4	3.9	-2.3	5.6	2.3	25.5
2010	-3.7	3.1	6.0	1.8	-8.1	-5.7	6.8	-4.7	9.0	3.8	0.1	6.5	13.9
2011	2.3	3.3	0.1	2.9	-1.3	-1.9	-2.3	-6.0	-7.6	11.1	-0.5	0.7	-0.5
2012	4.8	4.1	3.0	-0.7	-6.4	3.7	1.1	2.2	2.4	-1.8	0.5	0.8	13.9
2013	5.3	1.1	3.7	1.7	2.0	-1.5	5.2	-3.0	3.3	4.3	2.6	2.5	30.4
2014	-3.3	4.5	0.5	0.4									
TOTALS	41.1	8.2	41.1	57.7	32.0	6.2	22.7	9.7	-19.6	29.0	57.8	59.5	
AVG.	1.1	0.2	1.1	1.6	0.9	0.2	0.6	0.3	-0.6	0.8	1.7	1.7	
# Up	23	22	25	24	23	20	16	22	18	22	25	28	
# Down	13	14	11	12	12	15	19	13	17	13	10	7	

RUSSELL 1000 INDEX MONTHLY CLOSING PRICES SINCE 1979

	Jan	Feb	Mar	Apr	May	Jun	Jul	Aug	Sep	Oct	Nov	Dec
1979	53.76	51.88	54.97	55.15	53.92	56.25	56.86	60.04	60.05	55.78	58.65	59.87
1980	63.40	63.07	55.79	58.38	61.31	63.27	67.30	68.05	69.84	71.08	78.26	75.20
1981	71.75	72.49	75.21	73.77	73.90	73.01	72.92	68.42	64.06	67.54	70.23	67.93
1982	66.12	62.21	61.43	63.85	61.53	59.92	58.54	65.14	65.89	73.34	76.28	77.24
1983	79.75	81.45	84.06	90.04	89.89	93.18	90.18	90.65	91.85	89.69	91.50	90.38
1984	88.69	84.76	85.73	86.00	80.94	82.61	81.13	89.87	89.67	89.62	88.36	90.31
1985	97.31	98.38	98.03	97.72	103.02	104.65	103.78	102.76	98.75	103.16	109.91	114.39
1986	115.39	123.71	130.07	128.44	134.82	136.75	128.74	137.43	125.70	132.11	133.97	130.00
1987	146.48	152.29	155.20	152.39	152.94	159.84	166.57	172.95	168.83	131.89	121.28	130.02
1988	135.55	141.54	137.45	138.37	138.66	145.31	143.99	139.26	144.68	147.55	144.59	146.99
1989	156.93	152.98	155.99	163.63	169.85	168.49	182.27	185.33	184.40	179.17	181.85	185.11
1990	171.44	173.43	177.28	172.32	187.66	186.29	184.32	166.69	157.83	156.62	166.69	171.22
1991	179.00	191.34	196.15	195.94	203.32	193.78	202.67	207.18	204.02	206.96	198.46	220.61
1992	217.52	219.50	214.29	219.13	219.71	215.60	224.37	218.86	221.15	222.65	230.44	233.59
1993	235.25	236.67	241.80	235.13	240.80	241.78	240.78	249.20	247.95	250.97	246.70	250.71
1994	258.08	250.52	239.19	241.71	244.13	237.11	244.44	254.04	247.49	251.62	241.82	244.65
1995	250.52	260.08	266.11	272.81	282.48	289.29	299.98	301.40	313.28	311.37	324.36	328.89
1996	338.97	342.56	345.01	349.84	357.35	357.10	339.44	347.79	366.77	374.38	401.05	393.75
1997	416.77	417.46	398.19	419.15	445.06	462.95	499.89	475.33	500.78	483.86	504.25	513.79
1998	517.02	553.14	580.31	585.46	572.16	592.57	584.97	496.66	529.11	570.63	605.31	642.87
1999	665.64	643.67	667.49	695.25	679.10	713.61	690.51	683.27	663.83	707.19	724.66	767.97
2000	736.08	733.04	797.99	771.58	750.98	769.68	755.57	811.17	772.60	763.06	692.40	700.09
2001	722.55	654.25	610.36	658.90	662.39	646.64	637.43	597.67	546.46	557.29	599.32	604.94
2002	596.66	583.88	607.35	572.04	566.18	523.72	484.39	486.08	433.22	468.51	495.00	466.18
2003	454.30	446.37	450.35	486.09	512.92	518.94	528.53	538.40	532.15	562.51	568.32	594.56
2004	605.21	612.58	603.42	591.83	599.40	609.31	587.21	589.09	595.66	604.51	629.26	650.99
2005	633.99	646.93	635.78	623.32	644.28	645.92	670.26	663.13	668.53	656.09	679.35	679.42
2006	697.79	697.83	706.74	714.37	691.78	691.80	692.59	707.55	723.48	747.30	761.43	770.08
2007	784.11	768.92	775.97	807.82	835.14	818.17	792.11	801.22	830.59	844.20	806.44	799.82
2008	750.97	726.42	720.32	756.03	768.28	703.22	694.07	702.17	634.08	522.47	481.43	487.77
2009	447.32	399.61	433.67	476.84	501.95	502.27	539.88	558.21	579.97	566.50	598.41	612.01
2010	589.41	607.45	643.79	655.06	601.79	567.37	606.09	577.68	629.78	653.57	654.24	696.90
2011	712.97	736.24	737.07	758.45	748.75	734.48	717.77	674.79	623.45	692.41	688.77	693.36
2012	726.33	756.42	778.92	773.50	724.12	750.61	758.60	775.07	793.74	779.35	783.37	789.90
2013	831.74	840.97	872.11	886.89	904.44	890.67	937.16	909.28	939.50	979.68	1004.97	1030.36
2014	996.48	1041.36	1046.42	1050.20								

RUSSELL 2000 INDEX MONTHLY PERCENT CHANGES SINCE 1979

	Jan	Feb	Mar	Apr	May	Jun	Jul	Aug	Sep	Oct	Nov	Dec	Year's Change
1979	9.0	-3.2	9.7	2.3	-1.8	5.3	2.9	7.8	-0.7	-11.3	8.1	6.6	38.0
1980	8.2	-2.1	-18.5	6.0	8.0	4.0	11.0	6.5	2.9	3.9	7.0	-3.7	33.8
1981	-0.6	0.3	7.7	2.5	3.0	-2.5	-2.6	-8.0	-8.6	8.2	2.8	-2.0	-1.5
1982	-3.7	-5.3	-1.5	5.1	-3.2	-4.0	-1.7	7.5	3.6	14.1	8.8	1.1	20.7
1983	7.5	6.0	2.5	7.2	7.0	4.4	-3.0	-4.0	1.6	-7.0	5.0	-2.1	26.3
1984	-1.8	-5.9	0.4	-0.7	-5.4	2.6	-5.0	11.5	-1.0	-2.0	-2.9	1.4	-9.6
1985	13.1	2.4	-2.2	-1.4	3.4	1.0	2.7	-1.2	-6.2	3.6	6.8	4.2	28.0
1986	1.5	7.0	4.7	1.4	3.3	-0.2	-9.5	3.0	-6.3	3.9	-0.5	-3.1	4.0
1987	11.5	8.2	2.4	-3.0	-0.5	2.3	2.8	2.9	-2.0	-30.8	-5.5	7.8	-10.8
1988	4.0	8.7	4.4	2.0	-2.5	7.0	-0.9	-2.8	2.3	-1.2	-3.6	3.8	22.4
1989	4.4	0.5	2.2	4.3	4.2	-2.4	4.2	2.1	0.01	-6.0	0.4	0.1	14.2
1990	-8.9	2.9	3.7	-3.4	6.8	0.1	-4.5	-13.6	-9.2	-6.2	7.3	3.7	-21.5
1991	9.1	11.0	6.9	-0.2	4.5	-6.0	3.1	3.7	0.6	2.7	-4.7	7.7	43.7
1992	8.0	2.9	-3.5	-3.7	1.2	-5.0	3.2	-3.1	2.2	3.1	7.5	3.4	16.4
1993	3.2	-2.5	3.1	-2.8	4.3	0.5	1.3	4.1	2.7	2.5	-3.4	3.3	17.0
1994	3.1	-0.4	-5.4	0.6	-1.3	-3.6	1.6	5.4	-0.5	-0.4	-4.2	2.5	-3.2
1995	-1.4	3.9	1.6	2.1	1.5	5.0	5.7	1.9	1.7	-4.6	4.2	2.4	26.2
1996	-0.2	3.0	1.8	5.3	3.9	-4.2	-8.8	5.7	3.7	-1.7	4.0	2.4	14.8
1997	1.9	-2.5	-4.9	0.1	11.0	4.1	4.6	2.2	7.2	-4.5	-0.8	1.7	20.5
1998	-1.6	7.4	4.1	0.5	-5.4	0.2	-8.2	-19.5	7.6	4.0	5.2	6.1	-3.4
1999	1.2	-8.2	1.4	8.8	1.4	4.3	-2.8	-3.8	-0.1	0.3	5.9	11.2	19.6
2000	-1.7	16.4	-6.7	-6.1	-5.9	8.6	-3.2	7.4	-3.1	-4.5	-10.4	8.4	-4.2
2001	5.1	-6.7	-5.0	7.7	2.3	3.3	-5.4	-3.3	-13.6	5.8	7.6	6.0	1.0
2002	-1.1	-2.8	7.9	0.8	-4.5	-5.1	-15.2	-0.4	-7.3	3.1	8.8	-5.7	-21.6
2003	-2.9	-3.1	1.1	9.4	10.6	1.7	6.2	4.5	-2.0	8.3	3.5	1.9	45.4
2004	4.3	0.8	0.8	-5.2	1.5	4.1	-6.8	-0.6	4.6	1.9	8.6	2.8	17.0
2005	-4.2	1.6	-3.0	-5.8	6.4	3.7	6.3	-1.9	0.2	-3.2	4.7	-0.6	3.3
2006	8.9	-0.3	4.7	-0.1	-5.7	0.5	-3.3	2.9	0.7	5.7	2.5	0.2	17.0
2007	1.6	-0.9	0.9	1.7	4.0	-1.6	-6.9	2.2	1.6	2.8	-7.3	-0.2	-2.7
2008	-6.9	-3.8	0.3	4.1	4.5	-7.8	3.6	3.5	-8.1	-20.9	-12.0	5.6	-34.8
2009	-11.2	-12.3	8.7	15.3	2.9	1.3	9.5	2.8	5.6	-6.9	3.0	7.9	25.2
2010	-3.7	4.4	8.0	5.6	-7.7	-7.9	6.8	-7.5	12.3	4.0	3.4	7.8	25.3
2011	-0.3	5.4	2.4	2.6	-2.0	-2.5	-3.7	-8.8	-11.4	15.0	-0.5	0.5	-5.5
2012	7.0	2.3	2.4	-1.6	-6.7	4.8	-1.4	3.2	3.1	-2.2	0.4	3.3	14.6
2013	6.2	1.0	4.4	-0.4	3.9	-0.7	6.9	-3.3	6.2	2.5	3.9	1.8	37.0
2014	-2.8	4.6	-0.8	-3.9									
TOTALS	65.8	40.7	46.7	57.1	47.0	15.3	-10.5	9.0	-9.7	-18.0	63.6	98.2	
AVG.	1.8	1.1	1.3	1.6	1.3	0.4	-0.3	0.3	-0.3	-0.5	1.8	2.8	
# Up	20	21	26	22	22	21	17	20	20	19	23	28	
# Down	16	15	10	14	13	14	18	15	15	16	12	7	

RUSSELL 2000 INDEX MONTHLY CLOSING PRICES SINCE 1979

	Jan	Feb	Mar	Apr	May	Jun	Jul	Aug	Sep	Oct	Nov	Dec
1979	44.18	42.78	46.94	48.00	47.13	49.62	51.08	55.05	54.68	48.51	52.43	55.91
1980	60.50	59.22	48.27	51.18	55.26	57.47	63.81	67.97	69.94	72.64	77.70	74.80
1981	74.33	74.52	80.25	82.25	84.72	82.56	80.41	73.94	67.55	73.06	75.14	73.67
1982	70.96	67.21	66.21	69.59	67.39	64.67	63.59	68.38	70.84	80.86	87.96	88.90
1983	95.53	101.23	103.77	111.20	118.94	124.17	120.43	115.60	117.43	109.17	114.66	112.27
1984	110.21	103.72	104.10	103.34	97.75	100.30	95.25	106.21	105.17	103.07	100.11	101.49
1985	114.77	117.54	114.92	113.35	117.26	118.38	121.56	120.10	112.65	116.73	124.62	129.87
1986	131.78	141.00	147.63	149.66	154.61	154.23	139.65	143.83	134.73	139.95	139.26	135.00
1987	150.48	162.84	166.79	161.82	161.02	164.75	169.42	174.25	170.81	118.26	111.70	120.42
1988	125.24	136.10	142.15	145.01	141.37	151.30	149.89	145.74	149.08	147.25	142.01	147.37
1989	153.84	154.56	157.89	164.68	171.53	167.42	174.50	178.20	178.21	167.47	168.17	168.30
1990	153.27	157.72	163.63	158.09	168.91	169.04	161.51	139.52	126.70	118.83	127.50	132.16
1991	144.17	160.00	171.01	170.61	178.34	167.61	172.76	179.11	180.16	185.00	176.37	189.94
1992	205.16	211.15	203.69	196.25	198.52	188.64	194.74	188.79	192.92	198.90	213.81	221.01
1993	228.10	222.41	229.21	222.68	232.19	233.35	236.46	246.19	252.95	259.18	250.41	258.59
1994	266.52	265.53	251.06	252.55	249.28	240.29	244.06	257.32	256.12	255.02	244.25	250.36
1995	246.85	256.57	260.77	266.17	270.25	283.63	299.72	305.31	310.38	296.25	308.58	315.97
1996	315.38	324.93	330.77	348.28	361.85	346.61	316.00	333.88	346.39	340.57	354.11	362.61
1997	369.45	360.05	342.56	343.00	380.76	396.37	414.48	423.43	453.82	433.26	429.92	437.02
1998	430.05	461.83	480.68	482.89	456.62	457.39	419.75	337.95	363.59	378.16	397.75	421.96
1999	427.22	392.26	397.63	432.81	438.68	457.68	444.77	427.83	427.30	428.64	454.08	504.75
2000	496.23	577.71	539.09	506.25	476.18	517.23	500.64	537.89	521.37	497.68	495.94	483.53
2001	508.34	474.37	450.53	485.32	496.50	512.64	484.78	468.56	404.87	428.17	460.78	488.50
2002	483.10	469.36	506.46	510.67	487.47	462.64	392.42	390.96	362.27	373.50	406.35	383.09
2003	372.17	360.52	364.54	398.68	441.00	448.37	476.02	497.42	487.68	528.22	546.51	556.91
2004	580.76	585.56	590.31	559.80	568.28	591.52	551.29	547.93	572.94	583.79	633.77	651.57
2005	624.02	634.06	615.07	579.38	616.71	639.66	679.75	666.51	667.80	646.61	677.29	673.22
2006	733.20	730.64	765.14	764.54	721.00	724.67	700.56	720.53	725.59	766.84	786.12	787.66
2007	800.34	793.30	800.71	814.57	847.19	833.69	776.13	792.86	805.45	828.02	767.77	766.03
2008	713.30	686.18	687.97	716.18	748.28	689.66	714.52	739.50	679.58	537.52	473.14	499.45
2009	443.53	389.02	422.75	487.56	501.58	508.28	556.71	572.07	604.28	562.77	579.73	625.39
2010	602.04	628.56	678.64	716.60	661.61	609.49	650.89	602.06	676.14	703.35	727.01	783.65
2011	781.25	823.45	843.55	865.29	848.30	827.43	797.03	726.81	644.16	741.06	737.42	740.92
2012	792.82	810.94	830.30	816.88	761.82	798.49	786.94	812.09	837.45	818.73	821.92	849.35
2013	902.09	911.11	951.54	947.46	984.14	977.48	1045.26	1010.90	1073.79	1100.15	1142.89	1163.64
2014	1130.88	1183.03	1173.04	1126.86								

10 BEST DAYS BY PERCENT AND POINT

	BY PERCENT CHANGE				BY POINT CHANGE		
DAY	CLOSE	PNT CHANGE	% CHANGE	DAY	CLOSE	PNT CHANGE	% CHANGE
			DJIA 1901 TO 1949				
3/15/33	62.10	8.26	15.3	10/30/29	258.47	28.40	12.3
10/6/31	99.34	12.86	14.9	11/14/29	217.28	18.59	9.4
10/30/29	258.47	28.40	12.3	10/5/29	341.36	16.19	5.0
9/21/32	75.16	7.67	11.4	10/31/29	273.51	15.04	5.8
8/3/32	58.22	5.06	9.5	10/6/31	99.34	12.86	14.9
2/11/32	78.60	6.80	9.5	11/15/29	228.73	11.45	5.3
11/14/29	217.28	18.59	9.4	6/19/30	228.97	10.13	4.6
12/18/31	80.69	6.90	9.4	9/5/39	148.12	10.03	7.3
2/13/32	85.82	7.22	9.2	11/22/28	290.34	9.81	3.5
5/6/32	59.01	4.91	9.1	10/1/30	214.14	9.24	4.5
			DJIA 1950 TO APRIL 2014				
10/13/08	9387.61	936.42	11.1	10/13/08	9387.61	936.42	11.1
10/28/08	9065.12	889.35	10.9	10/28/08	9065.12	889.35	10.9
10/21/87	2027.85	186.84	10.2	11/13/08	8835.25	552.59	6.7
3/23/09	7775.86	497.48	6.8	3/16/00	10630.60	499.19	4.9
11/13/08	8835.25	552.59	6.7	3/23/09	7775.86	497.48	6.8
11/21/08	8046.42	494.13	6.5	11/21/08	8046.42	494.13	6.5
7/24/02	8191.29	488.95	6.4	11/30/11	12045.68	490.05	4.2
10/20/87	1841.01	102.27	5.9	7/24/02	8191.29	488.95	6.4
3/10/09	6926.49	379.44	5.8	9/30/08	10850.66	485.21	4.7
7/29/02	8711.88	447.49	5.4	7/29/02	8711.88	447.49	5.4
			S&P 500 1930 TO APRIL 2014				
3/15/33	6.81	0.97	16.6	10/13/08	1003.35	104.13	11.6
10/6/31	9.91	1.09	12.4	10/28/08	940.51	91.59	10.8
9/21/32	8.52	0.90	11.8	3/16/00	1458.47	66.32	4.8
10/13/08	1003.35	104.13	11.6	1/3/01	1347.56	64.29	5.0
10/28/08	940.51	91.59	10.8	9/30/08	1166.36	59.97	5.4
2/16/35	10.00	0.94	10.4	11/13/08	911.29	58.99	6.9
8/17/35	11.70	1.08	10.2	3/23/09	822.92	54.38	7.1
3/16/35	9.05	0.82	10.0	3/18/08	1330.74	54.14	4.2
9/12/38	12.06	1.06	9.6	8/9/11	1172.53	53.07	4.7
9/5/39	12.64	1.11	9.6	8/11/11	1172.64	51.88	4.6
			NASDAQ 1971 TO APRIL 2014				
1/3/01	2616.69	324.83	14.2	1/3/01	2616.69	324.83	14.2
10/13/08	1844.25	194.74	11.8	12/5/00	2889.80	274.05	10.5
12/5/00	2889.80	274.05	10.5	4/18/00	3793.57	254.41	7.2
10/28/08	1649.47	143.57	9.5	5/30/00	3459.48	254.37	7.9
4/5/01	1785.00	146.20	8.9	10/19/00	3418.60	247.04	7.8
4/18/01	2079.44	156.22	8.1	10/13/00	3316.77	242.09	7.9
5/30/00	3459.48	254.37	7.9	6/2/00	3813.38	230.88	6.4
10/13/00	3316.77	242.09	7.9	4/25/00	3711.23	228.75	6.6
10/19/00	3418.60	247.04	7.8	4/17/00	3539.16	217.87	6.6
5/8/02	1696.29	122.47	7.8	10/13/08	1844.25	194.74	11.8
			RUSSELL 1000 1979 TO APRIL 2014				
10/13/08	542.98	56.75	11.7	10/13/08	542.98	56.75	11.7
10/28/08	503.74	47.68	10.5	10/28/08	503.74	47.68	10.5
10/21/87	135.85	11.15	8.9	3/16/00	777.86	36.60	4.9
3/23/09	446.90	29.36	7.0	1/3/01	712.63	35.74	5.3
11/13/08	489.83	31.99	7.0	11/13/08	489.83	31.99	7.0
11/24/08	456.14	28.26	6.6	9/30/08	634.08	31.74	5.3
3/10/09	391.01	23.46	6.4	8/9/11	647.85	30.57	5.0
11/21/08	427.88	24.97	6.2	12/5/00	728.44	30.36	4.4
7/24/02	448.05	23.87	5.6	3/23/09	446.90	29.36	7.0
7/29/02	477.61	24.69	5.5	8/11/11	649.44	29.14	4.7
			RUSSELL 2000 1979 TO APRIL 2014				
10/13/08	570.89	48.41	9.3	10/13/08	570.89	48.41	9.3
11/13/08	491.23	38.43	8.5	9/18/08	723.68	47.30	7.0
3/23/09	433.72	33.61	8.4	8/9/11	696.16	45.20	6.9
10/21/87	130.65	9.26	7.6	11/30/11	737.42	41.32	5.9
10/28/08	482.55	34.15	7.6	10/4/11	648.64	39.15	6.4
11/24/08	436.80	30.26	7.4	11/13/08	491.23	38.43	8.5
3/10/09	367.75	24.49	7.1	10/27/11	765.43	38.28	5.3
9/18/08	723.68	47.30	7.0	5/10/10	689.61	36.61	5.6
8/9/11	696.16	45.20	6.9	8/11/11	695.89	35.68	5.4
10/16/08	536.57	34.46	6.9	10/16/08	536.57	34.46	6.9

10 WORST DAYS BY PERCENT AND POINT

	BY PERCENT CHANGE				BY POINT CHANGE		
DAY	CLOSE	PNT CHANGE	% CHANGE	DAY	CLOSE	PNT CHANGE	% CHANGE
DJIA 1901 to 1949							
10/28/29	260.64	−38.33	−12.8	10/28/29	260.64	−38.33	−12.8
10/29/29	230.07	−30.57	−11.7	10/29/29	230.07	−30.57	−11.7
11/6/29	232.13	−25.55	−9.9	11/6/29	232.13	−25.55	−9.9
8/12/32	63.11	−5.79	−8.4	10/23/29	305.85	−20.66	−6.3
3/14/07	55.84	−5.05	−8.3	11/11/29	220.39	−16.14	−6.8
7/21/33	88.71	−7.55	−7.8	11/4/29	257.68	−15.83	−5.8
10/18/37	125.73	−10.57	−7.8	12/12/29	243.14	−15.30	−5.9
2/1/17	88.52	−6.91	−7.2	10/3/29	329.95	−14.55	−4.2
10/5/32	66.07	−5.09	−7.2	6/16/30	230.05	−14.20	−5.8
9/24/31	107.79	−8.20	−7.1	8/9/29	337.99	−14.11	−4.0
DJIA 1950 to APRIL 2014							
10/19/87	1738.74	−508.00	−22.6	9/29/08	10365.45	−777.68	−7.0
10/26/87	1793.93	−156.83	−8.0	10/15/08	8577.91	−733.08	−7.9
10/15/08	8577.91	−733.08	−7.9	9/17/01	8920.70	−684.81	−7.1
12/1/08	8149.09	−679.95	−7.7	12/1/08	8149.09	−679.95	−7.7
10/9/08	8579.19	−678.91	−7.3	10/9/08	8579.19	−678.91	−7.3
10/27/97	7161.15	−554.26	−7.2	8/8/11	10809.85	−634.76	−5.6
9/17/01	8920.70	−684.81	−7.1	4/14/00	10305.77	−617.78	−5.7
9/29/08	10365.45	−777.68	−7.0	10/27/97	7161.15	−554.26	−7.2
10/13/89	2569.26	−190.58	−6.9	8/10/11	10719.94	−519.83	−4.6
1/8/88	1911.31	−140.58	−6.9	10/22/08	8519.21	−514.45	−5.7
S&P 500 1930 to APRIL 2014							
10/19/87	224.84	−57.86	−20.5	9/29/08	1106.39	−106.62	−8.8
3/18/35	8.14	−0.91	−10.1	10/15/08	907.84	−90.17	−9.0
4/16/35	8.22	−0.91	−10.0	4/14/00	1356.56	−83.95	−5.8
9/3/46	15.00	−1.65	−9.9	12/1/08	816.21	−80.03	−8.9
10/18/37	10.76	−1.10	−9.3	8/8/11	1119.46	−79.92	−6.7
10/15/08	907.84	−90.17	−9.0	10/9/08	909.92	−75.02	−7.6
12/1/08	816.21	−80.03	−8.9	8/31/98	957.28	−69.86	−6.8
7/20/33	10.57	−1.03	−8.9	10/27/97	876.99	−64.65	−6.9
9/29/08	1106.39	−106.62	−8.8	10/7/08	996.23	−60.66	−5.7
7/21/33	9.65	−0.92	−8.7	8/4/11	1200.07	−60.27	−4.8
NASDAQ 1971 to APRIL 2014							
10/19/87	360.21	−46.12	−11.4	4/14/00	3321.29	−355.49	−9.7
4/14/00	3321.29	−355.49	−9.7	4/3/00	4223.68	−349.15	−7.6
9/29/08	1983.73	−199.61	−9.1	4/12/00	3769.63	−286.27	−7.1
10/26/87	298.90	−29.55	−9.0	4/10/00	4188.20	−258.25	−5.8
10/20/87	327.79	−32.42	−9.0	1/4/00	3901.69	−229.46	−5.6
12/1/08	1398.07	−137.50	−9.0	3/14/00	4706.63	−200.61	−4.1
8/31/98	1499.25	−140.43	−8.6	5/10/00	3384.73	−200.28	−5.6
10/15/08	1628.33	−150.68	−8.5	5/23/00	3164.55	−199.66	−5.9
4/3/00	4223.68	−349.15	−7.6	9/29/08	1983.73	−199.61	−9.1
1/2/01	2291.86	−178.66	−7.2	10/25/00	3229.57	−190.22	−5.6
RUSSELL 1000 1979 to APRIL 2014							
10/19/87	121.04	−28.40	−19.0	9/29/08	602.34	−57.35	−8.7
10/15/08	489.71	−49.11	−9.1	10/15/08	489.71	−49.11	−9.1
12/1/08	437.75	−43.68	−9.1	4/14/00	715.20	−45.74	−6.0
9/29/08	602.34	−57.35	−8.7	8/8/11	617.28	−45.56	−6.9
10/26/87	119.45	−10.74	−8.3	12/1/08	437.75	−43.68	−9.1
10/9/08	492.13	−40.05	−7.5	10/9/08	492.13	−40.05	−7.5
8/8/11	617.28	−45.56	−6.9	8/31/98	496.66	−35.77	−6.7
11/20/08	402.91	−29.62	−6.9	8/4/11	664.65	−34.92	−5.0
8/31/98	496.66	−35.77	−6.7	10/27/97	465.44	−32.96	−6.6
10/27/97	465.44	−32.96	−6.6	10/7/08	538.15	−32.64	−5.7
RUSSELL 2000 1979 to APRIL 2014							
10/19/87	133.60	−19.14	−12.5	8/8/11	650.96	−63.67	−8.9
12/1/08	417.07	−56.07	−11.9	12/1/08	417.07	−56.07	−11.9
10/15/08	502.11	−52.54	−9.5	10/15/08	502.11	−52.54	−9.5
10/26/87	110.33	−11.26	−9.3	10/9/08	499.20	−47.37	−8.7
10/20/87	121.39	−12.21	−9.1	9/29/08	657.72	−47.07	−6.7
8/8/11	650.96	−63.67	−8.9	8/4/11	726.80	−45.98	−6.0
10/9/08	499.20	−47.37	−8.7	8/18/11	662.51	−41.52	−5.9
11/19/08	412.38	−35.13	−7.9	10/7/08	558.95	−36.96	−6.2
4/14/00	453.72	−35.50	−7.3	11/9/11	718.86	−36.41	−4.8
11/14/08	456.52	−34.71	−7.1	2/3/14	1094.58	−36.30	−3.2

10 **BEST** WEEKS BY PERCENT AND POINT

	BY PERCENT CHANGE				BY POINT CHANGE		
WEEK ENDS	CLOSE	PNT CHANGE	% CHANGE	WEEK ENDS	CLOSE	PNT CHANGE	% CHANGE
DJIA 1901 to 1949							
8/6/32	66.56	12.30	22.7	12/7/29	263.46	24.51	10.3
6/25/38	131.94	18.71	16.5	6/25/38	131.94	18.71	16.5
2/13/32	85.82	11.37	15.3	6/27/31	156.93	17.97	12.9
4/22/33	72.24	9.36	14.9	11/22/29	245.74	17.01	7.4
10/10/31	105.61	12.84	13.8	8/17/29	360.70	15.86	4.6
7/30/32	54.26	6.42	13.4	12/22/28	285.94	15.22	5.6
6/27/31	156.93	17.97	12.9	8/24/29	375.44	14.74	4.1
9/24/32	74.83	8.39	12.6	2/21/29	310.06	14.21	4.8
8/27/32	75.61	8.43	12.6	5/10/30	272.01	13.70	5.3
3/18/33	60.56	6.72	12.5	11/15/30	186.68	13.54	7.8
DJIA 1950 to APRIL 2014							
10/11/74	658.17	73.61	12.6	10/31/08	9325.01	946.06	11.3
10/31/08	9325.01	946.06	11.3	12/2/11	12019.42	787.64	7.0
8/20/82	869.29	81.24	10.3	11/28/08	8829.04	782.62	9.7
11/28/08	8829.04	782.62	9.7	3/17/00	10595.23	666.41	6.7
3/13/09	7223.98	597.04	9.0	3/21/03	8521.97	662.26	8.4
10/8/82	986.85	79.11	8.7	7/1/11	12582.77	648.19	5.4
3/21/03	8521.97	662.26	8.4	9/28/01	8847.56	611.75	7.4
8/3/84	1202.08	87.46	7.9	7/17/09	8743.94	597.42	7.3
9/28/01	8847.56	611.75	7.4	3/13/09	7223.98	597.04	9.0
7/17/09	8743.94	597.42	7.3	7/2/99	11139.24	586.68	5.6
S&P 500 1930 to APRIL 2014							
8/6/32	7.22	1.12	18.4	6/2/00	1477.26	99.24	7.2
6/25/38	11.39	1.72	17.8	11/28/08	896.24	96.21	12.0
7/30/32	6.10	0.89	17.1	10/31/08	968.75	91.98	10.5
4/22/33	7.75	1.09	16.4	12/2/11	1244.28	85.61	7.4
10/11/74	71.14	8.80	14.1	4/20/00	1434.54	77.98	5.8
2/13/32	8.80	1.08	14.0	7/2/99	1391.22	75.91	5.8
9/24/32	8.52	1.02	13.6	3/3/00	1409.17	75.81	5.7
10/10/31	10.64	1.27	13.6	9/28/01	1040.94	75.14	7.8
8/27/32	8.57	1.01	13.4	3/13/09	756.55	73.17	10.7
3/18/33	6.61	0.77	13.2	10/16/98	1056.42	72.10	7.3
NASDAQ 1971 to APRIL 2014							
6/2/00	3813.38	608.27	19.0	6/2/00	3813.38	608.27	19.0
4/12/01	1961.43	241.07	14.0	2/4/00	4244.14	357.07	9.2
11/28/08	1535.57	151.22	10.9	3/3/00	4914.79	324.29	7.1
10/31/08	1720.95	168.92	10.9	4/20/00	3643.88	322.59	9.7
3/13/09	1431.50	137.65	10.6	12/8/00	2917.43	272.14	10.3
4/20/01	2163.41	201.98	10.3	4/12/01	1961.43	241.07	14.0
12/8/00	2917.43	272.14	10.3	7/14/00	4246.18	222.98	5.5
4/20/00	3643.88	322.59	9.7	1/12/01	2626.50	218.85	9.1
10/11/74	60.42	5.26	9.5	4/28/00	3860.66	216.78	6.0
2/4/00	4244.14	357.07	9.0	12/23/99	3969.44	216.38	5.8
RUSSELL 1000 1979 to APRIL 2014							
11/28/08	481.43	53.55	12.5	6/2/00	785.02	57.93	8.0
10/31/08	522.47	50.94	10.8	11/28/08	481.43	53.55	12.5
3/13/09	411.10	39.88	10.7	10/31/08	522.47	50.94	10.8
8/20/82	61.51	4.83	8.5	12/2/11	687.44	47.63	7.4
6/2/00	785.02	57.93	8.0	4/20/00	757.32	42.12	5.9
9/28/01	546.46	38.48	7.6	3/3/00	756.41	41.55	5.8
10/16/98	546.09	38.45	7.6	3/13/09	411.10	39.88	10.7
8/3/84	87.43	6.13	7.5	7/1/11	745.21	39.46	5.6
12/2/11	687.44	47.63	7.4	10/14/11	675.52	38.87	6.1
3/21/03	474.58	32.69	7.4	7/2/99	723.25	38.80	5.7
RUSSELL 2000 1979 to APRIL 2014							
11/28/08	473.14	66.60	16.4	12/2/11	735.02	68.86	10.3
10/31/08	537.52	66.40	14.1	11/28/08	473.14	66.60	16.4
6/2/00	513.03	55.66	12.2	10/31/08	537.52	66.40	14.1
3/13/09	393.09	42.04	12.0	10/14/11	712.46	56.25	8.6
12/2/11	735.02	68.86	10.3	6/2/00	513.03	55.66	12.2
10/14/11	712.46	56.25	8.6	10/28/11	761.00	48.58	6.8
7/17/09	519.22	38.24	8.0	1/4/13	879.15	47.05	5.7
10/16/98	342.87	24.47	7.7	7/1/11	840.04	42.25	5.3
12/18/87	116.94	8.31	7.7	3/13/09	393.09	42.04	12.0
3/3/00	597.88	41.14	7.4	2/1/08	730.50	41.90	6.1

10 <u>WORST</u> WEEKS BY PERCENT AND POINT

	BY PERCENT CHANGE				BY POINT CHANGE		
WEEK ENDS	CLOSE	PNT CHANGE	% CHANGE	WEEK ENDS	CLOSE	PNT CHANGE	% CHANGE
DJIA 1901 to 1949							
7/22/33	88.42	−17.68	−16.7	11/8/29	236.53	−36.98	−13.5
5/18/40	122.43	−22.42	−15.5	12/8/28	257.33	−33.47	−11.5
10/8/32	61.17	−10.92	−15.2	6/21/30	215.30	−28.95	−11.9
10/3/31	92.77	−14.59	−13.6	10/19/29	323.87	−28.82	−8.2
11/8/29	236.53	−36.98	−13.5	5/3/30	258.31	−27.15	−9.5
9/17/32	66.44	−10.10	−13.2	10/31/29	273.51	−25.46	−8.5
10/21/33	83.64	−11.95	−12.5	10/26/29	298.97	−24.90	−7.7
12/12/31	78.93	−11.21	−12.4	5/18/40	122.43	−22.42	−15.5
5/8/15	62.77	−8.74	−12.2	2/8/29	301.53	−18.23	−5.7
6/21/30	215.30	−28.95	−11.9	10/11/30	193.05	−18.05	−8.6
DJIA 1950 to APRIL 2014							
10/10/08	8451.19	−1874.19	−18.2	10/10/08	8451.19	−1874.19	−18.2
9/21/01	8235.81	−1369.70	−14.3	9/21/01	8235.81	−1369.70	−14.3
10/23/87	1950.76	−295.98	−13.2	3/16/01	9823.41	−821.21	−7.7
10/16/87	2246.74	−235.47	−9.5	10/3/08	10325.38	−817.75	−7.3
10/13/89	2569.26	−216.26	−7.8	4/14/00	10305.77	−805.71	−7.3
3/16/01	9823.41	−821.21	−7.7	9/23/11	10771.48	−737.61	−6.4
7/19/02	8019.26	−665.27	−7.7	8/5/11	11444.61	−698.63	−5.8
12/4/87	1766.74	−143.74	−7.5	7/12/02	8684.53	−694.97	−7.4
9/13/74	627.19	−50.69	−7.5	7/19/02	8019.26	−665.27	−7.7
9/12/86	1758.72	−141.03	−7.4	10/15/99	10019.71	−630.05	−5.9
S&P 500 1930 to APRIL 2014							
7/22/33	9.71	−2.20	−18.5	10/10/08	899.22	−200.01	−18.2
10/10/08	899.22	−200.01	−18.2	4/14/00	1356.56	−159.79	−10.5
5/18/40	9.75	−2.05	−17.4	9/21/01	965.80	−126.74	−11.6
10/8/32	6.77	−1.38	−16.9	10/3/08	1099.23	−113.78	−9.4
9/17/32	7.50	−1.28	−14.6	8/5/11	1199.38	−92.90	−7.2
10/21/33	8.57	−1.31	−13.3	10/15/99	1247.41	−88.61	−6.6
10/3/31	9.37	−1.36	−12.7	3/16/01	1150.53	−82.89	−6.7
10/23/87	248.22	−34.48	−12.2	1/28/00	1360.16	−81.20	−5.6
12/12/31	8.20	−1.13	−12.1	9/23/11	1136.43	−79.58	−6.5
3/26/38	9.20	−1.21	−11.6	1/18/08	1325.19	−75.83	−5.4
NASDAQ 1971 to APRIL 2014							
4/14/00	3321.29	−1125.16	−25.3	4/14/00	3321.29	−1125.16	−25.3
10/23/87	328.45	−77.88	−19.2	7/28/00	3663.00	−431.45	−10.5
9/21/01	1423.19	−272.19	−16.1	11/10/00	3028.99	−422.59	−12.2
10/10/08	1649.51	−297.88	−15.3	3/31/00	4572.83	−390.20	−7.9
11/10/00	3028.99	−422.59	−12.2	1/28/00	3887.07	−348.33	−8.2
10/3/08	1947.39	−235.95	−10.8	10/6/00	3361.01	−311.81	−8.5
7/28/00	3663.00	−431.45	−10.5	10/10/08	1649.51	−297.88	−15.3
10/24/08	1552.03	−159.26	−9.3	5/12/00	3529.06	−287.76	−7.5
12/15/00	2653.27	−264.16	−9.1	9/21/01	1423.19	−272.19	−16.1
12/1/00	2645.29	−259.09	−8.9	12/15/00	2653.27	−264.16	−9.1
RUSSELL 1000 1979 to APRIL 2014							
10/10/08	486.23	−108.31	−18.2	10/10/08	486.23	−108.31	−18.2
10/23/87	130.19	−19.25	−12.9	4/14/00	715.20	−90.39	−11.2
9/21/01	507.98	−67.59	−11.7	9/21/01	507.98	−67.59	−11.7
4/14/00	715.20	−90.39	−11.2	10/3/08	594.54	−65.15	−9.9
10/3/08	594.54	−65.15	−9.9	8/5/11	662.84	−54.93	−7.7
10/16/87	149.44	−14.42	−8.8	9/23/11	627.56	−45.42	−6.8
11/21/08	427.88	−41.15	−8.8	10/15/99	646.79	−43.89	−6.4
9/12/86	124.95	−10.87	−8.0	3/16/01	605.71	−43.88	−6.8
8/5/11	662.84	−54.93	−7.7	5/7/10	611.63	−43.43	−6.6
7/19/02	450.64	−36.13	−7.4	7/27/07	793.72	−41.97	−5.0
RUSSELL 2000 1979 to APRIL 2014							
10/23/87	121.59	−31.15	−20.4	10/10/08	522.48	−96.92	−15.7
4/14/00	453.72	−89.27	−16.4	4/14/00	453.72	−89.27	−16.4
10/10/08	522.48	−96.92	−15.7	10/3/08	619.40	−85.39	−12.1
9/21/01	378.89	−61.84	−14.0	8/5/11	714.63	−82.40	−10.3
10/3/08	619.40	−85.39	−12.1	5/7/10	653.00	−63.60	−8.9
11/21/08	406.54	−49.98	−11.0	9/23/11	652.43	−61.88	−8.7
10/24/08	471.12	−55.31	−10.5	9/21/01	378.89	−61.84	−14.0
8/5/11	714.63	−82.40	−10.3	7/27/07	777.83	−58.61	−7.0
3/6/09	351.05	−37.97	−9.8	10/24/08	471.12	−55.31	−10.5
11/14/08	456.52	−49.27	−9.7	11/25/11	666.16	−53.26	−7.4

10 BEST MONTHS BY PERCENT AND POINT

	BY PERCENT CHANGE				BY POINT CHANGE		
MONTH	CLOSE	PNT CHANGE	% CHANGE	MONTH	CLOSE	PNT CHANGE	% CHANGE
			DJIA 1901 to 1949				
APR-1933	77.66	22.26	40.2	NOV-1928	293.38	41.22	16.3
AUG-1932	73.16	18.90	34.8	JUN-1929	333.79	36.38	12.2
JUL-1932	54.26	11.42	26.7	AUG-1929	380.33	32.63	9.4
JUN-1938	133.88	26.14	24.3	JUN-1938	133.88	26.14	24.3
APR-1915	71.78	10.95	18.0	AUG-1928	240.41	24.41	11.3
JUN-1931	150.18	21.72	16.9	APR-1933	77.66	22.26	40.2
NOV-1928	293.38	41.22	16.3	FEB-1931	189.66	22.11	13.2
NOV-1904	52.76	6.59	14.3	JUN-1931	150.18	21.72	16.9
MAY-1919	105.50	12.62	13.6	AUG-1932	73.16	18.90	34.8
SEP-1939	152.54	18.13	13.5	JAN-1930	267.14	18.66	7.5
			DJIA 1950 to APRIL 2014				
JAN-1976	975.28	122.87	14.4	OCT-2011	11955.01	1041.63	9.5
JAN-1975	703.69	87.45	14.2	APR-1999	10789.04	1002.88	10.2
JAN-1987	2158.04	262.09	13.8	APR-2001	10734.97	856.19	8.7
AUG-1982	901.31	92.71	11.5	OCT-2002	8397.03	805.10	10.6
OCT-1982	991.72	95.47	10.7	MAR-2000	10921.92	793.61	7.8
OCT-2002	8397.03	805.10	10.6	NOV-2001	9851.56	776.42	8.6
APR-1978	837.32	79.96	10.6	SEP-2010	10788.05	773.33	7.7
APR-1999	10789.04	1002.88	10.2	JAN-2013	13860.58	756.44	5.8
NOV-1962	649.30	59.53	10.1	OCT-1998	8592.10	749.48	9.6
NOV-1954	386.77	34.63	9.8	JUL-2009	9171.61	724.61	8.6
			S&P 500 1930 to APRIL 2014				
APR-1933	8.32	2.47	42.2	MAR-2000	1498.58	132.16	9.7
JUL-1932	6.10	1.67	37.7	OCT-2011	1253.30	121.88	10.8
AUG-1932	8.39	2.29	37.5	SEP-2010	1141.20	91.87	8.8
JUN-1938	11.56	2.29	24.7	APR-2001	1249.46	89.13	7.7
SEP-1939	13.02	1.84	16.5	AUG-2000	1517.68	86.85	6.1
OCT-1974	73.90	10.36	16.3	OCT-1998	1098.67	81.66	8.0
MAY-1933	9.64	1.32	15.9	DEC-1999	1469.25	80.34	5.8
APR-1938	9.70	1.20	14.1	OCT-1999	1362.93	80.22	6.3
JUN-1931	14.83	1.81	13.9	NOV-2001	1139.45	79.67	7.5
JAN-1987	274.08	31.91	13.2	JUL-2013	1685.73	79.45	4.9
			NASDAQ 1971 to APRIL 2014				
DEC-1999	4069.31	733.15	22.0	FEB-2000	4696.69	756.34	19.2
FEB-2000	4696.69	756.34	19.2	DEC-1999	4069.31	733.15	22.0
OCT-1974	65.23	9.56	17.2	JUN-2000	3966.11	565.20	16.6
JAN-1975	69.78	9.96	16.6	AUG-2000	4206.35	439.36	11.7
JUN-2000	3966.11	565.20	16.6	NOV-1999	3336.16	369.73	12.5
APR-2001	2116.24	275.98	15.0	JAN-1999	2505.89	313.20	14.3
JAN-1999	2505.89	313.20	14.3	JAN-2001	2772.73	302.21	12.2
NOV-2001	1930.58	240.38	14.2	APR-2001	2116.24	275.98	15.0
OCT-2002	1329.75	157.69	13.5	OCT-2011	2684.41	269.01	11.1
OCT-1982	212.63	24.98	13.3	SEP-2010	2368.62	254.59	12.0
			RUSSELL 1000 1979 to APRIL 2014				
JAN-1987	146.48	16.48	12.7	OCT-2011	692.41	68.96	11.1
OCT-1982	73.34	7.45	11.3	MAR-2000	797.99	64.95	8.9
AUG-1982	65.14	6.60	11.3	AUG-2000	811.17	55.60	7.4
DEC-1991	220.61	22.15	11.2	SEP-2010	629.78	52.10	9.0
OCT-2011	692.41	68.96	11.1	APR-2001	658.90	48.54	8.0
AUG-1984	89.87	8.74	10.8	JUL-2013	937.16	46.49	5.2
NOV-1980	78.26	7.18	10.1	FEB-2014	1041.36	44.88	4.5
APR-2009	476.84	43.17	10.0	OCT-1999	707.19	43.36	6.5
SEP-2010	629.78	52.10	9.0	DEC-1999	767.97	43.31	6.0
MAY-1990	187.66	15.34	8.0	APR-2009	476.84	43.17	10.0
			RUSSELL 2000 1979 to APRIL 2014				
FEB-2000	577.71	81.48	16.4	OCT-2011	741.06	96.90	15.0
APR-2009	487.56	64.81	15.3	FEB-2000	577.71	81.48	16.4
OCT-2011	741.06	96.90	15.0	SEP-2010	676.14	74.08	12.3
OCT-1982	80.86	10.02	14.1	JUL-2013	1045.26	67.78	6.9
JAN-1985	114.77	13.28	13.1	APR-2009	487.56	64.81	15.3
SEP-2010	676.14	74.08	12.3	SEP-2013	1073.79	62.89	6.2
AUG-1984	106.21	10.96	11.5	JAN-2006	733.20	59.98	8.9
JAN-1987	150.48	15.48	11.5	DEC-2010	783.65	56.64	7.8
DEC-1999	504.75	50.67	11.2	JAN-2013	902.09	52.74	6.2
JUL-1980	63.81	6.34	11.0	FEB-2014	1183.03	52.15	4.6

10 <u>WORST</u> MONTHS BY PERCENT AND POINT

	BY PERCENT CHANGE				BY POINT CHANGE		
MONTH	**CLOSE**	**PNT CHANGE**	**% CHANGE**	**MONTH**	**CLOSE**	**PNT CHANGE**	**% CHANGE**
			DJIA 1901 to 1949				
SEP-1931	96.61	–42.80	–30.7	OCT-1929	273.51	–69.94	–20.4
MAR-1938	98.95	–30.69	–23.7	JUN-1930	226.34	–48.73	–17.7
APR-1932	56.11	–17.17	–23.4	SEP-1931	96.61	–42.80	–30.7
MAY-1940	116.22	–32.21	–21.7	SEP-1929	343.45	–36.88	–9.7
OCT-1929	273.51	–69.94	–20.4	SEP-1930	204.90	–35.52	–14.8
MAY-1932	44.74	–11.37	–20.3	NOV-1929	238.95	–34.56	–12.6
JUN-1930	226.34	–48.73	–17.7	MAY-1940	116.22	–32.21	–21.7
DEC-1931	77.90	–15.97	–17.0	MAR-1938	98.95	–30.69	–23.7
FEB-1933	51.39	–9.51	–15.6	SEP-1937	154.57	–22.84	–12.9
MAY-1931	128.46	–22.73	–15.0	MAY-1931	128.46	–22.73	–15.0
			DJIA 1950 to APRIL 2014				
OCT-1987	1993.53	–602.75	–23.2	OCT-2008	9325.01	–1525.65	–14.1
AUG-1998	7539.07	–1344.22	–15.1	AUG-1998	7539.07	–1344.22	–15.1
OCT-2008	9325.01	–1525.65	–14.1	JUN-2008	11350.01	–1288.31	–10.2
NOV-1973	822.25	–134.33	–14.0	SEP-2001	8847.56	–1102.19	–11.1
SEP-2002	7591.93	–1071.57	–12.4	SEP-2002	7591.93	–1071.57	–12.4
FEB-2009	7062.93	–937.93	–11.7	FEB-2009	7062.93	–937.93	–11.7
SEP-2001	8847.56	–1102.19	–11.1	JAN-2014	15698.85	–877.81	–5.3
SEP-1974	607.87	–70.71	–10.4	MAY-2010	10136.63	–871.98	–7.9
AUG-1974	678.58	–78.85	–10.4	MAY-2012	12393.45	–820.18	–6.2
JUN-2008	11350.01	–1288.31	–10.2	FEB-2000	10128.31	–812.22	–7.4
			S&P 500 1930 to APRIL 2014				
SEP-1931	9.71	–4.15	–29.9	OCT-2008	968.75	–197.61	–16.9
MAR-1938	8.50	–2.84	–25.0	AUG-1998	957.28	–163.39	–14.6
MAY-1940	9.27	–2.92	–24.0	FEB-2001	1239.94	–126.07	–9.2
MAY-1932	4.47	–1.36	–23.3	JUN-2008	1280.00	–120.38	–8.6
OCT-1987	251.79	–70.04	–21.8	SEP-2008	1166.36	–116.47	–9.1
APR-1932	5.83	–1.48	–20.2	NOV-2000	1314.95	–114.45	–8.0
FEB-1933	5.66	–1.28	–18.4	SEP-2002	815.28	–100.79	–11.0
OCT-2008	968.75	–197.61	–16.9	MAY-2010	1089.41	–97.28	–8.2
JUN-1930	20.46	–4.03	–16.5	SEP-2001	1040.94	–92.64	–8.2
AUG-1998	957.28	–163.39	–14.6	FEB-2009	735.09	–90.79	–11.0
			NASDAQ 1971 to APRIL 2014				
OCT-1987	323.30	–120.99	–27.2	NOV-2000	2597.93	–771.70	–22.9
NOV-2000	2597.93	–771.70	–22.9	APR-2000	3860.66	–712.17	–15.6
FEB-2001	2151.83	–620.90	–22.4	FEB-2001	2151.83	–620.90	–22.4
AUG-1998	1499.25	–373.14	–19.9	SEP-2000	3672.82	–533.53	–12.7
OCT-2008	1720.95	–370.93	–17.7	MAY-2000	3400.91	–459.75	–11.9
MAR-1980	131.00	–27.03	–17.1	AUG-1998	1499.25	–373.14	–19.9
SEP-2001	1498.80	–306.63	–17.0	OCT-2008	1720.95	–370.93	–17.7
OCT-1978	111.12	–21.77	–16.4	MAR-2001	1840.26	–311.57	–14.5
APR-2000	3860.66	–712.17	–15.6	SEP-2001	1498.80	–306.63	–17.0
NOV-1973	93.51	–16.66	–15.1	OCT-2000	3369.63	–303.19	–8.3
			RUSSELL 1000 1979 to APRIL 2014				
OCT-1987	131.89	–36.94	–21.9	OCT-2008	522.47	–111.61	–17.6
OCT-2008	522.47	–111.61	–17.6	AUG-1998	496.66	–88.31	–15.1
AUG-1998	496.66	–88.31	–15.1	NOV-2000	692.40	–70.66	–9.3
MAR-1980	55.79	–7.28	–11.5	FEB-2001	654.25	–68.30	–9.5
SEP-2002	433.22	–52.86	–10.9	SEP-2008	634.08	–68.09	–9.7
FEB-2009	399.61	–47.71	–10.7	JUN-2008	703.22	–65.06	–8.5
SEP-2008	634.08	–68.09	–9.7	MAY-2010	601.79	–53.27	–8.1
AUG-1990	166.69	–17.63	–9.6	SEP-2002	433.22	–52.86	–10.9
FEB-2001	654.25	–68.30	–9.5	SEP-2011	623.45	–51.34	–7.6
NOV-2000	692.40	–70.66	–9.3	SEP-2001	546.46	–51.21	–8.6
			RUSSELL 2000 1979 to APRIL 2014				
OCT-1987	118.26	–52.55	–30.8	OCT-2008	537.52	–142.06	–20.9
OCT-2008	537.52	–142.06	–20.9	SEP-2011	644.16	–82.65	–11.4
AUG-1998	337.95	–81.80	–19.5	AUG-1998	337.95	–81.80	–19.5
MAR-1980	48.27	–10.95	–18.5	JUL-2002	392.42	–70.22	–15.2
JUL-2002	392.42	–70.22	–15.2	AUG-2011	726.81	–70.22	–8.8
AUG-1990	139.52	–21.99	–13.6	NOV-2008	473.14	–64.38	–12.0
SEP-2001	404.87	–63.69	–13.6	SEP-2001	404.87	–63.69	–13.6
FEB-2009	389.02	–54.51	–12.3	NOV-2007	767.77	–60.25	–7.3
NOV-2008	473.14	–64.38	–12.0	SEP-2008	679.58	–59.92	–8.1
SEP-2011	644.16	–82.65	–11.4	JUN-2008	689.66	–58.62	–7.8

10 BEST QUARTERS BY PERCENT AND POINT

	BY PERCENT CHANGE				BY POINT CHANGE		
QUARTER	CLOSE	PNT CHANGE	% CHANGE	QUARTER	CLOSE	PNT CHANGE	% CHANGE
DJIA 1901 to 1949							
JUN-1933	98.14	42.74	77.1	DEC-1928	300.00	60.57	25.3
SEP-1932	71.56	28.72	67.0	JUN-1933	98.14	42.74	77.1
JUN-1938	133.88	34.93	35.3	MAR-1930	286.10	37.62	15.1
SEP-1915	90.58	20.52	29.3	JUN-1938	133.88	34.93	35.3
DEC-1928	300.00	60.57	25.3	SEP-1927	197.59	31.36	18.9
DEC-1904	50.99	8.80	20.9	SEP-1928	239.43	28.88	13.7
JUN-1919	106.98	18.13	20.4	SEP-1932	71.56	28.72	67.0
SEP-1927	197.59	31.36	18.9	JUN-1929	333.79	24.94	8.1
DEC-1905	70.47	10.47	17.4	SEP-1939	152.54	21.91	16.8
JUN-1935	118.21	17.40	17.3	SEP-1915	90.58	20.52	29.3
DJIA 1950 to APRIL 2014							
MAR-1975	768.15	151.91	24.7	MAR-2013	14578.54	1474.40	11.3
MAR-1987	2304.69	408.74	21.6	DEC-2013	16576.66	1446.99	9.6
MAR-1986	1818.61	271.94	17.6	DEC-1998	9181.43	1338.81	17.1
MAR-1976	999.45	147.04	17.2	DEC-2011	12217.56	1304.18	12.0
DEC-1998	9181.43	1338.81	17.1	SEP-2009	9712.28	1265.28	15.0
DEC-1982	1046.54	150.29	16.8	JUN-1999	10970.80	1184.64	12.1
JUN-1997	7672.79	1089.31	16.5	DEC-2003	10453.92	1178.86	12.7
DEC-1985	1546.67	218.04	16.4	DEC-2001	10021.50	1173.94	13.3
SEP-2009	9712.28	1265.28	15.0	DEC-1999	11497.12	1160.17	11.2
JUN-1975	878.99	110.84	14.4	JUN-1997	7672.79	1089.31	16.5
S&P 500 1930 to APRIL 2014							
JUN-1933	10.91	5.06	86.5	DEC-1998	1229.23	212.22	20.9
SEP-1932	8.08	3.65	82.4	DEC-1999	1469.25	186.54	14.5
JUN-1938	11.56	3.06	36.0	DEC-2013	1848.36	166.81	9.9
MAR-1975	83.36	14.80	21.6	MAR-2012	1408.47	150.87	12.0
DEC-1998	1229.23	212.22	20.9	MAR-2013	1569.19	143.00	10.0
JUN-1935	10.23	1.76	20.8	SEP-2009	1057.08	137.76	15.0
MAR-1987	291.70	49.53	20.5	MAR-1998	1101.75	131.32	13.5
SEP-1939	13.02	2.16	19.9	JUN-1997	885.14	128.02	16.9
MAR-1943	11.58	1.81	18.5	DEC-2011	1257.60	126.18	11.2
MAR-1930	25.14	3.69	17.2	JUN-2003	974.50	125.32	14.8
NASDAQ 1971 to APRIL 2014							
DEC-1999	4069.31	1323.15	48.2	DEC-1999	4069.31	1323.15	48.2
DEC-2001	1950.40	451.60	30.1	MAR-2000	4572.83	503.52	12.4
DEC-1998	2192.69	498.85	29.5	DEC-1998	2192.69	498.85	29.5
MAR-1991	482.30	108.46	29.0	MAR-2012	3091.57	486.42	18.7
MAR-1975	75.66	15.84	26.5	DEC-2001	1950.40	451.60	30.1
DEC-1982	232.41	44.76	23.9	DEC-2013	4176.59	405.11	10.7
MAR-1987	430.05	80.72	23.1	SEP-2013	3771.48	368.23	10.8
JUN-2003	1622.80	281.63	21.0	JUN-2001	2160.54	320.28	17.4
JUN-1980	157.78	26.78	20.4	JUN-2009	1835.04	306.45	20.0
JUN-2009	1835.04	306.45	20.0	SEP-2009	2122.42	287.38	15.7
RUSSELL 1000 1979 to APRIL 2014							
DEC-1998	642.87	113.76	21.5	DEC-1998	642.87	113.76	21.5
MAR-1987	155.20	25.20	19.4	DEC-1999	767.97	104.14	15.7
DEC-1982	77.24	11.35	17.2	DEC-2013	1030.36	90.86	9.7
JUN-1997	462.95	64.76	16.3	MAR-2012	778.92	85.56	12.3
DEC-1985	114.39	15.64	15.8	MAR-2013	872.11	82.21	10.4
JUN-2009	502.27	68.60	15.8	SEP-2009	579.97	77.70	15.5
DEC-1999	767.97	104.14	15.7	DEC-2011	693.36	69.91	11.2
SEP-2009	579.97	77.70	15.5	JUN-2009	502.27	68.60	15.8
JUN-2003	518.94	68.59	15.2	JUN-2003	518.94	68.59	15.2
MAR-1991	196.15	24.93	14.6	DEC-2010	696.90	67.12	10.7
RUSSELL 2000 1979 to APRIL 2014							
MAR-1991	171.01	38.85	29.4	DEC-2010	783.65	107.51	15.9
DEC-1982	88.90	18.06	25.5	MAR-2013	951.54	102.19	12.0
MAR-1987	166.79	31.79	23.5	DEC-2011	740.92	96.76	15.0
JUN-2003	448.37	83.83	23.0	SEP-2013	1073.79	96.31	9.9
SEP-1980	69.94	12.47	21.7	SEP-2009	604.28	96.00	18.9
DEC-2001	488.50	83.63	20.7	MAR-2006	765.14	91.92	13.7
JUN-1983	124.17	20.40	19.7	DEC-2013	1163.64	89.85	8.4
JUN-1980	57.47	9.20	19.1	MAR-2012	830.30	89.38	12.1
DEC-1999	504.75	77.45	18.1	JUN-2009	508.28	85.53	20.2
SEP-2009	604.28	96.00	18.9	JUN-2003	448.37	83.83	23.0

10 <u>WORST</u> QUARTERS BY PERCENT AND POINT

	BY PERCENT CHANGE				BY POINT CHANGE		
QUARTER	CLOSE	PNT CHANGE	% CHANGE	QUARTER	CLOSE	PNT CHANGE	% CHANGE
DJIA 1901 to 1949							
JUN-1932	42.84	−30.44	−41.5	DEC-1929	248.48	−94.97	−27.7
SEP-1931	96.61	−53.57	−35.7	JUN-1930	226.34	−59.76	−20.9
DEC-1929	248.48	−94.97	−27.7	SEP-1931	96.61	−53.57	−35.7
SEP-1903	33.55	−9.73	−22.5	DEC-1930	164.58	−40.32	−19.7
DEC-1937	120.85	−33.72	−21.8	DEC-1937	120.85	−33.72	−21.8
JUN-1930	226.34	−59.76	−20.9	SEP-1946	172.42	−33.20	−16.1
DEC-1930	164.58	−40.32	−19.7	JUN-1932	42.84	−30.44	−41.5
DEC-1931	77.90	−18.71	−19.4	JUN-1940	121.87	−26.08	−17.6
MAR-1938	98.95	−21.90	−18.1	MAR-1939	131.84	−22.92	−14.8
JUN-1940	121.87	−26.08	−17.6	JUN-1931	150.18	−22.18	−12.9
DJIA 1950 to APRIL 2014							
DEC-1987	1938.83	−657.45	−25.3	DEC-2008	8776.39	−2074.27	−19.1
SEP-1974	607.87	−194.54	−24.2	SEP-2001	8847.56	−1654.84	−15.8
JUN-1962	561.28	−145.67	−20.6	SEP-2002	7591.93	−1651.33	−17.9
DEC-2008	8776.39	−2074.27	−19.1	SEP-2011	10913.38	−1500.96	−12.1
SEP-2002	7591.93	−1651.33	−17.9	MAR-2009	7608.92	−1167.47	−13.3
SEP-2001	8847.56	−1654.84	−15.8	JUN-2002	9243.26	−1160.68	−11.2
SEP-1990	2452.48	−428.21	−14.9	SEP-1998	7842.62	−1109.40	−12.4
MAR-2009	7608.92	−1167.47	−13.3	JUN-2010	9774.02	−1082.61	−10.0
SEP-1981	849.98	−126.90	−13.0	MAR-2008	12262.89	−1001.93	−7.6
JUN-1970	683.53	−102.04	−13.0	JUN-2008	11350.01	−912.88	−7.4
S&P 500 1930 to APRIL 2014							
JUN-1932	4.43	−2.88	−39.4	DEC-2008	903.25	−263.11	−22.6
SEP-1931	9.71	−5.12	−34.5	SEP-2011	1131.42	−189.22	−14.3
SEP-1974	63.54	−22.46	−26.1	SEP-2001	1040.94	−183.48	−15.0
DEC-1937	10.55	−3.21	−23.3	SEP-2002	815.28	−174.54	−17.6
DEC-1987	247.08	−74.75	−23.2	MAR-2001	1160.33	−159.95	−12.1
DEC-2008	903.25	−263.11	−22.6	JUN-2002	989.82	−157.57	−13.7
JUN-1962	54.75	−14.80	−21.3	MAR-2008	1322.70	−145.66	−9.9
MAR-1938	8.50	−2.05	−19.4	JUN-2010	1030.71	−138.72	−11.9
JUN-1970	72.72	−16.91	−18.9	SEP-1998	1017.01	−116.83	−10.3
SEP-1946	14.96	−3.47	−18.8	DEC-2000	1320.28	−116.23	−8.1
NASDAQ 1971 to APRIL 2014							
DEC-2000	2470.52	−1202.30	−32.7	DEC-2000	2470.52	−1202.30	−32.7
SEP-2001	1498.80	−661.74	−30.6	SEP-2001	1498.80	−661.74	−30.6
SEP-1974	55.67	−20.29	−26.7	MAR-2001	1840.26	−630.26	−25.5
DEC-1987	330.47	−113.82	−25.6	JUN-2000	3966.11	−606.72	−13.3
MAR-2001	1840.26	−630.26	−25.5	DEC-2008	1577.03	−514.85	−24.6
SEP-1990	344.51	−117.78	−25.5	JUN-2002	1463.21	−382.14	−20.7
DEC-2008	1577.03	−514.85	−24.6	MAR-2008	2279.10	−373.18	−14.1
JUN-2002	1463.21	−382.14	−20.7	SEP-2011	2415.40	−358.12	−12.9
SEP-2002	1172.06	−291.15	−19.9	SEP-2000	3672.82	−293.29	−7.4
JUN-1974	75.96	−16.31	−17.7	SEP-2002	1172.06	−291.15	−19.9
RUSSELL 1000 1979 to APRIL 2014							
DEC-2008	487.77	−146.31	−23.1	DEC-2008	487.77	−146.31	−23.1
DEC-1987	130.02	−38.81	−23.0	SEP-2011	623.45	−111.03	−15.1
SEP-2002	433.22	−90.50	−17.3	SEP-2001	546.46	−100.18	−15.5
SEP-2001	546.46	−100.18	−15.5	SEP-2002	433.22	−90.50	−17.3
SEP-1990	157.83	−28.46	−15.3	MAR-2001	610.36	−89.73	−12.8
SEP-2011	623.45	−111.03	−15.1	JUN-2002	523.72	−83.63	−13.8
JUN-2002	523.72	−83.63	−13.8	MAR-2008	720.32	−79.50	−9.9
MAR-2001	610.36	−89.73	−12.8	JUN-2010	567.37	−76.42	−11.9
SEP-1981	64.06	−8.95	−12.3	DEC-2000	700.09	−72.51	−9.4
JUN-2010	567.37	−76.42	−11.9	SEP-2008	634.08	−69.14	−9.8
RUSSELL 2000 1979 to APRIL 2014							
DEC-1987	120.42	−50.39	−29.5	SEP-2011	644.16	−183.27	−22.1
DEC-2008	499.45	−180.13	−26.5	DEC-2008	499.45	−180.13	−26.5
SEP-1990	126.70	−42.34	−25.0	SEP-2001	404.87	−107.77	−21.0
SEP-2011	644.16	−183.27	−22.1	SEP-2002	362.27	−100.37	−21.7
SEP-2002	362.27	−100.37	−21.7	SEP-1998	363.59	−93.80	−20.5
SEP-2001	404.87	−107.77	−21.0	MAR-2008	687.97	−78.06	−10.2
SEP-1998	363.59	−93.80	−20.5	MAR-2009	422.75	−76.70	−15.4
SEP-1981	67.55	−15.01	−18.2	JUN-2010	609.49	−69.15	−10.2
MAR-2009	422.75	−76.70	−15.4	DEC-1987	120.42	−50.39	−29.5
MAR-1980	48.27	−7.64	−13.7	JUN-2002	462.64	−43.82	−8.7

10 **BEST** YEARS BY PERCENT AND POINT

	BY PERCENT CHANGE			BY POINT CHANGE			
YEAR	CLOSE	PNT CHANGE	% CHANGE	YEAR	CLOSE	PNT CHANGE	% CHANGE
DJIA 1901 to 1949							
1915	99.15	44.57	81.7	1928	300.00	97.60	48.2
1933	99.90	39.97	66.7	1927	202.40	45.20	28.8
1928	300.00	97.60	48.2	1915	99.15	44.57	81.7
1908	63.11	20.07	46.6	1945	192.91	40.59	26.6
1904	50.99	15.01	41.7	1935	144.13	40.09	38.5
1935	144.13	40.09	38.5	1933	99.90	39.97	66.7
1905	70.47	19.48	38.2	1925	156.66	36.15	30.0
1919	107.23	25.03	30.5	1936	179.90	35.77	24.8
1925	156.66	36.15	30.0	1938	154.76	33.91	28.1
1927	202.40	45.20	28.8	1919	107.23	25.03	30.5
DJIA 1950 to APRIL 2014							
1954	404.39	123.49	44.0	2013	16576.66	3472.52	26.5
1975	852.41	236.17	38.3	1999	11497.12	2315.69	25.2
1958	583.65	147.96	34.0	2003	10453.92	2112.29	25.3
1995	5117.12	1282.68	33.5	2006	12463.15	1745.65	16.3
1985	1546.67	335.10	27.7	2009	10428.05	1651.66	18.8
1989	2753.20	584.63	27.0	1997	7908.25	1459.98	22.6
2013	16576.66	3472.52	26.5	1996	6448.27	1331.15	26.0
1996	6448.27	1331.15	26.0	1995	5117.12	1282.68	33.5
2003	10453.92	2112.29	25.3	1998	9181.43	1273.18	16.1
1999	11497.12	2315.69	25.2	2010	11577.51	1149.46	11.0
S&P 500 1930 to APRIL 2014							
1933	10.10	3.21	46.6	2013	1848.36	422.17	29.6
1954	35.98	11.17	45.0	1998	1229.23	258.80	26.7
1935	13.43	3.93	41.4	1999	1469.25	240.02	19.5
1958	55.21	15.22	38.1	2003	1111.92	232.10	26.4
1995	615.93	156.66	34.1	1997	970.43	229.69	31.0
1975	90.19	21.63	31.5	2009	1115.10	211.85	23.5
1997	970.43	229.69	31.0	2006	1418.30	170.01	13.6
1945	17.36	4.08	30.7	2012	1426.19	168.59	13.4
2013	1848.36	422.17	29.6	1995	615.93	156.66	34.1
1936	17.18	3.75	27.9	2010	1257.64	142.54	12.8
NASDAQ 1971 to APRIL 2014							
1999	4069.31	1876.62	85.6	1999	4069.31	1876.62	85.6
1991	586.34	212.50	56.8	2013	4176.59	1157.08	38.3
2003	2003.37	667.86	50.0	2009	2269.15	692.12	43.9
2009	2269.15	692.12	43.9	2003	2003.37	667.86	50.0
1995	1052.13	300.17	39.9	1998	2192.69	622.34	39.6
1998	2192.69	622.34	39.6	2012	3019.51	414.36	15.9
2013	4176.59	1157.08	38.3	2010	2652.87	383.72	16.9
1980	202.34	51.20	33.9	1995	1052.13	300.17	39.9
1985	324.93	77.58	31.4	1997	1570.35	279.32	21.6
1975	77.62	17.80	29.8	1996	1291.03	238.90	22.7
RUSSELL 1000 1979 to APRIL 2014							
1995	328.89	84.24	34.4	2013	1030.36	240.46	30.4
1997	513.79	120.04	30.5	1998	642.87	129.08	25.1
2013	1030.36	240.46	30.4	2003	594.56	128.38	27.5
1991	220.61	49.39	28.8	1999	767.97	125.10	19.5
2003	594.56	128.38	27.5	2009	612.01	124.24	25.5
1985	114.39	24.08	26.7	1997	513.79	120.04	30.5
1989	185.11	38.12	25.9	2012	789.90	96.54	13.9
1980	75.20	15.33	25.6	2006	770.08	90.66	13.3
2009	612.01	124.24	25.5	2010	696.90	84.89	13.9
1998	642.87	129.08	25.1	1995	328.89	84.24	34.4
RUSSELL 2000 1979 to APRIL 2014							
2003	556.91	173.82	45.4	2013	1163.64	314.29	37.0
1991	189.94	57.78	43.7	2003	556.91	173.82	45.4
1979	55.91	15.39	38.0	2010	783.65	158.26	25.3
2013	1163.64	314.29	37.0	2009	625.39	125.94	25.2
1980	74.80	18.89	33.8	2006	787.66	114.44	17.0
1985	129.87	28.38	28.0	2012	849.35	108.43	14.6
1983	112.27	23.37	26.3	2004	651.57	94.66	17.0
1995	315.97	65.61	26.2	1999	504.75	82.79	19.6
2010	783.65	158.26	25.3	1997	437.02	74.41	20.5
2009	625.39	125.94	25.2	1995	315.97	65.61	26.2

10 <u>WORST</u> YEARS BY PERCENT AND POINT

| | BY PERCENT CHANGE | | | | BY POINT CHANGE | | |
YEAR	CLOSE	PNT CHANGE	% CHANGE	YEAR	CLOSE	PNT CHANGE	% CHANGE
			DJIA 1901 to 1949				
1931	77.90	−86.68	−52.7	1931	77.90	−86.68	−52.7
1907	43.04	−26.08	−37.7	1930	164.58	−83.90	−33.8
1930	164.58	−83.90	−33.8	1937	120.85	−59.05	−32.8
1920	71.95	−35.28	−32.9	1929	248.48	−51.52	−17.2
1937	120.85	−59.05	−32.8	1920	71.95	−35.28	−32.9
1903	35.98	−11.12	−23.6	1907	43.04	−26.08	−37.7
1932	59.93	−17.97	−23.1	1917	74.38	−20.62	−21.7
1917	74.38	−20.62	−21.7	1941	110.96	−20.17	−15.4
1910	59.60	−12.96	−17.9	1940	131.13	−19.11	−12.7
1929	248.48	−51.52	−17.2	1932	59.93	−17.97	−23.1
			DJIA 1950 to APRIL 2014				
2008	8776.39	−4488.43	−33.8	2008	8776.39	−4488.43	−33.8
1974	616.24	−234.62	−27.6	2002	8341.63	−1679.87	−16.8
1966	785.69	−183.57	−18.9	2001	10021.50	−765.35	−7.1
1977	831.17	−173.48	−17.3	2000	10786.85	−710.27	−6.2
2002	8341.63	−1679.87	−16.8	1974	616.24	−234.62	−27.6
1973	850.86	−169.16	−16.6	1966	785.69	−183.57	−18.9
1969	800.36	−143.39	−15.2	1977	831.17	−173.48	−17.3
1957	435.69	−63.78	−12.8	1973	850.86	−169.16	−16.6
1962	652.10	−79.04	−10.8	1969	800.36	−143.39	−15.2
1960	615.89	−63.47	−9.3	1990	2633.66	−119.54	−4.3
			S&P 500 1930 to APRIL 2014				
1931	8.12	−7.22	−47.1	2008	903.25	−565.11	−38.5
1937	10.55	−6.63	−38.6	2002	879.82	−268.26	−23.4
2008	903.25	−565.11	−38.5	2001	1148.08	−172.20	−13.0
1974	68.56	−28.99	−29.7	2000	1320.28	−148.97	−10.1
1930	15.34	−6.11	−28.5	1974	68.56	−28.99	−29.7
2002	879.82	−268.26	−23.4	1990	330.22	−23.18	−6.6
1941	8.69	−1.89	−17.9	1973	97.55	−20.50	−17.4
1973	97.55	−20.50	−17.4	1981	122.55	−13.21	−9.7
1940	10.58	−1.91	−15.3	1977	95.10	−12.36	−11.5
1932	6.89	−1.23	−15.1	1966	80.33	−12.10	−13.1
			NASDAQ 1971 to APRIL 2014				
2008	1577.03	−1075.25	−40.5	2000	2470.52	−1598.79	−39.3
2000	2470.52	−1598.79	−39.3	2008	1577.03	−1075.25	−40.5
1974	59.82	−32.37	−35.1	2002	1335.51	−614.89	−31.5
2002	1335.51	−614.89	−31.5	2001	1950.40	−520.12	−21.1
1973	92.19	−41.54	−31.1	1990	373.84	−80.98	−17.8
2001	1950.40	−520.12	−21.1	2011	2605.15	−47.72	−1.8
1990	373.84	−80.98	−17.8	1973	92.19	−41.54	−31.1
1984	247.35	−31.25	−11.2	1974	59.82	−32.37	−35.1
1987	330.47	−18.86	−5.4	1984	247.35	−31.25	−11.2
1981	195.84	−6.50	−3.2	1994	751.96	−24.84	−3.2
			RUSSELL 1000 1979 to APRIL 2014				
2008	487.77	−312.05	−39.0	2008	487.77	−312.05	−39.0
2002	466.18	−138.76	−22.9	2002	466.18	−138.76	−22.9
2001	604.94	−95.15	−13.6	2001	604.94	−95.15	−13.6
1981	67.93	−7.27	−9.7	2000	700.09	−67.88	−8.8
2000	700.09	−67.88	−8.8	1990	171.22	−13.89	−7.5
1990	171.22	−13.89	−7.5	1981	67.93	−7.27	−9.7
1994	244.65	−6.06	−2.4	1994	244.65	−6.06	−2.4
2011	693.36	−3.54	−0.5	2011	693.36	−3.54	−0.5
1984	90.31	−0.07	−0.1	1984	90.31	−0.07	−0.1
1987	130.02	0.02	0.02	1987	130.02	0.02	0.02
			RUSSELL 2000 1979 to APRIL 2014				
2008	499.45	−266.58	−34.8	2008	499.45	−266.58	−34.8
2002	383.09	−105.41	−21.6	2002	383.09	−105.41	−21.6
1990	132.16	−36.14	−21.5	2011	740.92	−42.73	−5.5
1987	120.42	−14.58	−10.8	1990	132.16	−36.14	−21.5
1984	101.49	−10.78	−9.6	2007	766.03	−21.63	−2.7
2011	740.92	−42.73	−5.5	2000	483.53	−21.22	−4.2
2000	483.53	−21.22	−4.2	1998	421.96	−15.06	−3.4
1998	421.96	−15.06	−3.4	1987	120.42	−14.58	−10.8
1994	250.36	−8.23	−3.2	1984	101.49	−10.78	−9.6
2007	766.03	−21.63	−2.7	1994	250.36	−8.23	−3.2

DOW JONES INDUSTRIALS ONE-YEAR SEASONAL PATTERN CHARTS SINCE 1901

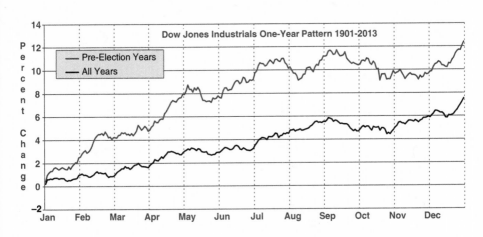

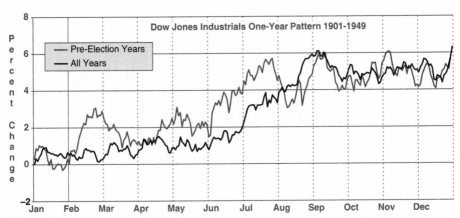

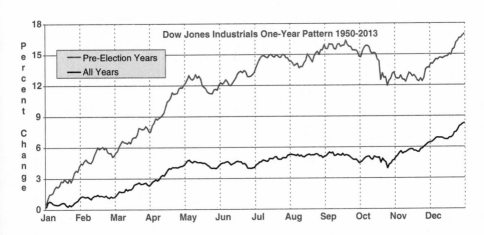

S&P 500 ONE-YEAR SEASONAL PATTERN CHARTS SINCE 1930

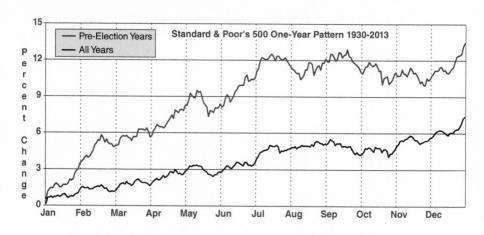

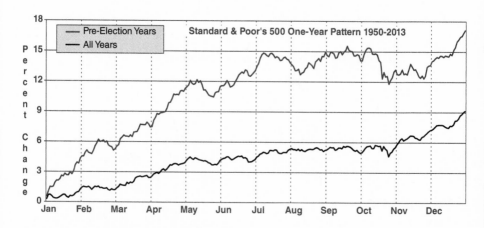

NASDAQ, RUSSELL 1000 & 2000 ONE-YEAR SEASONAL PATTERN CHARTS SINCE 1971

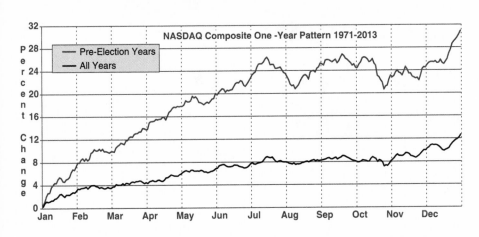

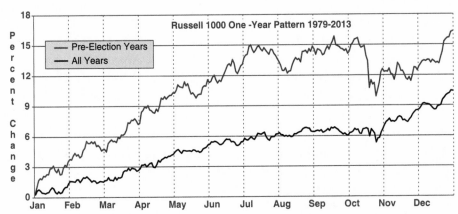

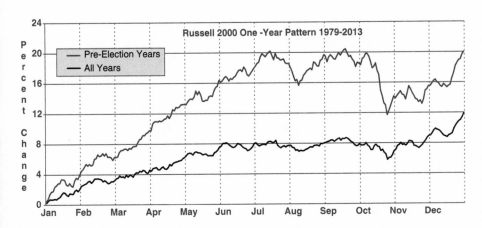

STRATEGY PLANNING AND RECORD SECTION

CONTENTS

175   Portfolio at Start of 2015

176   Additional Purchases

178   Short-Term Transactions

180   Long-Term Transactions

182   Interest/Dividends Received during 2015/Brokerage Account Data 2015

183   Weekly Portfolio Price Record 2015

185   Weekly Indicator Data 2015

187   Monthly Indicator Data 2015

188   Portfolio at End of 2015

189   If You Don't Profit from Your Investment Mistakes, Someone Else Will; Performance Record of Recommendations

190   Individual Retirement Account (IRA): Most Awesome Mass Investment Incentive Ever Devised

191   G.M. Loeb's "Battle Plan" for Investment Survival

192   G.M. Loeb's Investment Survival Checklist

These forms are available at our website www.stocktradersalmanac.com.

PORTFOLIO AT START OF 2015

DATE ACQUIRED	NO. OF SHARES	SECURITY	PRICE	TOTAL COST	PAPER PROFITS	PAPER LOSSES

ADDITIONAL PURCHASES

DATE ACQUIRED	NO. OF SHARES	SECURITY	PRICE	TOTAL COST	REASON FOR PURCHASE PRIME OBJECTIVE, ETC.

ADDITIONAL PURCHASES

DATE ACQUIRED	NO. OF SHARES	SECURITY	PRICE	TOTAL COST	REASON FOR PURCHASE PRIME OBJECTIVE, ETC.

SHORT-TERM TRANSACTIONS

Pages 178–181 can accompany next year's income tax return (Schedule D). Enter transactions as completed to avoid last-minute pressures.

NO. OF SHARES	SECURITY	DATE ACQUIRED	DATE SOLD	SALE PRICE	COST	LOSS	GAIN

TOTALS:
Carry over to next page

SHORT-TERM TRANSACTIONS (continued)

NO. OF SHARES	SECURITY	DATE ACQUIRED	DATE SOLD	SALE PRICE	COST	LOSS	GAIN

TOTALS:

LONG-TERM TRANSACTIONS

Pages 178–181 can accompany next year's income tax return (Schedule D). Enter transactions as completed to avoid last-minute pressures.

NO. OF SHARES	SECURITY	DATE ACQUIRED	DATE SOLD	SALE PRICE	COST	LOSS	GAIN

TOTALS:
Carry over to next page

NO. OF SHARES	SECURITY	DATE ACQUIRED	DATE SOLD	SALE PRICE	COST	LOSS	GAIN

TOTALS:

INTEREST/DIVIDENDS RECEIVED DURING 2015

SHARES	STOCK/BOND	FIRST QUARTER		SECOND QUARTER		THIRD QUARTER		FOURTH QUARTER	
		$		$		$		$	

BROKERAGE ACCOUNT DATA 2015

	MARGIN INTEREST	TRANSFER TAXES	CAPITAL ADDED	CAPITAL WITHDRAWN
JAN				
FEB				
MAR				
APR				
MAY				
JUN				
JUL				
AUG				
SEP				
OCT				
NOV				
DEC				

WEEKLY PORTFOLIO PRICE RECORD 2015 (FIRST HALF)

Place purchase price above stock name and weekly closes below.

STOCKS / Week Ending	1	2	3	4	5	6	7	8	9	10
JANUARY 2										
9										
16										
23										
30										
FEBRUARY 6										
13										
20										
27										
MARCH 6										
13										
20										
27										
APRIL 3										
10										
17										
24										
MAY 1										
8										
15										
22										
29										
JUNE 5										
12										
19										
26										

WEEKLY PORTFOLIO PRICE RECORD 2015 (SECOND HALF)

Place purchase price above stock name and weekly closes below.

STOCKS Week Ending	1	2	3	4	5	6	7	8	9	10
JULY 3										
10										
17										
24										
31										
AUGUST 7										
14										
21										
28										
SEPTEMBER 4										
11										
18										
25										
OCTOBER 2										
9										
16										
23										
30										
NOVEMBER 6										
13										
20										
27										
DECEMBER 4										
11										
18										
25										
1										

WEEKLY INDICATOR DATA 2015 (FIRST HALF)

	Week Ending	Dow Jones Industrial Average	Net Change for Week	Net Change on Friday	Net Change Next Monday	S&P or NASDAQ	NYSE Ad-vances	NYSE De-clines	New Highs	New Lows	CBOE Put/Call Ratio	90-Day Treas. Rate	Moody's AAA Rate
JANUARY	2												
	9												
	16												
	23												
	30												
FEBRUARY	6												
	13												
	20												
	27												
MARCH	6												
	13												
	20												
	27												
APRIL	3												
	10												
	17												
	24												
MAY	1												
	8												
	15												
	22												
	29												
JUNE	5												
	12												
	19												
	26												

WEEKLY INDICATOR DATA 2015 (SECOND HALF)

	Week Ending	Dow Jones Industrial Average	Net Change for Week	Net Change on Friday	Net Change Next Monday	S&P or NASDAQ	NYSE Advances	NYSE Declines	New Highs	New Lows	CBOE Put/Call Ratio	90-Day Treas. Rate	Moody's AAA Rate
JULY	3												
	10												
	17												
	24												
	31												
AUGUST	7												
	14												
	21												
	28												
SEPTEMBER	4												
	11												
	18												
	25												
OCTOBER	2												
	9												
	16												
	23												
	30												
NOVEMBER	6												
	13												
	20												
	27												
DECEMBER	4												
	11												
	18												
	25												
	1												

MONTHLY INDICATOR DATA 2015

	DJIA% Last 3 + 1st 2 Days	DJIA% 9th to 11th Trading Days	DJIA% Change Rest of Month	DJIA% Change Whole Month	% Change Your Stocks	Gross Domestic Product	Prime Rate	Trade Deficit $ Billion	CPI % Change	% Unem- ployment Rate
JAN										
FEB										
MAR										
APR										
MAY										
JUN										
JUL										
AUG										
SEP										
OCT										
NOV										
DEC										

INSTRUCTIONS:

Weekly Indicator Data (pages 185–186). Keeping data on several indicators may give you a better feel of the market. In addition to the closing DJIA and its net change for the week, post the net change for Friday's Dow and also the following Monday's. A series of "down Fridays" followed by "down Mondays" often precedes a downswing (see page 80). Tracking either the S&P or NASDAQ composite, and advances and declines, will help prevent the Dow from misleading you. New highs and lows and put/call ratios (www.cboe.com) are also useful indicators. All these weekly figures appear in weekend papers or *Barron's*. Data for 90-day Treasury Rate and Moody's AAA Bond Rate are quite important for tracking short- and long-term interest rates. These figures are available from:

Weekly U.S. Financial Data
Federal Reserve Bank of St. Louis
P.O. Box 442
St. Louis MO 63166
http://research.stlouisfed.org

Monthly Indicator Data. The purpose of the first three columns is to enable you to track the market's bullish bias near the end, beginning, and middle of the month, which has been shifting lately (see pages 92, 145, and 146). Market direction, performance of your stocks, gross domestic product, prime rate, trade deficit, Consumer Price Index, and unemployment rate are worthwhile indicators to follow. Or, readers may wish to gauge other data.

PORTFOLIO AT END OF 2015

DATE ACQUIRED	NO. OF SHARES	SECURITY	PRICE	TOTAL COST	PAPER PROFITS	PAPER LOSSES

IF YOU DON'T PROFIT FROM YOUR INVESTMENT MISTAKES, SOMEONE ELSE WILL

No matter how much we may deny it, almost every successful person in Wall Street pays a great deal of attention to trading suggestions—especially when they come from "the right sources."

One of the hardest things to learn is to distinguish between good tips and bad ones. Usually, the best tips have a logical reason in back of them, which accompanies the tip. Poor tips usually have no reason to support them.

The important thing to remember is that the market discounts. It does not review, it does not reflect. The Street's real interest in "tips," inside information, buying and selling suggestions, and everything else of this kind emanates from a desire to find out just what the market has on hand to discount. The process of finding out involves separating the wheat from the chaff—and there is plenty of chaff.

HOW TO MAKE USE OF STOCK "TIPS"

- The source should be **reliable**. (By listing all "tips" and suggestions on a Performance Record of Recommendations, such as the form below, and then periodically evaluating the outcomes, you will soon know the "batting average" of your sources.)

- The story should make sense. Would the merger violate antitrust laws? Are there too many computers on the market already? How many years will it take to become profitable?

- The stock should not have had a recent sharp run-up. Otherwise, the story may already be discounted, and confirmation or denial in the press would most likely be accompanied by a sell-off in the stock.

PERFORMANCE RECORD OF RECOMMENDATIONS

STOCK RECOMMENDED	BY WHOM	DATE	PRICE	REASON FOR RECOMMENDATION	SUBSEQUENT ACTION OF STOCK

INDIVIDUAL RETIREMENT ACCOUNT (IRA): MOST AWESOME MASS INVESTMENT INCENTIVE EVER DEVISED

MAX IRA INVESTMENTS OF $5,500* A YEAR COMPOUNDED AT VARIOUS INTEREST RATES OF RETURN FOR DIFFERENT PERIODS

Annual Rate	5 Yrs	10 Yrs	15 Yrs	20 Yrs	25 Yrs	30 Yrs	35 Yrs	40 Yrs	45 Yrs	50 Yrs
1%	$28,336	$58,118	$89,418	$122,316	$156,891	$193,230	$231,423	$271,564	$313,752	$358,093
2%	29,195	61,428	97,016	136,308	179,690	227,587	280,469	338,855	403,318	474,490
3%	30,076	64,943	105,363	152,221	206,542	269,515	342,518	427,148	525,258	638,994
4%	30,981	68,675	114,535	170,331	238,215	320,806	421,291	543,546	692,288	873,256
5%	31,911	72,637	124,616	190,956	275,624	383,684	521,600	697,619	922,268	1,208,985
6%	32,864	76,844	135,699	214,460	319,860	460,909	649,665	902,262	1,240,295	1,692,658
7%	33,843	81,310	147,884	241,258	372,221	555,902	813,524	1,174,853	1,681,635	2,392,423
8%	34,848	86,050	161,284	271,826	434,249	672,902	1,023,562	1,538,796	2,295,843	3,408,195
9%	35,878	91,082	176,019	306,705	507,782	817,164	1,293,186	2,025,605	3,152,523	4,886,426
10%	36,936	96,421	192,224	346,514	595,000	995,189	1,639,697	2,677,685	4,349,374	7,041,647
11%	38,021	102,088	210,045	391,958	698,493	1,215,022	2,085,404	3,552,048	6,023,428	10,187,848
12%	39,134	108,100	229,643	443,843	821,337	1,486,609	2,659,047	4,725,283	8,366,697	14,784,112
13%	40,275	114,479	251,195	503,085	967,176	1,822,233	3,397,621	6,300,172	11,647,933	21,500,837
14%	41,445	121,245	274,892	570,726	1,140,330	2,237,054	4,348,701	8,414,497	16,242,841	31,315,649
15%	42,646	128,421	300,946	647,956	1,345,916	2,749,763	5,573,401	11,252,746	22,675,938	45,652,055
16%	43,876	136,031	329,588	736,123	1,589,985	3,383,389	7,150,149	15,061,631	31,678,448	66,579,439
17%	45,138	144,100	361,069	836,762	1,879,695	4,166,271	9,179,470	20,170,648	44,268,235	97,100,943
18%	46,431	152,653	395,665	951,616	2,223,497	5,133,252	11,790,069	27,019,253	61,859,935	141,566,978
19%	47,756	161,720	433,676	1,082,661	2,631,368	6,327,131	15,146,529	36,192,731	86,416,412	206,267,876
20%	49,115	171,327	475,432	1,232,141	3,115,075	7,800,418	19,459,052	48,469,462	120,656,646	300,281,459

* At press time, 2015 Contribution Limit will be indexed to inflation.

G. M. LOEB'S "BATTLE PLAN" FOR INVESTMENT SURVIVAL

LIFE IS CHANGE: Nothing can ever be the same a minute from now as it was a minute ago. Everything you own is changing in price and value. You can find that last price of an active security on the stock ticker, but you cannot find the next price anywhere. The value of your money is changing. Even the value of your home is changing, though no one walks in front of it with a sandwich board consistently posting the changes.

RECOGNIZE CHANGE: Your basic objective should be to profit from change. The art of investing is being able to recognize change and to adjust investment goals accordingly.

WRITE THINGS DOWN: You will score more investment success and avoid more investment failures if you write things down. Very few investors have the drive and inclination to do this.

KEEP A CHECKLIST: If you aim to improve your investment results, get into the habit of keeping a checklist on every issue you consider buying. Before making a commitment, it will pay you to write down the answers to at least some of the basic questions—How much am I investing in this company? How much do I think I can make? How much do I have to risk? How long do I expect to take to reach my goal?

HAVE A SINGLE RULING REASON: Above all, writing things down is the best way to find "the ruling reason." When all is said and done, there is invariably a single reason that stands out above all others, why a particular security transaction can be expected to show a profit. All too often, many relatively unimportant statistics are allowed to obscure this single important point.

Any one of a dozen factors may be the point of a particular purchase or sale. It could be a technical reason—an increase in earnings or dividend not yet discounted in the market price—a change of management—a promising new product—an expected improvement in the market's valuation of earnings—or many others. But, in any given case, one of these factors will almost certainly be more important than all the rest put together.

CLOSING OUT A COMMITMENT: If you have a loss, the solution is automatic, provided you decide what to do at the time you buy. Otherwise, the question divides itself into two parts. Are we in a bull or bear market? Few of us really know until it is too late. For the sake of the record, if you think it is a bear market, just put that consideration first and sell as much as your conviction suggests and your nature allows.

If you think it is a bull market, or at least a market where some stocks move up, some mark time, and only a few decline, do not sell unless:

✓ You see a bear market ahead.
✓ You see trouble for a particular company in which you own shares.
✓ Time and circumstances have turned up a new and seemingly far better buy than the issue you like least in your list.
✓ Your shares stop going up and start going down.

A subsidiary question is, which stock to sell first? Two further observations may help:

✓ Do not sell solely because you think a stock is "overvalued."
✓ If you want to sell some of your stocks and not all, in most cases it is better to go against your emotional inclinations and sell first the issues with losses, small profits, or none at all, the weakest, the most disappointing, etc.

Mr. Loeb is the author of *The Battle for Investment Survival*, John Wiley & Sons.

G. M. LOEB'S INVESTMENT SURVIVAL CHECKLIST

OBJECTIVES AND RISKS

Security			Price	Shares	Date

"Ruling reason" for commitment

Amount of commitment

$_____

% of my investment capital

_____%

Price objective	Est. time to achieve it	I will risk _____ points	Which would be $_____

TECHNICAL POSITION

Price action of stock:

❏ Hitting new highs   ❏ In a trading range

❏ Pausing in an uptrend   ❏ Moving up from low ground

❏ Acting stronger than market   ❏ _____

Dow Jones Industrial Average

Trend of market

SELECTED YARDSTICKS

	Price Range		Earnings Per Share Actual or Projected	Price/Earnings Ratio Actual or Projected
	High	Low		
Current year Previous year				

Merger possibilities	Years for earnings to double in past
Comment on future	Years for market price to double in past

PERIODIC RE-CHECKS

Date	Stock Price	DJIA	Comment	Action taken, if any

COMPLETED TRANSACTIONS

Date closed	Period of time held	Profit or loss

Reason for profit or loss